THE CRITICAL RESPONSE TO RICHARD WRIGHT

Recent Titles in
Critical Responses in Arts and Letters

THE CRITICAL RESPONSE TO RICHARD WRIGHT

Edited by Robert J. Butler

Critical Responses in Arts and Letters, Number 16
Cameron Northouse, Series Adviser

GREENWOOD PRESS
Westport, Connecticut • London

Library of Congress Cataloging-in-Publication Data

The critical response to Richard Wright / edited by Robert J. Butler.
       p.   cm.—(Critical responses in arts and letters, ISSN
1057–0993 ; no. 16)
    Includes bibliographical references (p.   ) and index.
    ISBN 0–313–28860–7 (alk. paper)
    1. Wright, Richard, 1908–1960—Criticism and interpretation.
2. Afro-Americans in literature. I. Butler, Robert. II. Series.
PS3545.R815Z63   1995
813′.52—dc20   94–40142

British Library Cataloguing in Publication Data is available.

#31409595

Library of Congress Catalog Card Number: 94–40142
ISBN: 0–313–28860–7
ISSN: 1057–0993

First published in 1995

Greenwood Press, 88 Post Road West, Westport, CT 06881
An imprint of Greenwood Publishing Group, Inc.

Printed in the United States of America

∞

The paper used in this book complies with the
Permanent Paper Standard issued by the National
Information Standards Organization (Z39.48–1984).

10 9 8 7 6 5 4 3

COPYRIGHT ACKNOWLEDGMENTS

The editor and publisher gratefully acknowledge permission for the use of the following material:

Blyden Jackson, "Richard Wright: Black Boy from America's Black Belt and Urban Ghettos," *CLA Journal*, 12. June 1969, 287-309. Reprinted by permission of The College Language Association.

Phylon: "*Native Son*: The Personal, Social, and Political Background," Copyright (c) 1969, by Clark Atlanta University, Atlanta Georgia. Reprinted with permission.

Henry Seidel Canby, Review of *Native Son* by Richard Wright. *Book-of-the-Month-Club-News* February 1940: 2-3. Reprinted by permission of Book-of-the-Month-Club.

Charles Poore, Review of *Native Son* by Richard Wright. *The New York Times* March 1, 1940. Copyright (c) 1940 by The New York Times Company. Reprinted by permission.

Howard Mumford Jones, "Uneven Effect." Review of *Native Son* by Richard Wright. *Boston Evening Transcript* March 2, 1940: 1.

Margaret Wallace, "A Powerful Novel About a Boy from Chicago's Black Belt." Review of *Native Son* by Richard Wright. *New York Sun* March 5, 1940: 3.

Samuel Sillen, Review of *Native Son* by Richard Wright. *New Masses* 34 March 5, 1940: 24-25.

Donald B. Gibson, "Wright's Invisible Native Son," *American Quarterly*, 21, Winter 1969, 729-738. Copyright 1969. Reprinted by permission of the publisher, American Studies Association and the author.

Sylvia Keady, "Richard Wright's Women Characters and Inequality," Reprinted from *Black American Literature Forum*, (Now *African American Review*), Volume 10, Number 4, (1976): 124-28. Copyright (c) 1976 Indiana State University.

Robert Butler, "*Native Son* and Two Novels by Zola." Reprinted from *Black American Literature Forum*, (Now *African American Review*), Volume 18, Number 3, (1984). Copyright (c) Fall 1984 Indiana State University.

Orville Prescott, Review of *Black Boy, The New York Times*. Feb. 28, 1945: 21. Copyright (c) 1945 by The New York Times Company. Reprinted by permission.

James W. Tuttleton, "The Problematic Texts of Richard Wright, *The Hudson Review*. Reprinted by permission from *The Hudson Review*, Vol. XLV, No. 2 (Summer 1992). Copyright (c) 1992 by The Hudson Review, Inc.

Keneth Kinnamon, "The Library of America Edition of *Native Son*." Reprinted by permission of author.

Yoshinobu Hakutani, "The Library of America Edition of *The Outsider*. Reprinted by permission of author.

Eugene E. Miller, "Authority, Gender, and Fiction," *African American Review*, 27, Winter 1992, 687-691. Reprinted by permission of the author.

Robert Butler, "The Invisible Woman in *Rite of Passage*. Reprinted by permission of author.

Native Son by Richard Wright. Harper and Brothers, 1940. Copyright 1940. Passages reprinted by permission of HarperCollins Publishers.

Black Boy by Richard Wright. Harper and Brothers, 1945. Copyright 1945. Passages reprinted by permission of HarperCollins Publishers.

The Outsider by Richard Wright. Harper and Brothers, 1953. Copyright 1953. Passages reprinted by permission of HarperCollins Publishers.

For Mary Jo

Contents

Contents

Richard Wright Today

Series Foreword

Critical Responses in Arts and Letters is designed to present a documentary history of highlights in the critical reception to the body of work of writers and artists and to individual works that are generally considered to be of major importance. The focus of each volume in this series is basically historical. The introductions to each volume are themselves brief histories of the critical response an author, artists, or individual work has received. This response is then further illustrated by reprinting a strong representation of the major critical reviews and articles that have collectively produced the author's, artist's, or work's critical reputation.

The scope of *Critical Responses in Arts and Letters* knows no chronological or geographical boundaries. Volumes under preparation include studies of individuals from around the world and in both contemporary and historical periods.

Each volume is the work of an individual editor, who surveys the entire body of criticism on a single author, artist or work. The editor then selects the best material to depict the critical response received by an author or artist over his/her entire career. Documents produced by the author or artist may also be included when the editor finds that they are necessary to a full understanding of the materials at hand. In circumstances where previous isolated volumes of criticism on a particular individual or work exist, the editor carefully selects material that better reflects the nature and directions of the critical response over time.

In addition to the introduction and the documentary section, the editor of each volume is free to solicit new essays on areas that may not have been adequately dealt with in previous criticism. Also, for volumes on living writers and artists, new interviews may be included, again at the discretion of the volume's editor. The volumes also provide a supplementary bibliography and are fully indexed.

While each volume in *Critical Responses in Arts and Letters* is unique, it is also hoped that in combination they form a useful, documentary history of the critical response to the arts, and one that can be easily and profitably employed by students and scholars.

Cameron Northouse

Acknowledgments

This volume was made possible by the ongoing help and steady encouragement of many people. I wish to give special thanks to Dean Ellen Conley and Dr. Joan Connell of Canisius College for supporting my research with a course reduction and a summer fellowship. Without such generous assistance I would not have been able to complete this book. I am also deeply grateful to Mrs. Lucy Jagodzinski who typed the manuscript and saw it through so many revisions. Her tireless work, high spirits, and expertise were absolutely crucial to the success of this project. I am also very much in debt to my research assistants Jeffrey Siuda and Rachel Baron whose careful work and dedication were enormously helpful in all stages of this book's development. Sincere thanks are given also to my colleague and friend, Dr. James Dolan. His generosity, patience and technical acumen were immensely helpful in the formatting and printing of this book.

But most of all, I would like to acknowledge my wife, Mary Jo, and my children, Becky, Geoff, Mike, and Eric. Their understanding, belief, and support were vital resources that magically increased the more I drew from them.

Chronology

1908   Richard Wright is born on September 4, 1908 on a plantation twenty miles east of Natchez, Mississippi to Nathan Wright, a sharecropper, and Ella Wright, a country schoolteacher who gave up teaching soon after Richard was born for farm work. He grows up in one of the most poverty-stricken and rigidly segregated parts of the South.

1911-1912   Unable to support themselves on a farm, the Wrights move to Natchez to live with his maternal grandparents. His grandmother, Margaret Bolton Wilson, was a devoted Seventh-day Adventist and a strict head of the household.

1913-1914   In search of better employment, the Wrights move to Memphis, Tennessee where Nathan works as a night porter in a hotel and Ella works as a cook for a white family. The Wrights are left destitute when Nathan deserts the family for another woman.

1915-1916   Wright enters school in Memphis in the fall of 1915. In early 1916 his mother contracts a serious illness which weakens her health for the rest of her life and eventually makes her an invalid. Wright and his brother Leon are put in Settlement House, a Methodist orphanage where they stay for a month. The family then moves to Jackson, Mississippi where they live with his grandmother for the summer, and they move in the fall to Elaine, Arkansas to live with his Aunt Maggie and Uncle Silas, a saloon keeper.

1917-1918   After his Uncle Silas is murdered by whites who resent his prosperous business, the Wrights flee to West Helena, Arkansas and eventually back to Jackson where they take up residence again with Wright's grandmother. For the next two years, the Wrights move back and forth between Helena and Jackson. During this time, Wright's schooling is sporadic, and he becomes acutely aware of southern racism and violence, both of which leave indelible imprints on his consciousness and become important preoccupations in his fiction.

1919   Wright enters school in West Helena in fall. His mother's health deteriorates early in 1919 and he is forced to leave school to earn money for the family. When his mother suffers a paralyzing stroke, the family moves back to Jackson to live with his grandmother.

1919-1920   Wright moves to Greenwood, Mississippi to live with his aunt and uncle, Clark and Jody Wilson. When his mother suffers a cerebral blood clot that leaves her crippled, Wright moves back to Jackson to live with his grandmother. He enters Seventh-day Adventist school and rebels strongly against its strict discipline.

1921-1925   A period of serious and widespread racial discrimination against blacks and other minorities. The Ku Klux Klan is revived throughout the South and in various parts of the North, flourishing throughout the Twenties. Racial rioting takes place in many American cities in the years following World War I. Wright attends, with many interruptions, public and Seventh-day Adventist schools. In 1923, he enters the Smith-Robertson Public School and in 1925 graduates as valedictorian. Increasingly aware of southern racism and violence--brought to sharp focus when the brother of a high school friend is murdered by whites--he decides to leave Mississippi. He saves enough money from an assortment of menial jobs, and arrives in Memphis, Tennessee in November 1925.

1926   Starts to read widely and is especially drawn to H.L. Mencken's ideas criticizing American society and modern life. At this point, he also begins to read seriously American naturalists such as Theodore Dreiser, Sherwood Anderson, and Sinclair Lewis and is also strongly influenced by European realists Henrik Ibsen, Emile Zola, and Fyodor Dostoevsky. His period in Memphis is a profound psychological awakening that transforms his life and confirms his desire to be a writer.

1927-1931   Moves to Chicago in December, 1927 and shortly thereafter is joined by his mother and brother. After working as a waiter and helper in a grocery store, he passes a civil service examination and becomes a postal clerk, a job that enables him to work nights and spend his days reading and writing. He develops a strong interest in Edgar Allen Poe, and also begins to read works by T.S. Eliot, Charles Baudelaire, Andre Gide, Thomas Mann, Friedrich Nietzsche, Gustave Flaubert, and Nickolai Gogol. Soon after the stock market crash of 1929, he loses his position as a postal clerk and is forced to support himself and his family with a series of low-paying jobs; for much of this time he has no choice but to live in slum housing very much like that depicted in *Native Son*. In 1930, he works as an aide at the South Side Boys Club, where he is directly involved with young men from Chicago street gangs. He begins a novel entitled "Cesspool," a book about ghetto life in Chicago. In 1930, he takes a job with the Federal Negro Theatre and becomes a writer for the Illinois Writers Project.

1932-1933   Unable to support his family by selling insurance policies, Wright receives public assistance from the Cook County Welfare Department. He works as a street cleaner and gets a temporary job at the Post Office during the Christmas season. He is recruited by a fellow postal worker to join the John Reed Club, a literary organization sponsored by the Communist Party. He begins to write poems about revolution and is published in *Left Front*, the magazine of Midwestern John Reed Clubs. He is elected secretary of the Chicago John Reed Club.

1934   Wright officially joins the Communist Party and publishes poetry in leftist journals such as *Anvil* and *New Masses*. He becomes a member of the editorial board of *Left Front* and develops friendships with writer Nelson Algren and scholar Abraham Chapman. Wright continues to read widely in nineteenth and twentieth century fiction, especially works by Gertrude Stein, William Faulkner, Sherwood Anderson, Theodore Dreiser, Thomas Hardy, Fyodor Dostoevsky, Anton Chekov, and Leo Tolstoy.

1935   Continues to publish in leftist journals and submits "Cesspool" (later titled as *Lawd Today!*) to several publishers. He delivers a paper on

"The Isolation of the Negro Writer" at the American Writer's Conference in New York. Wright develops an important literary friendship with novelist James T. Farrell. He begins research on the history of blacks in Chicago for the Federal Writers' Project and also initiates work on "Big Boy Leaves Home."

1936   He helps to organize the South Side Writers' Group whose members include black writers and scholars such as Arna Bontemps, Frank Marshall Davis, Horace Cayton, and Margaret Walker. "Big Boy Leaves Home" is published in *The New Negro Caravan*, receiving praise from mainstream journals and newspapers.

1937   Has ideological differences with the Chicago John Reed Club over the issue of artistic freedom and moves to New York where he becomes Harlem editor of the Communist newspaper *Daily Worker*. "Blueprint for Negro Writing," an article calling for increased militancy in black literature, is published in *New Challenge* and "The Ethics of Living Jim Crow," an essay describing the racial injustices of the South, is published in *American Stuff: WPA Writers' Anthology*. His story "Fire and Cloud" wins first prize in *Story Magazine* contest. He begins outlining the novel which would become *Native Son*.

1938   *Uncle Tom's Children* is published, making Wright one of the Communist Party's outstanding young writers. He also becomes deeply interested in the Robert Nixon case, involving an 18-year-old black man accused of murdering a white woman. Wright does extensive research on the case and uses it as a documentary parallel to characters and events in *Native Son*.

1939   Is awarded a Guggenheim Fellowship of $2,500 and finishes *Native Son* on June 10. Marries Dhima Rose Meadman in August with Ralph Ellison serving as best man.

1940   *Native Son* is published on March 1 by *Harpers* as a Book-of-the-Month Club selection. In three weeks, it sells 215,000 copies and by early April it is a best-seller in America. When his marriage becomes strained, Wright travels through the South by himself and briefly visits his father, a poverty-stricken sharecropper. Later, he collaborates with Paul Green on a stage version of *Native Son* and begins work on *Twelve Million Black Voices*, a documentary study of the South featuring photographs by Edward Rosskam.

1941   Receives the Spingarn Medal awarded by the NAACP to an outstanding Negro. Marries Ellen Poplar, a white woman on March 12 despite her parents' strong objections to her marrying a black man. His doubts about being a member of the Communist Party intensify, partly because of the party's turning away from American racial issues in order to pursue a broader struggle against fascism in Europe. Wright begins to feel sharply divided between his commitment to opposing racial injustice in America and his loyalty to party ideology.

1942   Officially breaks with the Communist Party. *12 Million Black Voices* is published in October. He completes a manuscript version of "The Man Who Lived Underground," a short novel notable for its existential rather than Marxist vision of life.

1943   Visits the Deep South to give a lecture at Fisk University in April; the trip reacquaints him directly with the problems of the segregated South, triggering his desire to write his autobiography. By the end of the year, he has written *American Hunger*, an autobiography that covers his life up to his departure from Chicago in 1937.

1944   Wright's public disavowal of Communism, "I Tried to Be a Communist," is published in *The Atlantic Monthly*. "The Man Who Lived Underground" is published in *Cross Section*.

1945   *Black Boy*, a shortened version of Wright's autobiography, covering his childhood and adolescence in the South, is published in March as a Book-of-the-Month Club selection. Later in the year, he meets writer James Baldwin and helps launch Baldwin's career by assisting him in receiving a grant from the Eugene Saxton Foundation.

1946-1947   Decides to "exile" himself permanently in France, leaving the United States on May 1, 1946. His circle of friends in France includes existentialists Andre Gide, Jean-Paul Sartre, and Simone de Beauvoir, as well as American expatriate writers Gertrude Stein, Baldwin, and Chester Himes. He also develops close ties with the West Indian poet Aime Cesaire, writer George Padmore, and the African intellectual Leopold Senghor, each of whom is committed to viewing the situation of black people from a global, "third world" perspective.

1948   Reads extensively in existential philosophy, including works by Heidegger and Husserl. Becomes the focal point of an African-American expatriate colony in Paris which includes Baldwin and Himes. Develops friendships with European writers Carlo Levi, Arthur Koestler, and Ignazio Silone.

1950   Begins work on an existential novel which will eventually be published as *The Outsider*. Works intensively on a film version of *Native Son*, for which he writes the script and acts the role of Bigger Thomas. His relationship with James Baldwin sours when Baldwin publishes "Everybody's Protest Novel," which attacks *Native Son* as an artistically flawed piece of political and racial propaganda.

1951-1956   Publishes *The Outsider* in 1953 and *Savage Holiday* in 1954. Both novels reflect his increasing interest in French existentialism. In 1953, Wright visits the Gold Coast (now known as Ghana) where he observes firsthand an African nation in the process of liberating itself from colonial rule.

1955-1956   Participates in the Bandung Conference in Indonesia, which focuses on problems in the third world. His book *The Color Curtain* appears in March 1956 and places heavy emphasis on race as the crucial factor in resolving the problems of Western and third world cultures. In September 1956, he helps organize the First Congress of Negro Artists and Writers in Paris.

1957-1958   Works on a new novel, *Mississippi*, as the first installment in a trilogy centering on a black man's experience in the South and his exile in France. The first volume appears in 1958 as *The Long Dream*. *White Man, Listen!*, a book about black culture and politics, is published in October 1957.

1959   Wright plans to move to England because of increasing financial worries, a growing estrangement from friends in Paris, and a deepening distrust of the political situation in Gaullist France. He is not able to obtain a resident visa from British officials and has to remain in France while his wife and daughters, Rachel and Julia, relocate to London. In June he falls ill with amebic dysentery, and has persistent health problems.

1960   Begins a new novel, "A Father's Law" and collects his haiku poetry for publication. Finishes the final proofreading of *Eight Men*. Health problems continue with Wright being treated at a Dutch hospital for gastrointestinal problems. He enters a Paris hospital in November for further treatment of these problems and dies on November 28 from a heart attack. Wright is cremated along with a copy of *Black Boy* at the Père Lachaise cemetery on December 3.

Introduction

In *The Unfinished Quest of Richard Wright*, Michel Fabre points out that Richard Wright was from an early point in his life onward fascinated by the American success myth and how that myth was embodied in the novels of Horatio Alger. As a young man Wright was an "avid reader of Horatio Alger"[1] and as late as 1945 he reviewed the collected edition of Alger's works for *PM* magazine. Throughout his career he made complex use of the Alger myth, inverting it savagely in *Native Son* and "The Man Who Lived Underground" but affirming certain of its features in *Black Boy* and *American Hunger*. Fabre concludes that Wright could never quite shake the Alger myth which fired his imagination as a child: "All throughout his life Wright remained an American...brought up in spite of himself on Horatio Alger and the Bible. . . ."[2]

Fascinated by the myth of the self-made man, Wright did indeed live a life which, in some ways at least, bears a striking resemblance to the stories of personal transformation and dramatic success described in the Alger novels. As the chronology which prefaces this introduction should make abundantly clear, Wright was born into stark poverty, experiencing probably the most severe economic hardship endured by any major American writer, and through his own innate genius and extraordinary perseverance, became a world-famous writer who not only changed the direction of American and African-American literatures but also helped to transform the way modern people regard race. His beginnings could not have been more challenging, even surpassing the hardships encountered by Alger's raggedy young men. Born in 1908 in rural Mississippi to an illiterate sharecropper and a mother who had to turn from teaching to farm work in order to make more money, Wright faced throughout his childhood the bleakest poverty and the most extreme racism, living a life characterized by chronic hunger, emotional trauma, educational disadvantage, and social-disempowerment. Wright's family circumstances were deeply troubled by his father's desertion when Wright was five years old and by his mother's chronic health problems which date back to when Wright was eight. Moreover, Wright knew from first-hand knowledge the terrible racial violence of the segregated South--his uncle Silas was murdered by whites when Wright was only ten, and a brother of a high school friend was lynched for allegedly making sexual advances to a white girl. Given this social world of "total discrimination," Keneth Kinnamon has observed that it was remarkable that Wright became a novelist rather than a criminal: "That a novelist rather than a criminal emerged from the racial prejudice, poverty, family disorganization, and inadequate education that afflicted his early years is a phenomenon not easy to explain."[3]

Battling what Kinnamon has called "more than Algeresque odds,"[4] Wright left Mississippi in 1925 for Memphis and then in 1927 moved to Chicago where he lived for a decade. Like the typical Alger hero whose success in many ways is derived from hard work and self-education, Wright labored at a great variety of menial jobs, all the while engaging in an extraordinary process of self education. He not only read widely and deeply in American and European literature but also became an accomplished writer, who in 1937, won the *Story* magazine prize for fiction with "Fire and Cloud," a story which describes racial injustices in Mississippi. As John Reilly has pointed out, winning this prize (in a contest whose judges included Sinclair Lewis and Lewis Gannett) was a pivotal moment in Wright's life because it brought his literary apprenticeship to an end and prepared him for the larger project of publishing his first book, *Uncle Tom's Children*, in 1938.[5] In the seven years which followed, Wright achieved widespread success as a writer, publishing two major works--*Native Son* (1940) and *Black Boy* (1945)--which helped to transform American and African-American literatures.

Some of the initial reviews of *Uncle Tom's Children* certainly underscore Wright's Alger-like rise to literary success. Established critics and writers praised the book heavily, often citing it as evidence that an important new voice was emerging in American literature. Lewis Gannett (*New York Herald Tribune*, 25 March 1938), for example, admired the power and artistic skill of Wright's stories, adding that "Their spirit is a part of a new American history." Malcolm Cowley (*New Republic*, April 1938) hailed Wright as a "vigorous new talent" and Granville Hicks (*New Masses*, 27 March 1938) concluded that Wright was a "first-rate writer" who had "immeasurably strengthened" the literature of the American left. James T. Farrell (*Partisan Review*, 4 May 1938) strongly praised *Uncle Tom's Children* for its unflinching realism and emotional power, characterizing it as "a genuine literary achievement" by a "new American writer" of considerable importance. Countee Cullen (*The African*, April 1938) regarded Wright's book as "an impressive and important addition to American letters" because it envisioned racial conflict in bold new ways, realistically describing the militant demands of southern blacks in search of their fair share of the American Dream. Sterling Brown (*Opportunity*, April 1938) heartily agreed with Cullen, arguing that *Uncle Tom's Children*'s fresh rendering of southern life matched and perhaps even surpassed the power and artistry of Toomer's *Cane*.

As John Reilly has stressed, the majority of the early reviews of *Uncle Tom's Children* were "decidedly favorable"[6] and helped to make Wright an important new presence in the New York literary community. Not only was Wright honored by leftist groups and asked to participate in the League of American Writers, but he also became literary editor of *New Masses* and received a Guggenheim Fellowship in 1939. There were, however, some dissenting voices in certain early reviews which expressed serious reservations and strong criticisms of Wright's work. Some southern reviewers felt that *Uncle Tom's Children* failed to tell the full truth about race relationships in the South and therefore contributed to the problems it explored. James Saxon Childrens (*Birmingham New Age-Herald*, 1 May 1938), for instance, objected strenuously to Wright's "fierce story" because it oversimplified the "myriad conflicting sides" of southern culture when it demonized southern whites and "lashed out at the South as a whole." Herbert Agar, whose review appeared in both the *Louisville Courier-Journal* and the *Chicago Times*, made a similar complaint when he faulted the book for not being sufficiently balanced or complex to tell the full truth about race relationships in America.

But perhaps the most serious and enduring criticism of *Uncle Tom's Children* came from African-American novelist Zora Neale Hurston (*Saturday Review of Literature*, 2 April 1938) who accused Wright of not being able to "touch the broader or more fundamental phases of Negro life." Hurston's sharp criticism, perhaps in retaliation to Wright's equally critical review of her novel *Their Eyes Were Watching God* a year earlier, has several dimensions. First, she feels that Wright oversimplifies the psychological and emotional history of American blacks by grounding his book in a "Swamp of race hatred" and thereby failing to account for the "sympathy and understanding" which also is an important part of black culture. Secondly, she argues that Wright's art is propagandistic, centered in a narrowly Marxist thesis which naively proposes that solutions to the problems which the book explores can be found when the state takes "responsibility for everything" and the individual is given "responsibility for nothing." Thirdly, and most interesting for modern readers, is Hurston's charge that Wright has written a book for "black male readers," a series of stories in which all the action is driven by male "wish-fulfillment" and where the experience of women is either ignored or stereotyped. (This last criticism, little noticed when initial reviews of *Uncle Tom's Children* appeared, has become, as we shall see, a major issue confronting Wright's scholars today.)

These criticisms aside, Wright was well on his way to literary success with the publication of *Uncle Tom's Children* in 1938 and his being awarded a Guggenheim Fellowship a year later to complete another novel which he had been working on since 1937. When this novel appeared in 1940 as *Native Son*, Wright did indeed achieve the monetary and artistic success for which he had hungered for most of his life. Not only was the novel a Book-of-the Month Club selection which sold over 200,000 copies and became the number one best seller in American during its first month of existence,[7] but it was clear to many initial reviewers of the book that it was a seminal novel which was to change the course of modern literature.

The reviews of *Native Son* caused a fire storm of debate that burns brightly to the present day. Focusing sharply on fundamental issues which subsequent generations of critics would energetically discuss for more than fifty years, these reviews may be categorized into three basic types: 1) enthusiastic celebrations of a groundbreaking and paradigmatic novel; 2) vigorous denunciations of the book; and 3) troublingly split responses.

Many reviewers who praised the book did so because they saw in it a new and disturbing vision of black life in America which previous writers lacked either the background, understanding, or artistic skill to present in literature. Henry Seidel Canby (*Book-of-the-Month-Club-News*, Feb. 1940) boldly asserted that *Native Son* was "the finest novel written by an American Negro," a book so deeply grounded in black American experience that "only a Negro could have written it." Several other commentators explained the originality and depth of Wright's racial vision in terms of his creating a new kind of central character, a black person whose story provided a fresh perspective on African-American life. Milton Rugoff (*New York Herald Tribune Review of Books*, 3 March 1940) stressed that "the first extraordinary aspect of *Native Son* is that it approaches the tragedy of race, not through an 'average' member but through a criminal" and that such a character is skillfully probed by Wright to "connect one individual's pathology to the whole tragedy of the Negro spirit in a white world." Sterling Brown (*Crisis*, June 1940) praised *Native Son* as a "literary phenomenon" because it was the very first novel about American blacks which provided a "psychological probing of the consciousness of the outcast, the disinherited, the generation lost in the slum jungles of American civilization."

Some leftist critics, such as Samuel Sillen (*New Masses*, 5 March 1940), liked the book for its "revolutionary view of life" and its portrayal of the hero's "emancipatory" struggles against a capitalistic society intent on crushing him. Many other reviewers were also struck by the novel's extraordinary impact, its power to transform the reader's consciousness. May Cameron (*New York Post*, 1 March 1940) saw *Native Son* as an "intense and powerful" novel that moved with "tremendous force and speed" to shock the reader into a new awareness of the status of blacks in American society. Henry Hansen (*New York World Telegram*, 2 March 1940) observed that Wright's novel "packs a tremendous punch, something like a big fist through the windows of our complacent lives." Similarly, Margaret Wallace (*New York Sun*, 5 March 1940) sensed a "peculiar vitality" in the book which was likely not only to challenge the reader's views on race but which would also "father other books."

But many reviewers were equally vigorous in their condemnation of the novel. One day after its publication, Howard Mumford Jones (*Boston Evening Transcript*, 2 March 1940) strongly criticized *Native Son* on aesthetic grounds, describing its plot as melodramatic and its themes as "dull propaganda." Burton Rascoe (*American Mercury*, May 1940) aggressively attacked the early positive reviews and concluded "Sanely considered, it is impossible for me to conceive of a novel being worse." A number of reviewers faulted the book for a lack of realism, claiming that its vision of American life was overdrawn and unfair. David Cohn (*Atlantic Monthly*, May 1940), for example, described *Native Son* as "a blinding and corrosive study in hate," vehemently arguing that the actual condition of American blacks was considerably better than the book would allow. David Daiches (*Partisan Review*, May-June 1940) maintained that the novel failed in its attempt to be an "illustrative fable" of race relations in America because Bigger Thomas's violent actions are too extreme for him to be a representative figure. Alleging that "Mr. Wright is trying to prove a normal thesis with an abnormal case," Daiches felt that *Native Son* deteriorated into melodrama that destroyed its realism.

On an even more serious level, some reviewers sharply questioned Wright's conception of Bigger Thomas, claiming that the character actually reinforced the brutal stereotypes which the author wanted to challenge and destroy. Reverend Joseph McSorley (*Catholic World*, May 1940) asserted that Bigger Thomas was a "savage moron" whose portrayal had the unintended effect of "spreading and deepening distrust of the Negro." Jonathan Daniels, (*Saturday Review of Literature*, 2 March 1940), likewise, concluded that "the story of Bigger Thomas is the story of a rat," a dehumanized figure manipulated by the author to develop his political "tract."

A small number of reviewers had split responses to the novel, admiring it in certain ways but being troubled by it in other ways. Clifton Fadiman (*New Yorker*, 16 2 March 1940), for example, compares *Native Son* favorably to Steinbeck's *The Grapes of Wrath* and Dreiser's *An American Tragedy*, admiring its power and depth. But he finds that the novel has "numerous defects as a work of art," namely its excessive repetition and stereotyped white characters. Peter Monroe Jack (*New York Times Book Review*, 3 March 1940) characterizes Wright's novel as "extremely interesting" because it transcends its sociology and becomes "a memorable experience." But he feels that the books is marred by "much romantic nonsense" when Wright has Bigger undergo what he thinks is an unconvincing conversion at the end of the novel. Mary Carter-Roberts (*Washington Star*, 3 March 1940) praises Wright for writing a "splendid" story but considers Wright's portrayal of Bigger to be confused because she is unable to reconcile his view of Bigger as a victim of white society with what she thinks is his inability to supply concrete proof of Bigger's "supposedly crushed better nature" which would have flourished if he had lived in a just society.

In the five years after the publication of *Native Son* Wright increasingly turned to the writing of non-fictional prose. Although he did complete during this period one of his most important fictions, "The Man Who Lived Underground," most of his attempts at writing stories and novels were unsuccessful. (Indeed, he made one attempt to write a novel entitled "Black Hope" but was never able to complete it.) His most successful writing was in the form of autobiographical prose, an essay on *Native Son* entitled "How Bigger Was Born," a documentary book of photographs and commentary on the Deep South which he did with Edward Rosskam called *Twelve Million Black Voices*, an essay describing his break with the Communist Party titled "I Tried to Be a Communist" and his autobiographical masterpiece, *Black Boy*. Perhaps the charges made by some reviewers of *Uncle Tom's Children* and *Native Son* that these books were not "realistic" portraits of black American life drove Wright into autobiography as a means of authenticating his fiction. He clearly did, for example, write "How Bigger Was Born" to directly challenge Cohn's and Rascoe's claims that *Native Son* was an exaggerated and unfair account of race in America. Perhaps, too, Wright's leaving the Communist Party in 1942 and his growing interest in existentialism pushed him further into himself in an attempt to recover the philosophical coherence and meaning which Party ideology had formerly supplied. In any event, Wright's outstanding achievement during these years was the publication of *Black Boy*.

The critical responses to *Black Boy* were almost as animated and revealing as the initial reactions to *Native Son*. Many critics lavished even higher praise on it than *Native Son* received. Lewis Gannett (*New York Herald Tribune*, 28 Feb. 1945) argued that *Black Boy* "may be one of the great American autobiographies." Charles Lee (*Philadelphia Record*, 1 March 1945) made even stronger claims for the book, asserting that "*Black Boy* may very possibly go down as one of the most memorable books of our time, a kind of 20th century *Uncle Tom's Cabin*." Lee regarded *Black Boy* as a "much better book" than *Native Son* because it was not only "more potent" but also more realistic and more controlled as a work of art. In a similar way, John Paulus (*Pittsburgh Press*, 18 Feb. 1945) saw Wright's autobiography as a fundamentally American book which "could easily take its place alongside *The Autobiography of Benjamin Franklin* and *The Education of Edward Bok*." Although Lionel Trilling (*Nation*, 7 April 1945) was more measured in his praise, he nevertheless regarded *Black Boy* as "a remarkably fine book" which transcended sociological documentation and became a work of art arising from its author's "moral and intellectual power."

These positive reviews recall some of the high praise for Wright's earlier work but there is one area in which the critical reception of *Black Boy* is quite different from that received by either *Uncle Tom's Children* or *Native Son*. Leftist critics, still angry over

Wright's resigning from the Communist Party three years earlier, offered sharp criticisms of *Black Boy*, dramatically reversing their earlier estimate of him. Isador Schneider (*New Masses*, 3 April 1945) chided Wright for cultivating a vision centered in "hostility and alienation" which resulted in his losing sympathy with his fellow blacks in particular and the masses of all oppressed people in general. Schneider felt that when Wright rejected the leftist politics which had earlier enabled him to overcome the "isolation" which he now "defends" in *Black Boy*, he developed "an obsession with violence" which deeply mars his writing. Another leftist critic, Milton Mayer (*The Progressive*, 9 April 1945), likewise, deplores Wright's excessively personal vision, insisting that *Black Boy* is "not a great book" because it is merely "an account of singular events befalling a given person at a given time and place" rather than a more resonant study of racial problems in America. Furthermore, Mayer complains that when Wright lost his faith in Communism he lost a valuable resource which could not only help him to diagnose problems but imagine solutions to them. Because of this, he finds Wright's autobiography excessively negative, poking at the "scabs" of racial injustice in America but unable to suggest ways of healing these wounds.

The critical response to *Black Boy* differs from assessments of *Uncle Tom's Children* and *Native Son* in one other significant way. By 1945 a much larger group of African-American critics were submitting Wright's work to close scrutiny and this produced a fascinatingly mixed body of commentary. Several important black critics expressed substantial disappointment with Wright, citing the following passage from *Black Boy* which served as a focal point for their sharp disagreement with his interpretation of black American life:

> After I had outlived the shocks of childhood, after the habit of reflection had been born in me, I used to mull over the strange absence of real kindness in Negroes, how unstable was our tenderness, how lacking in genuine passion we were, how void of great hope, how timid our great joy, how bare our traditions, how hollow our memories, how lacking we were in those tangible sentiments that bind man to man, and how shallow was even our despair.[8]

This passage, which has continued to trouble many African-American readers up to the present day, was cited in W.E.B. Du Bois's review (*New York Herald Weekly Book Review* 4 March 1945) as evidence of Wright's "misjudgment of black folk." Du Bois challenged the veracity of Wright's account of black American experience, finding that it ignores all the positive features of black life in America. Instead, Du Bois considers *Black Boy* to be centered in a narcissistic "hero" whose self absorption becomes "almost pathological." Ben Burns (*Chicago Defender*, 3 March 1945) makes a similar complaint, judging Wright to be "a self-interested, anti-social rebel" who is "without feeling of solidarity with the Negro people." Indeed, Burns sees the book as "a sorry slander of Negroes" because it neglects to account for the positive features of black cultural life and the heroic struggles of blacks to achieve justice and equality in America. James Ivy (*The Crisis*, 52 April 1945) puts the case against Wright even more strongly, charging that he "put a sword in the back of his race." Like Du Bois and Burns, Ivy deplores Wright's bleak reading of the black past and what he feels is an excessively negative sense of the prospects for blacks in the future.

Many other African-American critics, however, were quick to defend Wright and his autobiography. Augusta Strong (*Congress View*, 2 May 1945) in a review which was included in the report of the National Negro Congress, aggressively challenged the idea that *Black Boy* was an "overdrawn" account of black life which did violence to the facts of the history of blacks in America. For Strong, *Black Boy* does indeed make "unpleasant reading" but it "carries the weight of absolute truth." Indeed, Strong insists that Wright is "our best Negro writer" because he has realistically portrayed the plight of southern blacks in American cities better than any previous writer. Alice Browning (*Negro Story*, 1 May-June 1945) likewise observes that *Black Boy* tells "a much-needed story" which faithfully records the injustices which most blacks in America have to face.

Horace Cayton (*Twice-a-Year*, Spring-Summer/Fall-Winter 1945) rescues Wright from the charge of excessive bitterness, explaining that such bitterness for blacks is a part of their "social reality." For Cayton *Black Boy* digs even more deeply into Negro life than Wright's early work because it examines in an uncompromisingly honest way the fears and hatreds which American society generates in black people. Ralph Ellison (*The Antioch Review*, Summer 1945), who would later make serious attacks on Wright's art, wrote perhaps the most sensitive review of *Black Boy*, likening it to a blues performance in which the pain of actual experience is realistically probed and then transcended with "a near-tragic, near comic lyricism." Approaching Wright's autobiography as a rich and complex work of art rather than as a political statement or a literal transcript of actual experience, Ellison argued that Wright was able to triumph over his personal disasters by forming those raw experiences into art which was coherent and balanced. In order to do this, Wright had to artfully fuse two cultures, his own southern black heritage and the larger Western world which enabled him to see his personal circumstances from a wider perspective. *Black Boy*, therefore, is rooted in Wright's complex double consciousness, which, on the one hand, derives from his own direct experiences in the South and, on the other hand, is vitally connected to Wright's reading of writers such as Dostoevsky and Joyce.

****

By 1945 the critical response to Wright's work had completed its first phase. Reviews of *Uncle Tom's Children*, *Native Son*, and *Black Boy* had generated an extremely broad variety of lively responses to Wright's work which ranged from utter condemnation to unqualified praise. But these reviews established Wright as an important young writer who would have a serious impact on African-American and American literatures. It is no surprise, therefore, to find one reviewer of *Black Boy*, Orville Prescott (*New York Times*, 28 February 1945), describing Wright in Algeresque terms as achieving "an honored rank among that traditionally American group, the self-made man." In 1945 Ralph Ellison had no difficulty in characterizing Wright as "an important writer, perhaps the most articulate Negro American."[9]

But by 1963 Ellison would substantially lower his estimate of Wright's work and influence, presenting him as a very limited "protest writer" whose "harsh naturalism" was outdated and artistically thin.[10] Between 1945 and the early 1960s Wright's reputation declined substantially and his place in African-American letters was challenged by a wide variety of younger critics and writers. What accounts for this sudden reversal in the critical response to Wright? Although there is no single definitive answer to this question, a number of factors contributed to Wright's diminished reputation. First of all, the writing he produced from 1945 to his death in 1960 clearly lacked the vitality, power, and artistic excellence of *Uncle Tom's Children*, *Native Son*, and *Black Boy*. By most accounts, novels such as *The Outsider* (1953) and *Savage Holiday* (1954) are uneven in quality and unfortunately helped to lower the critical estimate of Wright's work in general. Then too, the years immediately following World War II saw a decline in naturalism as a literary mode in favor of less doctrinaire, more experimental fictional styles and this left Wright--an acknowledged master of naturalistic fiction--in general disfavor with the new generation of critics. A pervasive disenchantment with leftist politics in the Cold War years also caused critics to look askance at Wright's work. (Although Wright's writing after *Native Son* was not informed by leftist ideas, he was, like James T. Farrell and John Dos Passos, unfairly labelled as a "thirties radical" and dismissed as obsolete.)

In addition, a perceived improvement in race relations after the war and a hope for the rapid integration of blacks into the mainstream of American life produced a desire for a more "universal" and less "race conscious" type of literature that would speak to the needs of a multiracial audience. William Gardner Smith, for example, urged the black American writer to move away from "propaganda" and toward an art centered in "universal" themes. He made Wright a special case in point, warning black novelists to avoid making their characters "an exaggerated Bigger Thomas with all the stereotyped characteristics three times over."[11] Hugh Gloster, who admired *Native Son* as "a masterpiece of proletarian fiction," nevertheless felt that such writing was too restrictive for the post-World War II Negro writer. Gloster generally faulted Wright for looking at American reality from too limited a perspective: "He sees only a segment of life, and even this limited part he views in its most violent and horrible aspects."[12] James Baldwin and Ralph Ellison state the case against Wright most pointedly in widely admired essays that seriously diminished Wright's literary reputation. Baldwin argued in "Many Thousands Gone" that "protest" novels like *Native Son* were intended to advance the cause of racial justice for American blacks but had the reverse effect because they were populated by one-dimensional characters who reinforced all the stereotypes which trapped black people in limited roles. He claimed that Wright constructed Bigger Thomas as "a monster created by the American republic" and "a social symbol revelatory of social disease"[13] rather than a fully developed, realistic character who could adequately reflect the richness of Afro-American experience. Ellison in "The World and the Jug" and interviews later collected in *Shadow and Act* likewise claimed that *Native Son* was artistically crude and that its vision of black life was too narrow because it was filtered through Bigger's limited perspective and Wright's excessive commitment to Marxist ideology.

One of the few major critics to come to Wright's defense during this period was Irving Howe who in "Black Boys and Native Sons" strenuously disagreed with the assessments of Wright made by Baldwin and Ellison. Howe argued that *Native Son* brought to a culmination the vital tradition of protest in black literature and chided younger black writers for abandoning this tradition. He praised *Native Son* for its "superbly aggressive" tone, "apocalyptic" mood and "clenched militancy." Moreover, he credited Wright with dramatically altering not only American literature but also the way Americans regard race:

> The day *Native Son* appeared, American culture was changed forever. No matter how much qualifying the book might later need, it made impossible a repetition of the old lies . . . . Richard Wright's novel brought out in the open, as no one had ever before, the hatred, the fear and violence that have crippled and may yet destroy our culture![4]

But as the reviews of *The Outsider* and *Savage Holiday* clearly indicate, Howe's emphatic praise of Wright was definitely a minority view. Indeed, it is jarring to move from the 1945 reviews of *Black Boy* to the reviews of *The Outsider* written just eight years later because these latter estimates seem informed by a general sense that Wright's work is in decline and that his exile from the United States has resulted in his losing touch with the African-American realities which endowed his earlier work with such force and vitality. Gone is the sense that Wright is an important new voice in American literature and what emerges instead is a greatly diminished estimate of the literary quality of Wright's work and the role it can play in understanding race in America.

Milton Rugoff (*New York Herald Tribune Book Review*, 22 March 1953), who had high praise for *Native Son* when it appeared in 1940, saw little to admire in *The Outsider*, complaining that the book was grossly unrealistic, "sheer melodrama" which was a "compost of sex and crime." Rugoff also found Wright's style to be "strained and fumbling" because it was centered in abstract ideas which Wright was not able to assimilate in a coherent work of art. Orville Prescott (*New York Times*, 18 March 1953) made a similar criticism, arguing that Wright's "philosophical novel" had moved too far away from his own concrete experience and thus was populated with "unreal" characters which made the novel "artificial" and lacking in the "impact" which was the trademark of *Native Son* and *Uncle Tom's Children*. Max Eastman (*The Freeman*, 4 March 1953) likewise saw *The Outsider* as a "thesis novel" which greatly oversimplified life. The reviewer for *Time* (30 March 1953) also panned the novel, asserting that "Wright has resorted to so much ludicrous coincidence, unlikely conversation, and soapbox bombast that his story is a bore."

The Outsider got an even harsher reception from African-American reviewers. Arna Bontemps (*Saturday Review*, 28 March 1953), who was a strong defender of *Native Son,* saw Wright's new novel as weak because it moved away from Wright's *forte*, an honest probing of American racial issues, and explored territory which he felt Wright was unsure of, the complexities of French existentialism. Disapproving of Wright's "roll in the hay with existentialism," Bontemps cautions Wright to redirect his attention to the subjects which gave such "narrative power" and "freshness of vision" to the books he wrote before exiling himself in France. Lorraine Hansberry (*Freedom*, 14 April 1953) agrees with Bontemps' view that Wright's residence in Europe weakened his writing but is much more severe in her estimate of the literary damage it caused. She claims that by 1953 Wright had "destroyed his talent" because he had forgotten the "beauty and strength" of working-class black people. By centering his novel instead on a monstrously violent black protagonist, Hansberry argues that Wright has reinforced the most brutally stereotypical notions about blacks, thus producing "a propaganda piece for the enemies of the Negro people." The reviewer for *Jet Magazine* (26 March 1953) offered an even more negative view of the novel, complaining that Wright's obsessive interest in violence and sensationalism had produced a "phony" book which was no better than "a cheap drugstore whodunit."

J. Saunders Redding, an enthusiastic champion of *Native Son* and *Black Boy*, was more measured in his evaluation of *The Outsider* but could find very few good things to say about it, characterizing it as a "disappointment." Like Bontemps, Eastman and Prescott, he sensed that the book's chief weakness was its being grounded in "abstraction" rather than arising naturally from concrete "reality." Because Wright's imagination was dominated by the "dogma of existentialism," he was unable to develop realistic characters or plausible narration. Redding also felt uncomfortable with another aspect of Wright's existentialism, his excessive preoccupation with his central character's inward life and his neglecting to connect that inward life to social, economic, and political dimensions of black life in America.

To be sure, there were some positive reviews of *The Outsider* but none had the unqualified praise which characterized the favorable reviews of books like *Native Son* and *Black Boy*. Granville Hicks (*New York Times Book Review*, 22 March 1953) characterized Wright as "one of the most important literary talents of our time" and described *The Outsider* as the first "consciously written" existential novel in American literature but even he pointed out serious flaws in the book, Wright's "persistent clumsiness in style" and his "sometimes incoherent" exposition of ideas. Harvey Curtis Webster (*The New Leader*, 6 April 1953), likewise, gave *The Outsider* a generally positive but mixed review, describing it as a "perhaps great" novel which nevertheless is "careless" and "often confusing." Catholic critics such as M.D. Reagan (*America*, 4 April 1953) and R.F. Grady S.J. (*Best Sellers*, 1 May 1953) praised the novel for its moving beyond narrowly racial themes to pursue more "universal" concerns, but both expressed reservations about Wright's preoccupation with sex and violence.

A rather clear indication of Wright's diminished reputation is the fact that his next novel, *Savage Holiday* (1954) was rejected by both Harper and World publishers and eventually appeared as an Avon paperback. Moreover, it received no American reviews. Wright did publish within the span of four years three works of nonfiction, *Black Power* (1954), *Pagan Spain* (1955), and *The Color Curtain* (1956) but these received mostly mixed and negative responses. *The Long Dream*, the first part of a proposed trilogy about a black man growing up in Mississippi and eventually moving to Paris in search of a new life, was published in 1957, but got a disappointing reception, especially from black critics such as Ted Poston and J. Saunders Redding. Even Granville Hicks, a long-time supporter of Wright's work, found the book melodramatic and crude.

Wright's last project, before he died so unexpectedly in November 1960, was to collect a number of his previously published and unpublished stories in a volume entitled *Eight Men*. The book appeared in 1961 and the reviews of it are another reminder of how much Wright's critical reputation had declined since its high point in the mid-1940's. Irving Howe (*New Republic*, 13 February 1961) deplored the fact that Wright was "hardly read today by serious literary persons; his name is barely known by the young." Although Howe felt that Wright deserved an "honored place" in twentieth-century American literature, he hesitated to regard Wright as a "writer of the first rank" because his literary "faults were grave and serious." For Howe, one of the most serious problems with Wright's later work was its "clumsy efforts" to break away from the naturalism of *Native Son* in favor of more "supple and terse" fictional forms. He argued that naturalism was Wright's "necessary mode of expression" because it allowed him to express his real subject, his past life in Mississippi and Chicago. But when Wright used more surrealistic techniques to express the existential themes of his later fiction the results were at best "uneven."

James Baldwin (*The Reporter*, 16 March 1961) gave Wright a mixed assessment for precisely the opposite reason, admiring him as a psychological writer who used physical details expressionistically and sharply criticizing his naturalistic fiction which he used for "social and polemical" purposes. Saunders Redding (*New York Herald Tribune Book Review*, 22 Jan. 1961), however, stuck to his views expressed in his review of *The Outsider* that Wright's best work was the naturalistic writing which predated his exile to Europe, arguing that the only stories in *Eight Men* which had merit were the ones written before 1945. Praising the "old Wright" who spoke out of "his supraconsciousness of being a Negro," he is saddened by the rootless "new Wright" whose work was deeply marred by nihilism. He concludes that *Eight Men* is "not one of the books by which Richard Wright deserves to be judged" because it is such a great falling-off in quality from masterpieces like *Uncle Tom's Children, Native Son* and *Black Boy*.

Richard Gilman (Commonwealth, 28 April 1962) is much harsher in its evaluation of both *Eight Men* and Wright's career in a review which was so negative that John Reilly has called it "the lowest point to which Wright's career ever sank."[15] Gilman regards *Eight Men* as "a dismayingly stale and dated book" and asserts that Wright was "simply not a good writer, not even a competent one." In an act of extraordinary critical arrogance, he reduces Wright's achievement to providing "extra-literary excitement" to readers who confuse literature with sociology. The review ends in a burst of sociological and literary naiveté, with Gilman claiming that Wright's brand of protest literature is obsolete and unnecessary, calling instead for Negro writers to develop a new literature which would explore "a common base" between whites and blacks transcending what he terms "artificial differences."

****

The next phase of the critical reception to Wright sharply challenged the predominantly negative response to his work from 1945 to the early 1960s. From the midsixties to the late seventies Wright's reputation as a writer and thinker was restored, even exceding the claims made for him early in his career. Today Wright is regarded not only as a major American writer but also a writer of considerable importance in world literature. Part of the reason for this dramatic reevaluation of Wright was the increasing militancy of the civil rights movement and a new interest in "black power," a phase Wright himself had coined. Whereas post-World War II critics were likely to view Wright's aggressive politics as an aesthetic liability, critics from the midsixties onward, particularly those connected with the Black Arts Movement, saw him as a model of the politically engaged writer. (While earlier critics were likely to view a character like Bigger Thomas as a dangerous stereotype of the "bad nigger" who would make people think twice about integration, critics now were apt to hail Bigger as a prototype of the revolutionary black hero who was not interested in assimilating into the mainstream.) Likewise, Wright's graphic portrayal of violence, which to critics like Baldwin and Redding was gratuitous and melodramatic, was to a newer generation of readers a necessary part of Wright's realism.

Probably the work that most vividly illustrates this shift in sensibility is Eldridge Cleaver's "Notes on a Native Son," published in *Soul on Ice* (1968). Cleaver strongly criticized writers like Baldwin for ignoring the sociology of black experience and praised Wright for the depth of his social and political vision. Wright's commitments to Marxism and black nationalism were seen by Cleaver as artistic advantages, for they enabled him to envision black life in broader, more coherent, and more resonant terms. Accordingly, Bigger Thomas becomes for Cleaver someone very different from the pathological monster Baldwin saw; on the contrary, he views Bigger as "the black rebel of the ghetto and a man."[16] In a similar way, Edward Margolies's *Native Sons* (1968) describes Bigger as a revolutionary figure rather than a sociological case study. Arthur P. Davis's *The Dark Tower* (1974) and Addison Gayle's *The Way of the New World* (1975) are later studies which also make a strong link between Wright's rebels and the tradition of black activism.

This dramatic reassessment of Wright as a social and political thinker led to an equally dramatic reevaluation of him as an artist. From the midsixties onward, much was written to call into question the earlier view that Wright was a "powerful" but artistically stunted writer. George E. Kent in 1969 observed that Richard Wright "seems all too prophetic, all too relevant, majestically awaiting the close critical engagement which forms the greatest respect that can be paid to a great man and a great writer."[17] In the years that followed, Wright's work, especially *Native Son*, received in scores of articles and books the "close critical engagement" it deserved but had been deprived of for such a long time. One of the best critical studies to appear at this time was Donald Gibson's "Wright's Invisible Native Son." Submitting *Native Son*, and especially Book Three to a close and sensitive reading, Gibson argued persuasively that critics who saw Bigger as a stereotyped monster fail to *see* the inward, personal self buried underneath Bigger's public mask. By the end of the novel, Bigger can transcend his outward environment through "solitary hours of minute introspection and self analysis" and can thus become a "private, isolated human" who is able "to face the consequences of his life."[18] Dan McCall's *The Example of Richard Wright* (1969) is another penetrating study that first describes the extraordinary hatred and violence of the world Wright experienced as an American black man and then raises the crucial question, "How does one write about such a world and how is it to be interpreted in literary art?"[19] Part of McCall's answer is his belief that Wright consciously moved away from a conventionally "realistic" style of fiction toward what he calls "psychodrama," a mode of gothic fiction in the tradition of Poe and Hawthorne that distorts outer reality as a way of dramatizing the world of the mind with symbolism.

McCall's book was followed three years later by another crucial study, Keneth Kinnamon's *The Emergence of Richard Wright*. This book, which has laid the groundwork for much subsequent exploration on Wright's fiction, carefully explores Wright's southern background and literary apprenticeship in Chicago and New York. Remaining chapters submit *Lawd Today!*, *Uncle Tom's Children* and *Native Son* to rigorous formal analysis. Kinnamon's analysis of *Native Son* is especially penetrating, demonstrating how Wright used his own experiences and the murder trial of Robert Nixon as a point of departure for his novel but then transformed these materials to produce a coherent work of art with universal implications. Carefully discussing the novel's structure, point of view, characterization, and symbolism, Kinnamon argues that each technique is artfully integrated to give full expression to "the theme of rebellion" that is the central meaning of *Native Son*. Although he admits that the novel is not without flaws, most notably an "unevenness in style" and a less than satisfactory Book Three, he finally regards *Native Son* not only as "a major document of the American racial dilemma" but also a book whose "art makes it . . . an important American novel."[20]

Three influential studies of the cultural background of Wright's fiction also emerged during this time. Blyden Jackson's biographical essay entitled "Richard Wright: Black Boy from America's Black Belt and Urban Ghettos" appeared in a 1969 special issue of *CLA Journal* devoted to Wright. Jackson placed Wright's fiction firmly in the context of his experience "deep within the world of the folk Negro," claiming that although Wright chose to live his adult life outside the South, his work is grounded in southern culture, which was both his "heart's home" and his "mind's tether."[21] George E. Kent's "Richard Wright: Blackness and the Adventures of Western Culture" appeared in the same special issue but approached Wright from another perspective, arguing that Wright's vision is centered in a broader context, his ambivalent response to the West. Kent sees Wright attracted in some ways to Western culture because of its tradition of Enlightenment rationalism that promises political freedom to oppressed people, but he also argues that Wright was deeply suspicious of other aspects of the West, especially its history of racism. Kent envisions Bigger Thomas as caught between these two opposite qualities of Western culture, for he is both victimized by Western racism and also achieves selfhood in a very Western way through "revolutionary will, individualism and self consciousness."[22] Houston Baker, like Jackson, examines Wright's work in the context of black folk culture. His chapter on Wright in *Long Black Song* (1972) presents *Native Son* as a landmark work in American literature because it is the first novel to capture adequately the full force and richness of black folk experience. Baker draws revealing parallels between Bigger Thomas and trickster heroes like Brer Rabbit, bad-man heroes like Stackolee, and revolutionary figures like Nat Turner.

From the late sixties to the beginning of the eighties no less than four biographies of Wright were published. But by far the best biography for literary purposes is Michel Fabre's *The Unfinished Quest of Richard Wright* (1973), the product of nearly a dozen years of research and writing. Fabre's book places Wright's work in a solid biographical context and is particularly good for its description of Wright's life in France and its detailed analysis of the actual composition of *Native Son* and *Black Boy*.

Several excellent comparative studies also emerge in this period. Kenneth Kinnamon's "Richard Wright's Use of *Othello*" (1969) points out a number of significant parallels between *Native Son* and Shakespeare's play. Stephen Corey's "The Avengers in *Light and August* and *Native Son*" (1979) compares William Faulkner's Percy Grimm with State Attorney Buckley from *Native Son*, demonstrating that both figures are used by their authors to portray the hatred and power of the white world. The most revealing comparative study, however, is Yoshinobu Hakutani's "*Native Son* and *An American Tragedy*: Two Different Interpretations of Crime and Guilt" (1979), which makes a number of subtle distinctions between Wright and Dreiser that were ignored by many earlier critics. Hakutani's analysis stresses that, however similar the two novels are in general situation, they are crucially different in structure and theme.

****

Strong interest in Wright's life, his work, and his influence continues in the 1980s and 1990s, although with not quite the same emphasis as in the preceding four decades. The focus of attention has shifted somewhat, with studies of Wright's political vision diminishing and analyses of his craftsmanship and literary sources increasing. The great majority of scholars and critics during this period are in general agreement about the centrality of Wright's position in African-American letters and his great importance in American and modern traditions, although some reappraisal of a negative sort has also developed, especially among those expressing dissatisfaction with Wright's portrayal of female characters. And with the publication in 1991 of the Library of America editions of Wright's major work, the critical response to Wright has entered an important new phase in which fundamental questions are now being raised about which texts are the most authentic representations of Wright's actual intentions and which texts are highest in literary quality. Which texts, in short, should be the "standard" texts used by scholars, critics, and general readers?

Many recent scholars continue to offer impressive evidence that Wright was certainly not the technically inept writer which many early reviewers and most critics of the post-World War II period had mistaken him to be. For example, Joyce Ann Joyce's *Richard Wright's Art of Tragedy* (1985) carefully examines Wright's craftsmanship in *Native Son*, analyzing his meticulous use of rhetorical strategies and literary techniques. Robert Butler's *Richard Wright's Native Son: The Emergence of a New Black Hero* (1991), likewise, argues that Wright's achievement in *Native Son* was "not only to project the experience of American black people in all its raw brutality but also to *form* it into a rich, coherent, balanced vision of life."[23] Yoshinobu Hakutani's "Creation of the Self in *Black Boy*" similarly takes exception with the early reviews and articles on *Black Boy* which saw that book as a raw slice of life, a direct transcript of Wright's actual experiences. Instead, Hakutani maintains that Wright carefully reshaped the literal events of his life to produce a complex work of art which was richly nuanced in its meanings. Houston Baker's masterful analysis of "The Man Who Lived Underground" in *Blues, Ideology and Afro-American Literature* also challenges earlier simplistic readings of that novel, making a convincing case for Wright's novella being a major work in Afro-American literary tradition.

Other recent scholarship has also tried to take a fresh look at Wright's place not only in black literary tradition but other traditions as well. Robert Stepto's *From Behind the Veil: A Study of Afro-American Narrative* (1979) places *Black Boy* in what Stepto calls one of the two main traditions of story-telling in Afro-American literature, "narratives of ascent" which describe a process of upward movement from South to North driven by a consciousness expanded and deepened by the achievement of literacy. In this sense, *Black Boy* "completes"[24] *Native Son* because it brings the hero beyond Bigger's physical immobility and incomplete psychological development. Michael Cooke places Wright squarely within the tradition of African-American literature which he describes as centered in the achievement of "intimacy," the connecting of the self with black community. Although characters like Bigger Thomas are initially described as alienated from both self and community, they experience genuine selfhood and become "a participant in the life of the spirit"[25] by establishing kinship with others. Tony Magistrale's "Wright's Crime and Punishment," on the other hand, links Wright with European literary tradition, exploring the striking points of similarity and difference between *Native Son* and Dostoevsky's *Crime and Punishment*. Michel Fabre's *The World of Richard Wright* (1985) examines Wright's connection with a wide range of literary influences including Poe, the American naturalists, Japanese haiku poets, the French existentialists, and African nationalists. Robert

Butler's "Richard Wright's *Native Son* and Two Novels by Zola: A Comparative Study" analyzes how Wright made extensive literary use of Zola's *La Bête Humaine* and *Thérèse Raquin* as he developed the themes, symbols and image patterns of *Native Son*. These studies by Magistrale, Fabre, and Butler each challenge the conventional notion that Wright was a crudely unlettered natural genius who created his fiction by simply transcribing his raw experiences; quite the contrary, these studies demonstrate that Wright was a self-taught but extremely literate man who was acutely aware of a rich diversity of literary traditions and could artfully *use* them, transforming them to express his own uniquely African-American vision of life.

There have been, however, some complaints about Wright's work in recent years. Bernard Bell's *The Afro-American Novel and its Tradition* (1987) takes a decidely negative view of *Native Son*, raising once again the objections made by Baldwin and others in the post-World War II years. Bell finds that Wright drew too bleak and narrow a vision of Afro-American life, neglecting the positive features of black culture. But the most serious recent criticism of Wright comes from critics expressing concern over the way Wright portrays female characters. Calvin Hernton, for example, in "The Sexual Mountain and Black Women Writers" used *Native Son* as an illustration of his thesis that "the complexity of black female experience has been fundamentally ignored" in modern black literature. In particular, he objects to Wright's portrayal of Bigger's mother and sister as "nagging bitches" and his depiction of Bessie as "a pathetic nothing."[26] Barbara Johnson likewise objects to a "careless misogyny"[27] in *Native Son*, claiming that Wright excuses Bigger's violence toward women by implying that white society forces Bigger into such actions. And Joseph Skerrett's "Composing Bigger: Wright and the Making of *Native Son*," while generally sympathetic to Wright, nevertheless concludes that much of the violence in the novel is rooted in Wright's repressed resentment and hostility toward women.

Maria K. Mootry puts the case most strongly in "Bitches, Whores, and Woman Haters: Archetypes and Typologies in the Art of Richard Wright." Surveying all of Wright's major fiction but centering on *Native Son*, Mootry demonstrates that Wright's work expressed a crude macho ethic that is "brutal and unfair to women." Mootry claims Wright portrays Mary Dalton as the "bitch goddess of American success," Bessie as a mindless whore, and Mrs. Dalton as a suffocating mother who embodies the demands of a racist society. Because of Bigger's inability to see women as human beings and to form human relationships with them, he is trapped by a "narcissism" that restricts his growth and plunges him into self-destructive violence.[28]

Perhaps the most dramatic development in the critical response to Richard Wright in the past decade has been the publication in 1991 of the Library of America editions of *Lawd Today!*, *Uncle Tom's Children*, *Native Son*, *Black Boy (American Hunger)* and *The Outsider*. Because these editions differ, sometimes in very substantial ways, from the standard editions, they raise important questions which will surely preoccupy Wright scholars for many years. For example, the manuscript of *Native Son* which Wright submitted to Harpers in 1939 was changed in a number of ways by editors who made abridgements and cuts in the text, especially in scenes where Wright's radical politics and his graphic descriptions of sex and violence were emphasized. In a similar way, the version of *Black Boy* which appeared in 1945 was significantly different from the version which Wright gave to his publishers in 1944. As originally written, the book was first called "Black Confession" and then "American Hunger." Moreover, it was comprised of two sections, "Southern Night" which detailed Wright's life in the South and "The Horror and the Glory" which described his experiences in Chicago, focusing sharply on his membership in and his eventually breaking from the Communist Party. Book-of-the-Month Club editors asked Wright to drop the entire second section and, when it appeared as *Black Boy*, it contained only his years in the South. (The second section was published posthumously in 1977 as *American Hunger*.) *Lawd Today!* when it was published in 1963 by Walker and Company was substantially altered by editors who "corrected" many of Wright's innovations in capitalization, punctuation, and usage, while also bowlderizing obscene words and "normalizing" colloquialisms. Wright also had serious difficulties with his editors at Harpers when he published *The Outsider*. He was forced to reduce the manuscript by one-sixth, compressing stream of consciousness passages which he considered important. Moreover, a copy editor, acting on his own judgment and without any permission from

Wright, removed two pages from the approved manuscript and eliminated other passages and words. Since Wright was given only two days to read the galleys, he was virtually powerless to object to these changes.

Needless to say, the strange editorial history of Wright's major writings raises serious critical questions. Which versions of Wright's major work should be considered definitive? Is the definitive text the one which is the best in terms of literary quality or Wright's actual intents? How does one determine Wright's intent, since many writers like Dreiser and Thomas Wolfe actually encouraged and profited from editorial assistance and Wright never left a record of being dissatisfied by the work of his editors? An even more difficult question is how does one determine literary quality, given a radically divided scholarly and critical community which can agree on painfully little these days? Other questions also arise. Can a definitive text be arrived at by simply choosing the manuscript Wright originally submitted to his publishers or choosing the book which eventually appeared? Or is the best text a mixture of these two versions? If so, how is this mixture to be achieved? Who has the authority and insight to determine the (W)right texts?

A lively debate has followed the publication of the Library of America's editions of Wright's work. Arnold Rampersad (*The New York Times Book Review* 29 December 1991) argues vigorously that the definitive texts should be those which undo the damage that was the result of editors whose "unconscious" racism led them to blunt the impact of "an extraordinarily forceful and brilliant black writer" who was intent on "speaking the unspeakable." James Campell (*Times Literary Supplement* 13 December 1991) disagreed sharply with Rampersad, claiming that, since there is no hard evidence that Wright actually disapproved of the changes insisted on by his editors, the standard editions should remain definitive. Wright's wife Ellen and their daughter Julia entered the argument in support of Rampersad when they insisted in a *TLS* letter of 31 January that *Native Son* and *Black Boy* were seriously damaged by editors who lacked the nerve and understanding to publish these books as Wright originally wrote them. James W. Tuttleton takes a middle view, claiming that "We need to have these restored passages" but that they "belong in the notes, not the text."[29]

Richard Wright's work thus continues to flourish because it continues to inspire a broad spectrum of deeply felt responses. The controversies ignited by the publication of his early fiction and the debates which flamed brightly through the forties, fifties, sixties, and seventies, burn brightly today, while taking on some new colors and not losing any of their original heat. Wright, who saw art in dialectical terms as a ceaseless pursuit of truths that were always changing, would surely be pleased by the knowledge that his writing continues to engage its readers in such vital, compelling ways.

****

The essays, chapters of books, and reviews in this volume are assembled to recapture these lively debates which have always been at the center of the critical response to Richard Wright. The book begins with two essays which put Wright's achievement in a solid biographical and historical context. Blyden Jackson's "Richard Wright: Black Boy from America's Black Belt and Urban Ghettos" argues eloquently that all of Wright's major writing is centered in his southern experience which was both his "heart's home" and his "mind's tether." Keneth Kinnamon's "*Native Son*: The Personal, Social, and Political Background" makes a careful and revealing connection between Wright's life and his masterwork, stressing that *Native Son* is more than a "purely personal scream of pain" or a "mere ideological tract"[30] because Wright could shape and transform his own experiences into a compelling work of art.

The section on *Native Son* begins with four initial reviews which give a clear idea of the wide range of spirited responses which that novel occasioned and how the issues raised in these reviews written shortly after the publication of the novel reverberate through Wright criticism to the present day. Is the novel a stunning new direction in American literature which is likely to "father" many more books, as Margaret Wallace suggests, or is it a crude piece of propaganda as Howard Mumford Jones maintains? Is the novel the first truly realistic portrayal of the life of urban black people, as many reviewers exclaimed or was it an "overdrawn" portrait of black life which was sensationistic and implausible? The three essays which follow these reviews explore these and many other related questions. Donald Gibson's "Wright's Invisible Native Son" argues that Wright was indeed correct in his assessment of the racial troubles in

America and critics like Baldwin were wrong when they tried to dismiss Bigger as a psychopathic monster. Sylvia Keady, on the other hand, in "Wright's Women Characters and Inequality," offers a strong feminist critique of *Native Son*, arguing that Wright's inability to imagine the experience of women in non-stereotyped terms was a major flaw in his vision. Robert Butler's essay shows how Wright was greatly influenced by Zola's novels, *La Bête Humaine* and *Thérèse Raquin*, providing him with thematic materials and techniques which he found useful in writing *Native Son*.

The sections on *Black Boy, The Outsider*, and *Eight Men* follow a similar pattern, establishing early responses to these works with reviews and then providing more nuanced and sophisticated readings by contemporary critics. The book concludes with a section entitled "Richard Wright Today," a series of essays which document the controversy brought on by the publication of the Library of America editions and also outline the critical tasks which need to be addressed by present and future Wright scholars. This volume's purpose, therefore, is not only to review past critical responses to Wright but to suggest new kinds of critical responses which might be used to explore parts of Wright's vision which have either been poorly understood or not examined. Just as Wright's career, as Michel Fabre has explained, was an "unfinished quest," so too must the critical response to that career be an ongoing process of vigorous and careful study.

NOTES

[1]Michel Fabre, *The Unfinished Quest of Richard Wright* (New York: William and Morrow, 1973), 51.

[2]Fabre, 529.

[3]Keneth Kinnamon, *The Emergence of Richard Wright: A Study in Literature and Society* (Urbana, Chicago and London: University of Illinois Press, 1972), 3.

[4]Kinnamon, 3.

[5]John Reilly, *Richard Wright: The Critical Reception* (New York: Franklin, 1978), XII.

[6]Reilly, XIII.

[7]Reilly, XIV.

[8]Richard Wright, *Black Boy: A Record of Childhood and Youth* (New York: Harper and Row, 1966), 45.

[9]Ralph Ellison, *Shadow and Act* (New York: New American Library, 1966), p 89.

[10]Ellison, 122.

[11]William Gardner Smith, "The Negro Writer: Pitfalls and Compensations," *Phylon* 11 (Fourth Quarter 1950), 298.

[12]Hugh Gloster, *Negro Voices in American Fiction* (Chapel Hill: University of North Carolina Press, 1948), 233-34.

[13]James Baldwin, *Notes of a Native Son* (Boston: Beacon, 1955), 41, 34.

[14]Irving Howe, "Black Boys and Native Sons," in *Twentieth Century Interpretations of Native Son*, ed. Houston Baker (Englewood Cliffs, : Prentice Hall, 1972), 65, 69, 63.

[15]Reilly, XXXVII.

[16]Eldridge Cleaver, *Soul on Ice* (New York: Dell, 1968), 106.

[17]George E. Kent, "Richard Wright: Blackness and the Adventure of Western Culture," *CLA Journal* 12 (June 1969), 340.

[18]Donald Gibson, "Wright's Invisible Native Son," *American Quarterly* 21, no.4 (Winter 1969), 731.

[19]Dan McCall, *The Example of Richard Wright* (New York: Harcourt, Brace and World, 1969), 77.

[20]Kinnamon, 143.

[21]Blyden Jackson, "Richard Wright: Black Boy from America's Black Belt and Urban Ghettos," *CLA Journal* 12 (June 1969), 289, 309.

[22]Kent, 341.

[23]Robert Butler, *Richard Wright's Native Son: The Emergence of a New Black Hero* (Boston: Twayne, 1991), 30.

[24]Robert Stepto, *From Behind the Veil: A Study of Afro-American Narrative* (Urbana and Chicago: University of Illinois Press, 1979), 128, 134.

[25]Michael Cooke, *Afro-American Literature in the Twentieth Century: The Achievement of Intimacy* (New Haven: Yale University Press, 1984), 97.
[26]Calvin Hernton, "The Sexual Mountain and Black Women Writers," *Black American Literature Forum* 18 (Winter 1984), 139.
[27]Barbara Johnson, "The Re(a)d and the Black," in *Richard Wright's Native Son*, ed. Harold Bloom (New York: Chelsea House, 1988), 120.
[28]Maria K. Mootry, "Bitches, Whores, and Woman Haters: Archetypes and Typologies in the Art of Richard Wright," in *Richard Wright: A Collection of Critical Essays*, ed. Richard Macksey and Frank E. Moorer (Englewood Cliffs: Prentice Hall, 1984), 127, 123, 127.
[29]James W. Tuttleton, "The Problematic Texts of Richard Wright," *The Hudson Review* 2 (Summer 1992), 271.
[30]Keneth Kinnamon, *"Native Son*:   The Personal, Social and Political Background," *Phylon*, XXX (Spring 1969), 72.

Biographical Overview

Richard Wright: Black Boy from America's Black Belt and Urban Ghettos

Blyden Jackson

Richard Wright was born in Mississippi, in a rural setting some twenty-five miles from the town of Natchez, on September 4, 1908. His father, whose given name was Nathan, has been variously described as a sharecropper and a mill worker. This is a distinction very much without a difference. For, wherever he went, whatever he did, essentially Nathan Wright was always and utterly a sharecropper. Essentially, moreover, any mill in which he labored would have been like him, as integral a part of the South's agrarian economy as a field of cotton or as any, and all, of the highly regional towns in Arkansas and Mississippi where his son, in an important adjunct of that son's progress toward a precocious manhood, acquired an intimate clinical knowledge of the fundamental nature of color caste in America.

Wright's father apparently was one of those Negroes about whose ethnic identity there can be little question. His skin was rather dark than light. He was also an absolute illiterate, never having set foot inside a school room in his entire life. In formal training, then, as well as in complexion, he differed from the young woman christened Ella Wilson whom he took in marriage. She was, Edwin Embree tells us, "light brown, good looking, [and] possessed a few years of book learning. [1] The relative lightness of her skin is understandable. She had a mother who was constantly being mistaken for white, as well as other Negro relatives equally lacking in discernible evidences of their Negro blood. Her good looks may have borrowed something from an Indian, added to a white and Negro, ancestry. Her son, our Wright, was to be "good" looking, too, with a cast of feature in which, as in his genealogy, Caucasian, Mongol and African would seem to blend, and with a skin more brown than black.

Any crossings of racial strains in Wright's genealogy, however, were not to be duplicated in his early experience of life. That was to be, until his most impressionable years were quite over, exclusively American Negro. It would seem, indeed, almost as if some tutelary spirit were presiding over his destiny, charged with strict obedience to an injunction from the Fates, "This boy must learn, comprehensively and powerfully, exactly what it means to be a Negro. Not a Negro of the black bourgeoisie who might go to Fisk (or even to an Eastern college) and join a Negro college fraternity, and perhaps journey every August to the Negro tennis 'nationals' and every Christmas holiday with his wife to her Negro sorority convention. No! This boy must be Negro as the masses of Negroes have been Negro. He must know at first hand their peasantry in the South, so pastoral in fable, so bitter in the fact, their groping folk exoduses to the North and West, the grubbiness of their existence in the ghettos of America's greatest cities above the Mason and Dixon line. He must emanate directly from the anonymous black throng, and what that throng has been forced to do, he must be forced to do also."

And so Wright's personal history does begin, as according to such an injunction it should, deep within the world of the folk Negro in the cotton-growing Delta, the world of all American worlds, when Wright was born, closest in form and substance to the plantation world of the ante-bellum South. Somewhere in the atavistic Delta countryside, probably in more than one sharecropper cabin--for sharecroppers have compulsively tended toward nomadism in their search for the ideal tenancy--Wright must have spent his very earliest years. His earliest published recollections, however, in *Black Boy,* his own account of his youth, place his family in Natchez. Wright then was four years old, with a brother, the only brother or sister Wright ever mentions, a year younger than himself. One can well imagine, at this still probationary stage in their lives, what must almost surely have been his parents' shared sentiments. They were young, and youth is notoriously buoyant. Undoubtedly they must have cherished some of those sanguine dreams of making things better for their children which tend to unite parents of every moment and milieu. And so these parents gathered their children and themselves and went up the big river (did they think of their many slave forebears who had come down the same stream?) to mount as it were, an assault on Memphis. They found, in Memphis, living quarters in a one-story brick tenement. The father found a job, as a night porter in a Beale Street drug store. But he found also, and all too soon, a temptress like the Circes of scriptural Babylon, another woman, unattached, who quickly blotted out from his mind whatever conventional plans he may have brought with him to Memphis. Before Wright was old enough to go to school, this father had completely forsaken the wife and the two small sons for whose presence in alien territory he was largely accountable. He left them just as they were in the one-story brick tenement. His person and all of his support he transferred to the other woman.

The three Wrights thus marooned were in parlous condition. There were whole days after the father's departure when they ate nothing simply because they had no money with which to purchase food. Wright's mother, on occasion, had taught school in the Delta. But Memphis was not the Delta and her formal training, after all, was meager by any standards. She took, therefore, the first job she could obtain, as a cook, while she dispatched to her relatives urgent appeals for funds which would enable her, with her sons, to retreat from Memphis. At the same time she did not neglect her sons' claims upon their father's interest. She haled the father into court on a petition for aid to these sons. A judge, who may have been more percipient than the mother, in her bitterness, supposed, accepted the father's stubborn avowal that he was doing all he could. She did not rest, however, with this rebuff from the law. Over Wright's strenuous objections she persuaded him to accompany her on an expedition which, virtual infant that he still was, yet seemed to him both shameful and futile. The two confronted her husband in the room which he was occupying with the woman who had supplanted her. Wright recreated the encounter in *Black Boy,* referring there to his father's mistress as the "strange woman." Wright's mother put her pride aside to beg her husband for money, not, she was careful to point out, to relieve her own distress, but to pay for the transportation of their two boys to a sister of hers in Arkansas. The father laughed in her face as he rejected her plea. And the "strange woman," true to her role, witting or not, of the ruthless siren from secular Negro folk song, threw her brazen arms possessively around the father's neck.

With Memphis Wright's mother was hardly more successful than with her husband. She had trouble not only in keeping a job. For she was already beginning to show a disposition toward invalidism. She found it difficult also, on the low-paying jobs which were the only means of gainful employment available to her, to provide even the mere creature necessities and the proper supervision for her boys. For a time, indeed, while he was barely six, Wright became a drunkard, enticed into daily tipsiness by the Negro clientele of a nearby saloon for their own ribald sport. Wright's mother put a period to this drunkenness by placing Wright, during the hours of the day while she was away from him, as she had to be, at work, under the strict surveillance of an older woman who lived near the Wrights. Yet Wright's mother still had the problem of a woefully insufficient income. She could not make ends meet. To avoid the rent she could not pay eventually she put her two sons in an orphanage. But it was an orphanage which traduced every principle of Good Samaritanism. Its queasy food was doled out in starvation rations. The unfortunate inmates did little except pull grass, a curious chore they were encouraged to perform because the orphanage could not afford to pay for the mowing of its lawns. To cap everything for Wright, the spinster in charge, whose very appearance and manner set Wright's teeth on edge, doted heavily on him and wanted to adopt him. Small wonder that Wright ran away from this Dickensian horror, albeit not for long. His deliverance came through his mother's relatives. They sent her, at last, the money to withdraw, with her sons, to that sister of hers in Arkansas.

The Wrights' trip to Arkansas was preceded by a stop in Jackson. The parents of Wright's mother lived there now, in a fairly large house of two stories given to them by one of their sons. If any dwelling in which Wright lived until he became a man could be called his home--and none could--this was to be it. In this dwelling he was to spend six years, his last six years of dependence, or semi-dependence, on anyone other than himself. But first he was taken to Arkansas, where he was to stay for four years interrupted only by one return to Jackson of short duration. His mother's sister in Arkansas had married prosperously. Her husband owned a thriving saloon in Elaine. The three Wrights were comfortable with him and well fed. But he was shot to death not long after the Wrights joined his household, Wright avers, by whites who coveted the business he would not relinquish, and his wife and the three Wrights, in dread of what might happen further, fled Elaine, under cover of the dark of night, for West Helena, another Arkansas town not far away. The four fugitives stayed in West Helena for a time, went back to Jackson, then retraced their steps to West Helena. The two women took menial jobs. Wright was even able to attend school with some regularity. He was in school in West Helena when the Armistice of 1918 was announced. But another night of terror came. When it passed, Wright's aunt was gone, vanished like a wraith along a trail that led into the fabled north, with a companion, only a vague figure to Wright, the man who had attached himself to her in West Helena. Behind them the escapees left a darksome shadow of something sinister and violent, perhaps dangerously inter-racial, that Wright never penetrated. In West Helena it now became as it had once been in Memphis. Wright's mother, left alone, found herself more than hard-put to try to provide for herself and two sons. Then came a morning of another kind of terror. Wright's brother shook Wright out of his sleep. The younger lad was frightened and frustrated, tremulous, and bewildered. He wanted Wright to look at their mother. Wright did, and called the neighbors, who summoned a doctor. The mother was paralyzed. Now the two boys, neither yet in his teens, were effectively alone. Within days they were back in Jackson with a mother who would never be able to fend for herself, or for them, again.

In Jackson new dispensations were arranged. Wright's brother was sent north to rejoin the aunt with whom the Wrights had lived in Arkansas. Wright was given a choice of residence with any of his other maternal aunts and uncles. He elected the uncle at Greenwood, Mississippi, nearest to his mother in Jackson. But he could not endure life with this uncle and the uncle's wife, kind though the couple tried their best to be. Soon Wright entrained once more for Jackson. He was returning to the house where his afflicted mother at least could give him some feeling of belonging.

The house in Jackson was dominated by his grandmother, a matriarch whose husband's only interest was his fantastic feud with Washington over a Civil War pension his right to which he had vainly tried for half a century to establish. The matriarch herself was a Seventh Day Adventist and like a member of a persecuted sect in the intensity of her zeal for the true faith. Her house was grim with the grimness of a genteel hopeless poverty. But it was even grimmer with the requirements of the matriarch's devotional austerities. Worse yet, protest as Wright would, he was forced into attendance at a Negro Seventh Day Adventist school in Jackson. Wright did not like the school. He vastly preferred the competitive environment of public education. He liked even less the teaching. This emanated from the sole instructor, a young aunt of Wright's, domiciled under the same roof with him, unsure of herself in her first professional assignment, and cherishing for Wright a temperamental detestation, intensified and enlarged by their teacher-pupil relationship, which he heartily reciprocated. Wright knew he could not continue at this school. Only when he threatened almost hysterically to leave his family altogether was he able, however, to wring from his grandmother permission to transfer from Seventh Day Adventist tutelage to the public schools. In Memphis he had had some months of primary training. He had spent perhaps more than a year all told in school in West Helena. He did not finish a term in Greenwood. His one consecutive experience of formal education that lasted long enough to be considerable came now in Jackson from 1921 to 1925. When, in June of the latter year, he had gone as far as he could go in the schools of Jackson and had finished their highest grade, a ninth grade which he noted constituted a review of the eighth, his formal education was completed.

Jackson offered Wright no future which Wright could accept with equanimity. He was a Negro in the South. He was trained to do nothing of the slightest consequence. Besides--and here was for him the greater rub--since he had first had whispered to him when he was eight or nine, by a girl schoolteacher boarding at his grandmother's, the story of Bluebeard, there had been, firm and unshakable in his will, the resolution to become a writer. Indeed he had already had a story published in the Jackson Negro weekly newspaper, a tale called "The Voodoo of Hell's Half-Acre," and had been rebuked by his grandmother for the language of the title as well as for the added sinfulness of telling, for any reason whatever, anything but the "truth." And still, he never seems to have thought seriously of any other permanent vocation but that of writing. Until, however, he could write, he had to live. He tried his hand at some of the "Negro" jobs available to him in Jackson. Not only were they leading him nowhere; he sensed, too, a danger in them. He sensed that, in his manner of performing the servile tasks associated with them, he was not acting "right." He was not conducting himself as a Negro should. An opportunity came for him to make a windfall in a petty swindle. He seized it, and supplemented his ill-gotten gains with the proceeds from his one excursion into burglary. Now through with crime for the rest of his days, and saying farewell only to his mother, he stealthily-quitted Jackson in the autumn of 1925 for Memphis. In Memphis for two years he worked at another, but better, Negro job with a large optical firm. His best job in Jackson had been also with an optical firm. He managed to re-unite with himself his mother and his brother as well as his aunt from his Arkansas days, who had lost, somewhere along her way, the vaguely figured companion with whom she had departed from West Helena. He saved some money. He began to read avidly on his own. He had access gratis to magazines and newspapers around the building in which he worked. Procuring books was not nearly so easy. He solved that problem with the help of a white employee of the optical firm. He would present himself at the public library with a list of books ostensibly from the employee, and with this employee's card, and thus acquire for his own use the loan of books he wanted to read. But, of course, Memphis was still not the environment for him. He broke one day, as diffidently as he could, to his employers at the optical firm the news that he was leaving, since he was in the position of being "forced" to "accompany" his aunt and his paralyzed mother to Chicago. He had arrived at the end of a first stage in his own life. Behind him was an impressionable youth spent in an urgent roving commission that had immersed him in the folk life of the American Negro at its very base even while it bereft him of any semblance of a normal childhood, a protected environment, or any convenient fantasies about the nature of social truth. Ahead of him, he hoped, would be a chance to learn to write. Chicago by 1927 may have come to constitute the ideal spot for a Negro writer who wanted thoroughly and reliably to understand the Negro as an American phenomenon. It is even doubtful whether Harlem, always the largest and greatest, and the best known, of American Negro ghettos,[2] was truly quite as representative of American Negro life between the two World Wars as the Black Belt of the South Side. For Harlem evinced, here and there in what it was able to compound with, a strangeness, an easygoing toleration of cosmopolitanism, that was not always American. And the Negro is the most wistfully American of all Americans. He wants to be accepted, on American terms by American people. From Harlem, for example, in the twenties a Negro of very sable hue, one Marcus Garvey, intoned his dream of black nationalism, a united Africa, every inch of it governed by black men in the interest, and with the support, of black people everywhere. "Up, you mighty race," he exhorted. And the black masses of America did respond to his exhortation. But it is instructive to examine dispassionately, indeed cynically, the nature of their response. They did not go to Africa. They never have, in sizable numbers to stay, under any persuasion. They long ago learned to want, with the rest of immigrant America, the best of two worlds, a respectable past in some distant overseas and a respectable here and now, or the reasonable hope of it, among their American neighbors.

Provisional Orders of the Black Legion, provisional duchies in Kenya and Uganda as hereditary rights, possessed a psychological value, on this side of the Atlantic, for Negroes who were bowed down beneath the weight of honorific European pasts to which they could lay no claim. The Black Belt of Chicago in the twenties, therefore, a teeming wedge within Chicago's South Side, extending seven miles south from Chicago's Loop, almost uniformly more than a mile wide, and growing like any good American boom town in everything except, significantly, its geographical boundaries, its 44,000 Negro inhabitants in 1910 having become 109,000 in 1920 and moving on to become the 237,000 of 1930, did not attract its large inpouring of Negroes from the South[3] because of any thirst those Negroes had for foreign conquest or Pan-Africanism. Chicago in the twenties had its own exhorter to black America. He was as sable of hue as Marcus Garvey. But Garvey was from Jamaica in the British West Indies. The mind of the American Negro was never quite in fact an open book to him. Robert S. Abbott, on the other hand, was, like most of Chicago's Negroes, from the American South, in his own case from Georgia. He had made his way to the Illinois Eldorado through the classrooms of Hampton Institute, where he acquired a mastery of printing. He had started, on the South Side in the early 1900's, a weekly newspaper, the *Chicago Defender,* which by the 1920's called itself the World's Greatest Weekly, and which did carry its message by then, in some form or other, into virtually every nook and cranny of Negro America. The "Up, you mighty race," which Abbott advocated was Negro migration from the South, and when he stood on his Mount Pisgah and crooned down to the Negro masses his telescopic view of the promised land which Negroes were to seek, one had only to eliminate Abbott's references to race to hear in accents pure the booster's voice of George F. Babbitt. Abbott came, indeed, at about the very time that Wright was settling in Chicago, to the campus of a Negro university and there told the undergraduates, in convocation assembled, but still agape from the epiphanic vision of Abbott's emergence from the plush recesses of a chauffeur-driven Rolls Royce, that in Chicago his money was enabling him to pass for white. He spoke not gloatingly, but as an Old Testament prophet dutifully expounding holy writ. His audience listened in a hush of unfeigned reverence.[4] For his audience knew of Jesse Binga, the Pullman porter who became president of one of Chicago's two Negro banks, of Oscar DePriest, the Negro who was to go to Congress from the South Side in 1928, of Daniel Hale Williams, the Chicago Negro surgeon who had operated on the human heart. With Abbott, indeed, this audience shared a black nationalism which began and ended only as a protest against the exclusion of the Negro from full participation in American life as the most conformist of Americans would have defined that life in the era of Harding and Coolidge. Abbott typified for this audience, therefore, what it truly dreamed of, or almost so. For, truth to tell, Abbott himself died without actually ever really "passing for white." Abbott belonged, really, only to a black bourgeoisie. And so, for that matter, did Binga and DePriest and Dr. Williams. What Abbott did have was a certain ease in the externalia of affluence. He did not have the psychological gratifications or the communal privileges of the elect. And still he, and his kind, were relatively fortunate. The vast bulk of Negroes in America in the twenties belonged to no kind of bourgeoisie. If they were not peasants on the land they were members of an urban proletariat.[5] The migrant Wright in 1927, a nineteen-year-old boy with no well-placed friends on the South Side, or anywhere else in Chicago, and no acquisitions in training or property that would invest him with economic or social power, had to become an addition to black Chicago's urban proletariat. Ten years of living with Chicago Negroes in the mass--Wright was to leave for New York in 1937--were to make him privy to the intimate condition of the black Chicagoan as nineteen years of residence in the upper region of the Mississippi Delta and its hinterland had made him privy to the intimate condition of the Southern Negro in that Negro's native habitat. He did not merely view the anonymous Negro masses of Chicago with a novelist's eye for material or a scientist's trained detachment. He existed for years as one of them. It may be hard to define the typical American Negro. It would certainly be impossible to define him, particularly as he was before the 1950's, without taking into account both the Negro of the agrarian and the small-town South and his often pathetically impotent cousin in the industrial North. For twenty-nine years of his life Wright never passed through a whole day without rubbing a fraternal shoulder with one, or both, of these Negroes.

His first job in Chicago was as a porter in a white delicatessen. He found this job by the simple expedient of getting on a street car, riding on it until he was out of the Black Belt, dismounting from his conveyance, and then trudging the cold winter streets until he saw a sign announcing that a porter was wanted. His next job was as a dishwasher in a white restaurant. He had taken, while he was portering, the Civil Service examination for the Chicago Postal Service. In 1929 he received a substitute clerkship in the Chicago Post Office. He tells of remembering the cries of newsboys hawking the story of the great stock-market crash to the Chicagoans past whom he was proceeding as he savored the contents of the letter which had brought him notice of his appointment. Work in the Post Office not only relieved him of menial labor. It gave him time and left him energy for reading and practice at writing. But the cries of the newsboys, had he but known it, had been at least as much of an omen for his life in Chicago as his letter. The Depression came and deepened. Through another examination he had raised his postal rating, but the mails were feeling the effects of the times. He was laid off at the Post Office, and again looking for any job he could find. A stint of duty as agent for various Negro insurance firms improved his knowledge of the Black Belt, but did not solve his problem of caring for the household for which he considered himself responsible. He went on relief and for a while swept streets as a relief worker at thirteen dollars a week. But after the relief authorities placed him as a worker at the South Side Boys' Club--with its provision of close, continuous scrutiny of young Negroes from the Black Belt streets, a job peculiarly appropriate for the writing he was now soon to accomplish--the tasks he performed for subsistence moved ever closer to the things he wanted to do as a matter of self-expression. He was transferred from the boys' club to an assignment as publicity agent for Federal Negro Theater. Then, still with WPA, he was transferred, again as publicity agent, to a white Federal Experimental Theater. Finally he came, still through the ranks of WPA, to the Federal Writers' Project, with which he became an acting supervisor of essays before he left Chicago.

So his life went through much of the 1930's. And yet his life was much more vivid, much fuller of the play of incident, once incident is conceived of as happenings in an inner, as well as an outer world, than any running account of it can suggest. For one thing he was reading, making himself into something of an intellectual, and talking, no longer to the unread, but to people, many of them keen youngsters like himself--in their keenness, at least, although they tended to be white--for whom the life of the mind carried far beyond the Philistias of an Abbott or a Garvey. For another thing, he was trying his hand at writing, practicing at the learning of a craft too exacting for dilettantes and amateurs, devoting long hours to the business of constructing sentences, a mystery he found that exposed itself only to relentless pursuit, and charging himself for the big job of writing a novel, in the spirit, it would seem, of Keats as Keats approached the parallel necessity, for him, of doing the long poem, *Endymion*. And for a final thing he had encountered Communism, an experience by no means unusual for the intellectually curious during the era of the Great Depression.

Wright has had his say about his bout with Communism in the essay he contributed to the symposium, *The God That Failed*. He made his acquaintance with it through the intermediation of the Chicago John Reed Club, an organization of left-wing writers and painters to which he was attracted by the recommendation of a young Jewish friend. He came home from his first evening at the club too excited to sleep. He read the magazines that had been pressed upon him there far into the night and, near the dawn, wrote a free-verse poem to exorcise tumultuous reactions.

When he was elected executive secretary of the club, in 1932, he joined the Communist Party. He says he tried to be a good Communist: He had not been drawn to the Party by "the economics of Communism, nor the great power of trade unions, nor the excitement of underground politics . . . [his] attention was caught by the similarity of the experience of workers in other lands, by the possibility of uniting scattered but kindred peoples into a whole."[6]

But the Party did not class him as a worker. It labeled him an intellectual and he discovered that the Party was suspicious of all intellectuals; that it was, indeed, suspicious of Richard Wright. In his own Party unit, a segregated cell located in the Black Belt of the South Side, even his black comrades seemed to consider him, as an intellectual, a curio.

The Party interfered with his writing, and he had joined it as a writer; had, in fact, had published in Party magazines some of his poetry and in the *New Masses* an article about Joe Louis. He held that a writer should write. The Party held that a writer at best should combine writing with political activity; but, failing that, should never shirk his assignments at the barricades. How very much in dead earnest the Party was in its proscription of art for politics Wright came to know, moreover, by direct experience. He had started on his novel, his major undertaking, when the Party communicated to him its decision that he was to organize a committee on the high cost of living. He expostulated, citing his novel. The Party was adamant, and the novel suffered while he organized.

Nor was the Party, for all of its uniting of peoples, free of color prejudice. In 1935 Wright was sent as a delegate to a writers' congress in New York. The white delegates were lodged without incident through a local committee on arrangements. Wright had to shift for himself to find a place to sleep. One night he spent in the kitchen of a white couple who seemed to be friends of one of his white fellow Chicago Communists. He ended, the next night, in Harlem at the YMCA branch there.

Indeed, when all was taken into account, Wright could not fail but notice a certain Gilbert-and-Sullivan derangement of the reasonable in much that the Party said and did. Only, the derangement was not intentional. It was not the consequence of levity or carelessness or, even, a spirit of high jinks. It was the result of solemn effort by solemn people unconsciously acting as addled as lunatics. It was actually true that a man who claimed to be a painter did, on one occasion, appear from out of the void to join the Chicago John Reed Club while Wright was serving as its executive secretary, suggest that he had powerful connections within the Party, cause a great furor with extravagant and palpably unjustified charges against one of the club's most respected members, and then, disappear with the club still somewhat intimidated by him before this tribune of the people was discovered to be nothing more nor less than a lunatic from Detroit somehow free of his usual confinement. How could happen? It was because of the way "normal" operations were actually conducted in the Party. And the Party could suit its words to its deeds. It could talk as fantastically as it behaved. It could, and did, prate of "counter-revolutionary" activity, "incipient Trotskyites," "bastard intellectuals" "anti-leadership attitudes," and something called "seraphim tendencies," a phrase which Wright came to discover signified, within the party "that one has withdrawn from the struggle of life and finds himself infallible."

It was, Wright could hardly avoid observing, the good Communists who thought themselves infallible. If the Party had tagged Albert Einstein a "bastard intellectual," to a good Communist so Einstein would have been, despite the inescapable originality of some of his best-known feats of intellect. And all these things were of a piece with a Communist practice that, perhaps, nettled Wright most, the imputation by a Party leader to a lesser light of damaging remarks which the lesser light (and less powerful comrade) had actually never uttered.

In one reflective moment Wright concluded of the Party that much of its both startling and maddening tendency to act in a most unreal fashion before obvious realities was attributable to its history in Russia. Under the czars the Russian Communists were conspirators. They had to be suspicious of everything, for the police were unremittingly in hot pursuit of them. And conventionally conditioned American Communists were behaving in the America of the 1920's as did their ideological forebears in czarist Russia.

The Communists, Wright felt, had given him some good things. He felt that he had found among them his first sustained human relationships. His early years, then, with no father since before he started to school, a mother too soon invalided, only relatives of lesser consanguinity with whom he invariably bickered, and a largely malicious environment outside this none too congenial family circle, may well have been even lonelier than he was ever to care to admit. Certainly he felt that he had learned from the Communists. They had made, he believed, the first organized search for the truth about the oppressed, and he never seems to have lost his respect for the Communist knowledge-in-detail of the lives of the workers of the world nor to cease to appreciate the magnitude of the capacity with which Communism would make "men feel the earth and the people on it."

For Communist social science, then, apparently he retained always an intellectual's regard. So, too, he apparently remained always grateful to the Party for its tonic effect on some of his early writing. Given, he believed, a new knowledge of the great world by Communist materials and a new elevation of spirit by Communist ideals, he produced some of his first work which seemed to him to express what he wanted to say. But, in the final analysis, too much of Communist practice outraged both his sense of independence and his sense of sanity. He had declared himself inactive in the Party well before May Day of 1936, not without some unpleasant reactions from the Party which he avers he tried to avoid. Apparently, his formal severance of membership from the Party did not come until 1944.

But by 1944 Wright was no longer living in Chicago. We may have seen that some poetry of his had been published. So, too, in 1936, had a novella of his in *New Caravan*. And we have seen, too, that he was planning, and trying to work, on a novel. This novel had become for him the something that must be done. And so in May of 1937 he went east. Nor did he go, moreover, without the knowledge that he was taking a risk which was all of his own making. He had taken a third Civil-Service examination on which he had achieved virtually a perfect score. Just now, when he was nerving himself for the great *Putsch* at writing, notice reached him of the appointment to a permanent clerkship in the Chicago Post Office at $2100 annually, a magnificent stipend in 1937. Like Cortez at Vera Cruz, however, he chose to burn his bridges behind him and he hitchhiked for the second time to New York City.

In New York he worked again with the Federal Writers Project. But he also worked at his writing and at trying to peddle his stories. He was not to be successful at selling his individual stories, but his novella "Big Boy Leaves Home," in 1937 won a prize in *Story* for the best story of the year, and Harper's printed four of his stories in *Uncle Tom's Children*. The book was a success. In 1939 Wright received a Guggenheim award to free him for creative work. In October, 1939, *Native Son,* his novel, was published, a dual selection of the Book-of-the Month Club. The novel sold well instantly and brought him recognition as well as profit. The Spingarn Medal, annual award of the NAACP to an American Negro for preeminent achievement, was presented to him in 1940. In 1941 *Native* Son was made into a play, Wright collaborating with Paul Green in the transformation, and produced on Broadway under the direction of Orson Welles. The late Canada Lee took the lead role of Bigger Thomas, and the play had a run of fourteen weeks in the metropolis before it was taken on the road. There could be no doubt, Wright's lean years were over.

The lean years of his personal life were over too. In 1940 Wright had married Ellen Poplar, a Jewish girl of New York City. Their first child was a daughter, Julia, born in 1942, the same year in which Wright's third book, *12 Million Black Voices,* was published. He and this wife were living now in Brooklyn, although Wright, accompanied by his first wife, had spent some time in 1940 in Mexico working on a second novel related to life in New York City which he apparently never finished.[7] He did finish, however, his own account of his early years, *Black Boy,* which was published in 1945. But World War II was ending now. Wright had hoped the peace would bring greater changes in the treatment of minorities in America than he was able to discern. An invitation to reside in France was extended to him by the Government of France. With his wife and Julia, he forsook Greenwich Village, to which the Wrights had moved from Brooklyn, and went to Paris. It was 1946 and the second stage of his life, his stage of residence in the North, had run its course.

He never returned, except for one visit, to the United States. Gertrude Stein had found for him, in the Latin Quarter, a large apartment. He settled down in a city where he was free to go and come as he had never been in the United States. This Paris became his home, although France never became the land of his citizenship. He was an expatriate American, never a naturalized Frenchman. Nor was he ever a sedentary boulevardier. Before he left America, he had spent some time in Mexico, but also, in 1945, in Quebec. First, now, he lived, in 1950, on his third continent, South America, where he went to the Argentine for the making, from the novel, *Native Son,* of a movie in which he played, without proving himself an actor, but also, only after having been drafted to do it, the role of Bigger Thomas. In Ghana in 1953 he lived for weeks on his fourth continent, Africa. His coverage of the Bandung Conference in 1955 carried him to Asia. He had set foot, then, on all the major land masses of the world except Australia. And he did move around, also, in western Europe. He lectured, and visited, at various times, in Italy, Holland, Germany, Denmark and the Scandinavian peninsula, and he made two extended trips to Spain for the writing of his *Pagan Spain.* Yet he made only one serious attempt really to detach himself from his acquired

Parisian background. In 1958 Julia was looking forward to going to college. A brilliant student with a most impressive scholastic record, the best in the lycee for her year, she received bids from Oxford and Cambridge. She chose Cambridge, but it was not deemed advisable for her to go there alone. Wright and his wife had a second child in 1947, another daughter, born in France and speaking only French, whom they named Rachel. Ellen Wright and Rachel left Wright alone in France to accompany Julia to England. Wright had now to himself both the apartment in the Latin Quarter and a farm house near the village of Ailly on the river Eure in Normandy which he had bought in 1957 as a place to which he could retire from his exposed position in sociable Paris and have the solitude and leisure a working writer tends to need. It took him, who had been for long a grown man before he acquired a felicitous domesticity, little time to make the decision to sell both the apartment and the house and cross the channel to London. He received, of course, from the English the customary tourist's visa. But when he applied for the residence visa which would have permitted him to live in England with his wife and Rachel and thus join them in their propinquity to Julia, he was surprised with a rejection. Friends of his in England interceded with the Home Office. He went himself there in person. The residence visa was not forthcoming. Convinced that the British did not truly want Negroes in Britain, although they also wanted not to seem not to want them, Wright returned to France, taking now an apartment in the rue Regis smaller than the one he had surrendered in anticipation of a transfer of his residence to England.

He had worked hard and published much during his years abroad: the three novels, *Savage Holiday*, a "white" novel not about the race problem which was brought out as a paperback original, *The Outsider* and *The Long Dream;* four books that were not fiction, *Black Power, Pagan Spain, The Color Curtain* and *White Man, Listen!; as* well as prepared for publication the collection of short stories, *Eight Men*, which would appear very shortly after his death. He had lectured before audiences in Europe, seen and unseen. He was beginning to write radio dramas for German radio. He had learned about the special Japanese poetic form, Hai-Kai and was experimenting with the application of this Oriental aesthetic discipline to Negro material. He was even, following an invitation from Nicole Barclay, committed to the writing, for her Barclay's Disques, a French record company, of the comment to accompany some of the recordings of jazz to be issued under that firm's name. Even without his family his days were full. For he was no recluse. He did more than write. He had helped in the organization of the Société Africaine de Culture. He was interested in its magazine, *Presence Africaine*. He had friends and visitors, many of both undoubtedly eminent. Many were French like Sartre. Some were Americans living in Paris, as with his good companion, Ollie Harrington whose cartoon character, Bootsie, may be the finest satire of its kind yet conceived by a Negro. Some were visiting foreigners, if any person of an intellectual or aesthetic bent can called a foreigner in Paris. Some were very much like himself, Negro writers, but Negro writers who were remaining in America. Indeed, on an autumn day in 1960 Langston Hughes arrived to visit him and found him in his apartment fully clothed, but lying on a bed under cover. The spectacle before Hughes seemed to require a witticism and Hughes laid under contribution an echo from the familiar vocabulary of the Negro evangelical faiths. "Man," he said, "You look like you're going to glory." Wright explained. There was no cause for alarm. In Africa, some years previously, he had contracted intestinal amoeba. Occasionally, therefore, it became wise to submit himself to a rather routine physical examination. He was merely waiting to be taken to the Eugene Gibez clinic, had dressed for his journey, and had decided to rest while waiting for his transportation. Hughes seems to have been Wright's last visitor. On Monday night, November 28, 1960, Wright was still awaiting his scheduled release to return to his apartment in the morning. His nurse had left him and he was alone when his night bell sounded. When the nurse responded, she found him dead. Death had claimed him suddenly and from a rather unexpected quarter. He had had a heart attack, not a fatal onslaught of the complaint which accounted, for his presence in the hospital. He must have died almost instantaneously, conceivably even before the full portent of this final seizure from which there could be no appeal was apparent to him.

His body was cremated, and his ashes quietly interred in a locker at the famed cemetery Pere La Chaise. It is a far cry from a Negro hovel in the Mississippi Delta to the inner haunts of an international aristocracy of talent in Paris, that *bon vivant's* elysium of the Western artist-intellectual. Indeed, it is a cry so very "far" in a certain sense of psychic distance as thus alone to constitute a fairly reliable index of the dauntlessness of Richard Wright's resolution and of the indefatigability of his enterprise--as well as, it may be added, of the extraordinary range of his overt experience of life. For the Richard Wright whom Hamlet's fell sergeant arrested so prematurely at such a great remove from his ancestral roots had achieved a miracle of sorts. He had conquered as his own Odysseus much more than land and sea, in the literal sense. He had really conquered, in effect, a succession of social worlds, and the truly significant pilgrimage he had managed to negotiate had been his migration in progressive stages of advance from the despised universe of the American Folk Negro across formidable barriers of custom and privilege into virtually a white man's status in a particularly privileged enclave of the white man's world.

Hence, undoubtedly we should give a most attentive ear to Wright when, in *Black Boy*, apropos the confrontation which became eventually his final meeting with his father (as it was, at its occurrence on a Mississippi plantation, his first in almost precisely a quarter of a century), after speaking of his father "standing alone upon the red clay...a sharecropper, clad in ragged overalls, holding a muddy hoe in his gnarled, veined hands, [8] he proceeds to declare:

> [when] I tried to talk to him [my own father] I realized that, though ties of blood made us kin, though I could see a shadow of my face in his face, though there was an echo of my voice in his voice, *we were forever strangers, speaking a different language, living on vastly distant planes of reality* [italics mine].[9]

We should, that is, note carefully Wright's own insistence, in terms that brook of no equivocation, upon the great and irreconcilable cultural abyss between himself and his unreconstructed parent. We should acknowledge, too, the ample apparent warrant for the lack of compromise in Wright's depiction of his position relative to his father. After all, Wright had written one book about Spain, another about a country in Africa, a third which dealt with the Bandung Conference, of which he had been an eye witness. Some of his short stories have European settings. One of his novels, even though it is his poorest, departs altogether from racism and its pitifully circumscribed areas of preoccupation. He clearly could not have written what he did write had he lived a life too much like that of his father's. Nor could he, for that matter, have married as he married, or talked as he came to talk, or thought as he came to think. An immensity of cultural variation did sunder him from his father, a whole buoyant mass of learned responses in concepts and behavior, for the assimilation of which he had, in all their blooming welter, discovered a more or less various capacity, but of the nature and uses of which his father had virtually not the slightest inkling. And yet ours is, when everything is said and done, a curious and inconsistent world in which, as an aspect of its sometimes inscrutably organic complexity, it is possible for two propositions which seem mutually to cancel each other out in their abstract logic not only both to be empirically true, but also, each to make the other, empirically, even truer. Just so, as there does seem to be incontrovertibly, good reason to aver of Wright and his father that they ended by becoming, toward each other, in all obvious respects, like total strangers, and evidence just as compelling for the contention that their alienation from each other was the almost unavoidable inescapable consequence of differences in the worlds into which they were cast as their lives continued, so it seems equally valid to maintain that they were, on the other hand, linked together by a bond which could never be severed and to argue that, in spite of the noticeable impact upon Wright of conditioning factors from the white worlds into which he had been able to insinuate himself, this bond was forged out of Wright's fellowship with his father in the world of the American Negro masses.

That fellowship dated, of course, from the moment Wright drew his first breath. It extended on Wright's side, however, actively only through the years of his youth, the formative years for any individual born into the human family, the plastic years during which all creatures so originated tend to acquire the deep-seated basic reactions which shape their characters for the remainder of their lives. Such years obviously are of no little import in the personal history of every person ever socialized. In the development of creative writers, whose trade depends to a consoderable extent upon exceptional receptivity to the stimuli from an external world, these very years are probably even more than ordinarily meaningful. Certainly, James Baldwin, who knew Wright on two continents and for more than half of Wright's adult life, found special significance in those years where Wright was concerned. For Baldwin once observed of Wright--in comparing, incidentally, Wright's sense of reality with the fondness of Sartre and Sartre's circle for ideal speculation-- "I always sensed in Richard Wright a Mississippi pickaninny, mischievous, cunning and tough. This seemed to be at the bottom of everything he did, like some fantastic jewel buried in high grass."[10] And while it is true that Baldwin here is making no issue of race, but merely playing upon a racial epithet to heighten the impression he wishes to convey of a Wright educated early, and lastingly, in a particularly bitter school of hard knocks, it is also true that Baldwin's contention opposes any conception of Wright as a creature totally emancipated from the world to which Wright's father still belonged when the father and son faced each other as we have been told they did in Wright's *Black Boy*. If we are to credit Baldwin, even at this last meeting Wright and his father were not total strangers. They did not live on vastly differant planes of reality. It may have seemed that they did, and in much that was most perceptible, even to Wright himself, no other conclusion may have appeared as reasonable. Yet Baldwin's phrase may haunt us, may tease us into further thought.

Mississippi pickaninny! It is an apt phrase. And it is even apter if we read it with a keen awareness both of its implications of Wright's indestructable affinities with his own youth and of his membership, which was irrevocable, in a peculiarly racial world. We may wish then, perhaps, to ponder deeply Redding's words, written soon after Wright's death, "In going to live abroad, Dick Wright had cut the roots that once sustained him; the tight-wound emotional core had come unravelled; the creative center had dissolved... ,"[11] and to add thereto Redding's veritable extension of those remarks a year later, "His heart's home [Wright's] and his mind's tether was in America. It is not the America of the moving pictures, nor of Thomas Wolfe, John P. Marquand and John O'Hara's novels, nor of the histories of the Allan Nevins and C.J.H. Hayes. It is the America that only Negroes know: a ghetto of the soul, a boundary of the mind, a confine of the heart. [12] For it may well be that Baldwin and Redding, in their separate fashions, have both pointed the way to the indispensable prelude for an understanding of Richard Wright, conceivably as a person, and certainly as a literary artist. It may well be that the picture of Wright which one should bear most in mind is not that of a Wright so visibly grown away from his father as to seem a visitor from another world as the father and the son finally encounter each other for a strained brief moment under a Southern sun, but rather the child described by Baldwin, and confirmed as a presence by Redding, who lurked always at the center of Wright's mind and heart, the child whose only real abode was the "America that only Negroes know," and whose only real release came in the fictive world of Wright's creation closest to the actual world that Wright had known in the Negro subculture of his youth.

Notes

[1]Edwin Embree, *13 Against the Odds* (New York, 1944), p. 26. "Good looking," it should be remembered, in American parlance almost invariably connotes "good" according to an Aryan standard of right and wrong in personal appearance.
[2]And, all through the twenties virtually, in ferment with the Harlem, or Negro, Renaissance.
[3]As late as the early 1940's St. Clair Drake and Horace Cayton in their careful study of the Negro in Chicago, *Black Metropolis* (New York, 1945), were to find (on p. 99) that over eighty out of every one hundred "Chicago" Negroes had been born in the South.
[4]The campus was that of Wilberforce University in southern Ohio. The date is uncertain. I was a contributor to the reverent hush.
[5]On the basis of the occupational distribution of Negroes, E. Franklin Frazier stipulates that, in the four northern cities containing, in 1940, Negro communities numbering 100,000 or more, a bourgeoisie element constituted a little more than a fifth of the total Negro population. Cf. Frazier, *Black Bourgeoisie* (Glencoe [Ill.], 1957), pp. 46-47.

Chicago was, of course, among these four cities. A Negro bourgeoisie was certainly proportionately no greater in the 1920's than in the 1940's.

[6]Richard Wright, "Richard Wright," in Richard Crossman, *ed.*, *The God That Failed* (New York, 1952), p. 106.

[7]This seems to have been the book which he also sometimes described as a novel about the status of woman.

[8]Richard Wright, *Black Boy* (New York, 1945), p.30.

[9]*Black Boy*, p. 30.

[10]James Baldwin, *Nobody Knows My Name* (New York,1945), p.184.

[11]J. Saunders Redding, "Richard Wright: an Evaluation," *Asmac Newsletter*, 3 (December 1940), 6.

[12]Redding, "Home Is Where the Heart Is," *The New Leader* (December 11, 1961), p.24.

From *CLA Journal*, 12 (Winter 1969), 287-309.

Native Son: The Personal, Social, and Political Background

Keneth Kinnamon

In the fiction of social protest, of which Richard Wright's *Native Son* (1940) is surely an outstanding example, the *donnée* has an interest almost equal to that of the artistic treatment. If the concern is with the relation of literature to society, one must not be content merely to grant the novelist his materials and concentrate on his fictional technique; one must examine carefully the factual substance on which the novelist's imagination operates. If this task is preliminary to literary criticism in the strict sense, it is necessary if that criticism is not to be impressionistic or narrowly aesthetic. An examination of Wright's fiction reveals that customarily he drew from personal experience and observation, the condition of the society about him, and his theoretic concerns. In *Native Son,* these elements may be identified respectively as certain episodes in Wright's life in Mississippi and Chicago, the social circumstances of urban Negroes and the Nixon trial, and Communist ideology.

Charles I. Glicksberg is speaking hyperbolically when he asserts that "Richard Wright is Bigger Thomas--one part of him anyway. Bigger Thomas is what Richard Wright, had circumstances worked out differently, might have become."[1] Nevertheless, there is some truth in the assertion, and not merely in the general sense, according to the formulation of James Baldwin, that "no American Negro exists who does not have his private Bigger Thomas living in the skull."[2] The general similarities between Wright at the age of twenty and the fictional protagonist *of Native Son* are obvious enough: both are Mississippi-born Negroes who migrated to Chicago; both live with their mother in the worst slums of the Black Belt of that city; both are motivated by fear and hatred; both are rebellious by temperament; both could explode into violence.

More specific likenesses were recovered from Wright's subconscious by Dr. Frederic Wertham, the eminent psychiatrist. When Wright, as a boy of fifteen, worked for a white family named Bibbs in Jackson, Mississippi, his duties included chopping wood, carrying coal, and tending the fire. The pretty young daughter of the family generally was kind to him within the limits of Southern custom, but when, on one occasion, he chanced upon her in her bedroom while she was dressing, "she reprimanded him and told him to knock before entering a room." The diffident and fearful young Negro handymate, the amiable white girl, the sexually significant situation--these elements, transmuted, found their way into *Native Son.* The name of the wealthy white family for whom Bigger works in the novel, *Dalton,* may itself bear an unconscious symbolic import. In the Chicago hospital where he worked as an orderly in 1931, Wright learned of Daltonism.[3] In their fashion, the Daltons in the novel strive toward color blindness, though they fall tragically short of achieving it.

Essentially, Bigger Thomas is a conscious composite portrait of a number of individual Negroes Wright had observed over the years. In that remarkable exercise in self-examination, *How "Bigger" Was Born,* Wright sketched five such Bigger prototypes he had known in the South. All of them were rebellious defiers of the jim crow order, and all of them suffered for their insurgency: "They were shot, hanged, maimed, lynched, and generally hounded until they were either dead or their spirits broken." In Chicago, especially when Wright worked at the South Side Boys' Club in the middle thirties, he observed other examples of the Bigger Thomas type--fearful, restless, moody, frustrated, alienated, violent youths struggling for survival in the urban jungle.[4]

The slum conditions of the South Side so vividly portrayed in *Native Son* had been the daily reality of a decade in Wright's life (1927-1937). He had lived in a cramped and dirty flat with his aunt, mother, and brother. He had visited hundreds of similar dwellings while working as an insurance agent.[5] The details of the Chicago environment in the novel have a verisimilitude that is almost photographic. The "Ernie's Kitchen Shack" of the novel, located at Forty-Seventh Street and Indiana Avenue, for example, is a slight disguise for an actual restaurant called "The Chicken Shack," 4647 Indiana Avenue, of which one Ernie Henderson was owner.[6] Similar documentary accuracy is observed throughout the book.

Aside from wide personal experience, moreover, Wright was becoming increasingly more interested in sociology at the time he was writing *Native Son*. The caseworker for the Wright family in Chicago was Mary Wirth, the wife of Louis Wirth of the University of Chicago, who was in the process of conducting an enormous research project on the urban ecology of the city. In Wirth's office Wright examined the files of the project and met Horace R. Cayton, a Negro research associate who was himself to become a distinguished sociologist and a warm friend of the novelist.[7] Sociological concepts, quite as much as Marxist theories, are apparent in the novel, especially in the final part.

In New York, too, where he moved in May, 1937, Wright became intimately acquainted with the conditions of Negro ghettos. Not only did he live for almost a year in Harlem, but as a participant in the Federal Writer's project of New York City, he wrote the Harlem sections of *New York Panorama* (1938) and *New York City Guide* (1939), two volumes in the American Guide Series. He also served during the last five months of 1937 as chief Harlem correspondent for the *Daily Worker,* contributing forty signed articles as well as numerous brief, unsigned dispatches. A fourth of the signed articles deal with hardship of life in Harlem. In one of these Wright reported on a hearing conducted by the New York State Temporary Commission on Conditions Among Urban Negroes. The questioning of Henry Dalton about his real estate policies by Boris Max in the last part of *Native Son* draws directly from this article.[8]

As if to confirm Wright's notions about the Bigger type and society's attitude toward him, when the writer "was halfway through the first draft of *Native Son* a case paralleling Bigger's flared forth in the newspapers of Chicago."[9] This case involved Robert Nixon and Earl Hicks, two young Negroes with backgrounds similar to that of Bigger. According to the first of a long series of highly sensationalistic articles in the *Chicago Tribune*, on May 27, 1938, Mrs. Florence Johnson "was beaten to death with a brick by a colored sex criminal ... in her apartment."[10] Nixon and Hicks were arrested soon after and charged with the crime. Though no evidence of rape was adduced, the *Tribune* from the beginning called the murder a sex crime and exploited fully this apparently quite false accusation.[11] Nixon was chosen for special attack, perhaps because he was darker and ostensibly less remorseful than Hicks. He was referred to repeatedly as the "brick moron," "rapist slayer," "jungle beast," "sex moron," and the like. His race was constantly emphasized. The casual reader *of Native Son* might consider the newspaper article which Bigger reads in his cell early in Book Three greatly exaggerated in its racism;[12] in point of fact, it is an adaptation of an actual piece in the *Tribune*. Although Nixon came from "a pretty little town in the old south--Tallulah, La.," the *Tribune* reporter wrote, "there is nothing pretty about Robert Nixon. He has none of the charm of speech or manner that is characteristic of so many southern darkies." The reporter proceeded to explain:

> That charm is a mark of civilization, and so far as manner and appearance go, civilization has left Nixon practically untouched. His hunched shoulders and long, sinewy arms that dangle almost to his knees; his outthrust head and catlike tread all suggest the animal.
> He is very black--almost pure Negro. His physical characteristics suggest an earlier link in the species.

Mississippi river steamboat mates, who hire and fire roustabouts by the hundreds, would classify Nixon as a jungle Negro. They would hire him only if they were sorely in need of rousters. And they would keep close watch on him. This type is known to be ferocious and relentless in a fight. Though docile enough under ordinary circumstances, they are easily aroused. And when this happens the veneer of civilization disappears...As he talked yesterday Nixon's dull eyes lighted only when he spoke of food. They feed him well at the detective bureau, he said. He liked coconut pie and strawberry pop. It was after a generous meal of these refreshments that he confessed two of his most shocking murders...These killings were accomplished with a ferocity suggestive of Poe's "Murders in the Rue Morgue"--the work of a giant ape.

Again the comparison was drawn between Nixon and the jungle man. Last week when he was taken...to demonstrate how he had slain Mrs. Florence Johnson, mother of two small children, a crowd gathered and there were cries of "Lynch him! Kill him"

Nixon backed against a wall and bared his teeth. He showed no fear, just as he has shown no remorse.[13]

The article concludes by quoting from a letter from the Louisiana sheriff of Nixon's home parish: "It has been demonstrated here that nothing can be done with Robert Nixon. Only death can cure him."[14]

This remedy was applied almost exactly a year after the murder of Mrs. Johnson. During this year the case became something of a local *cause célèbre*. The Chicago police quickly accused Nixon of a number of other murders, and the Los Angeles police did the same.[15] Early in the case the International Labor Defense became interested, providing Attorney Joseph Roth, white, to aid Negro lawyers in representing Nixon and Hicks.[16] Public emotion ran very high, stimulated by the lurid treatment given the case by the *Tribune*. A week after the crime the Illinois House of Representatives "approved a bill sponsored by State's Attorney Thomas J. Courtney of Cook County to curb moronic attacks." In debate on this bill, Nixon was mentioned prominently.[17] A complicated series of confessions and repudiations, charges of police brutality, and dramatic outbursts of violence[18] preceded the trial, which began in late July under Judge John C. Lewe after attorneys for the youths won a change of venue because of the prejudiced atmosphere.[19] The trial itself, despite some apparently contradictory evidence, was very brief, lasting just over a week before the jury reached a verdict of guilty on the first ballot after only one hour of deliberation. The death sentence was imposed on Nixon.[20] By this time, however, leaders of the Chicago Negro community were thoroughly aroused. The National Negro Congress, which had been providing legal representation for the two youths, continued its efforts on their behalf, including the sponsorship of a fund-raising dance.[21] Prominent Chicago Negro clergymen joined the struggle to save Nixon.[22] With the aid of such support, together with some irregularities in the evidence presented by the state, Nixon was able to win several stays of execution, but his struggle ceased in the Cook County electric chair three minutes after midnight, June 16, 1939.[23]

By the time Nixon was finally executed, Wright had completed *Native Son*. He did not need to wait the outcome of legal appeals and maneuvers to know the "Fate" (his title for Book Three of the novel) of Robert Nixon or of his fictional counterpart, Bigger Thomas. In any event, Wright's use of the Nixon case was that of a novelist, not that of an historian or journalist. He adapted whatever seemed useful to his fictional purpose, changing details as he wished. He followed the facts of the case fairly closely in his account of the newspaper treatment of Bigger Thomas. The inquest and trial scenes, also, resemble in certain respects their factual prototypes. Among the more significant distortions of Nixon material are those relating to Wright's polemic intent as a communist writer.

In the Nixon case the role of the International Labor Defense and its representative, Attorney Joseph Roth, was small and initiatory; it was soon replaced by the National Negro Congress. In *Native Son*, however, Wright magnifies the role of this organization (changing its name slightly to "Labor Defenders") and its radical Jewish attorney, Boris Max, who is made Bigger's sole lawyer. Another change illustrates even more vividly Wright's shift of emphasis in transforming fact to fiction. One of the murders for which Chicago police elicited confessions, later repudiated, from Nixon was that of a Mrs. Florence Thompson Castle a year before the murder of Mrs. Johnson. According to a newspaper report, in his account of this crime Nixon "told of picking up a lipstick belonging to Mrs. Castle and scrawling on the dresser mirror these words: 'Black Legion.' "[24] When Bigger in the novel wishes to divert suspicion to an extremist group, he selects leftists rather than fascists, signing the kidnap note to the Daltons in such a way as to implicate the Communist Party (p. 151).

As a fervent party member, Wright maintained a thoroughly communistic point of view in *Native Son*. The courtroom arguments of Max in the final section, of course, are patently leftist. He equates racial and class prejudice, both being based on economic exploitation (pp. 326-27). He repeats the basic party concept of the times regarding the collective status of Negroes in America: "Taken collectively, they are not simply twelve million people; in reality they constitute a separate nation, stunted, stripped, and held captive *within* this nation, devoid of political, social, economic, and property rights" (p. 333). He discerns in Bigger a revolutionary potentiality (pp. 337-38). Not all of Max's courtroom speech reflects so directly communist doctrine, but none of it is inconsistent with the party line on racial matters.

Communist material is obvious enough in the final section of the novel, but it is often implicit elsewhere. Early in Book One, for example, while Bigger and his friend Gus are loafing on the street they amuse themselves by "playing white," assuming roles of the white power structure. The youths are themselves nonpolitical, but the white activities Wright has them imitate are precisely those which he and other communists viewed as typical of the American capitalist system: warfare, high finance, and political racism (pp. 15-17). For Bigger's mother, religion is clearly presented as an opiate, as it is generally for the Negro masses. To accept the consolations of Christianity, Bigger comes to recognize, would be to lay "his head upon a pillow of humility and [give] up his hope of living in the world" (p. 215). The first movie that Bigger and a friend see in Book One, *The Gay Woman*, presents a Hollywood stereotype of a communist as a wild-eyed bomb thrower (pp. 27-28). Indeed, prejudice against communists is frequently depicted in the novel. On the other hand, party members Jan Erlone[25] and Boris Max are idealized portraits of selfless, noble, dedicated strivers toward the new social order.

These, then, are the main elements that went into the composition of *Native Son*. Much of the powerful sense of immediacy felt by the reader of the novel derives from the genesis of the work in the author's personal experience and observation. Though one may have reservations about the validity of Wright's communist ideological orientation, it provided him with an intellectual instrument with which to render meaningful the personal and social materials of the novel. The nice balance of subjective and objective elements in *Native Son* prevents the work from becoming either a purely personal scream of pain, on the one hand, or a mere ideological tract on the other. Whatever verdict one may finally reach about the artistic merits of *Native Son*, one must take into account the personal, social, and political materials out of which it grew.

Notes

[1]"The Furies in Negro Fiction," *The Western Review*, XIII (Winter, 1949), 110.
[2]"Many Thousands Gone," *Partisan Review*, XVIII (November-December, 1951), 678. This essay is reprinted in James Baldwin, *Notes of a Native Son* (Boston, 1955), pp. 24-45.
[3]Waldemar Kaempffert, "Science in Review: An Author's Mind Plumbed for the Unconscious Factor in the Creation of a Novel," *The New York Times*, September 24, 1944, Sec. 4, p. 11. This article asserts that the Bibbs girl loaned Wright money for his junior high school graduation suit, but Wright's autobiographical *Black Boy: A Record of Childhood and Youth* (New York, 1945) says that her mother did so (p. 156). Dr. Wertham comments briefly on his experiment with Wright in "The Dreams That Heal," his introduction to *The World Within: Fiction Illuminating Neuroses of Our Time*, ed. by Mary Louise Aswell (New York, 1947), xxi.
[4]"How 'Bigger' Was Born" (New York, 1940), pp. 6, 28-29. See also Wright's pamphlet *The Negro and Parkway Community House* (Chicago, 1941).

[5]The main source for this period of the novelist's life is Richard Wright, "Early Days in Chicago," *Cross-Section 1945*, ed. by Edwin Seaver (New York, 1945), pp. 306-42. This essay is reprinted, with minor changes, as "The Man Who Went to Chicago" in Wright's *Eight Men* (Cleveland and New York, 1961), pp. 210-50.

[6]Advertisement, *The Chicago Defender* January 3, 1933, p. 3.

[7]Horace R. Cayton, *Long Old Road'* (New York, 1965), pp. 247-48. Cayton gives further details in a symposium on Wright included in *Anger and Beyond: The Negro Writer in the United States*, ed. by Herbert Hill (New York, 1966), pp. 196-97. Having written the finest fictional portrayal of the South Side, Wright was the inevitable choice of Cayton and St. Clair Drake to write the introduction to their classic sociological treatise on the area, *Black Metropolis* (1945).

[8]"Gouging, Landlord Discrimination Against Negroes Bared at *Hearing*," *Daily Worker*, December 15, 1937, p. 6. Cf. *Native Son* (New York, 1940), pp. 276-79. Parenthetical page references in the text are to this edition.

[9]*How "Bigger" Was Born*, pp. 30-31.

[10]"Sift Mass of Clews for Sex Killer," *Chicago Daily Tribune*, May 28, 1938, p. 1.

[11]David H. Orro, a Negro reporter, wrote that police stated that Nixon and Hicks were "bent upon committing a sex crime," but that "authorities were unable to state whether the woman had been sexually attacked." "'Somebody Did It,' So 2 Youths Who 'Might Have Done It' Are Arrested." The *Chicago Defender*, May 28, 1938, p. 24. The date as printed is an error; this is actually the issue of June 4, 1938.

[12]Hubert Creekmore, the white novelist from Mississippi, charged that "the press is shown as chiefly concerned with unsubtle inspiration of hatred and intolerance. The manner and content of these newspapers exceed belief. Again Mr. Wright makes them present incidents and ideas which reflect his own mind rather than an editor's mind or the public mind." "Social Factors in *Native Son*," *The University of Kansas City Review*, VIII (Winter, 1941), 140.

[13]Charles Leavelle, "Brick Slayer Is Likened to Jungle Beast," *Chicago Sunday Tribune*, June 5, 1938, Sec. 1, p.6. Cf. *Native Son*, pp. 238-40.

[14]Leavelle, *op. cit.*

[15]"Science Traps Moron in 5 Murders," *Chicago Daily Tribune*, June 3, 1938, p. 1.

[16]"Robert Nixon Attacked By Irate Hubby," *The Chicago Defender*, June 11, 1938, p. 6.

[17]"Pass Courtney Moron Bill In Heated Debate," *Chicago Daily Tribune*, June 8, 1938, p. 1.

[18]When Nixon and Hicks were taken by police to the scene of the crime, a hostile, lynchminded mob required police control. Then "a dramatic incident occurred just as the police were about to leave with their prisoners. Elmer Johnson, the bereaved husband ... drove up with his two children, and his brother-in-law, John Whitton .... Johnson said nothing, but Whitton clenched his fists and shouted, 'I'd like to get at them.' Police hurried the prisoners away." "2 Accuse Each Other in Brick Killing." *Chicago Daily Tribune*, May 30, 1938, p. 2. Perhaps Elmer Johnson was merely waiting for a better opportunity, for, at the inquest he attacked the handcuffed Nixon savagely before police intervened. Shortly after this attack, Nixon attempted to retaliate. Johnson explained his intention to a reporter: "I hoped to hit him hard enough so his head would fly back and his skull would be cracked against the wall." "Beats Slayer of Wife; Own Life Menaced," *Chicago Daily Tribune, June 8*, 1938, p. 3. See also "Robert Nixon Attacked By Irate Hubby," p. 6. Cf. the incident in *Native Son* in which Bigger is attacked at the inquest (p. 265).

[19]"Brick Slayers' Trial Assigned To Judge Lewe," *Chicago Daily Tribune*, July 19, 1938, p. 6.

[20]"Guilty of Brick Murder; Gets Death In Chair," *Chicago Daily Tribune*, August 5, 1938, p. 2.

[21]"Dance Profits To Aid Nixon, Hicks," *The Chicago Defender*, August 20, 1938.

[22]"Nixon Plea To Be Given To Governor," *The Chicago Defender*, October 15, 1938, p. 6.

[23]"Nixon Dies In Chair," *The Chicago Defender*, June 17, 1939, pp. 1-2.

[24]"Brick Moron Tells of Killing 2 Women," *Chicago Sunday Tribune*, May 29, 1938, p. 5.

[25]Wright may have taken the first name from that of Jan Wittenber, a white friend who was active in the Chicago John Reed Club and served as secretary of the Illinois State International Labor Defense.

From *Phylon: The Atlanta University Review of Race and Culture,* 30 (Spring 1969) 66-72.

Native Son **(1940)**

Review of *Native Son*

Henry Seidel Canby

This powerful and sensational novel is very difficult to describe so as to convey its real purpose and its real strength. But it is important to describe it accurately, because it is certainly the finest novel as yet written by an American Negro--not that it was chosen by the Book-of-the-Month Club just because it was written by a Negro. It would have been chosen for its deep excitement and intense interest whether written by white, yellow, or black. Yet, nevertheless, this is a novel which only a Negro could have written; whose theme is the mind of the Negro we see every day; whose emotion is the emotion of that native born American under the stress of a social situation difficult in the extreme; whose point and purpose are not race war or propaganda of any kind, but to show how a "bad nigger" is made from human material that might have become something very different.

Superficially, *Native Son* is a crime story, adventurous, exciting, often terrible--with two murders, a chase and a gun fight over the roofs of Chicago, a trial, and what might have been, but was not, a rape. It is the old story of a man hunted down by society. But the reader will get through only a few chapters before he realizes that there is something different in this story. Bigger--and we all know Bigger--is no persecuted black saint. His family is a good family, as tenement families go; but he is a bad actor from the first. He is mean; he is a coward; he is on occasion liar, thief, and bully. There is no sentimentalism in the writer who created Bigger and made him chauffeur in the family of a wealthy philanthropist who spent some of the money wrung from Negro tenements on benefits for the race. Bigger is headed toward jail from the first chapter. When Mary Dalton, the flighty daughter of the philanthropist, asks Bigger to help along her intrigue with her Communist lover (also a negrophile), he has no compunctions. But he did not mean to kill her, he did not want to kill her, though he hated patronizing whites. Had her blind mother not come in at the fatal moment, the girl would have slept off her drunkenness, and Bigger would never have got beyond petty crime. With a skill which any master of the detective story might envy, Mr. Wright builds his book on the inevitable and terrifying results of an unpremeditated killing; the burning of the body; the false accusations; the murder of Bigger's Negro girl friend, lest she implicate him; the capture; the trial in which Mr. Max, the defending lawyer, pleads unsuccessfully the cause of a race driven toward crime, against a district attorney needing notoriety for his next election. And finally comes Bigger's confession--not of the murder which was not a murder, and of the rape which was not a rape, but of the obscure inarticulate causes which made him hate, and made him try to make up for his sense of inferiority by aggressive acts against the society in which he lived.

All this highly complicated story is handled with competence by Mr. Wright in a swift narrative style proceeding by staccato dialogue and with rapidly mounting suspense. The characters, too, are fully realized. There is a deadly satire in the portraits of the young radicals. Mary who is killed, and Jan, the Communist, who chooses Bigger to work on, not realizing that this kind of political pity is more offensive to a Negro than color prejudice. And the mob itself is a character, stirred up by sensational newspapers, getting blood-thirsty, wanting to lynch--the mob whose threatening roar is always in the background of the book and of the Negro's mind. Yet even in its characters this is not a vindictive book. Bigger dies without hate for anything, except the obscure circumstances which compelled him to be what he was. Max, his lawyer, with the ancient wisdom of the Jews, pleads for him on the broad basis of an America in grave danger from a conflict of races which only a deeper-going justice can ameliorate. Even the Negro evangelist who tries to bring back Bigger to the emotional religion which has helped so many men and women of his race, is presented with sympathy and pathos.

Indeed, two statements may be made with safety by the most conservative critic about this remarkable novel. No reader, however harrowed by its frank brutalities, will be able to stop in its engrossing story, which coils and mounts until a tale of crude violence broadens into a human tragedy. And no white man--and, I suspect, few Negroes--will finish this narrative without an enlargement of imagination toward the psychological problems of the Negroes in our society--and an appreciable extension of sympathy. This will hold, I prophesy, for South as well as North. Indeed, I suspect that this book and its probings will be less of a surprise to, and more readily understood by, Southerners than by Northerners. Mr. Wright himself was born and educated in Mississippi, and has lived his later life in the North. It is not the ex-slave of the South, or the almost-like-a-white-man Negro of the North, but the essential Negro-in-America of both, that he gets into Bigger and his book.

Let me repeat, this novel is no tract or defense plea. Like *Grapes of Wrath*, it is a fully realized story of unfortunates, uncompromisingly realistic, and quite as human as it is Negro. To the growing list of artistic achievements of a high quality, by a race which is, perhaps, singularly gifted in art, *Native Son* must surely be added, with a star for notable success.

From *Book-of-the-Month-Club News*, (February 1940) pp.2-3.

Review of *Native Son*

Charles Poore

Richard Wright's "Native Son," an enormously stirring novel of crime and punishment, is published this morning. It is a story to trouble midnight and the noon's repose, as Mr. Eliot once said about another matter, and to haunt the imagination many days.

It was widely praised long before publication. In deed, few other recent novels have been preceded by more advance critical acclamation, or lived up to the expectations they aroused so well. Mr. Wright is a Negro. His novel concerns a young Negro, Bigger Thomas, who twice commits murder before your eyes, and the whole dark background of his crimes. It is an extraordinarily difficult task he has undertaken--on the Dostoievskian scale--and the praise is soundly based on his accomplishment as a novelist.

Edward Weeks, editor of The Atlantic Monthly, calls "Native Son" a performance of great talent--powerful, disturbing unquestionably authentic." We'll question the authenticity of Bigger Thomas's ability to discuss the wider implications of his tragic destiny so expertly. But that is another matter. Henry Seidel Canby calls it "the finest novel yet written by an American Negro"--which it is, without a doubt. It would be a fine novel no matter who wrote it: though, to perpetrate an Irish bull in all sincerity, only a Negro could have written "Native Son." In a special introduction Dorothy Canfield Fisher makes the parallel with Dostoievsky, observes that this novel "can be guaranteed to harrow up any human heart capable of compassion or honest self-questioning," and shows how the story of Bigger Thomas bears out the studies in racial barriers carried out by the American Youth Commission under the chairmanship of Owen D. Young.

The praise has been cumulative. It gathered while "Native Son" awaited publication after it had been chosen (with Conrad Richter's "The Trees" . . .) by the Book-of-the-Month Club for March. Finally, we are told that the Guggenheim awards committee read "Native Son" in manuscript, and, on the strength of its strength, gave Mr. Wright--whose earlier book of stories, "Uncle Tom's Children," was also a prizewinner--one of its fellowships.

Mr. Wright drives his story forward at a furious yet skillfully controlled pace. The full drama is unfolded in just about two weeks. There is first of all the prophetic killing of a rat in the room where Bigger, his mother, his sister and his brother live in quarreling, desperate squalor. Then Bigger, who has a bad name as a braggart living by shady devices, goes out to meet the poolroom gang environment provides. He plans a hold-up he is afraid to carry out. To hide his cowardice he terrorizes one of his friends.

You see his character. That is the point. Mr. Wright is champion of a race, not defender of an individual wrongdoer. Bigger gets a job as chauffeur in the house of Mr. Dalton, who is a philanthropist toward Negroes and owner of many Negro tenements. Mary Dalton, the daughter of the house, and her friend Jan, a supernally noble radical, make him drink with them. Through an accident, Bigger kills Mary Dalton. That is the first murder.

There is a gruesome dismemberment to hide the crime. Bigger thinks of demanding money, and makes his girl, Bessie, help him. His crime is discovered. After that there is the flight, the second murder, deliberate and brutal, the manhunt spreading terror over the whole South Side, then the spectacular capture and the day of reckoning in court for all concerned.

It is a long time since we've read a new novelist who had such command of the technique and resources of the novel. Mr. Wright's method is generally Dreiserian; but he has written his American tragedy in a notably firm prose. He knows how to tell a story. He knows how to develop a character, how to show influences playing on a man or a situation. Reflection blends into action. Accents and intonations are caught. Ideas are dramatized with concrete and inescapable images. And dialogue goes crackling down the page.

Bigger is a symbol. But, as we have suggested, he is able to express what he symbolizes more fluently than seems natural, considering how clearly Mr. Wright has made us see his life. There is a constant, probing inquiry into the state of the world that creates people like Bigger Thomas. We do not doubt it. We cannot. But we can and do doubt that it could flow so coherently through Bigger's mind. It's better left to the lawyer's summation in the court-room scene.

"Native Son" is, in truth, one of those compelling books to which people pay the uneasy tribute of saying their picture is impressive but overdrawn. That places Richard Wright in very good company--from Charles Dickens to John Steinbeck. After all, we do not lack stories of quaint Negro life.

Apart from the ideas that give it volume, force and scope, "Native Son" has some magnificently realized scenes: in the early part, where Bigger, a stranger and afraid, as Houseman said, in a world he never made, gropes for freedom from the walls that hold him; in the flight across the roofs and the stand high over the world, in the jail where processions of people come to see him, at the inquest and in the howling mob outside the court. The measure in which it shakes a community is the measure of its effectiveness.

From *The New York Times*, (March 1, 1940), p. 19.

Uneven Effect

Howard Mumford Jones

"Native Son" enters the publishing world with such a fanfare of trumpets and beating of drums as somewhat to abash quiet folk who are looking for a good book to read. It is a Book of the Month Club selection. The dust jacket is occupied by a long quote from Henry Seidel Canby, and Henry certainly do let himself go: "highly complicated story," "handled with competence," "swift narrative style proceeding by staccato dialogue," "rapidly mounting suspense," "the characters, too, are fully realized." Mr. Edward A. Weeks, not unknown in these parts, is Mr. Canby's fellow traveler on the book jacket. He announces: "It has us all by the ears." A throwaway from Harper and Brothers declares that the author's life is as interesting as one of his own novels, and speaks darkly of the purchase of a razor at one stage of his development. Then there is a preface by Dorothy Canfield Fisher. I usually admire Mrs. Fisher, but she has constructed the worst written sentence of the year: "The other point I would like to make is that the author shows genuine literary skill in the construction of his novel in giving so few pages to show us in concrete detail the exact ways in which American society constantly stimulates the powerful full-blooded human organism to action, which is as constantly forbidden to him by our mores." I shall come back to that sentence presently.

The first impact of the novel on me was one of great power. In retrospect, however, I find that this sense of power fades, and, a week after having read it, I cannot remember the name of a single character except that of the hero-villain, and I have only a vague memory of anybody's personality except his.

I am compelled, contrary to rule, to reveal the plot in order to discuss the novel. It concerns a colored boy named Bigger. The novel opens admirably in a single room in the morning. In that room a colored family gets up, kills rats, dresses, and has breakfast. It is soon evident that Bigger is a bad nigger--I use the term without offence in its technical sense. He drifts down to a poolroom, almost kills a friend with a razor and almost commits a robbery. He is then engaged as a chauffeur for a white family known for its sympathy for Negroes. The daughter of the house is a "radical." She insists on being driven with a male Communist friend by Bigger to a Negro restaurant, where she and the Communist get more or less tight. The Communist leaves, Bigger takes the girl home, helps her to her room and there, fearful lest the family discover him, he smothers her. He then burns the body in the furnace. Native wit and white stupidity for a time fend off suspicion, but his refusal to shake the ashes arouses the interest of some newspaper reporters, and his guilt is surmised. He flees with his Negro sweetheart, whom he kills, is trapped on a roof, pleads guilty, is defended by a lawyer of vaguely radical tendencies, and is eventually electrocuted.

There are three tests for a tale of this sort. Is its plot well constructed and does it maintain interest? Are the characters credible? Does the story spring out of, or illustrate, any thesis?

Well, all murder stories are exciting, and when a black man kills a white girl, most of us, to put it mildly, are stirred. When in addition he threatens to carve his friend and bashes in the head of his sweetheart with a brick, a pleasant titillation of horror is felt along the spine. The pursuit-and-capture motive is sure-fire stuff. In melodrama, moreover, we expect villainy to be punished. Bigger is punished.

But what is "highly complicated" about this? The simplest of narrative techniques is employed--straight-line narrative as in "Robinson Crusoe." We begin with Bigger in an excellent domestic scene, and we follow him to the hour of his death. The story is about as complicated as "Three Blind Mice." It is evident to experienced readers from the beginning that retribution is bound to overtake Bigger, and the only question is how long the author can keep him from capture. If this be "rapidly mounting suspense," it is rapidly mounting suspense bought in the oldest of literary markets. As for the "staccato dialogue," it is often excellent, but the conversation bears about the same relation to the narrative in "Native Son" that it bears to the narrative in "The Three Musketeers."

What about the characters? There are none except Bigger, and Bigger wavers between being a poor colored boy and being a monster of amorality. Most of the time he is a monster of amorality whose proceedings we contemplate with horror, and we are startled in the last quarter of the tale to discover that all this time the author has been thinking of him as a misunderstood colored boy. The other characters exist either (a) to be knocked down or (b) to be set up in order to illustrate something.

What do they illustrate? A thesis. Mrs. Fisher's infractious sentence darkly hints that Bigger's character is the result of American society arousing desires in the "powerful full-blooded human "organism" which it does not satisfy. Mrs. Fisher of course does not mean that American society incites the "powerful full-blooded human organism" to murder and then disobligingly gives it no opportunity to kill. She has in mind the wrongs done by the white race to the colored man, and she thinks (and the author thinks) that Bigger's criminal career is traceable to this cause.

But the essential wrong done the colored race is not that it drives Negroes to murder, but that it does not drive them even to work. They are unemployed and stifled. Bigger, however, gets a job.

At this point the author drives him to murder. But the murder does not follow from this thesis, but from another thesis--the same thesis that Dreiser set forth in "The Hand of the Potter" and "The American Tragedy." It is determinism. Men do what they are born to do. Bigger happens to be a colored man. But if he had been of any other race, he would still have acted as his nature compelled him to act. He did not murder the white girl to avenge the black race; he murdered both girls because he was born that way. His sociological background does not "explain" the murder in terms of race-relationships, though his inheritance may "explain" his character. To say that American society incited this "powerful full-blooded human organism to action" is to confuse humanitarianism with determinism.

The novel seems to me imperfect and uneven. If it were all like its opening scenes, it would be a moving study of Negro life. If it were simply melodrama, it would, being shortened, have great emotional punch. If it were all like its last quarter, it would be dull propaganda. As it is, one is sympathetic with Bigger, then one shudders at him, and, lastly, one is glad when he is dead just as one is glad when the villains in Victor Hugo are dead. At times Mr. Wright shows a Dostoievsky-like insight; at other times he writes like a ten-twent-and-thirt melodrama.

Boston Evening Transcript, (March 2, 1940) book section, p. 1.

A Powerful Novel About a
Boy from Chicago's Black Belt

Margaret Wallace

Some novels--and not, by any means, only great novels--have a kind of life of their own, a peculiar vitality which amounts almost to independent being. They add something to the reader's mind which was not there before, and which cannot be lost or taken away. Usually they father other books in turn and may end by coloring the thinking of a generation which has scarcely heard of them. "Native Son," by Richard Wright, at a fair venture, is such a novel. Richard Wright's cruel and absorbing story of a Negro boy from Chicago's Black Belt leaves one with the feeling that never before, in fiction, has anything honest or important been written about the American Negro.

You may like this book or you may hate it. You may like it for its sheer excitement. It is a murder story and nothing on the list of current crime fiction is half so engrossing. You may hate it because, in spots, it is ugly and brutal enough to give you bad dreams at night. If you have a conscience sensitive to questions of social injustice it may remain to trouble you long after you thought you were through with it. In no case will you be able to put it aside and ignore it. It has a factual quality as hard and real as a paving stone.

Mr. Wright might have chosen for his protagonist--but by some grace of artistic insight did not choose--a "good Negro." Bigger Thomas at 20 is a big, surly, dangerous black boy. He had already served a term in reform school for stealing automobile tires. He and his mother and a younger brother and sister are living, on relief, in one ill-ventilated, rat-infested room for which they pay $8 a week. Bigger spends his time at movies, or hanging around a pool room planning petty crimes, always against members of his own race. He and his pals understood that the police did not search very diligently for thieves who preyed upon Negroes. It was really criminal, and therefore dangerous, to tamper with white property.

Always present, whether they mentioned it or not, was this cleavage between black and white. . . .If you were black they didn't even want you in the army, except to dig ditches.

"I know I oughtn't to think about it," Bigger said, "but I can't help it. . . .We black and they white. They got things and we ain't. They do things and we can't. It's just like living in jail. Half the time I feel like I'm on the outside of the world peeping in through a knot hole in the fence."

This is the hard core of fear and hatred central to Bigger's character. . . .The murder was accidental. Not so much a murder, really as a natural reaction to the interpretation Bigger knew would be placed on his presence in a white girl's bedroom. . . .Bigger's reaction to the murder--he accepts it as such, without bothering about extenuating circumstances--is not accidental. It is rooted in the past which has conditioned him. For the first time in his short life he has done something even the white world would regard as significant, and for the first time he is not afraid. This recognition is the great psychological triumph of the novel. Everything else follows inexorably. . . .

"Native Son" comes through heaped-up horror to an emotion not far removed from those Aristotle described as pity and terror. For abnormal as the events seem, a regular tabloid sensation in cheap melodrama, Richard Wright forces us to understand Bigger. We accept without question the convention which makes him, at least in thought, more articulate than he possibly could have been. We concede that, given this train of circumstances, he could have done nothing else. It is harder, though still not impossible, to accept him as representative of his race. The defense plea arranged by his Jewish lawyer. . .is an indictment of society already sufficiently indicted by the story as it stands.

Beyond question, "Native Son" is the finest novel yet written by an American Negro. It is an amazingly expert performance for a man so new to his trade, and we are informed that Richard Wright was awarded a Guggenheim fellowship to complete it. In all probability we shall hear more of him in the future. If by chance we should not, it would still be hard, on this showing alone, to deny him recognition as an important novelist.

From *New York Sun*, March 5, 1940, p. 3.

Review of *Native Son*

Samuel Sillen

The tremendous power of *Native Son* has its ultimate source in a revolutionary vision of life. It is, in the most profound sense, a philosophical novel, a creative affirmation of the will to live and to transform life. Wright has often said that the discovery of *meaning* in the suffering of an oppressed group dooms the social order that is responsible for the suffering. His novel is a dramatization of the tortured search for values by which Bigger Thomas is to struggle, live, and die. Every arrangement of a class society conspires to maim Bigger for refusing to submit without challenge. The overbearing environment which engenders his suffering mutilates the forms of his protest and aspiration. But if the process of discovery is tragic, it is also, in the end, emancipatory; and if Bigger is condemned to die at the moment he has learned to live, our own minds have been flooded with meaning. A bold conception of human dignity gives this novel its stature. The episodes of violence, the sensitive notations of life in a segregated community, and the subtle documentation of a social machine which grinds down human personality, are important only in so far as they materialize this conception.

Only a courageous novelist would have attempted so difficult a theme. Only a supremely gifted one could have executed it so perfectly. For Bigger Thomas, externally, is the stereotyped monster of a lynch-inciting press. So far as the police record is concerned, he is the murderer of Mary Dalton, the daughter of his wealthy white "benefactor." He is a "brutish sex-slayer." His Negro mistress is the victim of his "primitive blood-lust." His trial for murder is the subject for horrified editorials in the Jackson (Miss.) *Daily Star* and gory news columns in the Chicago *Tribune*. This is explosive material. And it does explode--in the faces of the stereotype makers. The police record is here turned into its opposite, an indictment not of an individual but of a brutal and discriminatory order.

Bigger Thomas is not a "sex-slayer" at all. He is a fear-ridden boy whose attitude of iron reserve is a wall between himself and a world which will not allow him to live and grow. A deepening sense of hysteria has accompanied the blocking of his normal impulses. "Playing white" with his friends on a Chicago street corner is a grim substitute for living white, for living in a world, that is, where one may presumably be an aviator, or a President or a millionaire or whatever one wants to be. Bigger acts tough toward his poverty-stricken family, sensing that if he allows the shame and misery of their lives to invade his consciousness his own fear and despair will become intolerable. The victim of movie-inspired fantasies, he cannot find a possible order or meaning in his relations to other people. He does not know, at the beginning of the novel, that his crushed existence is part of a much larger pattern which includes Negroes *and* whites.

The events which lead to Bigger's unintentional smothering of Mary, his burning of the body, his flight from the police, and his murder of his mistress, Bessie, who he fears will betray him, create a sense of dramatic excitement that catches us up in the tensions and rhythms of Bigger's life. Though he did not plan Mary's murder, Bigger accepts it as his own act. Like Dmitry Karamazov, who felt guilty because in his heart he had wished his father's death, Bigger feels that he has killed many times before, "only on those other times there had been no handy victim or circumstance to make visible or dramatic his will to kill." The murders give him a sense of *creation*. He feels that they have given a focus to the chaotic circumstances of his existence. The acceptance of moral guilt makes Bigger feel free for the first time.

But such a commitment to life was doomed to disillusion. After his capture, Bigger realizes that he is as defenseless in the face of death as he had been in the face of life: "a new pride and a new humility would have to be born in him, a humility springing from a new identification with some part of the world in which he lived, and this identification forming the basis for a new hope that would function in him as pride and dignity." Having renounced fear and flight, he must possess a conception of man's fate which will enable him to die. He cannot respect the submissive path of religion which his mother and Reverend Hammond urge him to follow. He must have an affirmative idea. And he discovers its spirit in the Labor Defender lawyer, Mr. Max, and the young Communist, Jan Erlone.

In an essay published two years ago, Richard Wright declared that "If the sensory vehicle of imaginative writing is required to carry too great a load of didactic material, the artistic sense is submerged." He might have added that when the artistic sense is submerged, the didactic material becomes ineffective. In *Native Son*, as in the stories of *Uncle Tom's Children*, he has skillfully avoided the danger. Idea and image are remarkably integrated. Only a critic whose esthetic senses are blunted or whose social prejudices are unalterable will attempt to shout this novel down with the old cry of "propaganda." And yet, like *The Grapes of Wrath*, it will jar men and women out of their routine ways of looking at life and sweep them toward a new conception of the way things are and the way they ought to be.

But an effort will undoubtedly be made by some people to distort the plain meaning of the book in order to bolster their own bigotry. The reader must be warned against the blurb by Henry Seidel Canby which appears on the jacket of the book, and I hope that the publishers will be persuaded to withdraw it as a gross and vicious misrepresentation. Canby describes Jan Erlone, the Communist, as a "negrophile"! He suspects that the book will be "less of a surprise to, and more readily understood by, Southerners than by Northerners." He relishes the "deadly satire in the portraits of the young radicals--Mary who is killed, and Jan, the Communist, who chooses Bigger to work on, not realizing that this kind of political pity is more offensive to a Negro than color prejudice."

This is the most blatant stuff I have ever read. It angles the novel away from itself to the very stereotype which the novel demolishes. For the plain fact is that the radicals, Mr. Max and Jan Erlone, are the only ones who make Bigger aware of his dignity as a human being. To be sure, this does not happen overnight. To be sure, Jan makes an initial blunder in treating Bigger as a comrade before Bigger has learned to believe in the very existence of comradeship. But if one reads the novel in its full sweep one cannot mistake the overwhelming significance of Bigger's final remark: "Tell...Tell Mister...Tell Jan hello." It is, at last, a dropping of the Mister, an affirmation of that solidarity with other human beings in which only Jan and Max have taught him to believe.

It is difficult to think of an American novel that provides a more brilliant analysis of the interplay of social and psychological factors in experience. Wright has fused the valid elements in the naturalistic and psychological traditions, and the result is something quite new. For lack of a better phrase, "dramatic realism" will do. Structurally, the novel is divided into three sections corresponding to the three acts of a play. The action is not chopped up into chapters; it moves in a long sweep toward three climaxes. The tonal unity and psychological tension which we associate with an intense drama can be sustained only with great difficulty in fiction. As a sheer achievement in structural craftsmanship, *Native Son* is worth careful study. There is nothing wayward, either in detail or in mood. It is the work of a writer who feels his material deeply and authentically at the same time that he can view it from an ideological perspective.

What this perspective is, Wright has explained elsewhere. The Marxist analysis of society, he holds, "creates a picture which, when placed before the eyes of the writer, should unify his personality, buttress him with a tense and obdurate will to change the world. And, in turn, this changed world will dialectically change the writer. Hence, it is through a Marxist conception of reality and society that the maximum degree of freedom in thought and feeling can be gained for the Negro writer. Further, this dramatic Marxist vision, when consciously grasped, endows the writer with a sense of dignity which no other vision can give. Ultimately, it restores to the writer his lost heritage, that is, his role as a creator of the world in which he lives, and as a creator of himself." *Native Son* is his first full-length embodiment of his conception in the warm and living terms of fiction. It is a first novel, but it places Richard Wright, incontrovertibly, in the first ranks of American literature in our time. There is no writer in America of whom one can say more confidently: He is the creator of our better world and our greater art.

From *New Masses*, 34 (March 5, 1940), 24-25.

Wright's Invisible Native Son

Donald B. Gibson

The difficulty most critics have who write about Richard Wright's *Native Son* is that they do not see Bigger Thomas.[1] They see him with their outer eyes, but not with the inner eyes, "those eyes with which they look through their physical eyes upon reality."[2] Of course there is certain sense in which everyone is invisible, a certain sense in which the observer creates the observed, attributing to him qualities whose nature depends upon the viewer's own character. When we see a man in muddy work clothes, we are likely to see him only as a laborer and to have aroused in us whatever ideas we have toward laborers. We rarely look at a man so dressed (assuming that he is unknown to us) and see a father, a churchgoer, taxpayer or fisherman, though the man underneath the clothing may theoretically be all these things. If we think about him, we automatically assume certain things about his life style--about his values, his economic and social position, and even his occupation. To the extent that the clothes determine what we see, the person beneath them is invisible to us.

The difficulty comes about when we assume that the outer covering is the essential person. Most critics of Wright's novel see only the outer covering of Bigger Thomas, the blackness of his skin and his resulting social role. Few have seen him as a discrete entity, a particular person who struggles with the burden of his humanity. Wright has gone to great lengths in the novel to create Bigger as a person, to invest the social character with particularizing traits, to delineate the features of a face. The final meaning of the book, as a matter of fact, depends upon the awareness on the part of the reader of Bigger's individuality. The lack of such awareness has led most critics to misread the novel, for almost all of them interpret it as though the social person, Bigger Thomas, were the *real* and essential person. The following bit of dialogue, however, suggests a different perspective.

> Max: "Well, this thing's bigger than you, son .... "
> Bigger: "They going to kill me anyhow."[3]

This exchange between Max and Bigger reveals that each is looking at the problem at hand in an essentially different way. Max is thinking of the social implications of the situation; Bigger's attention is focused on his own impending doom. Which view is the truer, the more significant in the content of the novel? Wright's critics have generally opted for the view of Max, but if Max's view is true, then most of the whole final section does not make sense. For a careful reading of that third section, "Fate," indicates that the focus of the novel is not on the trial nor on Max, but on Bigger and on his finally successful attempt to come to terms with his imminent death. It need be noted that the trial does not take up the entire third section of the novel as has been often said. In the edition cited above, the third section comprises 126 pages; the trial itself consumes 37 pages and Max's address to the jury, 17 pages. The length of Max's speech and his bearing on what has preceded in the novel to that point have led experienced readers to neglect what else happens in that final section. It has lead to many conclusions about the novel which are not borne out by the 89 pages of the last section describing what happens before and after the trial. The degree to which the reader focuses upon Max and Max's speech determines the degree to which Bigger is invisible to him.

In order to assess properly the meaning of the final section, it is necessary to understand what happens in the concluding pages of the novel. First of all, it is too simple to say as Baldwin does that "he [Bigger] *wants* to die, because he glories in his hatred and prefers, like Lucifer, rather to rule in hell than serve in heaven."[4] The point is that Bigger, through introspection, finally arrives at a definition of self which is his own and different from that assigned to him by everyone else in the novel. The many instances in the last of the three sections of the novel which show him exploring his deepest thoughts, feelings and emotions reveal Baldwin's statement to be patently false. Shortly after Bigger's capture and imprisonment he lies thinking in his cell.

> And, under and above it all, there was the fear of death before which he was naked and without defense; he had to go forward and meet his end like every living thing upon the earth .... There would have to hover above him, like the stars in a full sky, a vast configuration of images and symbols whose magic and power could lift him up and make him live so intensely that the dread of being black and unequal would be forgotten; that even death would not matter, that it would be a victory. This would have to happen before he could look them in the face again: a new pride and a new humility would have to be born in him, a humility springing from a new identification with some part of the world in which he lived, and this identification forming the basis of a new hope that would function in him as pride and dignity. (pp. 234-35)

This quotation not only refutes Baldwin's statement about Bigger's motivations, but it as well indicates the focus of the novel at this point is on Bigger Thomas the private person. The emphasis is on a problem that he faces as an isolated, solitary human whose problem is compounded   by race though absolutely not defined by racial considerations. There follows from the point in the novel during which the above quotation occurs a pattern of advance and retrogression as Bigger gropes his way, privately and alone, toward the "new identification," that "pride and dignity" referred to in the passage. From this point on Bigger feels by turns guilt, hate, shame, remorse, fear, anger, and through the knowledge of himself engendered through acquaintance with his basic thoughts and feelings moves toward a sense of identity. There is a good deal of emphasis placed upon the solitary nature of his problem. At least twice he advances to the point at which he recognizes that salvation for him comes only from himself, from his own effort and knowledge.

> He was balanced on a hair-line now, but there was no one to push him forward or backward, no one to make him feel that he had any value or worth, no one but himself. (p. 305)
> He believed that Max knew how he felt, and once more before he died he wanted to talk with him and feel with as much keenness as possible what his living and dying meant. That was all the hope he had now. If there were any sure and firm knowledge for him, it would have to come from himself. (p. 350)

If we see the quotation above (from pp. 234-235) as defining Bigger's essential problem, then it is evident that the passage must have relevance to the concluding pages of the novel. When Bigger has achieved the "new humility," the "pride and dignity" referred to there, if he has achieved it, it should be evidenced somewhere later in the novel. And so it is. During the final two pages of the novel, it is clear that Bigger no longer suffers, is no longer in terror about his impending death. "Aw, I reckon I believe in myself....I ain't got nothing else....I got to die" (p. 258--Wright's ellipses). He accepts himself as never before, and in realizing his identity is able to evaluate his past actions objectively. "I didn't want to kill!...But what I killed for, I am! It must have been pretty deep in me to make me kill! I must have felt it awful hard to murder...."

Because he has come to terms with himself, because he no longer hates and despises himself as he has during most of his life, it is no longer necessary for him to feel hatred. For this reason he is able to pass along through Max a reassuring word to his mother: "Just go and tell Ma I was all right and not to worry none, see? Tell her I was all right and wasn't crying none..."(p. 358). Had he "died in hatred," as Bone says,[5] he would hardly have called out his final words to Max, "Tell Jan hello..." (p. 359). These words indicate that Bigger's accepted the consequences of his actions and hence himself. He has no choice--if he is to achieve the degree of reconciliation to his fate necessary for him to face death and therefore assert his humanity--but to recognize that he is what he has done.

The two perspectives of Bigger Thomas contained in the novel exist in tension until in the final pages the focus shifts away entirely from the social emphasis. No matter what the social implications are, the fact is that he, the private, isolated human must face the consequences. It is no wonder that Bigger is totally unable to understand Max's speech during the trial. He grasps something of the tone, but the meanings of the words escape him, for Max is not really thinking about Bigger the existential person, the discrete human entity. When Bigger and Max converse privately, they understand each other reasonably well. But during the trial Max is talking about a symbol, a representative figure. Hence the significant problem becomes not whether Max will save Bigger--the answer to that question is a foregone conclusion--but whether Bigger will save himself in the only possible way, by coming to terms with himself. This we see him doing as we observe him during long, solitary hours of minute introspection and self-analysis.

Probably the critic most responsible for the perception of Bigger Thomas as a social entity and that alone is James Baldwin, who conceived some rather convincing arguments about the limitations of the protest novel and especially of *Native Son.*

> All of Bigger's life is controlled, defined by his hatred and his fear. And later, his fear drives him to murder and his hatred to rape; he dies, having come, through this violence, we are told, for the first time, to a kind of life, having for the first time redeemed his manhood.[6]

Baldwin, for all the persuasiveness of his language, has failed to see Bigger the person. For it is clear enough that Bigger's feeling of elation, of having done a creative thing simply in murdering is not the final outcome. It is rather early in the novel when he feels release, free from the forces which have all his life constrained him. But after his capture he feels he is not free; he still has himself to cope with. His final feeling is not --as the concluding pages of the novel explicitly show--exaltation for having "redeemed his manhood." Very soon after the first murder, to be sure, he does feel that it has had some redeeming effect.

> The thought of what he had done, the awful horror of it, the daring associated with such actions, formed for him for the first time in his fear-ridden life a barrier of protection between him and a world he feared. He had murdered and had created a new life for himself. It was something that was all his own, and it was the first time in his life he had had anything that others could not take from him. (p. 90)

But this response occurs after all about one-fourth of the way through novel. These are not the feelings Bigger has at the end. One need only imagine this passage as among Bigger's thoughts as we last see him in order to see how inappropriate it would be as a concluding statement. He is not in the mood of prideful self-assertion which he feels so often from the time he disposes of Mary's body until his crime is discovered. Instead, the conclusion finds him feeling a calm assurance and acceptance of self. There is neither irony nor condescension in his final "Tell Jan hello," nor does the last scene in the denotative meanings of its words and the tone project "hatred and fear" on Bigger's part.

Baldwin's eloquent statement at the end of "Everybody's Protest Novel" describing how the protest novel fails does not describe the content of Wright's novel.

> The failure of the protest novel lies in its rejection of life, the human being, the denial of his beauty, dread, power, in its insistence that it is his categorization alone which is real and which cannot be transcended.[7]

The statement itself is not to be questioned; its applicability to *Native Son* is. There is too much in Wright's novel which suggests that Bigger's response to his situation does not stem from his categorization, his Negroness, but from his humanness. What has the following response occurring after Bigger has returned from hearing his sentence, to do with his "categorization?"

> In self-defense he shut out the night and day from his mind, for if he had thought of the sun's rising and setting, of the moon or the stars or clouds or rain, he would have died a thousand deaths before they took him to the chair. To accustom his mind to death as much as possible, he made all the world beyond his cell a vast grey land where neither night nor day passed, peopled by strange men and women whom he could not understand, but with those lives he longed to mingle once before he went. (p. 349)

These are not the thoughts and the feelings of a Negro, as such, but of a man who is about to die and who struggles to cope with the fact. Race, social condition, whatever category a reader might have placed him in, have no relevance here. There are many such passages in the third section of the book showing Bigger's individual response to his situation. For example, the following:

> He had lived and acted on the assumption that he was alone, and now he saw that he had not been. What he had done made others suffer. No matter how much he would long for them to forget him, they would not be able to. His family was a part of him, not only in blood, but in spirit. (p. 254)
> He would not mind dying now if he could only find out what this meant, what he was in relation to all the others that lived, and the earth upon which he stood. Was there some battle everybody was fighting, and he had missed it? (p. 307)
> His face rested against the bars and he felt tears roll down his cheeks. His wet lips tasted salt. He sank to his knees and sobbed: "I don't want to die....I don't want to die...." (p. 308)

His interpretation of the opening scene of the novel is likewise a measure of the degree to which Baldwin does not see Bigger.

> Rats lived there too in the Thomas apartment...and we first encounter Bigger in the act of killing one. One may consider that the entire book, from that harsh "Brring!" to Bigger's weak "Good-by" as the lawyer, Max, leaves him in the death cell is an extension, with the roles inverted, of this chilling metaphor. [8]

This metaphor would be true if Bigger were only the social figure which critics have seen. But the figure on the final pages of the novel, no matter what he is, is not a rat. He does not die as a rat does; he is neither fearful nor desperate.

An alternative reading is offered by Edwin Burgum in his essay on *Native Son* in which he says of Bigger's killing of the rat and flaunting it in the faces of his mother and sister: "His courage is that overcompensation for fear called bravado. It passes beyond the needs of the situation and defeats its own end here as in the later crises in the novel."[9] This interpretation gets beyond the problem of comparing Bigger with a rat. Certainly Wright's sympathies are with Bigger to a greater degree than his being likened to a rat implies.

It must be admitted that Bigger Thomas, the social figure whom Baldwin and others have seen, has a prominent place in the novel and is by no means a figment. He is a representative figure to Buckley, to the policemen investigating the murder of Mary, and to the public at large. Wright makes it amply evident that the desire on the part of these people do away with Bigger reflects a primitive desire to perform ritual murder and thereby, to do away with the potential threat posed by all other Negroes through sacrificing the representative black figure. But readers need to avoid the error of the characters in the novel by distinguishing Bigger's qualities as a representative figure and his qualities as a particular person (difficult though this may be in our time and in our society)who, exclusive of race, faces death.

If he were nothing, if this were all, then why could not he die without hesitancy? Who
and what was he to feel the agony of a wonder so intensely that amounted to fear?
Why was this strange impulse always throbbing in when there was nothing outside of
him to meet it and explain it? Who or what had traced this restless design in him?
Why was this eternal reaching for something that was not there? Why this black gulf
between him and the world: warm red blood here and cold blue sky there, and never a
wholeness, a oneness, a meeting of the two? (pp. 350-51)

Feeling such things as these and about to die in the electric chair, Bigger ceases to be
representative of the Negro and becomes every man whose death is imminent--that is,
every man.

The view of Bigger as representative (and hence invisible) comes about in part
because Wright's novel has been too frequently seen as a "Negro" novel or a protest
novel, and all the limitations of these categories have been ascribed to it. It has been
extremely difficult for even the most sophisticated readers to see Bigger's humanity
because the idea of an ignorant, uneducated, criminal Negro coming to terms with the
human condition, as Bigger finally does, is an alien idea. The novel should be
compared not only to *Crime and Punishment,* the work with which it is most frequently
compared, but with *The Stranger* as well. Wright's and Camus' novels were published
two years apart (1940 and 1942 respectively) and there are many striking parallels
between them. The most fruitful result of such a comparison may be to lift Wright's
novel out of the context of the racial problem in America and to place it in larger
perspective, or at least to reveal the extent to which *Native Son* is not so limited as it
has appeared to be.

The limited view has also been responsible for the interpretation of the novel as a
propaganda piece for the Communist Party. [10] On the contrary the novel points up the
limitations of a system of ideas which by its very nature is incapable of dealing with
certain basic human problems. Bigger is saved in the end, but not through the efforts of
the Party, which constantly asserts that the individual cannot achieve meaningful
salvation. This further implies that the thought processes leading to Wright's break with
the Party were already in motion as early as 1939, and that his formal public
announcement of the break in 1944 [11] was a result of much earlier distress. The
interpretation of the novel as a propaganda piece for the Communist Party stems from
the notion that Max is Wright's spokesman. As a result, a good deal of weight is placed
upon Max's address to the jury. Though there is enough evidence to suggest that Max's
personal view of Bigger allows for his existence as a discrete individual, the strategy he
chooses to defend Bigger requires that he deal with him largely on an abstract level
with the intention of convincing his hearers that the abstraction is embodied within the
particular individual before them. Thus he says:

> "This boy represents but a tiny aspect of a problem whose reality sprawls over a
> third of this nation." (p. 330)
> "Multiply Bigger Thomas twelve million times, allowing for environmental and
> temperamental variations, and for those Negroes who are completely under   the
> influence of the church, and you have the psychology of the Negro people." (p. 333)

The effect of his words on many is simply to enhance Bigger's invisibility.

Rather than being Wright's spokesman, in truth, Max presents one side a dialogue
whose totality is expressed through the dual perspective contained in the novel. [12] Max
is indeed a sympathetic character, but for all his good intentions, he has limitations. He
never, for example, entirely understands what Bigger is getting at during their
conversations. Only in end, during their final meeting, does he come to have some
notion of fact that he is not superior to Bigger, that he knows no more than Bigger
about the kinds of questions the condemned man is asking and consequently is not in a
position to explain anything. When Bigger tells Max that he *is* what he has *done*
("What I killed   for, I *am!)*", Max's response is to recoil in horror, for even he
ultimately is unable to accept any definition of a man outside his own preconceived
idea. Max cannot accept the implications of Bigger's conclusions nor, indeed, can he
fully understand the position that Bigger has finally arrived at. Wright makes this point
doubly clear with the line, "Max groped for his hat like a blind man." Now given the

nearly explicit meanings which sight and blindness have had in the novel prior to this, it can hardly be a fortuitous simile. Not even Max is completely capable of recognizing and accepting the truth of Bigger's humanity.

Though Max's motivations are good, founded as they are upon his basic good character and good feeling, he is unable finally to save Bigger for Bigger's salvation comes about through his own efforts, through his eventual ability to find freedom from the constraints of his past. All the characters in Wright's major works after *Native Son* achieve the same kind of freedom, or at least the promise of such freedom, in one way or another. This is true of the central character of *Black Boy* (which is more fictional in technique and intention than commonly recognized), *The Long Dream, The Outsider* and "The Man Who Lived Underground." *Native Son* resolves the tension between the two alternatives, the one seeing the salvation of individuals through social change, the other seeing the salvation of individuals through their own efforts. After *Native Son,* Wright was never again to suggest the possibility of any individual's achieving meaningful social salvation. The inescapable conclusion is that Wright lost faith entirely in social solutions to human problems and came to believe that ultimately the individual alone can save himself. During that final meeting between Max and Bigger it is made abundantly clear that Bigger has through the course of the third section of the novel come to terms with his most pressing problem, his impending doom. In so doing he achieves the only meaningful salvation possible. (Max speaks first.)

> "But on both sides men want to live; men are fighting for life. Who will win? Well, the side ..with the most humanity and the most men. That's why.. y-you've got to b-believe in yourself, Bigger ...."
> Max's head jerked up in surprise when Bigger laughed.
> "Aw, I reckon I believe in myself....I ain't got nothing....I got to die." (p. 358)

Now if the conclusions I have come to are valid, then two highly significant corollaries follow: 1) Wright did not simply emerge from the naturalistic school of Dreiser, Dos Passos and Farrell; he did not simply adapt the techniques and thoughts of the naturalists to the situation of the black man.[13] 2) The existential thinking of his later work did not derive from the influence on him of Camus, Sartre and other French existentialists, but grew out of his own experience in America.[14]

I do not want to argue that Wright was not strongly influenced by American literary naturalism; certainly he was. But he was not as confined by the tradition as has been generally believed. If my thesis about *Native Son* is correct, then Wright is not an author whose major novel reflects phases of a dying tradition, but he is instead one who out of the thought, techniques and general orientation of the naturalistic writers developed beyond their scope. *Native Son,* as I have described it in this essay looks forward rather than backward. It is a prototype of the modern existential novel and a link between the fiction of the 1930s and a good deal of more modern fiction.

A kind of condescension and a preconception about the potential of a self-educated black man from the very depths of the South have combined to obscure the sources of Wright's proclivity toward existentialism. The comments made by two writers and critics who were friends of Wright make the point.

> REDDING: Dick was a small-town boy--a small-town Mississippi boy--all of his days. The hog maw and the collard greens. He was fascinated by the existentialist group for a while, but he didn't really understand them.
> BONTEMPS: Essentially, of course, Wright was and remained not only an American but a Southerner. Negroes have a special fondness for that old saw, "You can take the boy out of the country, but you can't take the country out of the boy.[15]

In order to understand the sources of the existentialist concern in Wright's work and thought, one need only to note the quality and character of the life described by Wright in *Black Boy* and realize as well that existentialism may be described as a mood arising out of the exigencies of certain life situations rather than as a fully developed and articulated systematic philosophy which one chooses to hold or rejects. Though we cannot say that existentialism resulted directly from the experience of Europeans under Nazi occupation, we can certainly say that the occupation, the war itself, created circumstances conducive to the nurturing and development of the existential response. Europeans during the war, especially those engaged in underground activities, daily faced the imminent possibility of death, and the constant awareness of impending death was largely responsible for the emergence of a way of interpreting the meaning of life consonant with that awareness. *Black Boy* of course does not describe a wartime situation, but one cannot help but feel the constant pressure on the person described there, a pressure from a world which threatens unceasingly to destroy him. The earliest of Wright's memories is of an episode which results in his being beaten unconscious, and this at a very young age. Thereafter we see described in the book the progress of an inward, alienated individual, distrustful of all external authority, who learns that his survival depends upon the repudiation of the values of others and a strong reliance upon his own private and personal sense of values. The existential precept, "existence precedes essence," stems as a mood from Wright's experience as described in *Black Boy*, but as a condition of his life and not as a consciously held philosophical principle. Herein lie the sources of Bigger Thomas' response to the condition brought about by his crime, capture and condemnation.

A comment made by Wright in response to an unfriendly review of *Native Son* is relevant as a final observation.

> If there had been one person in the Dalton household who viewed Bigger Thomas as a human being, the crime would have been solved in half an hour. Did not Bigger himself know that it was the denial of his personality that enabled him to escape detection so long? The one piece of incriminating evidence which would have solved the "murder mystery" was Bigger's humanity under their very eyes. [16]

We need only make the proper substitutions to see the relevance Wright's comment to the views of most critics of his novel. "The denial of his personality," and the failure on their part to see "Bigger's humanity under their very eyes" have caused him to be invisible, to be Wright's own invisible native son.

NOTES

[1]Limitations of space preclude naming all the critics I have in mind. A few of them are the following: James Baldwin, "Everybody's Protest Novel" and "Many Thousands Gone, "*Notes of a Native Son* (Boston, 1955), pp. 13-23, 24-45; Robert Bone, *The Negro Novel in America*(New Haven, 1958), pp. 140-52; Hugh M. Gloster, *Negro Voices in American Fiction* (Chapel Hill, N.C., 1948), pp. 222-34; John Reilly, "Afterword," *Native Son* (New 1966). Critics most nearly exceptions are: Edwin Berry Burgum, *The Novel and the World's Dilemma* (New York, 1963), pp. 223-40; Esther Merle Jackson, "The American Negro and the Image of the Absurd," *Phylon*, XXIII (1962), 359-71; Nathan A. Scott, "Search for Beliefs: The Fiction of Richard Wright," *University of Kansas City Review*, XXIII (1956), 19-24.
[2]Ralph Ellison, *Invisible Man* (New York, 1952), p. 3.
[3]*Native Son* (New York, 1940), p. 312. Subsequent quotations from the novel are from this edition.
[4]*Notes of a Native Son*, p. 44.
[5]*The Negro Novel*, p. 150.
[6]*Notes of a Native Son*, p. 22.
[7]P.23. Edward Margolies explores the opposite view of Wright's novel in *Native Sons: A Critical Study of Twentieth-Century American Authors* (New York, 1968), pp. 85-86.
[8]P. 34.
[9]P. 232.
[10] Richard Sullivan, "Afterword" to *Native Son*, Signet, 1961.
[11]"I Tried to be a Communist," *Atlantic Monthly*, CLXV (Aug. 1944), 61-70; (Sept. 1944), 56.
[12]Margolies believes that the duality of perspective referred to here is unresolved. Pp. 79-80.
[13]Wright's relation to the naturalistic tradition was first articulated by Alfred Kazin, *Native Grounds* (New York, 1942), p. 372, and later by Bone in *The Negro Novel*, pp. 142-43.

[14]Margolies concurs with this conclusion. P. 68.

[15]Saunders Redding and Arna Bontemps in "Reflections on Richard Wright: A Sympos-ium," *Anger and Beyond*, ed., Herbert Hill (New York, 1966), p. 207. Further comments on Wright and existentialism occur on pages 203,205,208, 209.

[16]"I Bite the Hand that Feeds Me," *Atlantic Monthly*, CLXV (June 1940), 826.

From *American Quarterly* 21, (Winter 1969), 729-738.

Richard Wright's Women Characters and Inequality

Sylvia Keady

After reading a large number of Richard Wright's short stories and novels, I came to feel that his characterization of women must be termed prejudiced and stereotyped. He emphasizes certain aspects and characteristics of his female characters while leaving out features of equal or greater importance. I intend to demonstrate through an analysis of several of Wright's female characters that his writings have a sexist bias. In order to define the phenomena of male sexual bias and female stereotyping more accurately, I shall draw on the feminist theories espoused in Kate Millett's *Sexual Politics* and Simone de Beauvoir's *The Second Sex*.

Literature, insofar as it mirrors the world, reflects the predominant attitude which frequently values men and masculine pursuits more highly than women and feminine pursuits. And since male values and consequently male concerns, problems, and dilemmas prevail, it follows that women characters are used to reveal, justify, and enhance masculine problems. "To be more explicit," Cynthia Griffin Wolff remarks, "the bias is carefully chosen so that certain types of masculine behavior (toward women and toward the world in general) must be justified. The stereotypes of women vary, but they vary in response to different masculine needs. The flattering frequency with which women appear in literature is ultimately deluding: they appear not as they are, certainly not as they would define themselves, but as conveniences to the resolution of masculine dilemmas."[1] It will become apparent that in Wright's novels the female characters frequently function as vehicles through which the hero's problems and difficulties are further increased or solved.

In a male-dominated society, women do not develop the symbols and stereotypes with which they are described. The image of women as we know it and read about it was created by men and fashioned to suit their needs. The function of the male's gender-linked otherness is to provide a means of control over a subordinate group and a rationale which justifies and explains the oppression of those in a lower order. According to Kate Millett's summary of stereotypes,

> . . . the ascribed attributes of blacks and women reveal that common opinion associates the same traits with both: inferior intelligence, an instinctual or sensual gratification, an emotional nature both primitive and childlike, an imagined prowess in or affinity for sexuality, a contentment with their own lot which is in accord with a proof of its appropriateness, a wily habit of deceit, and concealment of feeling. Both groups are forced to the same accommodational tactics: an ingratiating or supplicatory manner invented to please, a tendency to study those points at which the dominant group are [sic] subject to influence or corruption, and an assumed air of helplessness involving fraudulent appeals for direction through a show of ignorance.[2]

To the characteristics ascribed to women, we may add passivity, slyness, and the inability to grasp subtle principles of conduct, large aspirations, and grand designs. Most of Wright's female characters fit into the above stereotypes since they are frequently described as being childlike, whimpering, and stupid. Wright did not attribute characteristics of a mature mentality to them. Frequently his male characters lack the ability to rationalize, but the female characters are the bottom of the scale of human intelligence. Aunt Sue in "Bright and Morning Star" is an exception. She takes up a gun to kill Booker, the stool pigeon. However, she is a motherly figure, desexualized by her age and appearance. Wright's other females are mainly young and sexually active.

Kate Millett asserts that "patriarchy's chief institution is the family. It is both a mirror of and a connection with the larger society; a patriarchal unit within a patriarchal whole" (Millett, p. 33). The main contribution of the family is the socialization of the young "into patriarchal ideology's prescribed attitudes toward the categories of role, temperament, and status" (Millett, p. 35). *The Long Dream* gives the reader an insight into the workings of a typical patriarchal family. The father, Tyree, is a powerful figure within the family and the Black Belt. The mother is a submissive being who does not assert herself until after her husband's death. Throughout the major part of the novel and during Fish's most formative years, the mother figure is portrayed as meek and passive. With Gladys he continues the kind of relationship which he had with his mother. "The comfort he drew from her [his mother] was sensual in its intensity, and it formed the pattern of what he was to demand later in life from women. When he was a man and in distress, he would have to have them, but his need of them would be limited, localized, focused toward obtaining release, solace."[3]

Fish's family life, his environment, and his peers are operative in forming his image of woman, whose mission is to give herself to man in order to serve his sexual desires.

> Black girls, with their giggling and talking, were no longer negative creatures who did not "understand," but a substratum of life whose chief traits were marking time until he and his black brothers were old enough to go to them and give them their duties and destinies. And, to Fishbelly, this interpretation of woman was as it should have been; it was in this fashion that his environment had presented woman to him. Indeed, the pending gift of woman was something delightful, a gratuitous pleasure that nature had somehow showered down upon the male section of life alone, and he waited for that gift as one would wait for a new and different kind of Christmas with Santa Clauses going up instead of coming down chimneys. He and his gang joked loud and long about the physical pleasures they would inherit, but as yet their knowledge was hearsay. *(Dream,* p. 77)

Fish's initiation into sex takes place when his father takes him to his own whorehouse. Before they leave he gives his son fatherly advice: "'A woman's just a woman .... When you had one, you done had 'em all'"*(Dream,* p. 137). By the time Fish meets Gladys his sexual behavior has taken on the pattern of

> *vip*
> *Vaim*
> *Thank you*
> *Ma'am...*   (*Dream,* p. 159)

The sexual experiences of many of Wright's male characters constitute a victory of masculine diligence and wit over females. "The more difficult the assault the greater the glory, but any victory is pointless if it cannot be boasted of and sniggered over" (Millet, p. 303). Sex, i.e., the victory over woman, is not good unless it is approved and applauded by a peer-group jury. Zeke's boastful account of his first sexual experiences to his high school friends in *The Long Dream* demonstrates the necessity of peer-group approval--as does a similar conversation between Al, Jake, Slim, and Bob in *Lawd Today.* Every woman whom they see is described in terms of her physical contours and her possible prowess in bed. They talk about "the first meat"[4] they ever had, bragging about their first sexual victories. During a break from their post-office work they look at pornographic photos, again talking about woman as "meat" that is being had and handled:

> "He's riding her like a stallion!"
> "He's riding her like a bicycle!"   (*Lawd*, p. 161)

Wright's humor -- if we can call it that -- is the humor of the men's room where, in fact, parts of these conversations take place. The humor depends on a whole series of shared assumptions, attitudes, and responses which constitute a bond of male companionship. The joke succeeds only if sex is hard to get, secretive, and comic. "Meat" must also be transparently stupid.

The major female characters in *The Long Dream, Native Son, Lawd Today, The Outsider,* and "Bright and Morning Star" exemplify Wright's patriarchal bias. Gladys in *The Long Dream* is portrayed as an unintelligent and passive woman who is grateful that Fish intends to save her from the whorehouse. While taking her for a ride through the streets of the white area, he wants to talk to her about the inequities of black and white. However, Gladys does not respond intelligently and consistently with her own bad experiences with whites, and Fish realizes "that her mind was incapable of comprehending the elementary complexity of it all" (*Dream,* pp. 190-91). "Yeah, poor little Gladys was just a woman and didn't know"(*Dream,* p. 192). Gladys is Fish's emblem of spending ability and status, and it is in this light that we have to see his wish to set her up in an apartment. When he tells her of his intention to move her out of the Grove, her reaction is one of utterly grateful submission: she flings herself into his arms and cries. Wright's women whimper and cry easily; after all, "A woman's business is emotion and her trade is carried on in cash of tears."[5] Gladys looks at Fish, after he has told her of his intention to set her up in an apartment, with "eyes that were begging redemption, salvation" (*Dream, p.* 192). "He had never before seen a woman in the throes of redemption, had never before witnessed the light in the face of a woman whose destiny had been changed in the twinkling of an eye" (*Dream,* p. 192). Of course it is a man who redeemed poor little fallen Gladys "in the twinkling of an eye."

Bessie in *Native Son* and Lil in *Lawd Today* are equally dull and mindless, and drown what little mind they have in either liquor or religion. Both function as road blocks to the actions and pursuits of the male characters. Neither Jake nor Bigger is an intelligent, rationalizing man. However, they are shown as active, whereas the women are portrayed as passive and acted upon. Lil is, in the beginning of the novel, like a bullied child who is continually ordered around, which, in the hero's view, degrades her while it aggrandizes him. At the beginning of *Lawd Today* Jake sits at the breakfast table and reads the newspaper, which incites him to muse about Roosevelt, Hitler, Einstein, crime, Communism, and race problems. Lil, in the meantime, is absorbed in reading *Unity,* a religious pamphlet, and does not respond to his musings. Her silence provokes Jake to an angry response.

> "Woman, what makes you so dumb? Don't you ever try using your brains sometimes? Don't you never think of nothing that's serious?"
> "I don't know, Jake." (*Lawd*, p. 31)

In this oppressive marriage Jake's post-office job and her presumed right to be supported by her husband are Lil's only weapons against him. " 'All I want from you is support,' "she cries, "'and I'm going to get it or get your job' "(Lawd, p. 19). Lil fits into the stereotype of the passive and dependent woman who will carry her lot rather than attempt to change it. Even after Jake, in a drunken stupor, beats her up at the end of the novel, she cries, wraps herself into her coat, and sinks to the floor, sobbing, " 'Lawd, I wish I was dead' "(Lawd, *p.* 189). Since the focal point of the novel is the meaninglessness of a Black male's day, Lil functions to increase Jake's masculine problems by complaining and creating difficulties for him at the post-office.

Bessie in *Native Son* uses liquor to numb her mind, and it is her blindness and passivity which Bigger hates in her as well as in his sister and mother. Bessie likes liquor and sex, and since Bigger provides her with both she likes him too. "... only it was Bessie he was looking at now and seeing how blind she was. He felt the narrow orbit of her life: from her room to the kitchen of the white folks was the farthest she ever moved."[6] Bigger's orbit of life is equally narrow. He, however, is somewhat aware of his situation and acts to create a meaning for his life, albeit through killing a white woman. When Bigger first comes to Bessie's room, she is portrayed as the jealously teasing and coaxing female who wants to be reassured that her lover still desires her. Only after Bigger has shown her the roll of dollar bills which he stole from Mary Dalton is she willing to go to bed with him. Bessie is a mindlessly accommodating woman when she agrees to be Bigger's accomplice in his intended kidnap. Her reaction to Bigger's request is one of helpless agony that results in sobbing and ultimately in accommodating Bigger's will. "'If I do it, it's 'cause you want me to,' she sobbed" (*Native*, p. 140). She is equally weak in asserting herself against Bigger's sexual attack in the abandoned house. "Bessie was still, inert, unresisting, without response. He kissed her again and at once she spoke, not a word, but a resigned and prolonged sound that gave forth a meaning of horror accepted" (*Native*, p. 219). This sex act is described only from Bigger's point of view, as is the earlier one in Bessie's room. "Imperiously driven, he rode roughshod over her whimpering protests, feeling acutely sorry for her as he galloped a frenzied horse down a steep hill in the face of a resisting wind" (*Native*, p. 219). This description illuminates the hatred of the flesh, the willingness to liken a woman to a domesticated animal, and the refusal to permit her any autonomy. The woman's body serves to placate male desires and is reduced to function, as Simone de Beauvoir puts it, as "injection vessel and bidet."[7] This form of sexual intercourse can be likened to rape, of which Bigger is, in fact, accused. "In rape, the emotions of aggression, hatred, contempt, and the desire to break or violate personality, take a form consummately appropriate to sexual politics" (Millett, p. 44). "Patriarchal force also relies on a form of violence particularly sexual in character and realized most completely in the act of rape"(Millett, p. 44).

Within the context of sexual abuse of women, prostitution should be mentioned. "In prostitution, male desire can be satisfied on no matter what body, such desire being specific but not individualized as to object. . . . So long as the prostitute is denied the rights of a person, she sums up all the forms of feminine slavery at once" (de Beauvoir, p. 619). Any time the female body becomes the object of male sexual pleasure in Wright's novels, we do not have two equal partners engaging in intercourse. Woman becomes "woman as body of woman for his senses" (*Outsider*, p. 236). Prostitution is the epitome of this exploitation of women. Prostitutes appear frequently in Wright's novels: Blanche and Rose in *Lawd Today;* Gladys, Maybelle, Maud, and Vera in *The Long Dream;* and Jenny in *The Outsider.* Except for Gladys and Jenny, the prostitutes only appear as peripheral figures.

Jenny's first appearance in Cross's room captures the mercenary and exploitative aspect of prostitution. Jenny was "selling herself" (*Outsider*, p. 92), and although Cross thinks of her only in terms of "this fetching little tart" (*Outsider*, p. 93), he "was suddenly hungry for her; she was woman as body of woman..." (*Outsider*, p. 93). Jenny is selling and Cross is buying: " 'Listen, I'm selling, you're buying. Pay now or nothing doing,' she said, 'I know how men feel when they get through' "(*Outsider*, p. 94). After Cross is "through" it hurts his male pride that he has made no impression on Jenny. Jenny is considered only in terms of the brief sexual pleasure which will relax Cross's taut nerves. "When the spasm was over he lay with his hand gently touching her face, mutely thanking her for the benediction that she had shed upon his distraught senses" (*Outsider*, pp. 113-14). It is worth noting that Cross's sexual feelings toward Jenny and Eva are described with almost identical terminology. Both women are regarded in terms of "woman as body of woman" (*Outsider*, pp. 93,236). Both women place a "benediction" (*Outsider*, pp. 114, 321) upon Cross's distraught mind by giving their bodies to him. Wright makes no distinction in describing the significance and meaning of sexual intercourse between Cross and Jenny and between Cross and Eva, although Jenny is a prostitute and Eva is the only woman whom Cross loves.

The sex act as well as the moment after sexual intercourse is exclusively described through male eyes. Both Bigger and Cross feel a moment of respite. "Some hand had reached inside of him and had laid a quiet finger of peace upon the restless tossing of his spirit" (*Native*, p. 128). Both Cross and Bigger want to rid themselves quickly of the women after they have had intercourse. Cross gets rid of Jenny by making her believe that he will go west with her. Bigger gets rid of Bessie by bashing in her head with two bricks, killing her immediately after he has had intercourse with her. It is apparent that the women function as sources of short respite who quickly, however, become burdensome because the male characters' problems and pursuits are more important. They also function as obstacles whose removal increases the male characters' dilemmas.

Sarah in "Long Black Song" fits another stereotype, that of the intellectually inferior woman with an instinctual, primitive, and childlike nature. These attributes manifest themselves in her thoughts, which wander aimlessly from concern for her child to longing for her former lover. Sarah is portrayed as a highly sensuous woman whose nebulous thoughts have sexual overtones. Her sensuousness and her desire for sexual gratification overwhelm her when a white man embraces her. She tries to fight against her sexual desire by recalling to her confused mind the fact that he is white. But she is overcome by her sexual feelings and leads him into her bedroom. The heroic character of the story is Silas, Sarah's husband, who comes back from town to find the white man's handkerchief in his bed. Sarah functions as a vehicle in the story to show the tragedy of a hard-working Black man whose wife has cheated on him with a white man. Her thoughtless action creates an opportunity for Silas to become a tragic figure, to behave manly, proudly and courageously. He kills the white man and wounds his partner when they come back in the morning to get the money for the "graphophone." Before the sheriff comes to kill him, Silas stands before his house and talks "out of his life, out of a deep and final sense that now it was all over and nothing could make any difference."[8] Silas burns to death in his own house, which the white men set afire. Briefly before the white men come to kill Silas, Sarah runs across the fields to rescue herself and the baby. While she is walking away from the house, her thought pattern is described as illogical and emotional: ". . . she could not put her finger on it [her thoughts on life] and when she thought hard about it it became all mixed up, like milk spilling suddenly" ("Song," p. 126). The domestic imagery of the spilling milk would hardly be used to describe a man's confused mind.

The women characters in *The Outsider* are slightly more articulate, especially Gladys and Eva. However, their main purpose is to enhance Cross's entrapment. This function is particularly evident in the first part of the novel which leads to Cross's desire to leave his old life for a new one. His mother, Dot and Gladys weigh him down with their emotional and revengeful demands upon him. "He had just left one woman, his mother, who had hurled at him her life draped in the dark hues of complaint and accusation, who had tried futilely to rouse compassion in him by dramatizing the forlorn nature of her abandoned plight; now he was on the way to struggle with yet another woman. And after Dot there loomed the formidable figure of his wife" (*Outsider*, p. 34). Cross is entrapped by the three women--one of whom, Dot, is threatening to sue him for rape. The second one, Gladys, will not give him a divorce; and his mother is entangling him in a net of complaints and accusations.

Dot is frequently described as childlike. "In their relationship he had found her a passionate child achingly hungry for emotional experience" (*Outsider*, p. 32). Dot is certainly intellectually inferior and is incapable of following the greater schemes and thoughts that emanate from a man's mind. She is a patient listener when Cross talks to her about his "analytical tirades" (*Outsider*, p. 34). "He never quite knew how much of what he told her she understood, but she always listened patiently, now and then timidly venturing a detatched question of two, but never commending or blaming. He came at last to believe that she accepted the kind of talk in which he indulged as a mysterious part of man's equipment, along with his sexual organs" (*Outsider*, pp. 33-34). Just as man's penis is natural to him, so is man's "innate" ability to think and talk about abstract matters. In comparison, women stand in quiet admiration, especially since they possess neither characteristic.

Dot is portrayed as using the accommodational tactics of an assumed air of helplessness, while, at the same time, scheming to trap Cross into marrying her by threatening to sue him for rape. This manner of deviousness is the only resource for Dot, who is pregnant and wants the security of a marriage. Gladys is similarly helpless and in need of a man to depend upon when she first meets Cross. Like Dot, Cross finds her to be a good listener. She, too, is craving a secure relationship with a man because a woman is nothing until she has a man to make her into something. "He understood now; it was the helplessness of dependence that made her fret so. Men made themselves and women were made only through men" (*Outsider, p.* 51).

Eva in *The Outsider* fits the stereotype of the childlike, helpless, and devoted woman intent on pleasing her male partner. While Eva serves Cross's lunch he studies her face:

"How did this child--for there was an undeniable childishness about her--fit into his dark broodings and interpretations of Gil's politics?" (*Outsider,* p. 202). Eva has to be a helpless and oppressed victim of the Communist Party in order for Cross to experience the necessity of human involvement and love. Eva functions as Cross's cure from his aimless life and his self-hatred. "Yes, he would make of that girl his life's project, his life's aim; he would take her hand and lead her and, in leading her, he would be leading himself out of despair toward some kind of hope..." (*Outsider,* p. 293). Eva's frailty and helplessness stir in Cross feelings of protectiveness and desires for love. However, he has to be punished for his past violations of human lives and has to atone for his lawlessness. His punishment takes place when Eva, the only woman he ever loved, kills herself.

Cross criticizes and despises the desire the members of the Communist Party have for power and their oppression of Eva as an artist. We can assume that Cross is voicing Wright's own disgust with the Party, which he expresses in *The God that Failed.* He, like Eva, was suppressed as an artist, and an intellectual. He had been told that "Intellectuals didn't fit well into the Party, Wright."[9] Wright fought to maintain his individuality while he was a member of the Party; however, he had to learn that being a member meant unquestioning submission to the power of the Party. While Wright criticizes through Cross the oppressive tactics of the Communist Party, he seems to have no awareness of the oppressive situations into which he places his female characters. He certainly allows them none of the individuality which he cherishes so highly in his refusal to submit to the will of the Party: "But they [the Party members] had never been able to conquer their fear of the individual way in which I acted and lived, an individuality which life had seared into my bones" (*God,* p. 135).

It is apparent that Wright's female characters fit into the stereotypes summarized at the beginning of this study. They do not exist as equal partners and full human beings but function as conveniences for the resolution or development of masculine dilemmas. This treatment of female characters is inconsistent for a writer like Wright, who describes in most of his works the effects of being a member of an oppressed minority in a racist and hostile environment. He describes the need of Blacks to live a whole life without suppression, and in his essay "How 'Bigger' Was Born," defends "a *human* right, the right of a man to think and feel honestly.''[10] Wright claims to be striving for the realization of the charters of the Bills of Rights so "that every man and woman should have the opportunity to realize himself, to seek his own individual fate and goal, his own peculiar untranslatable destiny" (" 'Bigger,'" p. xxv). However, Wright gives his female characters neither the attributes nor the opportunities within the narrative context to think, act, and feel freely. Although he depicts clearly the oppression of Blacks, he appears unconscious of creating female characters who, regardless of race, are exploited and suppressed. Karl Marx writes in his *Economic and Philosophic Manuscripts of 1844* that from the relationship between man and woman one can "judge man's whole level of development."[11] The relationship between man and woman, therefore, "reveals the extent to which man's *natural* behavior has become *human,* or the extent to which *human* essence in him has become a *natural* essence--the extent to which his *human nature* has come to be *nature to him*" (ibid.). Marx also says that from the character of this relationship follows how much man has "come to be himself and to comprehend himself" (ibid.). If we apply Marx's definition of the male-female relationship as an indicator of man's and society's development to Wright's novels, we have to conclude that Wright is unaware that a free and equal relationship between men and women is a major ingredient for liberating a whole race and society.

NOTES

[1]"A Mirror for Men: Stereoptypes of Women in Literature," in *Women: An Issue,* ed. Lee R. Edwards, Mary Heath and Lisa Baskin (Boston: Little, Brown and Co., 1972), p. 207.
[2]*Sexual Politics* (Garden City: Doubleday, 1970), p. 57.
[3]*The Long Dream* (New York: Ace Publishing Corp., 1958), p. 56.
[4]*Lawd Today* (New York: Walker and Co., 1963), p. 159.
[5]*The Outsider* (New York: Harper and Row, 1953), p. 44.

[6]*Native Son* (New York: Harper and Row, 1940), pp. 131-32.
[7]*The Second Sex*, trans. and ed. by H. M. Parshley (New York: Vintage, 1952), p. 232.
[8]"Long Black Song," in *Uncle Tom's Children* (NewYork: Harper and Row, 1940). p. 125.
[9]Richard Wright, et al., *The God That Failed*, ed. Richard Crossman (NewYork: Bantam Books, 1949), p. 115.
[10]Intro. to *Native Son* (New York: Harper and Row, 1940), p. xxii.
[11]*Economic and Philosophical Manuscripts of 1844*, by Karl Marx, ed. with an intro. by Dirk J. Struik, trans. by Martin Milligan (New York: International Publishers, 1964), p. 134.

From *Black American Literature Forum* 10 (Winter 1976): pp. 124-128.

Wright's *Native Son* and Two Novels by Zola: A Comparative Study

Robert Butler

Toward the end of *Black Boy* Richard Wright stresses that his discovery of literature was an awakening experience for him: "A vague hunger would come over me for books, books that opened up new avenues of feeling and seeing." Indeed, he admits that "reading was like a drug, a dope. The novels created moods in which I lived for days." His discovery of Mencken's *Book of Prefaces* was particularly crucial, for it opened up to him the world of modern fiction which he immediately saw as a powerful correlative to his own lived experience: "All my life had shaped me for the realism of modern novels and I could not get enough of them."[1] He mentions Dreiser, Zola, Crane, Ibsen, and Anderson, among others, as writers who were especially strong influences upon him. As Houston A. Baker has observed, Wright's selection of naturalism as a literary mode was not an ideologically self-conscious choice as it was for novelists such as Dos Passos and Steinbeck, who grew up in worlds quite remote from the more brutal determinants of the naturalistic universe. Rather, it was the recognition that his own life was closely mirrored in the naturalistic fiction which he read so avidly:

> Comparing Wright's life with almost any of Emile Zola's protagonists, one immediately recognizes the similarity. Wright's existence in the Black Belt and the urban ghettos of America was one in which events seemed predetermined by heredity ... and the environment seemed under divine injunction to destroy[2]

Naturalism for Wright, therefore, was no mere literary convention but something which gave him "a sense of life itself,"[3] a vital and coherent rendering of his own disturbing experiences.

Although several studies have explored the relationship between Wright and other novelists from the realist/naturalist tradition, no one to date has examined the remarkable similarities between *Native Son* and two novels by Emile Zola, *Thérèse Raquin* and *La Bête Humaine*.[4] Although one could not argue with full assurance that Wright used these two novels as actual sources, it seems clear that his keen interest in naturalism would have led him almost inevitably to Zola, the founder of the movement and a writer who, like Wright, saw fiction as a necessary mode of social criticism. As social critics, Wright and Zola were in strong agreement, offering visions of their respective societies as being on the verge of paying historical dues of long standing. Zola's France, which was collapsing because it could no longer support itself under the burdens of chronic injustice and massive historical change, could offer Wright a striking parallel to his own America. Just as the Second Empire was dissolved as a consequence of France's defeat in the Franco-Prussian War, America in the Thirties was threatened by worldwide depression and war.

Of all Zola's novels, *Thérèse* and *La Bête* would have been especially compelling for Wright since they are exhaustive studies of the psychology of violence, a matter which heavily preoccupied Wright throughout his career. These two novels, like *Native Son*, center on scenes of killing which are used as terrifying epiphanies of the social worlds their authors examined. To Wright's and Zola's powerfully inversive imaginations, modern society had become a parody of itself. Instead of protecting life and fostering human value, it had degenerated into an environment of fear which blocked man's most deeply creative impulses, thereby bringing on terrible acts of self-destruction.

It is this all-pervasive atmosphere of fear which vibrates so powerfully throughout *Native Son* and *Thérèse Raquin* that links the two novels in the most immediate way. Nearly every scene in Wright's book is dominated by this emotion, from the opening sequence, which portrays a terrified rat arousing equally strong fear in people who must destroy it, to the final scene, in which Max is seen as "full of terror."[5] As Wright pointed out in "How 'Bigger' Was Born," the novel's initial scene is used as a "type of concrete event that would convey the motif of the entire scheme of the book."[6] The Thomases' one-room apartment is a microcosm of the universe imagined in the novel, a world in which all people, regardless of race, social class, or economic status, are controlled by a wide variety of crippling fears. In the same way, *Thérèse Raquin* gives us a world which is essentially gothic. Laurent, despite his placid exterior, enters an existence of deepening terror after his illicit relationship with Thérèse is established. Camille, who has deluded himself that life is a serene affair, gets his one horrified look at reality when Laurent grabs him by the throat and drowns him. From this point on, Laurent and Thérèse must face "an intolerable life of ceaseless terror,"[7] as they try unsuccessfully to handle the demons in themselves which their violence has unleashed.

Such fear-dominated existences have two basic rhythms, apathy and violence. Wright says of Bigger: "These were the rhythms of his life: indifference and violence ..." (*NS*, p.31). When he is not emotionally paralyzed by an environment which denies him significant forms of action, he blindly lashes out against his world, ironically creating situations which get progressively more frightening. The same can be said of the characters populating Zola's novel. Either, like Camille, they succumb to a complete lassitude, or they alternate, like Laurent and Thérèse, between frenzied violence and sickly torpor. Growing up, Thérèse had always repressed her "burning desires" and as an adult lives an outward life in which she appears "dull and half awake" (*TR*, p. 72). After she has been aroused by Laurent's "brutal" (*TR*, p. 62) lovemaking, though, her turbulent inner nature asserts itself more strongly, culminating in her helping to murder Camille. From then on, her life fluctuates between a "dismal apathy" (*TR*, p. 241) and hysteria.

She resembles Bigger in several other important ways. Just as he has been emotionally stunted by the death of his father in a race riot and by a mother overburdened with responsibilities, she is an orphan who is brought up by an aunt who shrinks from any real contact with life. Bigger is stifled by Mrs. Thomas's otherworldly religion, and Thérèse is nearly suffocated by Madame Raquin's shallow faith in the goodness of bourgeois life. Thérèse, whose mother is reputed to be the offspring of an African tribal chieftain and who therefore may have black blood, is also forced, like Bigger, to be a skillful mask-wearer. Circumstances force him to hide behind the stereotypical image of the dumb, submissive Negro and she must use a "mute, impenetrable mask" (*TR*, p.73) to physically and emotionally survive. Both characters, therefore, are required to live very similar double lives. Growing up in the Raquin household, Thérèse must give the impression of accepting such a pallid life, just as Bigger must never give any overt signs that he ever questions the passive role which white society imposes on him. Much of Thérèse's later vehemence toward Camille is a consequence of this repression, in the same way that Bigger's violence against Mary is the result of his hidden emotions finally coming to the surface. And Thérèse's "skillful acting" (*TR*, p. 136) as grieving widow in the second half of the novel clearly parallels Bigger's artful role-playing after Mary's death.

To stress the split nature of their characters' lives, Wright and Zola use a number of motifs which bear an uncanny similarity to each other. The growing discrepancy between the characters' public and private selves is dramatized in each novel by nightmare images which are nearly identical. For example, the white cat which becomes an externalization of Bigger's deepest fears and guilt is exactly mirrored by the tabby cat which functions as a major symbol in *Thérèse*. Laurent feels "chilled to the bone" (*TR*, p. 71) by the cat because it has observed his adultery and also seems to have a premonition of Camille's murder. Tormented by a sense that "the creature must know everything" (*TR*, p. 168), Laurent finally destroys it. Bigger is haunted by the white cat in a comparable way. He always associates it with omniscience and malice, two qualities which epitomize his view of the white world. Although the cat is soft and white like Mary, it is also distant and cold like her parents. It therefore touches down on his fears of being caught, for, in a dark world that has made him an invisible man, the cat actually saw him bring Mary's corpse into the basement. Like Zola's cat, Wright's has "round green eyes" (*NS*, p. 90) which activate all Bigger's anxieties. In a later scene in which the cat leaps onto Bigger's shoulder when he is being questioned by reporters, he feels that "the cat had given him away" (*NS*, p. 190). Although he rationally understands that such fears are groundless, like Laurent, he reacts instinctively to the cat. So rattled is he by the whole experience that he fails to properly attend the furnace. This eventually gives him something real to worry about since the clogged grate results in smoke filling the room, forcing the reporters to investigate the furnace and then discovering one of Mary's bones in it. Like Laurent, who successfully arranges for a perfect crime with his rational mind but is then destroyed by his irrational fears, Bigger is undone by the subconscious self which the cat calls into action.

Bigger's compulsive imagining of Mary's severed head is also closely paralleled by Laurent's persistent vision of Camille's dead face. Although neither character feels any conscious remorse for his victim, each is plagued with enormous anxiety springing from the subconscious. Bigger is haunted at several key points by "that lingering image of Mary's bloody head" (*NS*, p. 108), and Laurent has recurrent nightmares of Camille's face. When Laurent tries to withdraw into his painting for relief, matters get worse, for all of his portraits show his victim's "ghastly face" (*TR*, p. 165). Neither man is able to come to psychological grips with such nightmare images, and, as a result, each is driven into deeper levels of fear.

Each novel also employs images of impaired vision as an important formal pattern which is tied in with its central themes. As James Nagel, Robert Bone, and others have pointed out, images of blindness go to the core of *Native Son*, portraying a dark world in which human identity and solidarity are radically undermined.[8] In exactly the same manner, *Thérèse* portrays a universe in which people are so locked into their own perceptions that they never are able to really "see" themselves or the ones around them. Camille, his mother, and their friends all fail to discern the true relationship between Laurent and Thérèse until it is too late. As Thérèse points out, "All these folks are blind" (*TR*, p. 70). The animal passions which drive the characters also cancel out vision. Laurent's lust for Thérèse breaks out with "blind fury" (*TR*, p. 73), and he kills Camille in a fit of "blind animal instinct" (*TR*, p. 122). Significantly, he and Thérèse avoid each other's eyes at their wedding and are tormented by Madame Raquin's accusing looks after she has discovered the truth: Like Max in *Native Son*, who deliberately remains a "blind man" (*NS*, p. 392) because he cannot deal with the dark compulsions operating in his world, they are intent on avoiding a true look at each other. When their eyes are fully opened, they die, just as Bigger's clarified vision at the end of Wright's novel is accompanied by Bigger's own imminent death.

In other words, *Thérèse* and *Native Son* are grounded in outlooks which radically question all traditional values and conventional assumptions. It is not surprising therefore, that both novels make skillful use of inverted religious imagery. The Raquin household, for example, is described as having "the vague atmosphere of the cloister" (*TR*, p. 36) and is viewed by some as "a temple of peace" (*TR*, p. 253), even though it is the setting for some very unholy passions. Madame Raquin, whose eyes beam with "divine radiance" (*TR*, p. 204) before she knows about the facts of her son's death, is "unable to feast her eyes enough" (*TR*, p. 256) on the double suicide which concludes the novel. Entering the novel as a sort of deluded Christian God, she leaves the book as an avenging fury. Even though Thérèse tries to make use of her as a "prayer stool" (*TR*, p. 233) in an attempt to win forgiveness, Madame Raquin only becomes more intent on revenge as she hears such confessions. Thérèse, who had earlier tried to win "salvation" (*TR*, p. 138) by marrying Laurent, finds only damnation by the end of the novel.

Bigger's existence is also reduced to emptiness with ironically inverted religious imagery. His society is presided over by people such as Mr. Dalton, an ironic "god" (*NS*, p. 164) who brings about great suffering even while engaged in apparent works of

Christian mercy. And Bigger's mother's otherworldly yearnings are consistently portrayed as mere escape. Although the spiritual she sings in the first chapter imagines life as a mountain railroad operated by a brave engineer who will get the train safely to its appointed destination, her own life consists of meaningless stasis. Likewise, Mary Dalton's singing of "Swing Low, Sweet Chariot" while being chauffeured by Bigger is undercut by terrible ironies—she will indeed be taken "home" in her father's expensive "chariot" where she will be killed rather than saved. To further intensify this irony, Wright describes Bigger as in "an attitude of prayer" (*NS*, p. 91) as he later decapitates Mary. Indeed, almost all of Bigger's acts of violence are associated with such religious inversions, for they give him "a new life" (*NS*, p. 101), which is a conversion to death. Ultimately, such a religiously drained world is presented as an appalling void, "a world whose metaphysical meanings had vanished."[9] *Thérèse Raquin* evokes the same frightening universe.

The affinities between these two novels are important because they echo each other in nearly all of their important metaphorical patterns and much of their outer action. But the parallels between Wright's book and Zola's *La Bête Humaine* are even more revealing. *La Bête*, published twenty-three years after *Thérèse*, would have engaged Wright's imagination on its deepest levels because it arises from a more thoroughgoing naturalism and an even more relentless probing of human psychology. Whereas *Thérèse* can be read as " a cautionary tale on the sixth and seventh commandments,"[10] in which two murderers are treated with poetic justice, *La Bête* works on a more complex and disturbing tragic level, as does *Native Son*. At the root of these two novels is not a disgusting murder which is allegorically punished but a profound analysis of human duality. Both novels envision human nature as a strong war between a fierce drive to love and create and an equally strong compulsion to hate and destroy. And each author understood the volcanic energy of these opposed impulses at the core of human nature, an energy which has little to do with any simple moral categories. They knew that if *eros* is blocked then *thanatos* would erupt with devastating results. Even more unsettling, however, is the terrible suspicion in their minds that such impulses are perhaps made of the same materials. The central question raised by *La Bête* is simply this: "Were [sexual] possession and killing the same thing in the dark inner resources of the human brute?"[11] Precisely the same disturbing question resonates throughout *Native Son*.

The most revealing technique used in each novel to explore this question is the elaborate system of inverted sexual imagery employed so pervasively in the books' central episodes. *Native Son* and *La Bête* almost always describe lovemaking in terms of violence and violence in terms of lovemaking. The implications behind these startling inversions strongly suggest that man's creative and destructive tendencies have become snarled, thus locking him in a psychological trap. The death of Mary Dalton, perhaps the most revealing scene Wright ever wrote, is a brilliant illustration of this entrapment. The episode begins in a simple erotic way, with Mary trying to sexually arouse Bigger. In the car she tells him he is "very nice," deliberately sprawls her legs "wide apart" (*NS*, p. 80), and leans her head on his shoulder. When she catches him looking at her exposed legs, she laughs and asks him to carry her out of the car, while her "dark eyes looked feverishly at him" (*NS*, p. 81). Although she is intoxicated, she is much more in control of herself than she allows Bigger to realize. Swaying against him, she asks him to take her up the "back way" (*NS*, p. 82) to her room. Although she is surely conscious enough to give him directions and reject his advances if she wishes, she does not resist "the tips of his fingers feeling the soft swell of her breasts" (*NS*, p. 82). Indeed, she clearly desires to make love to him, her world's forbidden fruit. As he carries her up the stairs, "she pulled heavily on him, her arm around his neck" (*NS*, p. 82) and her hair brushing his lips. Fully aroused now, Bigger feels "possessed" (*NS*, p. 83) by her, *his* world's forbidden fruit.

Several erotic images are then used to describe the two entering Mary's room. As his fingers spread over Mary's back, "her face came toward him and her lips touched his" (*NS*, p. 84). Although he wants to leave after he has "laid" (*NS*, p. 84) her on the bed, he is overtaken by sexual desires. When he tightens his fingers on her breasts and kisses her twice, she moves toward him, clearly encouraging his actions.

Mrs. Dalton's entry into the room abruptly turns their lovemaking into death-making. But Wright artfully persists in using erotic images to describe the scene, turning them inside out for shockingly ironic effect. As Mrs. Dalton approaches them, all of Bigger's violent tendencies become "erected": "... he grew tight and full, as though about to explode" (*NS*, p. 84). When Mary's fingernails tear at him, he covers her entire face with a pillow, and her suffocation is described in terms of copulation:

> Mary's body surged upward and he pushed downward upon the pillow with all of his weight, determined that she must not move or make any sound that would betray him.... Again Mary's body heaved and he held the pillow in a grip that took all of his strength. For a long time he felt the sharp pain of her fingernails biting into his wrists. (*NS*, p. 84-85)

After her "surging and heaving" (*NS*, p. 85) body finally relaxes and Mrs. Dalton leaves the room, Bigger orgasmically utters "a long gasp" (*NS*, p. 85). In the weird afterglow of this strange experience, he is depicted as "weak and wet with sweat" (*NS*, p. 85), listening for some time to his heavy breathing filling the darkness.

Many key scenes in *La Bête* brilliantly invert sexual images for the same remarkable effects. The most striking example is Jacques' killing of Severine in the eleventh chapter. Severine, whose dark curls and "delicate milk-white skin" (*BH*, p. 237) create a significant physical resemblance to Mary Dalton, makes Mary's mistake of naively thinking of her sexuality as unconnected with man's destructive impulses. Both women use their physical attractiveness with disastrous results, unleashing powerful forces which they neither understand nor control. Just as Mary tries to sexually manipulate Bigger for her own pleasure, Severine uses her body as a kind of bribe in exchange for Jacques' murder of her husband Roubaud. The net effect in both cases is the same, with both women being suddenly killed.

Zola's scene is suffused with startling inversions. As Jacques and Severine make love, they are described with grotesque images of violence, "crushing" (*BH*, p. 323) each other in embraces which result in physical "exhaustion" (*BH*, p. 323). At one point she equates their lovemaking with the act of his physically devouring her: "Kiss me, go on, hard, hard! As though you were eating me up so that there's nothing left of me ..." (*BH*, p. 330). As they imagine their murder of Roubaud, they become sexually aroused, and Severine actually suggests that they be naked as they perform their murder. She unwittingly becomes a victim of this linkage between sex and violence when his erotic needs are suddenly displaced by his lust for murder, an act which gratifies him more deeply. Aroused fully by her language and "the voluptuous curve of her bosom" (*BH*, p. 330), he throws her on her back, drags her over by the bed, and uses his knife to get the "fuller possession" (*BH*, p. 330) he could not achieve with his penis. Like Bigger, he feels his virility most deeply when killing a woman. The muscles "that had gone flabby" are finally "worked up" (*BH*, p. 327) by his act of insane violence. The scene ends with Severine's screaming out a question which no doubt would have occurred to Mary Dalton, had she lived: "'Why me? Why?'" (*BH*, p. 331).

The novel is replete with such astonishing scenes. Roubaud's brutal beating of Severine in the first chapter follows the same pattern of sudden reversal. Starting in an uncomplicated erotic way, it becomes near murder when she stimulates but does not satisfy his sexual cravings. Very much in love with his wife whom he idolizes, he tries "to smother her in kisses" (*BH*, p. 24) and then almost literally kills her when he finds out about her previous affairs with Grandmorin, her elderly guardian. Their grisly murder in a later scene is presented as a strange kind of rape, with Severine holding down the old man's legs while Roubaud savagely applies the phallic knife to Grandmorin's throat. The "fulfillment" (*BH*, p. 72) which Roubaud gets from the act is deeply tied to his twisted sexual nature, as is the pleasure achieved by Severine, who gets revenge on Grandmorin for his sexual abuse of her.

Her later description of the murder to Jacques in the eighth chapter stresses this. As she relates the awful story, they both become sexually excited and make love like beasts "disemboweling each other" (*BH*, p. 230). Her version dwells on the intense sexual satisfactions provided by the act. Straddling Grandmorin's legs while Roubaud slits his throat, she undergoes a kind of orgasm: "'And I didn't see anything but felt it all, the impact of the knife in his neck, the long tremor of his body, and death in three hiccuping gasps ...'" (*BH*, p. 231). Jacques vicariously experiences the same feelings as he forces her to repeat the story, highlighting details such as the knife entering the body and the spasms that resulted.

As sensationalistic as is this outer action in the two novels, the authors' real emphasis is on the motives which lie behind it. Both *Native Son* and *La Bête* focus most importantly on an exhaustive analysis of the psychology of violence and the larger issues it raises. In fact, these novels may be seen as an inversion of Lord Acton's idea that power corrupts and absolute power corrupts absolutely: Zola and Wright present deterministic worlds in which the central characters are reduced to something approaching absolute impotence. Given such an existence, they respond to violence with fascination, for it endows their lives with a kind of power. Thus Bigger feels "elation" and "control" (*NS*, p. 102) after killing Mary because he has finally rebelled against pressures to which he had always submitted. In a society which threatens to paralyze him economically, socially, and politically, violence is a form of action which gives him a kind of independence, a sort of "wholeness" (*NS*, p. 225). Similarly, Jacques and Severine regard their violence as supremely meaningful activity. In helping to kill a high-ranking official in French society who has totally controlled her adulthood, Severine feels "more alive than in a whole lifetime" (*BH*, p. 235), just as Bigger sees his own violence as a form of highly concentrated experience. And the same "terrified pride" (*NS*, p. 101) which Bigger feels after killing Mary is found in Jacques' intense reaction to murdering Severine:

> Yes he had done it. Boundless joy and awful exultation bore him aloft in the complete contentment of his eternal desire. He felt a surprising pride, an enhanced sense of his male sovereignty .... (*BH*, p. 332)

Jacques, who has been emotionally paralyzed by the illness which he has inherited, attains a kind of freedom from violence. Bigger, who has been morally frozen by the racist society which has destroyed his family and deprived him of meaningful options, finds the same release in violence. In a world of dead ends, it provides the only kind of "new life (*NS*, p. 101) available to him.

It is important to realize that Zola and Wright enrich their characters by giving them extremely complicated responses to the women they have killed. Although neither Bigger nor Jacques feels any conscious pangs of conscience from his actions and at times actually gloats over them, their subconscious natures evoke genuine human guilt and compassion. Here, too, the central characters of *La Bête* should be distinguished from the main characters of *Thérèse*. Although Laurent and Thérèse lead radically divided lives because of the disparity between their rational and irrational selves, they are never able to feel any deeply positive human emotion such as love or real sorrow. At worst, they feel nothing, and at best they experience compulsive fear. Jacques and Bigger are much more complex as human beings and, therefore, can not be easily dismissed as simple monsters. Ironically, their brutal actions stem from a blocked desire to love rather than an intrinsic lust for killing.

Bigger's humanity is brought into focus with a number of devices which indicate that, on the most essential levels of his being, he can see Mary and others as human. Although his conscious self, that part of him shaped by environment, prompts him to view whites as "a great natural force" (*NS*, p. 109) to simply "blot out," his inner self makes possible more humane reactions. The dream he has in Book Two immediately after he takes perverse satisfaction in ransoming Mary is clear evidence of this duality. In it he imagines himself on a street corner holding a package containing a human head. When ringing church bells and a strange red glare "like that which came from the furnace (*NS*, p. 156) activate Bigger's conscience, he panics and runs away, trying to hide from the increasing number of white people who appear. The dream ends with his throwing the head at the whites who begin to "close in " (*NS*, p. 156) on him. Significantly, the head is not Mary's, but his own. The dream, therefore, can not be interpreted simply as dramatizing Bigger's animal fear of being caught and punished, although it partly reflects this idea. On its deeper levels it illuminates his very moral perception that, in killing Mary, he has destroyed part of himself.[12] Bigger is not the pathological monster created by society which James Baldwin characterizes him as[13] but a complex human being who transcends the stereotypes attached to him.

Zola develops the same kind of double view of Jacques, a character who feels a strange kind of "peace" (*BH*, p. 355) from his violence but is also humanly disturbed by it. For example, he is able to cavalierly discuss his wife's death with Philomène but then in private feels something altogether different:

> Jacques shivered as though he were coming out of a dream. Sometimes it happened like this that in spite of the total absence of remorse and the senses of relief and physical well being in which he had lived since the murder, Severine passed through his mind and touched the kindly man in him to the point of tears. (*BH*, p. 340)

The same duality is apparent at the trial. Although outwardly he is "perfectly controlled" and does not feel "the slightest emotion" (*BH*, p. 357) about the crime, inwardly he is tormented by the image of his lover's face. On this level, he "still worshipped her, a great pity overwhelmed him and he wept bitterly for her ..." (*BH*, p. 357).

Other striking parallels between the two books should also be stressed. Both novels systematically employ images of blindness, animality, and paralysis to portray their grimly naturalistic universes. Their use of setting is also quite similar—the major scenes in each novel are almost always acted out during rainstorms or snowstorms, again reflecting the deterministic implications of these scenes. And their endings also have much in common, connecting the personal disasters of the central characters with large-scale cultural disintegration. Zola depicts riots in Paris and the breakout of the Franco-Prussian War as an appropriate backdrop for the deadly fight in which Jacques and Pecqueux engage while their train runs wildly out of control. So too does Max's courtroom speech in Book Three provide an apocalyptic vision of an entire society experiencing disruptions which Bigger's story has worked out in microcosm. Unless basic structural changes are made in American life, history will be "'a wheel of blood'" (*NS*, p. 362) bringing about a violent revolution which will destroy the "'foundations'" (*NS*, p. 368) of civilization.

The trials in the novel are compelling metaphors of this sort of cultural decay, reflecting worlds which are fundamentally corrupt and blind. French society refuses to "see" the real implications behind Grandmorin's murder because it is not willing to take a hard look at the widespread social corruption which his life symbolized.

The so-called "certainties" established in his case are "blinding" (*BH*, p. 349) because people do not want to disturb the status quo. Likewise, nearly everybody associated with Bigger's trial is "blind" because they do not want to face the fact that he is indeed a "native son" whose crimes reflect the equally criminal nature of an unjust society. More specific comparisons further link the trials in each novel. Zola's Denizet uses his role as prosecutor to advance his own political career while Wright's Buckley exploits Bigger's case demogogically to strengthen his position in an upcoming election. Cabuche, like Bigger, is made a convenient scapegoat, being reduced to a "ravening beast" (*BH*, p. 355), as his counterpart is depicted as a "'black mad dog'" (*NS*, p. 375) and a '"treacherous beast'" (*NS*, p. 376). In both cases, the public imagination feels the need to lower its victims to an animal level to justify its own brutal treatment of them. Both novels also explore the bitter irony of defendants being convicted of the wrong murder. Bigger is wrongfully punished for killing Mary while his actual murder of Bessie never is made a real issue. Roubaud, who did in fact murder Grandmorin, is not believed when he confesses, but is instead falsely convicted of being an accomplice in his wife's death.

Although Zola's and Wright's novels are clearly made from strikingly similar bolts of imaginative cloth, they are finally different in several important ways. If it is true that Wright may have used Zola's vision and techniques as ways of seeing his own world more clearly, it is also true that he felt the need to stress certain distinctive features of his own experience. *Native Son* is a deeply disturbing novel calculated to deprive its readers even of "the consolation of tears."[14] But it is not so categorically pessimistic as either *La Bête* or *Thérèse*. At the root of Zola's universe are problems which are irremediable, such as Jacques' "hereditary taint" (*BH*. p. 66) or Thérèse's fundamentally perverse sexuality and weak nervous system. Bigger's problems are quite different, coming from socially imposed determinants which can be changed rather than an intrinsic weakness which can not be altered. As both Max and Wright make clear, Bigger's natural impulses, such as his desires to fly, make love to Mary, or feel solidarity with other people, are sound. It is only when these creative feelings are stifled that they are displaced by the urge to destroy. If Bigger were given valid options for growth, he would have not been forced into his final terrible awareness: "'What I killed for I am'" (*NS*, pp. 391-392).

Hence the narrative structures in Wright's and Zola's novels are different in subtle but crucial ways. In both *Thérèse* and *La Bête* we are given fables of human disintegration in which determinants portrayed in the opening scene set in motion a rigid chain of events which eventually destroy all of the major characters. The world presented at the outset of *Native Son* is also a miniature version of the entire novel, but it depicts a world which is not hopeless. Rats can be eliminated from housing; slums can be cleaned up; economic and political systems may be reformed; and racist ideas may be changed. Although Wright gives us no easy assurances that any of this will be done and actually stresses the extreme difficulty of producing this kind of change, he does not deny that such a transformation is possible. While writing *Native Son* he was seriously committed to the Marxist belief that history need not be a futile wheel of blood but can in fact move toward a more humane world. Even after he abandoned Communism, Wright never repudiated the position of a maverick radical affirming the possibility of meaningful social change. And his deeply felt existential yearnings, which are strongly apparent in *Native Son*, centered around a faith in man's ability to create a human self even in an absurd world.

Whereas Zola's characters undergo an inevitable breakdown which eventually rots the self and dissolves human values, Bigger can grow despite a world of harsh, but not absolute, determinants. He does become aware of himself and his world through suffering and, like the hero of Ellison's *Invisible Man*, can truthfully tell us at the end of his novel that he may be invisible but is no longer blind. And unlike Jacques, whose atavistic compulsions make it impossible for him to form any viable human relationships, Bigger can transcend his pathological view of whites to form a kind of friendship with Jan and a real understanding of Max that involves both irony and compassion. He can also finally resolve his bitter feelings toward his mother, seeing her as more a victim than a failure. His concern for her feelings at the end of the novel offers clear proof of his human growth, standing in such vivid contrast to the hatred and "iron reserve" (*NS*, p. 14) with which he regards her in the opening scene. Without ever becoming sentimental or making affirmations which the text of the novel could not support, Wright gave us a fictive world too rich for simple despair. Although growing out of the deep soil of naturalistic masterpieces such as *Thérèse Raquin* and *La Bête Humaine*, *Native Son* flowered in its own unique way.

NOTES

[1]Richard Wright, *Black Boy* (New York: Harper & Brothers, 1945), pp. 275, 273, 274.
[2]Baker, *Long Black Song* (Charlottesville: Univ. of Virginia Press, 1972), p. 127.
[3]*Black Boy*, p. 274.
[4]Michel Fabre has pointed out that it was possible that Wright, who was profoundly influenced by a number of modern novelists and often "tried hard to imitate his idols," may have read Zola in Memphis or in his early Chicago years (*The Unfinished Quest of Richard Wright* [New York: William Morrow, 1973], pp. 68-69).

There are many excellent discussions of Wright's imaginative assimilation of realist/naturalistic fiction. See especially Kenneth Reed's "*Native Son:* An *American Crime and Punishment*," *Studies in Black Literature*, Summer 1970, pp. 33-34; and Yoshinobu Hakutani's "*Native Son* and *An American Tragedy*: Two Different Interpretations of Crime and Guilt," *Centennial Review*, 23 (1973), 208-26. See also Granville Hicks' "Dreiser to Farrell to Wright," *Saturday Review*, 46 (30 Mar. 1963), 37-38.

Several unpublished doctoral dissertations have explored the affinities between Wright's work and other American naturalistic fiction. Susan McBride's "Richard Wright's Use of His Reading of Fiction, 1927-1940" (Univ. of Pennsylvania 1975) surveys Wright's interest in Dreiser, Farrell, Hemingway, and Stein, among others, but does not discuss his reading of Zola. Alvin Starr's "The Influences of Stephen Crane,

Theodore Dreiser, and James T. Farrell" (Kent State Univ. 1974) also does not discuss Zola.

[5]Wright, *Native Son* (1940; rpt. New York: Harper & Row, 1966), p. 392. All subsequent references to the text are to this Perennial Classic edition and will appear parenthetically.

[6]"How 'Bigger' Was Born," included as the introduction to the Perennial Classic edition of *Native Son*, p. xix.

[7]Zola, *Thérèse Raquin*, trans, Leonard Tancock (New York: Penguin Books, 1962), p. 172. All subsequent references to the text are to this edition and will appear parenthetically.

[8]See Nagel's "Images of 'Vision' in *Native Son*," *University Review*, 36 (1969), 109-15; and Bone's *The Negro Novel in America* (New Haven, CT: Yale Univ. Press, 1965), pp. 147-49.

Two other useful studies of this matter are James Emanuel's "Fever and Feeling: Notes on the Imagery in *Native Son*," *Negro Digest*, Dec. 1968, pp.16-24; and Thomas LeClair's "The Blind Leading the Blind: Wright's *Native Son* and a Brief Reference to Ellison's *Invisible Man*," *CLA Journal*, 13 (1970), 315-20. Recently, Priscilla Ramsey has added to the discussion with "Blind Eyes, Blind Quests in Richard Wright's *Native Son*," *CLA Journal*, 24 (1980), 48-60.

[9]"How 'Bigger' Was Born," p. xix.

[10]Leonard Tancock, "Introduction to *Thérèse Raquin*," in the Penguin Books edition (1962), p. 16.

[11]Zola, *La Bête Humaine*, trans. Leonard Tancock (New York: Penguin Books, 1977), p. 182. All subsequent references to the text are to this edition and will appear parenthetically.

[12]Wright develops this important theme at many key points in the novel. In Book One, for example, Mary and Bigger are subtly compared when Mrs. Thomas characterizes her son as "'plain black plumb crazy'" (*NS*, p. 12) and Mr. Dalton describes Mary as "'that crazy daughter of mine'" (*NS*, p. 154). For all their obvious dissimilarities, Bigger and Mary are alike in several important ways. They are both radically misunderstood by their parents and rebel strongly against the roles expected of them by society. Both also are blind to many dangerous realities in their worlds and pay a heavy price for this. And they are also the "forbidden fruit" tabooed by their respective cultures. In many revealing ways, therefore, Bigger's killing of Mary is actually a killing of himself, especially that "soft" and humane self he is so intensely afraid of. Bigger, who in the novel's opening scene is described as a person who "would either kill himself or someone else" (*NS*, p. 14), ironically accomplishes both tasks in destroying Mary.

[13]*Notes of a Native Son*. (Boston: Beacon Press, 1955) pp. 22-23.

[14]"How 'Bigger' Was Born," p. xxvii.

Black Boy (1945)

Review of *Black Boy*

Orville Prescott

Richard Wright is a famous writer now, the author of one of the most widely read and hotly debated novels of recent years, "Native Son," an acknowledged leader of his race. But the way was long, and the road was rocky. Not very many years ago he was just "a black boy in Mississippi," which means few men in the world have begun life under a burden of graver handicaps or faced more difficult obstacles. That he has gone so far, accomplished so much, entitles Mr. Wright to an honored rank among that traditionally American select group, the "self-made men." His success story does him great credit. The troubles he knew in his childhood and youth were terrible, the wounds he received deep. He carries indelible scars and still burns with bitter fury. The life he knew as a child is not over. It has not changed. Hundreds of thousands of other little black boys are enduring it today. Such a life is usually completely outside the comprehension of white Americans, either Southern or Northern. But those who care to can now share it in Mr. Wright's "Black Boy: A Record of Childhood and Youth."

This is a story from America's own lower depths. No nostalgic memories of childhood are these, no sentimental yearnings for innocent years when the hills were so much higher. Mr. Wright's childhood was an obscene and monstrous nightmare, a malign inferno that might well have destroyed him utterly. He survived, but not unscathed. "Black Boy" is not the work of an objective artist or of an open mind. It could not have been. The neuroses, the overemphasis, the lack of balance and the emotion recollected in turmoil are the bitter fruit of an old injustice.

Mr. Wright in this explosive autobiography does not suggest any constructive means for improving the lot of the Negro in this country. Like Lillian Smith, he can only display suffering and cruelty with harsh dramatic power, he can only arouse anger and sympathy. If enough such books are written, if enough millions of people read them, maybe, some day, in the fullness of time, there will be a greater understanding and a more true democracy.

Richard Wright grew up in the slums of Memphis and in the rural slums of Arkansas and of Mississippi near Jackson. His father deserted his mother, so the poverty he knew was double the usual lot. The two dominant influences of his childhood were hunger and fear, a gnawing hunger that kept him weak and half-starved and a fear that grew and multiplied and filled his entire life. He feared his mother's anger, the whippings of his uncles and aunts, the abuse of other children, ghosts, white men with their inexplicable and capricious cruelties, fear itself. Terror was his companion night and day, violence the norm of all experience. Foul language and foul habits, ignorance and superstition, primitive religious fanaticism surrounded him on all sides. The proud, sensitive, intelligent child looked up from below at a grotesque, outrageous world.

Some of the evils he knew were caused by poverty and ignorance alone and would not have been much different in Ireland or Iran. But even these evils were intensified by the shibboleth of color and many others were caused by race alone. Mr. Wright's uncle was murdered by a white man and no one dared even to protest. A boyhood acquaintance was lynched. He learned to be servile and obsequious, to say "sir" to drunken and contemptible white men, to conceal his thoughts and emotions beneath a mask of humble good humor and deference. Not to do so, to forget the "sir" or the "mister," to aspire to learn a skilled trade, to show resentment of sneers, condescension and abuse, was to invite "trouble." And trouble could mean death.

"Black Boy" only takes Mr. Wright into his late teens when he escaped to Chicago. His experiences there and in radical politics will doubtless be material for another book. It could conceivably be an intellectually more interesting book, one more concerned with thought and ideas. But it could hardly be a more emotionally dreadful one. Part of the raw shock of "Black Boy" is caused by Mr. Wright's excessive determination to omit nothing, to emphasize mere filth. This springs from a lack of artistic discrimination and selectivity. He has not added to the bleak tragedy of his story; he has only distorted it and confused it with such material.

It is also obvious in reading "Black Boy," and Mr. Wright admits it, that his is not a typical story. He felt isolated from Negroes as well as from whites; other Negroes resented their lot but did not feel at all so acutely as he did. Perhaps with the hindsight of the years in which he has brooded and with a natural literary instinct to capitalize and dramatize his emotions Mr. Wright has exaggerated his sufferings. It would be only human if he had.

"Black Boy" has little subtlety, little light and shade, no restraint. It is written in a continuously strained and feverish manner. It is over-written. But it is powerful, moving and horrifying. It is certain to be extravagantly praised and roundly condemned. It will be widely read.

From *The New York Times*, February 28, 1945, p. 21.

Black Hunger

Charles Lee

Richard Wright's autobiography, "Black Boy" may very possibly go down as one of the most memorable books of our time, a kind of 20th century "Uncle Tom's Cabin."

Though it may not cause the immediate sensation stirred up by the author's lurid best-seller, "Native Son," it is in our judgment much the better book, more potent, more dramatic if less theatrical, more accurate in its aim, more telling in impact. Indeed it is the raw material out of which that unforgettable novel was forged.

Subtitled "A record of Childhood and Youth," Wright's new work is quiveringly animate. Life breathes in its pages with a reality and an intensity given only to the great recorders of the human scene. The result is that "Black Boy" is as intimate a personal story as you have ever read, fearlessly candid, a revelation of the clockwork beneath the ticking of one man's heart. But it is not an exhibitionist exposure, not self-exploitation, neither is it the product of masochism; it is, instead, a laying open of personality, at obviously great pain, in the interest of a cause, a cause greater than self and worthy of the sacrifice of soul's peace and privacy, the cause of human dignity, in this particular case the cause of the American Negro.

Wright is today recognized as both an outstanding member of his race and a distinguished artist, and could easily coast along on the esteem and riches which his talent has won him. But he is no coaster. He is a crusader. He does not only dirge, he is hotly angry, he points, he speaks out, he challenges. And on his feet, not his knees.

"Black Boy" is no Hollywood serving of magnolia and julep; it is a piece of immediate Danteian reality made in the U.S.A., a candid-camera recording of the virulent Fascist tumor that exists in our democratic body. The cure? Democracy itself. Not the promulgation of ideals, but their acceptance; the practice of all those attitudes which make for a decent respect between men, regardless of race, color and creed.

As Wright unfolds the bleak story of his incredibly underprivileged life from Mississippi odd-jobs man to Chicago writer--nor in the telling of it does he spare the sins of his people or minimize his own faults--it reduces itself to a series of gnawing hungers, hunger for food, for friendship, for love, for normality, for security, for the things of the spirit and mind, in the end, in near-madness and dreams, for a totally different existence.

Living in one squalid house after another, starved for even subsistence sustenance, set upon by gangs, let to wander the streets (he was a drunkard at six), clutching his rags, threatened with hell by religious fanatics, poorly schooled, never medicated, brutally beaten by his own family, nearly killed by whites and living in constant terror of their sadistic whimsies and coded arrogance, Wright's miracle is that he did not end up as either the degraded, grinning "non-man" caricature of humanity resignedly accepted by his fellows as the typical Negro's lot, or a murderer. Yet more wonderful is that out of this day-and-nightmare of a life he arose a commanding artist in realism (he details his artistic and intellectual beginnings, crediting most to his mother and H.L. Mencken), a man not softened but ennobled by suffering and dedicated, in the belief that it can and must be won, to the battle for those educative, economic and, fundamentally, spiritual conditions which are necessary to the democratization of Negro life.

From *Philadelphia Record*, (March 1, 1945).

Richard Wright Looks Back

W. E. Burghardt Du Bois

This book tells a harsh and forbidding story and makes one wonder just exactly what its relation to truth is. The title, "A Record of Childhood and Youth," makes one at first think that the story is autobiographical. It probably is, at least in part. But mainly it is probably intended to be fiction or fictionalized biography. At any rate the reader must regard it as creative writing rather than simply a record of life.

The hero whom Wright draws, and maybe it is himself, is in his childhood a loathsome brat, foul-mouthed and "a drunkard." The family which he paints is a distressing aggregation. Even toward his mother he never expresses love or affection. Sometimes he comes almost to sympathy. He wonders why this poor woman, deserted by her husband, toiling and baffled, broken by paralysis and disappointment, should suffer as she does. But his wonder is intellectual inability to explain the suffering. It doesn't seem for a moment to be personal sorrow at this poor, bowed figure of pain and ignorance.

The father is painted as gross and bestial, with little of human sensibility. The grandmother is a religious fanatic, apparently sincere but brutal. The boy fights with his aunt. And here again the artist in Richard Wright seems to fail. He repeats an incident of fighting his aunt with a knife to keep her from beating him. He tells the tale of his grandfather, a disappointed veteran of the Civil War, but tells it without sympathy. The Negroes whom he paints have almost no redeeming qualities. Some work hard, some are sly, many are resentful; but there is none who is ambitious, successful or really intelligent.

After this sordid, shadowy picture we gradually come upon the solution. The hero is interested in himself, is self-centered to the exclusion of everybody and everything else. The suffering of others is put down simply as a measure of his own suffering and resentment. There is scarcely a ray of light in his childhood: he is hungry, he is beaten, he is cold and unsheltered. Above all, a naturally shy and introverted personality is forced back upon itself until he becomes almost pathological. The world is himself and his suffering. He hates and distrusts it. He says "I was rapidly learning to distrust everything and everybody."

He writes of a mother who wanted him to marry her daughter. "The main value in their lives was simple, clean, good living, and when they thought they had found those same qualities in one of their race they instinctively embraced him, liked him and asked no questions. But such simple unaffected trust flabbergasted me. It was impossible!"

He tells of his own pitiful confusion, when as an imaginative, eager child he could not speak his thought: "I knew how to write as well as any pupil in the classroom, and no doubt I could read better than any of them, and I could talk fluently and expressively when I was sure of myself. Then why did strange faces make me freeze? I sat with my ears and neck burning, hearing the pupils whisper about me, hating myself, hating them."

Then here and there for a moment he forgets his role as artist and becomes commentator and prophet. Born on a plantation, living in Elaine, Ark., and the slums of Memphis, he knows the whole Negro race! "After I had outlived the shocks of childhood, after the habit of reflection had been born in me, I used to mull over the strange absence of real kindness in Negroes, how unstable was our tenderness, how lacking in genuine passion we were, how void of great hope, how timid our joy, how bare our traditions, how hollow our memories, how lacking we were in those intangible sentiments that bind man to man, and how shallow was even our despair."

Not only is there this misjudgment of black folk and the difficult repulsive characters among them that he is thrown with, but the same thing takes place with white folk. There is not a single broad-minded, open-hearted white person in his book. One or two start out seemingly willing to be decent, but as he says of one white family for whom he worked, "They cursed each other in an amazingly offhand manner and nobody seemed to mind. As they hurled invectives they barely looked at each other. I was tense each moment, trying to anticipate their wishes and avoid a curse, and I did not suspect that the tension I had begun to feel that morning would lift itself into the passion of my life."

From the world of whites and the world of blacks he grows up curiously segregated. "I knew of no Negroes who read the books I liked, and I wondered if any Negroes ever thought of them. I knew that there were Negro doctors, lawyers, newspaper men, but I never saw any of them."

One rises from the reading of such a book with mixed thoughts. Richard Wright uses vigorous and straightforward English; often there is real beauty in his words even when they are mingled with sadism: "There was the disdain that filled me as I tortured a delicate, blue-pink crawfish that huddled fearfully in the mudsill of a rusty tin can. There was the aching glory in masses of clouds burning gold and purple from an invisible sun. There was the liquid alarm I saw in the blood-red glare of the sun's afterglow mirrored in the squared planes of whitewashed frame houses. There was the languor I felt when I heard green leaves rustling with a rainlike sound."

Yet at the result one is baffled. Evidently if this is an actual record, bad as the world is, such concentrated meanness, filth and despair never completely filled it or any particular part of it. But if the book is meant to be a creative picture and a warning, even then, it misses its possible effectiveness because it is as a work of art so patently and terribly overdrawn.

Nothing that Richard Wright says is in itself unbelievable or impossible; it is the total picture that is not convincing.

From *New York Herald Tribune*, (March 4, 1945), p 2.

Richard Wright Adds a Chapter to Our Bitter Chronicle

Lillian Smith

The story is being told. Little by little, it grows clearer in our minds, this tragic, painful life of shame which white folks and black folks have lived together in America. In turning the leaves of his life, Richard Wright has turned many a bitter page of America's chronicle. We read again of that ugly blend of poverty and ignorance, of fanatical religious zeal and fanatical sex fear, of the white man's desperate, regressive concern with skin color and of the Negro's terrible loneliness. We know that black and white are caught in the web, strangers stripped of human dignity, hating and fearing each other, yet pushed into shameful intimacy by that web's tightly interwoven strands.

As a white Southerner, I find few surprises in this book. It is an old, familiar thing of pain and guilt to us who were born there: this story of a black boy whose culture refused him the right to be human and forced him to crawl through dark, underground, evil, slimy ways into the sunlight of faraway places--whose culture tells every black child, born in the South, that not for one day can he feel at home there.

The wonder is that the creative potentials of his personality developed so consistently. The wonder is that Richard Wright today is a sane, creative, highly intelligent artist and man, bringing presents back to the very culture that spat him out when he was a child.

How did it happen? What early experiences of warmth and tenderness and human worth did he have that convinced him of his own dignity, that tied him to reality and kept him from totally rejecting the good with the bad? We should know. Yet his book does not tell us.

His childhood is still, in large part, a closed door to him. He has not yet found the key that will unlock old memories and bring back deeply buried childhood feelings. He tells little incidents, little, heartbreaking, pitiful and sometimes amusing anecdotes. But they are told with a strange lack-of-feeling tone, with little of that quality of imagination that interprets even as it narrates, and gives focus and perspective even as it conveys a sense of nearness.

When he writes of his boyhood, Richard Wright becomes the artist. He makes us experience with him that restless, striving period of growth when manhood was something he craved more than food, when he found, and fell in love with the world of ideas and books.

He shows us again here the power of prose, the warm, urgent use of word and phrase that made us recognize his great talent in *Native Son* . . . .

From *PM* (March 4, 1945) p. m 15.

Creation of the Self in Richard Wright's *Black Boy*

Yoshinobu Hakutani

Black Boy is generally acclaimed not only as the finest autobiography written by a black author but as one of the greatest autobiographies ever written in America. Critics, however, are not in agreement on what kind of autobiography it is. W.E.B. Du Bois, for instance, wondered about the authenticity of the book, saying, "The [sub]title, 'A Record of Childhood and Youth,' makes one at first think that the story is autobiographical. It probably is, at least in part. But mainly it is probably intended to be fiction or fictionalized biography. At any rate the reader must regard it as creative writing rather than simply a record of life."[1] Yet even if one regards the book as a creative work rather than an actual record of life, and despite its felicities of language, *Black Boy*, Du Bois felt, falls short of its possible effectiveness because it is "so patently and terribly overdrawn."[2] Those who are not impressed by the book criticize the excessive emphasis on violence, meanness, and despair in Wright's work. Moreover, they are not convinced of the authenticity of *Black Boy* as an autobiography because they feel that the world, bad as it is, cannot be so bad as Wright says it is.

Even those who are convinced of its authenticity do not necessarily consider it a higher accomplishment than *Native Son*. When the book appeared, many distinguished writers became its advocates: Sinclair Lewis, William Faulkner, Gertrude Stein, Henry Miller, Ralph Ellison, Lionel Trilling. Among them Faulkner, who perhaps knew black life in the South as well as anyone, wrote to Wright that he was deeply moved by *Black Boy*, but commented that what is said in it is better said in *Native Son*. "The good lasting stuff," Faulkner wrote, "comes out of one individual's imagination and sensitivity to and comprehension of the sufferings of Everyman, Anyman, not out of the memory of his own grief."[3] This response by a fellow novelist suggests that *Black Boy* suffers as a work of art since Wright's method here is less impersonal than it is in a novel like *Native Son*. To Faulkner, art cannot be created when too much is made of one's own life; dealing with impersonal forces of nature and society in such a novel as *Native Son* requires a sense of detachment. For this reason Faulkner said, "I hope you will keep on saying it, but I hope you will say it as an artist, as in *Native Son*."[4]

Faulkner's evaluation is based on the assumption that *Black Boy* is an autobiography. But the narrator of the book takes such an impersonal attitude that the book as a whole may not sound like a usual autobiography. As Du Bois has noted, there is a genuine paucity of personal love or affection expressed toward Wright's mother in *Black Boy*.[5] The young Wright amply expresses his awe and wonder at his suffering mother: He is unable to understand the reason that she was deserted by her husband, broken by paralysis, and overwhelmed by every imaginable circumstance she had to face. His reaction, as a narrator, is intellectual rather than personal. By contrast, in Theodore Dreiser's autobiography of his youth, *Dawn*, the narrator's wonder at his equally suffering mother is tinged with personal sorrow and sympathy. In short, Wright's intention in *Black Boy* seems to have been to portray his experience with naturalistic objectivity, rather than from a personal point of view.

A literary naturalist is expected to establish a milieu taken from life and, into it, project characters who then act in accordance with that milieu. The naturalist must record, without comment or interpretation, what actually happens. If Wright regarded himself as a fictional persona in *Black Boy*, he would be less concerned with either his own life or his own point of view. The focus of his interest in the book would be on the events that occurred outside of his life. It is understandable, then, that Wright's account of his own life would not be entirely authentic. One might even suspect that Wright's self-portrait would abound with fictional accounts, and, indeed, many differences between *Black Boy* and his life have been pointed out. One reviewer's objection to the book as autobiography is based on discrepancies found between Wright's accounts in the book and "The Ethics of Living Jim Crow."[6] For example, *Black Boy* describes a fight between Wright and a group of white boys in which he was injured behind the ear and later ushered to a doctor by his mother, whereas in his "Ethics of Living Jim Crow," Wright relates that "a kind neighbor saw me and rushed me to a doctor, who took three stitches in my neck." Also in *Black Boy* Wright often refers to his mother as a cook "in the white folks' kitchen" and describes her as less intellectual than she really was.[7] In fact, Ella Wilson, his mother, before her marriage to his father, was well educated for a black woman and taught school. Edwin R. Embree, who intimately knew Wright's youth and early literary career, testifies that "his mother, light brown, good looking, possessed of a few years of book learning, got jobs a few months as a teacher at \$25.00 a month."[8]

These alterations, however, are not a major reason for calling *Black Boy* a fictionalized biography. Even though parts of the book are fictional, it is nevertheless autobiographical and should not be equated with a novel. No one for a moment can overlook the fact that it portrays Wright himself, and if it concerns others, their lives are necessarily intertwined with his. But the most important distinction *Black Boy* bears as autobiography is Wright's intention to use his young self as a mask. The attitudes and sentiments expressed by the young Wright are not totally his own but represent the responses of those he called "the voiceless Negro boys" of the South.[9] Such a technique makes *Black Boy* a unique autobiography just as a similar technique makes *Native Son* a unique novel (Wright tells us that Bigger Thomas is a conscious composite portrait of numerous individual blacks he has known in his life[10]).

II

The uniqueness of Wright's autobiography can be explained in another way. Since he is a spokesman for the voiceless black youths of the South he had known in his life, he must be objective and scientific in his observations. Thus *Black Boy*, though not intended as such, is a convincing sociological study. Like sociology, it not only analyzes a social problem but offers a solution to the problem it treats. Wright's purpose is to study the way in which black life in the South was determined by its environment, and, to borrow Zola's words, his desire to "disengage the determinism of human and social phenomena so that we may one day control and direct these phenomena."[11] Wright is constantly trying to make his investigation systematic and unbiased. He is concerned with the specific social forces in the environment of a black boy: white racism, black society, and his own family.

James Baldwin has accused Wright of his belief that "in Negro life there exists no tradition, no field of manners, no possibility of ritual or intercourse, such as may, for example, sustain the Jew even after he has left his father's house."[12] Unlike Baldwin, who grew up in a highly religious black community in Harlem, Wright in the deep South witnessed "the essential bleakness of black life in America" (p. 33). The central issue, however, is whether such human traits as, in Wright's words, "tenderness, love, honor, loyalty, and capacity to remember" are innate in the Negro tradition, as Baldwin says, or are "fostered, won, struggled and suffered for," as Wright believed (p. 33). Elsewhere Wright tells us that he "wrote the book to tell a series of incidents strung through my childhood, but the main desire was to render a judgment on my environment .... That judgment was this: the environment the South creates is too small to nourish human beings, especially Negro human beings."[13] Wright, therefore, squarely places the burden of proof upon white society, contending with enough justification given in *Black Boy* that the absence of these human qualities in black people stemmed from years of white oppression.

To Wright, the effect of white oppression in the South was visible in the black communities of the Mississippi Delta. By the time he became fourteen he was able to read and write well enough to obtain a job, in which he assisted an illiterate black insurance salesman. On his daily rounds to the shacks and plantations in the area, he was appalled by the pervasiveness of segregated life: "I saw a bare, bleak pool of black life and I hated it: the people were alike, their homes were alike, and their farms were alike" (p. 120). Such observations later infuriated not only white segregationists but many black citizens, who wrote letters to the FBI and denounced *Black Boy.* Letters called him "a black Nazi" and "one of the biggest spreaders of race hatred." Another black protester complained: "I am an American Negro and proud of it because we colored people in America have come a long way in the last seventy years .... We colored people don[']t mind the truth but we do hate lies or anything that disturb[s] our peace of mind."[14]

What had, at first, disturbed Wright was not the failure of many blacks and whites alike to see the facts of racism, but their inability to recognize malice in the minds of white racists. *Black Boy* recounts an incident in which Wright was once wrongfully accused of addressing a white employee at an optical company without using the title "Mr." Another white employee later corroborated the accusation by telling Wright: "'Didn't you call him *Pease*? If you say you didn't, I'll rip your gut string loose with this f-k-g bar, you black granny dodger! You can't call a white man a liar and get away with it!'" (p. 166). Consequently Wright was forced to leave his job. Resenting a black man's obtaining what they considered a white man's occupation, these white men deliberately created a falsehood to deny Wright a livelihood.

In retrospect, however, Wright realizes that such grudges as white men held against black men did not seem to derive from the white men themselves. He theorizes that they were not acting as individual men, but as "part of a huge, implacable, elemental design toward which hate was futile" (p. 170). Wright's autobiography does not for one moment concern itself with the theme of evil, as romantic fiction or tragic drama sometimes does.[15] *Black Boy* is intended as a sociological document rather than a novel; what such a document shows is the fact that the oppressors are as much victims of the elemental design of racism as are the oppressed. The center of Wright's interest, then, rests on deciphering this design.

In *Black Boy* Wright is continually at pains to show that white people have a preconceived notion of a Negro's place in the South: He serves them, he is likely to steal, and he cannot read or write. The tabooed subjects that Southerners refused to discuss with black men included "American white women; the Ku Klux Klan; France, and how Negro soldiers fared while there; Frenchwomen; Jack Johnson; the entire northern part of the United States; the Civil War; Abraham Lincoln; U.S. Grant; General Sherman; Catholics; the Pope; Jews; the Republican Party; slavery; social equality; Communism; Socialism; the 13th, 14th, and 15th Amendments of the Constitution" (p. 202). Sex and religion were the most accepted subjects, for they were the topics that did not require positive knowledge or self-assertion on the part of the black man. White men did not mind black men's talking about sex as long as it was not interracial. Sex was considered purely biological, and like religion it would not call for the will power of an individual. Although blacks were physically free, the South had replaced traditional slavery with a system by which their freedom of speech and movement was closely monitored and restricted. The culprit was not any individual white man; it was the complicity of white society that had allowed the design of slavery to renew itself in the twentieth-century South.

What underlies this new design of slavery? Most significantly, black men are classified as animals, a mentality inherited from the old days of slavery. Not only are black people considered to be white men's servants, but they are expected to entertain them as though blacks were animals in the zoo. Crimes perpetrated on fellow blacks are not condemned as such. Wright cites an incident in which his foreman at a company he worked for instigated antagonism between Wright and a black employee at another company so that they would try to stab each other. Wright, avoiding the trap, agreed instead to fight a boxing match to satisfy the white employees' whim. "'I suppose,'" Wright reasoned, "'it's fun for white men to see niggers fight .... To white men we're like dogs or cocks'" (pp. 207-208). Even killing among black men would not prick the white men's consciences. Such an attitude echoes that of the white public at the trial of Bigger Thomas for the murder of Bessie Mears, his black girlfriend, in *Native Son*.

Another degrading assumption white men hold about black men is that, since they are treated as animals, they are not supposed to possess intellectual capabilities. The reason for the young Wright's losing employment is often related to his intelligence, which poses a threat to the white man's sense of superiority. Wright points out, for instance, that some black men tried to organize themselves and petitioned their white employers for higher wages and better working conditions. But he correctly observes that such a movement was swiftly avenged by further restrictions and brutality. Throughout the book Wright continues to demonstrate the fact that Southern whites would rather have blacks who stole goods and property than blacks who were conscious, however vaguely, of the worth of their own intelligence and humanity. For Wright, racism induces black deceit and encourages black irresponsibility. Ironically, blacks are rewarded in the degree that they can make the whites feel safe and maintain their moral superiority.

Needless to say, the forces of racism have devastating effects on black life. Critics, both black and white, have complained that Wright in *Black Boy* lacks racial pride. It is true that he is critical of the black community in the South, but it is not true that he places the blame on the black community itself. His intention is to show that a racist system produced the way of life that was forced upon black people. In terms of social determinism, *Black Boy* provides a literary experiment to demonstrate uniformity in Negro behavior under the influence of social forces.[16]

Most black people, he admits, do adjust to their environment for survival. But in doing so they lose individuality, self-respect, and dignity. This is perhaps the reason that Benjamin Davis, Jr., a black leftist critic, attacked Wright's portrayal of the Southern black community: "*Black Boy* says some wholly unacceptable things about the Negro's capacity for genuine emotion."[17] To Wright, however, it is the circumstances in which Negroes find themselves that cause the personalities to warp, and this in turn results in various forms of hypocritical and erratic behavior. The most striking example of this appears in an incident with an elevator boy the young Wright encountered in Memphis. The black boy, who professed that "he was proud of his race and indignant about its wrongs," never hesitated to expose his buttocks for a white man to kick so he could solicit a quarter from the white man. Wright tells us he felt "no anger or hatred, only disgust and loathing," and that he confronted this youth:

"How in God's name can you do that?"
"I needed a quarter and I got it," he said soberly, proudly.
"But a quarter can't pay you for what he did to you," I said.
"Listen, nigger," he said to me, "my ass is tough and quarters is scarce." (p. 200)

About white men's sexual exploitation of black women, Wright is as much critical of black women as of white men, because black women expect and readily condone white men's behavior. Once a black maid who had been slapped playfully on her buttocks by a white nightwatchman told the indignant Wright who had witnessed the incident: "'They never get any further with us than that, if we don't want 'em to'" (p. 174).

Understandably such portraits of black men and women made some readers feel that Wright unduly deprived black people of their personal honor and dignity. For Ralph Ellison, Wright's autobiography lacks "high humanity," especially among its blacks. As Dan McCall correctly argues, however, "Wright is trying to show us how this gross state came about. He refuses to dress up his Negroes in an imported Sunday best because he has a far larger task before him."[18] Wright explains:

I began to marvel at how smoothly the black boys acted out the roles that the white race had mapped out for them. Most of them were not conscious of living a special, separated, stunted way of life. Yet I knew that in some period of their growing up—a period that they had no doubt forgotten—there had been developed in them a delicate, sensitive controlling mechanism that shut off their mind and emotions from all that the white race had said was taboo. (p. 172)

One of the remarkable insights *Black Boy* offers is that social determinism takes its heaviest toll in Wright's family life. One would assume that if black boys are mistreated in society at large, they would at least be protected in their family. But in Wright's early childhood his father deserted his wife and children; not only did Wright become a casualty of the broken family, but his father himself was a victim of the racial system in the deep South. Wright observes about his father: "From the white landowners above him there had not been handed to him a chance to learn the meaning of loyalty, of sentiment, of tradition" (p. 30).

Consequently, the young Wright was subjected to the crushing blow of family antagonisms.[19] His grandmother's Seventh-Day Adventist doctrine as practiced at home epitomizes this hostility and strife. Wright saw "more violent quarrels in our deeply religious home than in the home of a gangster, burglar, or a prostitute .... The naked will to power seemed always to walk in the wake of a hymn" (p. 119). While Granny held on to the helm of the family, several of Wright's uncles also attempted to administer their authority. One of them, enraged by Wright's impolite mannerisms, scolded his nephew for not acting as "the backward black boys act on the plantations"; he was ordered "to grin, hang my head, and mumble apologetically when I was spoken to" (p. 138). It seems as though black adults, subjected to racism in white society, in turn felt compelled to rule their children at home. The black adults had grown up in the world in which they were permitted no missteps in a white-dominated society. The fact that Wright's worst punishments, such as those he had given by his mother for setting fire to his grandmother's house, were inflicted by his closest relatives suggests how completely black life was dominated by white racism.

III

Despite the naturalistic philosophy that underlies Wright's vision of black life, the miracle of *Black Boy* is that its hero, by the time he left for Chicago, had not become the patient, humorous, subservient black man of the white myth. Nor did he end up as either the degraded, grinning, and perpetually frustrated Negro or a murderer like Bigger Thomas of *Native Son*. Throughout the book Wright is at great pains to create a manhood as a direct challenge to the overwhelming forces of society. *Black Boy* reveals how self-creation can be thwarted and mauled, but unlike James Farrell's *Studs Lonigan* or Dreiser's *An American Tragedy*, the hero's spirit remains unbroken. Most importantly, however, what distinguishes *Black Boy* from any other naturalistic work is that it is the story of a man estranged from his own race by sensitivity and intellect, yet segregated from the white race by the color of his skin.

Finding himself in no-man's-land, the young Wright attempted to create his own world. Although *Black Boy* is predominantly a portrayal of Southern society, it is also a self-portrait. Despite the devastating effects of the society upon his own life, he came to the conclusion that anything was "possible, likely, feasible, because I wanted everything to be possible" (p. 64). Early in the book he rationalizes this passion for ego: "Because I had no power to make things happen outside of me in the objective world, I made things happen within. Because my environment was bare and bleak, I endowed it with unlimited potentialities, redeemed it for the sake of my own hungry and cloudy yearning" (p. 64).

About this process of self-creation, critics have charged that he deliberately degrades black life to dramatize the emergence of the self as a hero.[20] But given his life as we know it today, one can scarcely deny the authenticity of the events recounted in the book, nor are the episodes about racism unbelievable or unconvincing. Although Du Bois argues that "the suffering of others is put down simply as a measure of his own suffering and resentment,"[21] it is understandable that Wright did so in order to make his own life representative of the voiceless black boys, as well as to indicate that they too are capable of self-creation.

Whether or not our hero is too selfish and proud an achiever to be credible can be judged by how convincingly his maturation is portrayed. In his early childhood Wright acquired a hatred for white people, not based on his own experience, but derived from other Negro children. Like any child, black or white, Wright had his vision circumscribed by blinders and colored glasses. As he grew older, however, he realized that the roots of racial hatred did not exist in any individuals, but stemmed from an inherited system. The white race was as much its victim as the black race. From this vantage point, he took social determinism to be a threat to his autonomy and began to wage a battle. By the time he was nineteen, he became aware that his life experiences "had shaped me to live by my own feelings and thoughts" (p. 221).

It was the crushing effects of environment and temperament that Wright learned so well from his immediate relatives. When he was a young boy, one of his uncles was murdered by his white business competitors; his grandmother was a religious fanatic. The greatest blow to his childhood came from his own father, who succumbed to the temptation of sex and alcohol. When he saw his father again a quarter of a century later, he realized that, "though ties of blood made us kin, though I could see a shadow of my face in his face, though there was an echo of my voice in his voice, we were forever strangers, speaking a different language, living on vastly distant planes of reality" (p. 30). Not only is Wright denying the influence of heredity on his own character, but he is distinguishing two men subjected to the same environment. His father, Wright concludes, "was a black peasant who had gone to the city seeking life, but ... whose life had been hopelessly snarled in the city, and who had at last fled the city—that same city which had lifted me in its burning arms and borne me toward alien and undreamed-of shores of knowing" (p. 31).

What, then, were the forces in his life that young Wright had learned to ward off in his struggle for independence? Throughout his youth he witnessed how deeply superstitious religion had trapped the minds and hearts of black people. As a child he was impressed with the elders at church for the inspiring language of their sermons: "a gospel clogged with images of vast lakes of eternal fire, of seas vanishing, of valleys of dry bones,... of the lame walking; a salvation that teemed with fantastic beasts having multiple heads and horns and eyes and feet" (p. 89). But such sensations departed quickly once he left the church and saw the bright sunshine with the crowded people pouring into the streets. To him none of these religious ideas and images seemed to have anything to do with his life. He knew not only that religion had a capacity to mesmerize people in the black community, but also that it was used by "one individual or group to rule another in the name of God" (p. 119).

As some critics have noted, *Black Boy* is relatively free from the hero's references to his own sexual awakening.[22] Sex in *Black Boy* is treated much like religion, for Wright knew during his adolescent years that one could easily be victimized by sexual forces. The only time sexual attraction is mentioned is in connection with a church service in which Wright, at twelve, was infatuated with the elder's wife. The fact that the woman is depicted in grotesquely physical terms rather than spiritual and felicitous images ("a black imp with two horns; ... a scaly, naked body; wet, sticky fingers; moist, sensual lips; and lascivious eyes") suggests that he is indeed debasing his sexual attraction (p. 98). That he could easily fend off such biological forces can be contrasted with Fishbelly Tucker's unsuccessful struggle with his sexual problems in the *The Long Dream*. In that novel, sex is dealt with in its sordid context; the hero's ritual of initiation into manhood is performed in a house of prostitution.

Although *Black Boy* is strung with a series of episodes that illustrates various forms of racial oppression, the center of attention lies in our hero's transcendence of the oppression. Racial oppression is caused not only by the external forces of society but by the internal problems of the oppressed. "Some," Wright admits, "may escape the general plight and grow up, but it is a matter of luck.[23] To the hero of *Black Boy*, most of them were victims of racial prejudice, failures in the battle for survival. No small wonder an anonymous reviewer, calling *Black Boy* "the most ferocious exercise in misanthropy since Jonathon Swift," was appalled by the hatred Wright expresses toward both whites and blacks.[24] Obviously, the reader misunderstood Wright's intention, for the book is not meant to be a satire like *Gulliver's Travels*, in which the narrator assails and loathes every conceivable human vice and depravity. Rather, *Black Boy* is Wright's honest attempt to refute a naturalistic philosophy of life. Our hero is a catalyst in accomplishing this task.

In "Blueprint for Negro Writing," Wright asserts that "Themes for Negro writers will rise from understanding the meaning of their being transplanted from a 'savage' to a 'civilized' culture in all its social, political, economic, and emotional implications."[25] In *Black Boy*, his chief aim is to show how this youth, whom the South called a "nigger," surmounted his obstacles in the civilized culture. The most painful stance he took in this struggle was to be an intense individualist; he created selfhood and exerted his will at the risk of annihilation. In scene after scene both the black and the white community kept piling crushing circumstances upon him, but no matter how unbearably they were pressed down on him, he refused to give in. Only under such pressure can one discover one's self. For others, this process of creation might have been aided by chance, but for him "it should be a matter of plan." And himself an exemplar, Wright defined the mission as "a matter of saving the citizens of our country for our country."[26]

One could be puzzled by this youth's individuality and fortitude if the seed of manhood had not been sown in the child. Despite a critic's disclaimer to the contrary, *Black Boy* contains ample evidence for the child's precocity and independence.[27] Wright's earlier self is presented even to the point of betraying his vanity: When he moved to his grandmother's house after his family was deserted by his father, he took pride in telling the timid children of the new neighborhood about his train ride, his cruise on the *Kate Adams* on the Mississippi River, and his escape from the orphanage (p. 33). Moreover, the young child is presented as a rebel who refuses to compromise with the dictates of society and family. Once he was dismayed to find out that the man who had beaten a black boy was not the boy's father. Though Wright was told by his mother that he was "'too young to understand,'" he responded with a resolution: "'I'm not going to let anybody beat me'" (p. 21). This youthful attitude gave rise to an even more awesome resolution, of which he later became capable when he heard the story of a black woman who had avenged her husband's murder. According to the rumor, when she was granted permission to claim her husband's body for burial, she took with her a shotgun wrapped in a white sheet and, while kneeling down before the white executioners, shot four of them—a tale that served as the exact prototype of "Bright and Morning Star." *Black Boy* records the young Wright's belligerency:

> I resolved that I would emulate the black woman if I were ever faced with a white mob; I would conceal a weapon, pretend that I had been crushed by the wrong done to one of my loved ones; then, just when they thought I had accepted their cruelty as the law of my life, I would let go with my gun and kill as many of them as possible before they killed me. The story of the woman's deception gave form and meaning to confused defensive feelings that had long been sleeping in me. (p. 65)

Becoming a rebel inevitably led to being a misfit. In Wright's life, however, it is his innate character that allowed this to happen. How self-assertive the young Wright was can be best demonstrated in a comparison between him and his playmates. Although he identified himself with a mistreated group, there was a crucial difference between him and other black children. They constantly complained about the petty wrongs they suffered, but they had no desire to question the larger issues of racial oppression. Their attitude resembles that of the young Fishbelly in *The Long Dream*; just like his father before him, Fishbelly servilely worships the powerful white people. He falls in love with the values of the white world because such demeanor can offer him material rewards and make his manhood easier and less painful to achieve. The young Wright, on the other hand, found among the black boys no sympathy for his inquiring mind. As a result he was forced to contemplate such questions for himself.

As early as twelve years old, Wright held "a sense of the world that was mine and mine alone, a notion as to what life meant that no education could ever alter, a conviction that the meaning of living came only when one was struggling to wring a meaning out of meaningless suffering" (pp. 87–88). His decision to leave the South seven years later, the final action of our hero, was based upon such conviction, as if the seed of manhood had already been in the child. Without mental companionship to rely on, however, he withdrew and turned inward like the anti-hero of an existentialist novel. In his recoil he had once again discovered that the revelation of all truths must come through the action and anguish of the self. It was at this point in his ordeal that he came in contact with the works of such American realists such as H. L. Mencken, Theodore Dreiser, and Sherwood Anderson. It was their ideas, he tells us, that literally delivered his brooding sensibility to a bright horizon, a vision that "... America could be shaped nearer to the hearts of those who lived in it" (p. 227). It was also at this time that he decided to head North to discover for himself that man could live with dignity and determine his own destiny. Because he knew he could not make the world, he sought to make things happen within him and caught a sense of freedom; in doing do he discovered the new world.

NOTES

[1]"Richard Wright Looks Back," *New York Herald Tribune Book Review*, 4 Mar. 1945, p. 2.
[2]Ibid.
[3]"Letter to Richard Wright," in *Richard Wright: Impressions and Perspectives*, ed. David Ray and Robert M. Farnsworth (Ann Arbor: Univ. of Michigan Press, 1973), p. 143.
[4]Ibid.
[5]"Richard Wright Looks Back," p. 2.
[6]See Beatrice M. Murphy, *Pulse*, 3 (Apr. 1945), 32-33.
[7]Richard Wright, *Black Boy: A Record of Childhood and Youth* (New York: Harper & Brothers, 1945), p. 17. Later references are to this edition and indicated in parentheses.
[8]See "Richard Wright: Native Son," in *13 Against the Odds* (New York: Viking, 1944), pp. 25-26.
[9]See "The Handiest Truth to Me to Plow Up Was in My Own Life," *P.M. Magazine*, 4 Apr. 1945, p. 3.
[10]"How 'Bigger' Was Born," in *Native Son* (1940; rpt. New York: Harper & Row, 1966), p. xii.
[11]"The Experimental Novel," in *Documents of Modern Literary Realism*, ed. George J. Becker (Princeton: Princeton Univ. Press, 1963), p. 181.
[12]*Notes of a Native Son* (1955; rpt. New York: Bantam Books, 1968), p. 28.
[13]"The Handiest Truth," p. 3.
[14]See Addison Gayle, *Richard Wright: Ordeal of a Native Son* (Garden City, NY: Anchor Press/Doubleday, 1980), pp. 173-74. According to Gayle, Senator Bilbo of Mississippi condemned *Black Boy* on the floor of the U.S. Senate on June 7, 1945, as "the dirtiest, filthiest, lousiest, most obscene piece of writing that I have ever seen in print ... it is so filthy and dirty .... it comes from a Negro, and you cannot expect any better from a person of his type" (p. 173).
[15]In general I agree with Dan McCall, who says: "Wright knew that all the evil could not be laid to a man. He reused to create a 'white villain.' ... In *Black Boy* we see no villains; we do not even see a series of villains. We see men utterly helpless; varieties of foulness, stunted minds" (*The Example of Richard Wright* [New York: Harcourt, 1969], p. 128).
[16]Edward Margolies observes: "Wright traps the reader in a stereotyped response--the same stereotyped response that Wright is fighting throughout the book: that is, that all Negroes are alike and react alike" (*The Art of Richard Wright* [Carbondale: Southern Illinois Univ. Press, 1969], p. 19).
[17]"Some Impressions of *Black Boy*," *Daily Worker*, 1 Apr. 1945, p. 9.
[18]*The Example of Richard Wright*, pp. 118-19.
[19]*Black Boy* as autobiography can be closely compared with Angelo Herndon's *Let Me Live* (1937). Both writers depict the forces of segregation that had devastating effects on their educations and job opportunities. Both describe poverty and hunger in the plights of their families. But, while Wright grew up without his father and with his bedridden mother and hostile relatives, Herndon could rely on the traditional family loyalty—a father with trust and confidence in his son and a warm-hearted, loving mother.
[20]W.E.B Du Bois writes: "After this sordid, shadowy picture we gradually come upon the solution. The hero is interested in himself, is self-centered to the exclusion of everybody and everything else" ("Richard Wright Looks Back," p. 2). John M. Reilly also argues that Wright "will not risk telling experiences inconsistent in any way with his image of himself as an alienated peasant youth in rebellion against the hostile Southern caste system .... Wright suppresses his connections with the bourgeoisie. Had he mentioned these connections, Wright might have modified the picture of a bleak and hostile environment, but there is no question of falsification" ("Self-Portraits by Richard Wright," *Colorado Quarterly*, 22 [Summer 1971], 34).
[21]"Richard Wright Looks Back," p.2.

[22]Edward Margolies considers sex in *Black Boy* in terms of "violence (the dangers inherent in relationships with white prostitutes); bravado (adolescent boys speaking of their prowess); adultery (his father's abandonment of his wife for another woman); obscenities (which Wright learned at the age of six); or condescension and rejection (Wright's fending off the daughter of his landlady in Memphis because she was incapable of understanding the depths of his sensibilities)" (*The Art of Richard Wright*, pp. 17-18). Katherine Fishburn maintains that *The Long Dream* has more detail and a much more thorough treatment of a young black's sexual maturation than *Black Boy* (*Richard Wright's Hero: The Faces of a Rebel-Victim* [Metuchen, NJ: Scarecrow, 1977], p. 14).

[23]"The Handiest Truth," p. 3.

[24]*Newark Evening News*, 17 Mar. 1945.

[25]In *Richard Wright Reader*, ed. Ellen Wright and Michel Fabre (New York: Harper & Row, 1978), p. 47.

[26]"The Handiest Truth." p. 3.

[27]Reviewer F.K. Richter observed that *Black Boy* is an unconscious demonstration of Aristotle's entelechy, that manhood resides in childhood. But he maintains that because Wright fails to provide indispensable factors that made the child grow, "the book loses some of its value as autobiography and non-fiction and takes on, however slightly, a quality of fiction" (*Negro Story*, 1 [May-June 1945], 93-95).

From *Black American Literature Forum*, 19 (Summer 1985), 70-75.

Sociology of an Existence: Richard Wright and the Chicago School

Carla Cappetti

A reciprocal interest between sociology and literature marked much of the writing of the 1930s. A number of cultural links—forged in the attempt to confront, portray, condemn or predict the "social reality"—provided the intellectual environment for such exchange. Three important links consisted of the John Reed Clubs, the League of American Writers, and the Federal Writers' Project; in the products of these groups—the proletarian literature, the social writings, as well as the guidebooks, history books, life-stories and folklore collections—one can clearly notice the affinity of interests between literary and sociological discourse. The career of Richard Wright for a whole decade ran parallel to these three phases. Like James Farrell and Saul Bellow, he had discovered the kinship of literature and sociology under the aegis of the Chicago School of Urban Sociology. His two-volume autobiography--*Black Boy* and *American Hunger*--remains a most emblematic product of such intellectual grafting.[1] More specifically, it remains a remarkable expression of the tendencies which made the convergence of sociology and literature possible: on the one hand the tendency towards a more subjective sociology which rediscovered the subjectivity of the individual beneath its uniform-looking statistics; on the other the tendency towards a more objective literature which rediscovered the individual's unbreachable ties with his or her culture and environment. The following discussion will explore these themes through the privileged observation point of *Black Boy* and *American Hunger*.[2] Richard Wright's appropriation of a theoretical framework from sociology and the content of the exchange will provide the two main axes of study.

Richard Wright's association with the Chicago School of Urban Sociology—our departure point here and an important phase in his career—has been an obligatory point of reference for his biographers. With greater or lesser detail, Wright's biographers have generally summarized the facts, dates, and names of his sociological readings and friendships.[3] Louis Wirth, Robert Park, Horace Cayton, Franklin Frazier--the main names on the list—are also the names that spell out the early theories of "urbanism," "juvenile delinquency," "human behavior," "urban environment." These theories first tried to explore disgregation within families and to study the transition from rural to urban environments of both Blacks and immigrants. While greatly indebted to Wright's biographers for gathering and organizing the main data of this rapport, the present study aims at rendering problematical this aspect of Wright's intellectual itinerary. Two critical debates are specifically relevant to the essay's argument. The first, a methodological one, includes Robert Bone and John Reilly, and is concerned with the cultural constructs which a literary text appropriates from a larger cultural whole in order to redefine certain aspects of experience. The second debate, which includes John McCluskey and Günter Lenz, is concerned with analyzing the themes of culture, tradition, family and community in Wright's work.

In "Richard Wright and the Chicago Renaissance," Robert Bone has attempted to reformulate the literary periodization of Afro-American literature so as to allow for a Chicago Renaissance alongside the more famous Harlem one.[4] His essay adds no new information on Wright's study of sociology. However, Bone succeeds in framing the question within a significant literary-historical setting—the Chicago Renaissance. In the process, he uncovers an important element of Wright's relationship with the Chicago sociologists when he suggests that one should link the documentary spirit of the Chicago School with that of Naturalism, its literary counterpart; or when he points to the "quasiliterary" methods involved in the sociologist's use of "case studies" and "life-stories." As Bone points out, "these forms at bottom are versions of the narrative art; hence their affinity with fiction and autobiography."[5] Although primarily concerned with a larger discussion of the Chicago Renaissance, Bone's essay contains both an invitation to rethink the "literary thirties" alongside the "sociological thirties," and an implicit suggestion that studying Wright's relationship with the Chicago sociologists can represent a first step in such a direction.

A further exploration of Bone's idea is contained in John Reilly's essay "Richard Wright Preaches the Nation: *12 Million Black Voices.*" Reilly openly rejects the idea that Richard Wright may have "stumbled" fortuitously on social theory.[6] Instead he suggests it was the result of an active search for "explanatory concepts." Focusing on *12 Million Black Voices,* Reilly highlights the main concepts which Wright appropriated in order "to tell not only his own individual story, but also the story of other Blacks, whose experience, the Chicago School assured him, were his own."[7]

Reilly's and Bone's essays provided the present study with important methodological clues on the literary use of sociological constructs and the development of urban sociology itself. For both critics, in fact, cultural constructs are neither natural nor accidental phenomena. With Reilly and Bone the following discussion shares a methodological assumption: cultural constructs are mental tools actively sought and shaped in order to deal with new or changed realities.

A second critical debate over the contents of Wright's autobiographical construct—culture, tradition, family, and community—is relevant to the present study. A number of critics have discussed Wright's handling of these themes, as the question is central to his autobiography and to much of his work, from the early *Lawd Today* (1937), to his late works on Africa, *Black Power* (1954), and on Spain, *Pagan Spain* (1957). Two of the most antithetical among the recent contributions are those of John McCluskey and Günter Lenz. The former discusses the problem of placing an important figure such as Richard Wright at the center of Afro-American literary tradition, considering Wright's "uneasy relationship with Afro-American vernacular," his dismissal of the church as an "ineffective and uncreative force," and finally his unwillingness "to use the positive elements from his own culture."[8] McCluskey spots a major contradiction in Wright's work: on the one hand are Wright's official pronouncements in favor of the use of folklore and folk idioms—found for example in "Blueprint for Negro Writing" (1937); on the other hand is his writing praxis, one which consistently creates heroes who have "weak, if non-existent" relationships with the Black community, and one in which heroes are consistently "isolated men at odds with the world, fragmented victims and outsiders."[9]

Lenz, to the contrary, argues that *Black Boy* represents Wright's attempt to "[communicate] the meaning of Southern folk heritage" and "to interpret his own life as part of a communal and cultural heritage."[10] Using "Blueprint for Negro Writing" as evidence of Wright's "reassessment of folklore," Lenz writes that the essay is "a far cry from his lament (in *Black Boy*) about the 'cultural barrenness of black life' and its traditions."[11] Lenz makes no mention of the fact that "Blueprint" had been published some eight years prior to the autobiography and thus can hardly be used as evidence of Wright's newly achieved consciousness. In general, Lenz's attempt to trace some of the precursors of an Afro-American folk-culture reevaluation—in this case, Richard Wright and Zora Neale Hurston—is admirable. However, as the ensuing discussion intends to show, one can hardly simplify the complexities and ambiguities which made Wright's relationship with his own culture most contradictory.

The present essay agrees with McCluskey and other critics in viewing Wright's work as soaked in irreconcilable contradictions between the individual and the group—i.e. culture, tradition, family, community. It also hopes to explore those contradictions and their motivations as embedded in Wright's relationship with the Chicago urban sociologists. Concentrating on *Black Boy* and *American Hunger,* the essay pursues Bone's and Reilly's concern with both literature and sociology in the 1930s, and Wright's personal relationship with the Chicago School of Urban Sociology. The essay investigates Wright's sociological imagination in two main directions. The first part discusses the struggle between the individual and the group as the construct which both structures the autobiography and underlies its main concepts. Around this construct Richard Wright and the Chicago sociologists converge in conceptualizing some important aspects of reality. The second part concentrates on the cooperation of sociology and literature in formulating the two points of view of "informant" and "participant observer" as they emerge from *Black Boy* and *American Hunger.*

I

> Personal evolution is always a struggle between the individual and society—a struggle for self-expression on the part of the individual, for his subjection, on the part of society—and it is in the total course of this struggle that the personality—not as a static 'essence' but as a dynamic, continuing evolving set of activity—manifests and constructs itself.

With these words Thomas and Znaniecki, two early Chicago sociologists, postulated a dichotomy which is crucial to the understanding of *Black Boy* and *American Hunger.* [12] This notion constitutes the common ground on which a sociological theory and a literary text stand: the former articulating and evolving it into a set of concepts and categories, the latter dramatizing it and demonstrating its functioning in the concrete details of a life-story.

The struggle between individual and society forms the backbone of Wright's autobiography, just as it controls the two main categories used in the text—the concept of "personality" and the concept of "environment." "Environment" here becomes an all inclusive term, indicating the group, the community, the culture, tradition, authority. Against these formidable institutions and the threats which they produce, the individual "personality" must strive for self-realization. These institutions become tangible living bodies, more real than the single individuals who form them. They are the formidable challenges against which Richard Wright, the only individual who seems consciously to oppose the racist South, must contend.

In *Black Boy* and *American Hunger* three types of institutions confront the individual and organize his life-story: the family to which he belongs by blood; the South—epitomized by religion, school, and the racist white world—to which he belongs by culture; and the Communist Party to which he belongs by choice. As a ritual reenactment of the pyromaniacal action of the first scene, the autobiography develops through numberless episodes in which the hero sets symbolic fires to the institutions which surround him. This seems to be the only way to keep his personality intact, until the choice of isolation, which closes the autobiography, emerges as the only alternative to the oppression of the group.

The hero's relationship with the family covers the first half of *Black Boy.* It develops through a progression from passive to resentful submission, to successful rebellion against the authority of this institution and of the entire family environment. Attempts at self-expression provide the ground for most of the confrontations. Young Richard is punished for printing "four-letter words describing physiological and sex-functions" which he had just learned in school (pp. 32-33). He is punished for listening to the "Devil's stuff," the story of "Bluebeard and His Seven Wives" (p. 47). He is punished for speaking words "whose meaning he did not fully know .... 'When you get through, kiss back there,' he said, the words rolling softly but unpremeditatedly" (p. 49). Many other times he is "slapped across the mouth" for saying something wrong.

Far from being a simple catalogue of beatings and punishments, the narrative illustrates the child's growing ability to rebel against his environment and its institutions, and describes the process through which his personality shapes itself and is in turn shaped. Moreover, each time he successfully emerges from a confrontation with a family member, the hero is able to keep his personality intact only through a progressive denial of kinship and through a growing sense of isolation. In the first confrontation with his father, the narrator describes the old man as a "stranger to me, always somehow alien and remote" (p. 17). By lynching the kitten that is disturbing his father's sleep he subverts his father's authority, and ignites a process of estrangement of which the actual writing of the autobiography is the culmination:

> A quarter of a century was to elapse ... when I was to see him again .... I realized that, though ties of blood made us kin, though I could see a shadow of my face in his face, though there was an echo of my voice in is voice, we were forever *strangers,* speaking in a different language, living on vastly distant planes of reality. (p. 42, my emphasis)

Through a denial of kinship ties, the individual can thus subtract himself from the familial institution and from its violence against the personality.

Similar if more violent confrontations take place between Richard and Aunt Addie. She is the embodiment of three institutions—school, family, and religion—which try to annihilate the individual personality. As she is preparing to give Richard another lashing, and as he is considering whether or not to defend himself, reflections on the values of blood ties once more come to the foreground:

> I was trying to stifle the impulse to go to the drawer of the kitchen table and get a knife and defend myself. But this woman who stood before me was my aunt, my mother's sister, Granny's daughter; in her veins my own blood flowed; in many of her actions I could see some elusive part of my own self; and in her speech I could catch echoes of my own speech. (p. 119)

In spite of blood and, if need be, by spilling blood, Richard decides to defend himself. The result is a violent struggle of "kicking, scratching, hitting, fighting as though we were *strangers,* deadly enemies, fighting for our lives" (p. 120, my emphasis). Unlike the pupils in Aunt Addie's school whose personalities are "devoid of anger, hope, laughter, enthusiasm, passion, or despair" and who are "claimed wholly by their environment and could imagine no other," Richard's personality defies submission to these institutions (pp. 115-16).

The institution of the family, we soon discover, defines only the first environment which shapes and threatens Richard. It is merely the first universe within and against which he develops as a distinct personality. Richard must now face the racist white South. Although no biological law binds him to it, Richard must constantly carry its culture within himself while trying to escape from it. This culture cannot be fought with knives and razors since it pervades the social world—of religion, school, and racism—in which young Richard must live and work.

External to the family and yet hardly distinguishable from it, religion comes uninvited to Richard, first in the guise of the Seventh-Day Adventist Church of his fanatical grandmother and later in the guise of the Black Methodist Church of his more moderate mother and friends. The budding strength of his personality enables Richard to resist, at first, the potent machinery of family and friends, and their attempts to save his soul:

> The hymns and sermons of God came into my heart only long after my personality had been shaped and formed by uncharted conditions of life . . . and in the end I remained basically unaffected. (p. 124)

In a later episode, however, Richard finds himself seduced by the social environment of the Methodist Church:

> I entered a new world: prim, brown, puritanical girls--black college students ... black boys and girls .... I was so starved for association with people that I allowed myself to be seduced by it all. (pp. 166-67)

When a revival begins, Richard is urged to attend and join the Church: "'We don't want to push you,' they said delicately, implying that if I wanted to associate with them I would have to join" (p. 167). Much like the family, the Church embodies and sanctions a group which confronts the individual by asking him either to be a part of it or to remain alone. "It was hard to refuse," when refusal means returning to imprisonment within the family. Besieged by the preacher, the congregation, and his mother, Richard—in the company of a few other lost sheep—finds himself trapped into allegiance to the group:

> We young men had been trapped by the community, the tribe in which we lived and of
> which we were a part. The tribe, for its own safety, was asking us to be at one with it
> .... In essence, the tribe was asking us whether we shared its feelings. (pp. 169-70)

Walking home "limp as a rag," feeling "sullen anger and a crushing sense of shame,"
the newly baptized Richard has lived the nightmare which underlies the entire
narrative: the domination of the group over the individual through the power of social
consensus. This episode first articulates a vision which will become increasingly more
pronounced throughout the autobiography. The congregation—or the tribe—merges as
a powerful abstract living body which, while formed by individuals, exists in and of
itself, over and against the very individuals who at some level compose it. This reified
perception becomes more evident in the portrayal of two other institutions—the school
and racism. It culminates with the experiences in the Communist Party—in this
autobiography, the most reified of all groups.

Outside of the family, yet still in the South, while the individual's soul finds
nourishment in the church, his intellect must find it in school. Central to the hero's
experiences within the educational institution is the confrontation over the speech that
he is to deliver as class valedictorian. In another variation of the theme "group versus
individual," three groups—family, school friends, and whites—ally themselves together
against the hero. Assigned to deliver the graduation speech, Richard discovers that his
principal has already written one. No other student has ever refused to comply, and if
he will not submit, Richard will give up the chance to teach in the school system. For
Richard, however, complying with the principal means complying with the racist
South: "He was tempting me, baiting me; this was the technique that snared black
young minds into supporting the southern way of life" (p. 194). It means complying
with his more submissive school friends—"My class mates, motivated by a desire to
'save' me, pestered me until I all but reached the breaking point,"—as well as with his
family, both groups fervently opposing his determination (p. 196). Shortly before
giving his own speech, the narrator remembers "I was hating my environment more
each day" (p. 196).

A new and larger environment opens up for Richard the moment he steps out of
school. Waiting for him is the white world with its institutions of racism, segregation,
and violence. While much more powerful and threatening, this world allows Richard to
distance himself from his previous environment and from its values.

> The truth was that I had—even though I had fought against it—grown to accept the
> value of myself that my old environment had created in me, and I had thought that no
> other kind of environment was possible. (p. 240)

Richard's experiences among whites illustrate various degrees of Black submission or
adaptation to the "culture of terror" from which the hero will soon flee. Wright chooses
two individuals in the store of his recollections to illustrate how a personality can
become identical with its social environment. In Jackson, Grigg wants Richard to learn
how to act "like a black" around white people; Grigg says he hates whites, yet submits
completely to their authority. When he made fun of whites and began to laugh, "he
covered his mouth with his hand and bent at the knees, a gesture which was
unconsciously meant to conceal his excessive joy in the presence of whites" (p. 204).
Similarly, in Memphis, Richard meets Shorty, "the most amazing specimen of southern
Negro" (p. 248). Shorty is willing to do anything for a quarter and even lets himself be
kicked by a white man after having clowned around for him in the most shameless
way.

Painfully aware of the destruction of individual personality which the environment
produces on both Grigg and Shorty, Wright presents Richard as the antithesis of
submission and adaptation. Beaten for not saying "sir," fired for his looks, driven out
of a job, forced to fight with another Black boy for the amusement of whites, Richard
discovers in the "civilized" culture seeping through to him from books and magazines
the sustenance which his own culture does not provide:

> From where in this southern darkness had I caught a sense of freedom?... The external
> world of whites and blacks, which was the only world that I had ever known, surely

had not evoked in me any belief in myself. The people I had met had advised and demanded submission .... It had been only through books .... Whenever my environment had failed to support or nourish me, I had clutched at books. (p. 282)

Finding in books—the symbol of what is culturally farthest from the white and Black South—a way both to survive and escape his environment, Richard gives himself a new cultural birth and reads his way out of the "darkness in daytime" postulated in the epigraph. Finally heading North and reflecting on his experiences in the South, the narrator provides a summary of those events. Here emerge unmistakably the principles of selection beneath the apparent formlessness of a life-story:

I had been what my *surroundings* had demanded, what my *family*—conforming to the dictates of the whites above them—had exacted of me, and what the *whites* had said that I must be. Never being fully able to be myself, I had slowly learned that the *South* could recognize but a part of a man, could accept but a fragment of his *personality*. (p. 284, my emphasis)

More than simply a record of Wright's experiences, *Black Boy* is a selection of episodes organized around the categories of family, South, environment, and personality. The reality which Wright constructs—and which the above quotation synthesizes—shares much with that constructed by Thomas and Znaniecki. This construct organizes Wright's life-story into a series of confrontations between the individual and the surrounding institutions. A similar construct organizes *The Polish Peasant*—a pathbreaking study in the use of personal documents—into an

... institutional analysis which proceeded first in terms of the basic units of the primary group, then the community, and finally a selected series of large-scale organizations, which included such elements as the educational system, the press, and co-operative and voluntary associations.[13]

The contradictions inherent in the relationship between individual and group reach the starkest point in *American Hunger,* the second part of the autobiography. Here, the last stage of Wright's individual confrontation with the group unfolds through his relationship with the Communist Party. Unlike the family and the South, the Party represents a social organization which Richard chooses to join. However, like the family and the South, the Party provides a system of kinship and community; once again, the alternative to allegiance is isolation.

Thomas and Znaniecki, in *The Polish Peasant,* had described the social and political reorganization which follows the disgregation of primary groups such as family and community subsequent to immigration. They also had contrasted the rationality of "common ends and means" underlying the new forms of cooperation with the "unreflective social cohesion brought about by tradition" of the primary group.[14] The city represents for these authors both the destruction of community but also its reconstitution at a higher level as conscious cooperation. As an immigrant to the "flat black stretches ... black coal ... grey smoke ... dank prairies" of Chicago, Wright experienced this precise transition from primary groups to social reorganization. Yet, far from experiencing the new forms of cooperation which Thomas and Znaniecki had optimistically prophesied, Richard is once more painfully confronted by an overwhelming institution.

The Communist Party feeds Wright's secular hunger for a sustained relationship without racism, for an intellectual light which can dissolve the epigraphic "darkness in the daytime" and the "[groping] at noonday as in the night." At the same time, the Party becomes an abstract power opposed to his personality, transcending yet subsuming all of the preceding institutions from which he fled.

The Party, much like the family, is constructed as a kinship system. Both contain a degree of "oneness" which is dearly, if fearfully, portrayed in the purge trial of Ross, another member:

Ross was one with all the members there, regardless of race or color: his heart was theirs and their hearts were his; and when a man reaches that state of *kinship* with others, that degree of *oneness,* or when a trial has made him *kin* after he has been sundered from them by wrongdoing, then he must rise and say .... "I'm guilty. Forgive me." (pp. 124-25, my emphasis)

Like a religion, the Party hinges around a "common vision" and notions of guilt. However, unlike religion, it relies not on "mysticism" or the "invoking of God," but rather on a "moral code that could control the conduct of men, yet it was a code that stemmed from practical living, and not from the injunctions of the supernatural" (p. 121). Control is once more in the foreground—control by the group, the environment, the society. The Party, no less than the family and the church, exacts a high toll from its members.

The similarities between the Party and the racist South are also highlighted. At Ross's trial Wright has a momentary vision of his fellow comrades as being free of racial hate and prejudice, but quickly realizes that the South has followed him yet in another guise: "I had fled men who did not like the color of my skin, and now I was among men who did not like the tone of my thoughts" (p. 119). The South has followed him in the shape of another group which isolates minority thoughts. It also has followed him as the agent of distrust and suspicion between Wright and other Blacks. In Memphis, the South had instilled fear between two Black boys who became unable to trust one another, so that whites could have the pleasure of seeing them fight. As in a déjà-vu experience, the Communist Party breaks up the friendship between Wright and Ross by once again casting the seed of suspicion:

We two black men sat in the same room looking at each other in fear. Both of us were hungry. Both of us depended upon public charity .... Yet we had more doubt in our hearts of each other than of the men who had cast the mould of our lives. (p. 84)

Wright constructs the Party—as the family and the South before—as a tangible and living body; the Party is more of a real character than almost any other character, excepting Wright himself. Rather than being the accumulated consciousness—or lack of consciousness—of the individuals who form it, the Party becomes, in Wright's allegorical universe, the personification of institutionalized control. Much like his view of the family and the South, Wright has created an institution as a body with its own discipline, beliefs and truths. Totally missing is an image of the Party as embodying a relationship, a dynamic between people fighting their historical battles. Instead, when the object becomes animated—Frankenstein-like—it turns against its creator.

The purge trial of Ross is the apex of the process. This trial is signifiant in two ways. On the one hand it culminates and epitomizes Wright's view of social reality. Here is the concept of the individual versus group formalized in a trial which states that the two contending litigants are the individual and the group. Ross is crushed in the process and represents all of those who were crushed previously in the autobiographical universe by the various looming institutions which populate it:

His hands shook. He held onto the edge of the table to keep on his feet. His personality, his sense of himself, had been obliterated. Yet he could not have been so humbled unless he had shared and accepted the vision that had crushed him, the common vision that bound us all together. (p. 124)

Once again Wright survives annihilation. On the other hand, the trial is significant because it contains the outline of what would become an official nightmare of American culture in the age of McCarthyism and the Cold War—the nightmare of the individual's loss of self and annihilation by "the Party." Certainly the Communist Party offered a convenient target for working out deep social tensions over the relationship between individual and group.

As the autobiography itself reveals, the tensions dramatized in Ross's trial—and some of those dramatized in the McCarthy trials as well—must be seen as the tip of an iceberg. Beneath them are the South, the family, and many other social institutions, all on trial by proxy.[15] In such a context, the concept of "personality" which Wright uses with stubborn insistence emerges as an attempt to build a bulwark against the rising tides of massification and loss of identity, a bulwark whose blueprint was signed by the

Chicago sociologists themselves. It is in this regard that Wright's debt to the Chicago School is most evident. Clearly related to the dichotomy which structures the narrative into cyclical and ever larger clashes between individual and group, the two categories of "personality" and "environment" theoretically formalize the distinction. The concepts allow Wright to confront the threats posed to the individual by the rural racist environment in the South and by the urban massified environment in the North. Through the use of these categories Wright tried to become the sociologist of his own life:

> I hungered for a grasp of the framework of contemporary living, for a knowledge of the forms of life about me, for eyes to see the bony structures of personality, for theories to light up the shadows of conduct. (p. 26)

In sociology, more than in any other discipline, Richard Wright found the means to anchor his creative effort to the depths of social life.

II

In the first part of this essay one aspect of the relationship between sociology and literature has emerged: first, in the common assumptions underlying *The Polish Peasant* and Wright's autobiography; secondly, in the analogous way of structuring the text from family to community to immigration to reorganization; finally, in the use of similar categories as explanatory tools for the reality thus constructed. A different aspect of the parallel enterprise of sociology and literature stems more directly from the methodology which the Chicago sociologists developed. These new scientists of society provided Wright with the conceptualization of two important points of view: the informant and the participant-observer. The notion of the "informant" identifies the individual as a meaningful unit and transforms autobiography from a religious-confessional document into a sociological one. At the same time, the notion of "participant-observer" identifies the social scene as a complex reality which can be properly captured only from within—as experienced by participants or through the total immersion of a sociologist. The sociological products of these two notions are well illustrated in the anthology *The Social Fabric of the Metropolis: Contributions of the Chicago School of Urban Sociology*.[16] The essays in this anthology move easily from a neo-Dickensian description of Chicago, to a Taxi-Dance hall, to a Street Gang, etc. Through the voices of different informants, a number of social worlds are explored with the depth that only an insider can have.

The concept of informant articulates and organizes Wright's life-story into a representative case study. The concept of participant-observer, with its implications of both being part of and observing a social reality, allows the literization of its most significant internal aspects. The development of the concept of informant, the use of personal documents and life-stories in the field of social sciences, owe much to Thomas and Znaniecki's study *The Polish Peasant*. Both sociologists had strong backgrounds in literary study and an equally strong determination to deal not only with objective social structures but with subjective reality as well. Thomas and Znaniecki had found in letters and life-stories of Polish immigrants important sources for their study. The methodological result was

> ... a synthesis of the anthropologist's or ethnographer's participant observations, the case study method of the social worker, and the content analysis procedures of the traditional humanistic disciplines.[17]

Not only Thomas and Znaniecki, but many other Chicago sociologists as well, eagerly found in personal documents a power of generalization which no statistical set of data could match, a power derived from the concreteness of the specific flesh-and-bone individual as opposed to the more general but abstract statistical picture:

> If we knew the full life-history of a single individual in his social setting, we would probably know most of what is worth knowing about social life and human nature![18]

Richard Wright's mentor and guide through the shelves of sociological writings, the Chicago sociologist Louis Wirth, expressed with these words the crucial idea of the informant as a "writer" and of the writer as "informant."[19]

By deciding to write his own autobiography, Wright took up the challenge of the sociologist. Writing himself into a casestudy, Wright became the informant of himself as a Black youth growing up in the South and emigrating to Chicago. Through the concept of informant Wright articulated the story of the self in search of meaning and order. At the same time, he could make that story representative both of the specific experiences of Black people and of the more general facts of "social life" and "human nature."

Wright's attempt to draw a series of biographical sketches of "Negro Communists" well epitomizes his ultimate objective in becoming his own informant, sociologist, historian, and anthropologist. Ross's lifestory was to be the first one:

> Southern-born, he had migrated north and his life reflected the crude hopes and frustrations of the peasant in the city. Distrustful but aggressive, he was a bundle of the weaknesses and virtues of a man living on the margin of a culture. I felt that if I could get his story I would make known some of the difficulties inherent in adjustment of a folk people to an urban environment; I would make his life more intelligible to others than it was to himself. I would reclaim his disordered days and cast them into a form that people could grasp, see, understand and accept. (pp. 78-79)

Wright's view of Ross's life-story contains both the sociological idea of the individual as "typical," as representative of a group and of its experiences, and the literary idea of narration as a search for order and meaning. Clearly sharing with Louis Wirth a belief that all of the significant aspects of a society merge in the individual's life-story, Wright eventually discovered in his own life-story all the tiles of the mosaic that he was trying to compose. Furthermore, by becoming his own informant rather than the recorder of other people's life-stories, he could portray the development of his own consciousness:

> A dim notion of what life meant to a Negro in America was coming to consciousness in me .... I sensed that Negro life was a sprawling land of unconscious suffering, and there were but few Negroes who knew the meaning of their lives, who could tell their story. (p. 7)

In these words, from *American Hunger,* Wright's three-fold role as informant, participant-observer, and sociologist become unmistakably connected by a hyperbolic-looking curve reaching into the height of consciousness and meaning. As an informant, Wright can tell his own story as "few" Blacks can; as a participant-observer, he can depict "the sprawling land of unconscious suffering" of Black life; finally, as a sociologist—through the lens of sociological consciousness—he can give meaning to his own and to Black people's life-stories.

As a participant-observer, Wright described, in some of the best pasages of his autobiography, the social worlds in which he found himself immersed along the path of his narrative. These passages reveal the insight of the informant which the Chicago sociologists had postulated; at the same time, Wright's passages—unlike the sociologists'—are endowed with a language which closely captures speech, and are unified by the overall plot. In the role of participant-observer, Wright produces a remarkable sketch in *Black Boy* of the street-gang language and psychology:

> I would stumble upon one or more of the gang loitering at a corner, standing in a field, or sitting upon the steps of somebody's house.
> "Hey." Timidly.
> "You eat yet?" Uneasily trying to make conversation.
> "Yeah, man. I done really fed my face." Casually.
> "I had cabbage and potatoes." Confidently.
> "I had buttermilk and black-eyed peas." Meekly informational.

And the talk would weave, roll, surge, veer, swell .... The culture of one household
was thus transmitted to another black household, and folk tradition was handed from
group to group. (pp. 88-92)

In this conversation Wright depicts what Louis Wirth had called the "cultural milieu" of
the street gang, its "moral and social codes."[20] It is Richard the gang-boy who, through
his special gift for words, captures the ocean-like quality of the conversation; at the
same time, it is Wright the sociologist who subtitles it, interprets it, stage-directs it, but
most importantly distances himself in order to describe it.

While sharing with many Chicago sociologists a dislike for the uniformity of the
rural world, Wright was less optimistic in viewing the urban environment as a "new
way of life."[21] Once more as a participant-observer he described the waitresses with
whom he worked in Chicago: "I learned about their tawdry dreams, their simple hopes,
their home lives, their fear of feeling anything deeply, their sex problems, their
husbands" (p. 12). For Wright the "urbanism" which the waitresses represent is a
despicable world filled with "radios, cars, and a thousand other trinkets ... the trash of
life .... The words of their souls were the syllables of popular songs" (p. 14) —the
world of mass consumerism.

Again as a participant-observer, Wright describes the other pole of "urbanism" which
those who are excluded from the "trash of life" represent: the world of juvenile
delinquents. Chicago sociologists heavily focused on this phenomenon and on its
correlation with mass migration, social contact, and cultural transition. This is how
Wright, who worked at the Chicago South Side Boy's Club, describes in *American
Hunger* the world of juvenile delinquents:

> Each day black boys between the age of eight and twenty-five came to swim, draw, and
> read. They were a wild and homeless lot, culturally lost, spiritually disinherited,
> candidates for the clinics, morgues, prisons, reformatories, and the electric chair of the
> state's death house. For hours I listened to their talk of planes, women, guns, politics,
> and crime. Their figures of speech were as forceful and colorful as any ever used by
> English-speaking people. (p. 88)

In the role of participant-observer, Wright thus capitalizes on his first-hand experiences
in different social realities. The ability to encompass many social and cultural
experiences had once been the prerogative of the Picaro, the literary archetype who
symbolized the individual's freedom from social and cultural ties. Was this prerogative
now becoming embodied in a sociological archetype—the immigrant? Having moved
away, the immigrant can look back from a distance while at the same time still being
part of what he is observing. As a participant-observer Wright became precisely this
archetype: the immigrant-Picaro whose story confirms the achieved freedom from
cultural and social strings.

III

> My problem was here, here with me, here in this room, and I would solve it here alone
> or not at all .... I would hurl words into this darkness and wait for an echo, and if an
> echo sounded, no matter how faintly, I would send other words to tell, to march, to
> fight, to create.[22]

A belated product of the 1930's sociological imagination, *Black Boy* and *American
Hunger* reveal some important aspects of the relationship between literature and
sociology. Structured around the paradigm "individual versus group," Richard Wright's
autobiography clearly shares with the Chicago urban sociologists a way of constructing
reality into an opposition of individual on the one side and primary groups, community,
culture, and institutions on the other. With the strength of such a construct, Wright
infused a classical form—the ex-slave narrative—with a most modern perception:
rather than traveling from bondage to freedom, Wright's autobiographical persona is
condemned to travel from bondage to bondage forever, never to reach freedom. With
the weakness of such construct, Wright committed the sociological fallacy of separating
the individual—in this case himself—from his institutions, culture, environment, in

order to show their effect on his personality. In the process, the subjective possibility for change, which the social reality as a relationship between social beings encompasses, became lost. Wright's last words are uttered in the emptiness of his total isolation, one from which he hoped to cause change and achieve self-expression. Unfortunately, those words turned out to be not the call "to fight" that Wright had envisaged, but the testament of the 1930s dying movement.

NOTES

[1]Not only the literature of the 1930s benefited from its affair with sociology. Sociologists as well profited from this infatuation as the literary titles of their monographs often indicated: *The Hobo, The Gang, The Ghetto, The Strike, The Gold Coast and the Slum, The Jack-Roller, Brothers in Crime, Delinquent Boys.* Their use of language is often literary—the imagery, metaphors, hyperboles of their descriptions; they were also concerned with narrative techniques, point of view, and first person accounts.

[2]All references in the text are to *Black Boy: A Record of Childhood and Youth* (New York: Harper and Row, 1966) and to *American Hunger* (New York: Harper and Row, 1983). *Black Boy* and *American Hunger* were originally composed as part of a single manuscript—to be called "American Hunger"—which Wright completed in 1943. Following the suggestion of his publisher, Wright agreed to publish the first part as a separate text. The parts dealing with his experience in the Communist Party came out separately in two installments in the *Atlantic Monthly*, a few months later the well known "I Tried to Be a Communist" appeared. If one excludes Constance Webb's limited edition of 1946, it was not until *1977* that the second part was published integrally. [For diverging opinions on the reasons for such a choice see Michel Fabre, *The Unfinished Quest of Richard Wright*, (New York: Morrow, 1973), pp. 254-56; John M. Reilly, "The Self-Creation of the Intellectual: *American Hunger* and *Black Power*," in *Critical Essays on Richard Wright*, ed. Yoshinobu Hakutani, (Boston: G.K. Hall, 1982), pp. 213-14; Robert Kirsch, *Los Angeles Times*, 29 May 1977, pp. 1, 71; Darryl Pinckney, *Village Voice*, 4 July *1977*, pp. 80-82; and Bruno Cartosio, "Due scrittori afroamericani: Richard Wright e Ralph Ellison," *Studi americani*, 15 (1971), 395-431.] Most importantly for us here, Richard Wright composed the two parts as one text. Since the structure and the movement of the autobiography are central to our discussion, it is methodologically crucial to consider the two parts in their aesthetic and dialectical unity, or dis-unity. As Cartosio has noted, by reintegrating the text one can also notice the remarkable parallelism between the autobiography and *Native Son*. It is, in fact, in the last part of both texts that the equilibrium between narration and commentary gives way to a "didactical-moralistic anxiety" beneath which lay poorly hidden the unresolved contradictions of a whole generation.

[3]The most complete account of such a relationship remains Fabre's *The Unfinished Quest*. References can also be found in Edward Margolies, *The Art of Richard Wright* (Carbondale, Illinois: University of Southern Illinois Press, 1969), p. 11; Dan McCall, *The Example of Richard Wright* (New York: Harcourt, Brace, 1969), p. 194; John A. Williams, The *Most Native of Sons* (New York: Doubleday, 1970), p. 82; Keneth Kinnamon, *The Emergence of Richard Wright: A Study in Literature and Society* (Urbana, Illinois: University of Illinois Press, 1972), pp. 196-97; Robert Felgar, *Richard Wright* (Boston: Twayne, 1980), pp. 39-40, 138; and Addison Gayle, *Richard Wright: Ordeal of a Native Son* (New York: Anchor Press, 1980), pp. 148 ff.

[4]Robert Bone, "Richard Wright and the Chicago Renaissance," forthcoming in *Afro-American Literature: Reconstruction of a Literary History*, eds. John M. Reilly and Robert B. Stepto, (New York: Modern Language Association).

[5]Bone, pp. 24-25.

[6]John M. Reilly, "Richard Wright Preaches the Nation: *12 Million Black Voices*," *Black American Literature Forum*, 16 (Fall 1982), 116-19.

[7]Reilly, "Richard Wright," 116, 117.

[8]John McCluskey, Jr., "Two Steppin': Richard Wright's Encounter with Blue Jazz," *American Literature*, 55 (1983), 332-44.

[9]McCluskey, pp. 333, 336, 338, 343. McCluskey is not the only one who has pointed out such contradictions, although his is one of the most insightful discussions on this

point. Other illuminating remarks can be found in Charles T. Davis, "From Experience to Eloquence: Richard Wright's *Black Boy* as Art," in *Chants of Saints: A Gathering of Afro-American Literature, Art and Scholarship,* eds. Michael Harper and Robert Stepto, (Urbana, Illinois: University of Illinois Press, 1979), pp. 428-29; Houston A. Baker, Jr., "Racial Wisdom and Richard Wright's *Native Son,*" in Hakutani's *Critical Essays,* pp. 215 ff; Nina Kressner Cobb, "Richard Wright and the Third World," *Critical Essays,* pp. 230 ff. Among the recently published discussions on *Black Boy* and *American Hunger,* I found particularly inspiring Reilly's "The Self Creation of the Intellectual," and Donald B. Gibson's "Richard Wright: Aspects of his Afro-American Literary Relations," both in *Critical Essays.* Also inspiring is Robert J. Butler's "The Quest for Pure Motion in Richard Wright's *Black Boy,*" *MELUS,* 10 (Fall 1983), 5-17.
[10]Günter H. Lenz, "Southern Exposures: The Urban Experience and the Reconstruction of Black Folk Culture and Community in the Works of Richard Wright and Zora Neale Hurston," *New York Folklore,* 7 (Summer 1981), 3-39.
[11]Lenz, pp. 12, 18, 21.
[12]Cited in Robert Park, "Sociological Methods of W.G. Sumner, and W.I. Thomas and F. Znaniecki," in *Methods in Social Science. A Case Book,* ed. S. Rice, (Chicago: University of Chicago Press, 1931), p. 166. Due to the time and space limits imposed upon this essay, I sacrificed in part the discussion of the Chicago School of Urban Sociology, a discussion which deserves far more attention. I often refer to the Chicago School as if it were a homogeneous entity, when, in fact, the group included as many theories and methodologies as individuals; it refers also to this intellectual school as if it were identifiable with the 1930s, when, in fact, by that time a "second generation" had already taken over. As it will soon become clear, the sociological study from which I largely draw is W.I. Thomas and F. Znaniecki, *The Polish Peasant in Europe and America,* 5 vols. (Chicago: University of Chicago Press, 1918-1920). Thomas did not belong to the second generation of sociologists, those with whom Richard Wright might have been more easily acquainted. My apology for not emphasizing more those sociologists which we know Wright had read (see note 18) is twofold: first, I was not tracing the lost map of Wright's sociological readings through the extant fragments scattered in his works; secondly, as my reading of Chicago sociologists progressed, I noticed that the focus of my concern—structure, concepts, point of view—found in *The Polish Peasant* unified within a single text many aspects of Wright's sociological constructs.
[13]Morris Janowitz, ed., Introd., *On Social Organization and Social Personality,* by W.I. Thomas (Chicago: University of Chicago Press, 1969), p. xxxv.
[14]Park, p. 163.
[15]Through a collective process of projection the Communist Party became a symbol for the individual's loss of identity, for the fear of losing oneself in a changed social reality. A desired and increasingly unattainable goal—one's social identity as part of a community, a culture, a group—was turned into an undesirable one. The self as a social being became the enemy to be fought for the survival of the individual being. As in a modern version of the passion plays, the Communist Party was made to bear the cross for a society moving away from culture and community and into mass civilization.
[16]James F. Short, ed., Introd., *The Social Fabric of the Metropolis: Contributions of the Chicago School Of Urban Sociology* (Chicago: University of Chicago Press, 1971), p. xi-xivi.
[17]Janowitz, p. xxiii.
[18]Louis Wirth, *The Ghetto* (Chicago: University of Chicago Press, 1928), p. 287.
[19]Cf. Fabre, *The Unfinished Quest;* Fabre provides a wealth of details on Wright's friendship with Louis Wirth—Mary Wirth's role as social worker of the Wright's household, Wright's first readings of sociology, his later collaboration with Horace Cayton and St. Clair Drake on their *Black Metropolis* (New York: Harcourt, Brace, 1945) and on his own *12 Million Black Voices* (New York: Arno, 1941). Cfr. Fabre, pp. 232-34, 293-402, 201, 249, 267. Further information on the specific authors studied by Wright can be found in his prefaces to *Black Metropolis,* pp. xviii-xix and to *12 Million Black Voices,* pp. xix-xix.
[20]Louis Wirth, *On Cities and Social Life,* ed. A. Reiss (Chicago: University of Chicago Press, 1964), pp. 234-37.

[21]Louis Wirth, "Urbanism as a Way of Life," in *Louis Wirth: On Cities and Social Life,* (Chicago: University of Chicago Press, 1964), pp. 60-83.
[22]Wright, *American Hunger,* pp. 134-35.
The title of this article is derived from a statement by Irving Howe. Howe believed that "The sociology of his [Wright's] existence formed a constant pressure on his literary work, and not merely in the way this might be true for any writer, but with a pain and ferocity that nothing could remove." From Howe's "Black Boys and Native Sons" reprinted in Critical Essays on Richard Wright, *p. 40.
Special thanks to Werner Sollors whose seminar at Columbia University on kinship and ethnicity inspired this research.*

From *MELUS* 12 (Summer 1985), 25-43.

Introduction to the HarperPerennial Edition of *Black Boy (American Hunger)*

Jerry W. Ward, Jr.

The first edition of *Black Boy* (1945) is a classic example of American autobiography, a subtly crafted narrative of a young man's coming of age in the United States. For slightly more than three decades, this version of Richard Wright's story of the journey from innocence to experience in the Jim Crow South stood as tragic witness to the collective, as well as the individualized, realities of movement from childhood to manhood in a particular time and place. One could question the reliability of Wright's memory, try to discriminate between fiction and fact in the densely woven texture of the autobiography, or inquire why Wright himself never capitulated to the dehumanizing norms of early twentieth-century Southern culture. It was impossible to deny, however, that *Black Boy* was a work of stunning imagination and mythic power; here was a book that nicely blended the meaning, the challenge, and the significance of being Southern, black, and male in America.

Readers were confronted with a different challenge when *American Hunger*, the unused portion of Wright's original manuscript of his autobiography, was published in 1977. *Black Boy* has provided a certain pleasure of the text for readers, prior to the turbulent 1960s, who tended to be less than thorough in analyzing the institutionalized nature of racism in the United States. Migration to the North was accepted as an essential prelude to black people's enjoying the full blessings of liberty and citizenship; Wright's story of his life up to his leaving Memphis for Chicago reinforced belief that the South was a socially unreconstructed region where blacks who asserted their basic human rights invited retribution or death. *American Hunger* suggested that what Wright had all along envisioned was certainly a fuller depiction of his American education. His "hazy notion that life could be lived with dignity, that the personalities of others should not be violated, that men should be able to confront other men without fear or shame" in the North was swiftly transformed by the urban environment into clear ideas about the pervasive constrictions placed on authentic human freedom in the North as well as in the South. That such barriers were different in kind and degree did matter. Nevertheless, what mattered more was Wright's recognition that the Promised Land in America was nowhere. The posthumously published segment of Wright's autobiography exposed the deepest ironies of equality in America.

In short, Wright's early experiences in the North were variations, within a bleak urban setting, of what had happened to him in the South. *Black Boy* documented in vivid and painful detail Wright's southern education from the age of four to that day in 1927 when he boarded a north-bound train "without a qualm, without a single backward glance." Readers who were not aware that other fragments of Wright's autobiography had been published prior to 1977 might assume that his reflection on childhood and youth ended with hope and promise. They could not know until the unexpurgated edition was published that Wright really ended his reflections on the South with a terse indictment: "This was the culture from which I sprang. This was the terror from which I fled." (303)

The autobiographical inscription of the relations between a sensitive, intelligent, spiritually hungry native son and a racist social order (in the South) had ended textually (in 1945) with the prospect that perhaps human beings could attain "some redeeming meaning for their having struggled and suffered here beneath the stars." *Black Boy*, so much in the tradition of the slave narrative, belonged also, as Ralph Ellison discerned in one of the earliest reviews, to the tradition of the blues. It was an elegant gesture of testifying "both [to] the agony of life and the possibility of conquering it through sheer toughness of spirit." Yet *American Hunger*, the continuation of Wright's autobiography, seemed to be a lamentation, an extended riff on his hazy notion that wholeness and decency and redemption lay up North. The analytic imagination that informed the Southern portion of Wright's life experience itself was transformed from a blues to a jazz mode in *American Hunger*. In that sense, readers—regardless of ethnic or racial identity—who might have felt free to cast aspersions on the South were compelled to inspect the dirty laundry of race, oppression, and class in the North.

The publication of Wright's autobiography in its entirety for the first time in October 1991 by the Library of America, despite an understandable reluctance to claim that the meaning of his story is radically changed, did make possible greater access to Wright's intention in creating autobiography and extended the possibilities of how one reads the text. This is to say, the unexpurgated text provides grounds for the claim that Wright originally wanted less to shape from his life a representative myth of growing up Southern than an American story which speaks to "the hunger for life that gnaws in us all, to keep alive in our hearts a sense of the inexpressibly human." Such a story, if it were to be an adequate critique of individuality and ethnicity, required the wholeness of Wright's southern and northern experiences. Reading the story whole (or maybe holistically), we have a stronger appreciation of the artistry in Wright's reflective movement from homegrown optimism to tested knowledge. The facts of publishing history that led to a truncated edition of Wright's autobiography being issued in 1945 is of greater interest to literary scholars than to common readers, but the restored text provides for a new opportunity to explore the authority of Wright's confirming the referentiality of autobiography, the complex contract to be maintained between autobiographer and reader. As readers, we become more aware of Wright's position and our positioning ourselves with reference to his text.

Wright's position as writer and thinker, of course, can be described briefly by recalling salient features of his life and works. Born on September 4, 1908, on a Mississippi plantation some twenty miles from Natchez, Richard Wright was driven by the desire to satisfy hunger until his death in the Eugene Gibez Clinic (Paris) on November 28, 1960. During his boyhood, Wright described his hunger as physical, especially after his father deserted the family. The absence of a father and of food became interchangeable for the young boy. As a young man reflecting on black childhood and youth in the South, Wright exposed this wound: "As the days slid past the image of my father became associated with my pangs of hunger, and whenever I felt hunger I thought of him with a deep biological bitterness." (18) Even after Wright achieved success as a writer, he was subject to the idea and the effect of abstract hunger. It became pervasive.

It could not be satisfied by the success of *Uncle Tom's Children* (1938), the fame and financial security that followed the publication of *Native Son* (1940), nor the impact of *Black Boy* that made Wright something of a spokesman for an entire generation of black Americans. In fact, material success only served to intensify Wright's awareness that hunger of the spirit is implacable. He could write passionately, eloquently, about the meaning of suffering in the lives of the oppressed and exploited people. He had the authority of his own experiences, and he seemed to have felt the necessity of expressing suffering as if it were personal. There is no question that Wright was sincere in his efforts to alert the world to the deepest feelings of people shaped or mangled by oppression. Their feelings dovetailed so neatly with his own. What is at issue in our efforts to understand Richard Wright is how the consciousness of a man who craves the unattainable makes his vision particular and often reflective of the visions of others.

In the books that followed *Black Boy*, Wright yearned for authority and freedom of an unusual kind. Like Cross Damon, the hero of *The Outsider* (1953), Wright longed to be existentially free, ultimately responsible to the "self" he endeavored to create through the act of writing. If one posits that this novel involves intellectual autobiography, the book gives us keys for explaining the intrusive "self" in Wright's later works. Whether he was analyzing the independence movement in Africa (*Black Power*, 1945), reporting on the Bandung Conference (*The Color Curtain*, 1956), or examining the intricacies of a culture (*Pagan Spain*, 1957), Wright was never the distanced observer. He was essentially the brother in suffering, the brother who had the strength to speak. The voice in *White Man, Listen!* (1957) is not that of victimized millions but rather that of the man who feels outraged as he beholds the world's injustice and disorder. In *The Long Dream* (1958), the last book published before his death, Wright sought to create in Rex "Fishbelly" Tucker a childhood and youth that fate had denied him. Wright's work was strongly determined by autobiographical impulses. *Black Boy (American Hunger)* permits us to grasp afresh why Wright's life as a wronged human being was so powerful a stimulus for creative work.

Recreating and inscribing himself in a particularized moment of American history from angles available to an African American male, Wright did not intend, as those who would censor his autobiography contend, to corrupt, scandalize, or blaspheme. On the contrary, his autobiography is designed to illuminate how obscene was denial of access to full participation in the democratic process by law, custom, and the practice of race. *Black Boy (American Hunger)* embodies its own defense as a classic response to the call of the most sacred American principles regarding human rights. The primal causes in the making of this autobiography were Wright's analytic brilliance and the cultivated hell the United States was for black Americans between 1900 and 1945. Far from being topical, Wright's autobiography transcends the limits of simplistic correspondence between historical fact and narration to achieve a necessary language for projecting the ambiguities of human existence that manifest themselves in the rhetoric of dream and nightmare, in what can be perceived and in what is metaphysical. The necessary language assumes special importance in black autobiography of the twentieth century, because the autobiographical "selves" often think it obligatory to guard against "enslavement" by the very medium used to tell a free story.

Black Boy (American Hunger) does explain the universal potentials of the person who is socialized to be black and male in an oppressive society. Richard Wright selected the symbolic moments that he deemed most representative of his own life experiences from a broad range. The text establishes the probability that, as autobiographical act, it spoke specifically for Wright. And Wright spoke specifically, as he did in *12 Million Black Voices* (1941) for a very distinct community, a group that knew intimately "Southern Night," the title Wright chose for the first portion of his autobiographical manuscript, and "The Horror and the Glory," the paradoxical title of the second portion. One of the special qualities of *Black Boy (American Hunger)* is its masterful exploitation of what Bakhtin named "the dialogical imperative" and of what many black Americans would identify as "signifying." Indeed, the significance of the autobiography as a situating of the self in American history (and by extension, situating other Americans) may change according to a reader's affinities, social experiences, associations, and knowledge of literary conventions. The autobiography's meanings, on the other hand, remains fixed.

As autobiography, Wright's text demands attention to matters of a decidedly flexible genre and to the facts of race and gender at the time the manuscript was written. To be inattentive to the material complexity in which the book was formed would only conceal the dynamics of those historical, psychological, and intellectual processes that informed its production and transmission. It is precisely the facts of race and gender in the United States that expose the literary qualities of a work that emerged from a definite socio-historical matrix. The task requires that we know American history in the multicultural sense, and we must also know not to confuse literature with social documents, or at least how to come to grips with a blurred genre.

Autobiography is not sociology, however rich its sociological implications might be. Thus, the opening paragraph of "Southern Night" begins with a conflict of desires that deeply frustrates the four-year-old self Wright recalls. The language draws attention to what might traditionally and uncritically be accepted as the masculine desire to run, play, and shout. Such desire is frustrated by the feminine admonition (scolding) to "make no noise," to be still, to not touch—the cliché of woman's guardianship of cultural behavior is presented as the source of anger, fretfulness, and impatience. Using casual references to a commonplace exchange between mother and child, Wright entices us into a web of gendered relations that are powerfully symbolic in the subtext of the autobiography. This is the beginning of what we might call Wright's engendered vision, or the male child's recognition of woman's dominance; it induces fear. By the end of "The Horror and the Glory," it is clear that the matured, male self recognizes that race and society cooperate to displace gender and, to a certain extent, to reverse its discursive location. That is to say, Wright came to understand that the power to structure gender (male and female) in early twentieth-century America seemed to be an exclusive privilege of certain white males. The black boy is forever denied the achievement of manhood, so defined. The black male is to be made a permanent child and denigrated into the posture of the stereotyped female—victim, umempowered! The subversive literary force of *Black Boy (American Hunger)*, which deserves deeper investigation, is contained in the book's ultimate explanation of how gendering makes whites "as miserable as their black victims" and makes some men as miserable as women. It matters greatly that Wright uses fused gender and race themes in structuring his autobiography, because he thus projects a strong cultural consciousness of how best to transform the forces of society into the forceful shape of literature.

Wright makes splendid use of the abused male prototype that is so well presented in Frederick Douglass's 1845 *Narrative*. Playing subject to his own objectification, such a narrator has the option of accommodating oppression, becoming the destructive and self-destructive rebel, or resisting, through a spiraling quest for the safe space where integrity, balance, and wholeness might be achieved. For Douglass and for Wright, the space is that which can be opened by literacy. It might be noted, for example, that the protagonist Bigger Thomas in Wright's *Native Son* becomes destructive and self-destructive in part because he lacks a certain control of language. By contrast, what we find in *Black Boy (American Hunger)* is one man's record, partially authentic and partially fictional, of how literacy enables one to emerge from harrowing experiences with integrity and balance intact. The achievement is also based on self-control and discipline and the peculiar qualities of hunger broadly understood. A man possessing the power of language cannot be a hapless victim.

The graphic portrait of the abused male as a young man details something of Wright's predisposition toward individualism, self-reliance, and nonconformity. His growth experiences foretoken the need for self-discovery, about himself as the representative voice of black youths, and about the society he inhabited. It can be argued that as an artist Wright highlighted the negativity of accommodating and becoming in order to strengthen the act of transcending resistance that *Black Boy (American Hunger)* is.

The book is a record of Wright's consummate exploitation of outsideness, his prowess in manipulating language and its codes. Part of his success is demonstrated by his ability to subvert the discourse of the dominant culture and bring it under the terms of his own control. Nowhere is this clearer then in his strategy for borrowing books from the segregated public library in Memphis. Not only does he forge (the dual meaning seems intended) his own notes to borrow the books, but he names himself "nigger" to insure his success.

> That afternoon I addressed myself to forging a note. Now, what were the names of books written by H. L. Mencken? I did not know any of them. I finally wrote what I thought would be a foolproof note: *Dear Madam: Will you please let this nigger boy*—I used the word "nigger" to make the librarian feel I could not possibly be the author of the note—*have some books by H. L. Mencken?* I forged the white man's name. (291)

Wright ensured that readers could not avoid confronting what is endemic in a closed society, for he re-enacts a situation quite familiar in a slave narrative, borrowing a generic convention that tells in brief compass the profound insights and aspirations of the oppressed. What Wright valorizes is the possibility of such narration to name the lie upon which American society has historically fed: the beautiful and truly noble democratic theories of life, liberty, and the pursuit of happiness. The reality for a substantial number of Americans has been death, unfreedom, and the flight from despair. *Black Boy (American Hunger)* is to some degree, then, an accounting for this reality, a critique of American optimism betrayed. It deconstructs the myth.

The continuing value of *Black Boy (American Hunger)* is located in its providing engaging ways for us to use autobiography to think about how our lives are shaped by law and custom, by ethnic encounters and intraracial negotiations, by desire and psychological defeat and intrepidity. The book challenges our stereotypical thinking about South and North; it questions the profit of using the symbolic geographical designations loosely. In Part I, "Southern Night" (Chapters I-XIV), the autobiographical self learns that his people "grope at noon-day as in the night," believing in a better world up North. In Part II, "The Horror and the Glory" (Chapters XV-XX), Northern exposure results in the self's "knowing that all I possessed were words and a dim knowledge that my country had shown me no examples of how to live a human life." (452) There is no hiding place in regional differences. But what touches us most deeply as readers is the autobiography's concluding words:

> I would hurl words into this darkness and wait for an echo, and if an echo sounded, no matter how faintly, I would send other words to tell, to march, to fight, to create a sense of the hunger for life that gnaws in us all, to keep alive in our hearts a sense of the inexpressibly human. (453)

In the humanistic affirmation of such a conclusion is a foreshadowing of the charge that would come several decades later to ask not what our country could do for us, but rather what we might do for our country. Read carefully as an affirmative literary work of art, *Black Boy (American Hunger)* serves a liberating function: It provides the opportunity to remember and to be renewed.

From the HarperPerennial edition of *Black Boy (American Hunger)* (New York: 1993), xi-xxi.

The Outsider (1953)

Review of *The Outsider*

Orville Prescott

It is thirteen years since the publication of Richard Wright's famous novel, "Native Son," and eight since that of his even more celebrated autobiography, "Black Boy." Both those books were bitterly angry, fiercely eloquent denunciations of the racial discriminations and social and economic pressures that condition the lives of Negroes. And both were so powerfully written that they established Mr. Wright as the leading American Negro writer of his generation. His new novel, his first book since "Black Boy," is published today.

"The Outsider" marks a complete reversal in the direction of Mr. Wright's literary career. It is just as preoccupied with violence as the earlier books, just as harshly effective in its melodrama and its narrative impact. But the first two books were concentrated on the plight of the Negro and they interpreted it in terms of the sins of society, emphasizing the dominant power of environment in the tradition of literary naturalism. "The Outsider" has a Negro for its hero; but it is not primarily his plight as a Negro, but as a thinking, questioning man in the perplexing twentieth century that concerns Mr. Wright. And instead of a realistic sociological document he has written a philosophical novel, its ideas dramatized by improbable coincidences and symbolical characters. "The Outsider" has the plot interest of a rousing murder story, and its characters are as unreal as they are in most murder stories. And because of their unreality "The Outsider" seems artificial and lacks the persuasive impact that only fully individualized characters can give to fiction. But this partial fictional failure is compensated for to some extent by the interest of Mr. Wright's ideas.

This is the story of Cross Damon, a Negro mail sorter on the night shift in a South Chicago post office. Cross was consumed with despair, guilt, shame and self-loathing, trying to anesthetize his overpowering sense of dread with whisky. He was in debt. His mistress was pregnant and his wife, from whom he was separated, was threatening legal steps. So when Cross had a chance to let another man's body be mistaken for his in a subway wreck he never hesitated. He fled from all personal responsibility, feeling no obligations to his wife or children or mistress. And to make good his escape, he impulsively murdered his best friend.

It is one of the unbelievable things in "The Outsider" that Cross should act so suddenly and violently when he is presented as meditative, introspective, addicted to self-analysis and philosophical speculation. But Cross did not stop with one murder. In New York he murdered three more people! Cross' murders and his battle of wits with the District Attorney in his efforts to conceal his guilt make lively if incredible reading. But there are other factors in "The Outsider" that are of considerably more interest.

One of these is Cross' relations with several leaders of the Communist party and Cross' (for Mr. Wright's) analysis of the driving force behind communism as nothing except a lust for naked power. If power over the nation is a remote ambition, power over lesser members of the party is a present and delicious satisfaction. Idealistic talk about crusading for the working class is just hypocritical cant, which the Communist leaders don't believe themselves, Cross realized. Believing in no faith or ideals or ethical restraints, the Communists just want to reorganize the world with themselves in positions of power on top.

And Cross felt that he understood the Communists because he, too, believed in nothing. An outsider in American society because of his black skin, he was much more of an outsider because of his conviction that existence was senseless, that society had no moral claims upon him, that there were no divine or traditional or logical laws that applied to him. Cross believed that life was an incomprehensible disaster and human beings were "nothing in particular." So, if no ideas were necessary to justify his acts, he could kill impulsively to satisfy a passing whim or for his own convenience.

Cross had reached these nihilistic depths only after reading widely, particularly in several existentialist writers. He was a highly intelligent and widely informed man, but he used his intelligence and his information only to destroy himself and others. He despised the Communists for their cruelty and duplicity; but he could not see that if he despised such sins he ought logically to love kindness and honesty. He saw the confusion and suffering and fear of the modern world and the only step he could find to take was abdication from human responsibilities, failing to see that in times of change and crisis there is more need than ever for loyalty to responsibilities.

Toward the end of "The Outsider" Richard Wright has devoted a dozen pages to a speech in which Cross outlines his philosophy of negation and despair. It is a fair assumption, I think, that Mr. Wright deplores Cross' moral weakness and irrational behavior, but that he finds much cogency in Cross' philosophy. That men as brilliant as Richard Wright feel this way is one of the symptoms of the intellectual and moral crisis of our times.

From *The New York Times* (18 March, 1953), 29.

Review of *The Outsider*

Arna Bontemps

Richard Wright's boisterous new novel, "The Outsider" arrives like a band of brigands from the hills with horses snorting, guns blazing, bent on shooting up the town. It will be difficult to sleep through this new assault on our nerves . . . . Mr. Wright's novel reopens the intriguing and often disputed question of the Negro's place in contemporary American fiction.

In the past, of course, the central problem has been the stereotype, and perhaps it is wrong to place too much blame on the creative writer for the more or less standard portrayals of Negroes. We now know that there are minds that need such stereotypes for their comfort, that the root of the matter is a national attitude and that the recurrence of these over-simplified types cannot be honestly accounted for without reference to the sociological environment in which they exist.

In these terms it is possible to trace a sort of evolution of stereotypes. One recalls the shiftless, improvident, and musical predecessors of the slumshocked Depression folk. New phantoms glide in as the older ones glide out, and the otherwise serious reader is consoled without being convinced. Thus it was, no doubt, that the latest racial stereotype of the Negro as problem emerged.

This was the prevailing attitude when Ralph Ellison's "Invisible Man" appeared last year. It is the dominant one this year as Wright's first novel since "Native Son" comes up for attention.

When "Native Son" was published in 1940, Richard Wright was given the acclaim usually reserved for writers of major importance. Thousands of readers were shocked speechless by it, and most of them had not completely recovered five years later when "Black Boy" was published. By this time Wright's position in the ranks of American writers seemed clear. That this was the most impressive literary talent yet produced by Negro America was only rarely disputed. Interest in him as a personality was widespread.

The fact that he was largely self-educated and that he sprang from the sharecropping element in Mississippi served to point up the sharpness of his insights, the restlessness of his mind. While much of his strength was in his narrative power, much more was in the freshness of his vision, his daring exploration of a more or less taboo subject matter. Readers detected a correlation between his own odyssey and the world of fiction and semi-fiction which he created.

His first book, for example, "Uncle Tom's Children," reflected his discovery of Communism and his application of this dogma to the struggles of a sensitive migrant boy newly arrived in Chicago's black belt. "Native Son" came next, and again the writer's frame of reference was Communism; but equally apparent here was his preoccupation with another discipline quite new to him, sociology. "Black Boy" was written while Wright was learning about psychoanalysis and reflects an awakened interest in the subconscious roots of personality.

"The Outsider," his first book in eight years, and his first novel in thirteen, has now appeared, and almost the first observation one can make of it is that the black boy from Mississippi is still exploring. He has had a roll in the hay with existentialism of Sartre, and apparently he liked it. Wright went to France with his family in 1948. This would have been true to form for almost any American writer, ready to enjoy the fruits of two best sellers in a row. For the boy who had not been allowed to draw books from the main public library in Memphis, it was more than understandable.

But what would it do to him as a writer, some asked. Certainly the works on which his reputation was based had been sparked by anger, anger at indignities and racial discrimination. Would Wright be able to write at all away from the conditions that riled him? Months and years passed with no word from Wright. Nelson Algren charged him with powdering-out on his old stamping grounds, and Wright admitted to someone that he had café-itus. He was sitting and enjoying himself. He was reading and thinking. If he was writing, he was not telling anyone about it. And if this was the whole story, who could blame him?

Oddly enough, however, Richard Wright has gone back to the Chicago of his earlier books for the people and the situations of the novel he was writing meanwhile. Cross Damon is a postal clerk with a college education. Nervous, disturbed, drinking too much--even in the opinion of his hearty, non-critical buddies--he carries on his mind a problem which he cannot share. It is this problem which Wright, the good storyteller, sets out to unravel, and knowing Wright, one soon suspects that he knows where it is going. But one is mistaken.

Cross Damon's problem has nothing to do with color. This may surprise those who have been led to believe that all Negroes on the south side of Chicago eat, sleep, and breathe racial thoughts. Cross's difficulty is much older and even more puzzling. Its name is woman.

A more hag-ridden young man than the fretting and sweating hero of "The Outsider" is hard to imagine. His wife, mother, and sweetheart are closing in on him as the story opens. While refusing to divorce him, the wife from whom he is separated increases her demands beyond all conscience. The mother pounds at him for his drinking and wenching and his neglect of her. The sweetheart, whom he has gotten in trouble, reveals that she is two years younger than he had known and that makes him guilty of statutory rape in Illinois; she can send him to prison. Hopelessly trapped, Cross yields to his wife's blackmail and borrows $800 against his salary. He has boarded the subway with the cash in his pocket when his deliverance comes: a hideous wreck.

When he drags himself out of the mess of glass and steel and makes his way to the platform, nurses, doctors, and crowds of people are waiting. But Cross is all right. He can walk to the ambulance. The attention of the bystanders shifts back to the broken bodies still being rescued, and Cross remembers that he has left his overcoat in the wreckage. Well, never mind. And never mind about that ambulance. The attention of the bystanders shifts back to the broken stretcher on which a hopelessly mangled body is carried, he doesn't bother. He heads for a restaurant. He is at a table waiting for his order when the radio bulletins begin to come over the air. Soon the announcer is naming victims. Cross hears his own name called. That gives him the notion that is crucial to Wright's story. He will play dead. He will run away, take a new name, make a new life.

The second-half of the novel is the author's account of this strange flight by a man whose furies are many. Almost immediately Cross starts killing through fear, and a string of murders dot his trail thereafter. He meets a Communist and decides to join the Party as a means of giving himself some sort of identity, though he has no interest in its aims. He finds love as he rushes feverishly, but by then the end is clear. He can neither escape from himself nor from the society in which he lives.

Richard Wright's mind has always run to melodrama, and in "The Outsider" it does just that, but with him melodrama is a device rather than an end. His real concern is with such matters as his hero's awareness of "his body as an alien and despised object over which he had no power, a burden that was always cheating him of the fruits of his thoughts," with his version of the time-honored debate between body and soul, with "woman as body of woman," with guilt, with fear, and with the havoc that can follow them. Cross's dilemma in his story is that "each act of his consciousness sought to drag him back to what he wanted to flee." As Wright tells it, "The Outsider" makes gripping reading . . . .

From *Saturday Review* (28 March, 1953), 15-16.

Review of *The Outsider*

Lorraine Hansberry

Remembering Richard Wright's *Black Boy* and *Native Son*, certain sharp literary experiences yet hang in our minds. Experiences etched hard and true by the skill of the young Negro writer from the South. We remember, that whatever his weaknesses as a writer--he had power. He had the ability to scoop out the filth and sickness of white supremacy and present it to his readers with a stark and terrible realism. And we still remember how that power almost realized itself once when a strong hint of its mighty potential escaped in a short story called *Bright and Morning Star*.

It is 18 years since Richard Wright wrote that powerful little glimpse of the promise of dignity achieved through human struggle. And now Richard Wright has written *The Outsider*.

The Outsider is a story of sheer violence, death and disgusting spectacle, written by a man who has seemingly come to despise humanity. The hero is Cross Damon, a twenty-six year old Negro postal clerk on Chicago's Southside. For 45 pages Wright describes Damon's deterioration into a drunkard who leaves his wife and children, has an affair with a fifteen year old girl, murders one of his best friends, fakes a new identity and murders three other people and finally winds up being shot in the street by some grotesque characters who are supposed to be agents of the Communist Party. And that is the story.

Cross Damon is someone you will never meet on the Southside of Chicago or in Harlem. For if he is anything at all, he is the symbol of Wright's new philosophy--the glorification of--nothingness.

Richard Wright has been away from home for a long time. He has forgotten which of the streets of the Southside lie south of others, an insignificant error, except that it points up how much he has forgotten other things. In one passage he describes in great detail the contents of a garbage can. And a stark, real description it is. But nowhere in his four hundred pages can he bring himself to describe--say, the beauty or strength in the eyes of the working people of the Southside. It seems that he has forgotten.

As a propaganda piece for the enemies of the Negro people, of working people and of peace, *The Outsider* has already been saluted with a full page spread of praise by the *New York Times Sunday Book Supplement* (3-22-53). On the other hand it has been appointed to the trash category by the Negro newsweekly, *Jet* (3-20-53) which summed the book up simply and accurately, ". . . his almost psychopathic lust for violence gets the better of him in this second novel and his story becomes as completely phony and unreal as a cheap drugstore whodunit."

Such is the pronouncement on Negro America's onetime most promising writer. Richard Wright is correct in one thing: he is an outsider, he is outcast from his own people. He exalts brutality and nothingness; he negates the reality of our struggle for freedom and yet works energetically in behalf of our oppressors; he has lost his own dignity and destroyed his talent. He has lost the bright and morning star--but the Negro people have not.

From *Freedom* (April 1953), 7.

Richard Wright and the
French Existentialists

Michel Fabre

If Richard Wright's interest in existentialism was generally interpreted by American reviewers during his lifetime as a regrettable concession to literary fashion or an incongruous "roll in the hay" with "a philosophy little made to account for Negro life,"[1] critics and scholars have by now recognized and seriously examined the place and nature of the existentialist world view in Wright's novels, if not in his entire body of writings. For a time, there even existed a tendency to overemphasize the influence of the French school of existentialism, as opposed to the German school or preexistentialist writers like Dostoevsky and Nietzsche. Partly with the aim of restoring a proper balance, I have already attempted to document the actual contacts and collaboration—mostly political—between Wright and such leading French existentialist thinkers and writers as Sartre, Camus, and de Beauvoir, while providing a more precise, if more sobering, view of possible literary influences.[2] In this article, I will reconsider this relationship, focusing upon the convergence of philosophical views and their possible impact on the shaping of Wright's only existentialist novel. I will touch well upon the emotional and ideological coloring that the discovery of French existentialism imparted to Wright's "metaphysical decade," as we might call the years of meditation, pessimism, questioning, and self-examination that resulted in the writing and publication of *The Outsider*.

Wright's encounter with French existentialism took place in the mid-1940s at a crucial time in his career, when, having rejected Communism, if not Marxist perspectives and explanatory principles, he was for the first time without the sustenance and burden of an ideology. Also, in contemplating the possibilities left open for human values in the industrialized West at the close of World War II, he had become utterly disillusioned. His correspondence with Gertrude Stein, among others, documents his rejection of the consumerism and materialistic goals of American life—what Henry Miller described at the time as *The Air Conditioned Nightmare*. As Wright turned to Europe as a repository of humanistic concerns in the tradition of the Enlightenment, the pronouncements of the leading French intellectuals—existentialists like Sartre, Camus, and de Beauvoir (each of whom visited the United States on lecture tours and made public their reactions to the American and the European situation)—undoubtedly played a part in reinforcing Wright's own pessimistic leanings.

Wright's existentialism, however, should by no means be limited to his contacts with the French existentialist group from the mid-'40s to the mid-'50s. His interest in an existentialist world view both predates and postdates those contacts. On the one hand, works like *Native Son* and *Black Boy* already express an existential vision of life, couched in Dostoevskyan terms, which is closely linked with the oppressed, traumatic, and precarious aspects of the Afro-American experience. On the other hand, Wright's genuine interest in and knowledge of Kierkegaard and Heidegger, among the German school of existentialists, lasted throughout his later life and became just as integral a part of his *Weltanschuung* as Marxism. This paper does not deal, therefore, with all the dimensions of Wright's existential philosophy. It concentrates, rather, upon the period (roughly from 1946 to 1953) that saw the genesis of *The Outsider* in order to emphasize possible convergences between Wright's outlook and that of the French existentialists, when it does not prove possible to speak of outright influences.

Wright had three major general preoccupations at the time: how to inject a personal philosophy into Marxist theory; how to restore morality to political action; and how to save mankind from atomic destruction through the reactivation of humanistic values.

The publication of *Native Son* and its reception by the American left-wing and Communist intelligentsia had raised for Wright the problem of how far a Marxist writer could go in presenting a humanist, or personalized, version of his ideology. Aside from all the misunderstandings, the problem arose: did the writer who accepted Marxism enjoy the liberty of expounding a personalized philosophy? In 1937 Wright had outlined his literary program in "Blueprint for Negro Writing" in the CP-sponsored *New Challenge*, but he had not renounced ideas expressed in earlier pieces, often unpublished, like "Personalism," and he remained very much a humanist. A close analysis of Max's speech in *Native Son* reveals he is attempting to state certain ideas and concepts that are implicit in Marxist philosophy but that, since Marx and Lenin were more interested in politics and economics than in literature, were not previously stated in humanistic terms. Wright had perceived the important failure of Marxism to treat the human personality. In attempting to remedy that, revolutionary novelists like Gorki and Malraux were compelled to use a sort of mysticism for which they were faulted by Communist critics.

On another level, Wright's autobiographical essay "I Tried to Be a Communist" (1944) concerned, among other things, the morality of politics (i.e., the morality of American Communism) and how it was shaped by the nature of race relations in American society. Wright's exposure of its faults, which pointed to what was vital to the theory of (Marxist) action, was in fact an example of that morality in action. After the explosion of the atomic bomb in 1945, he felt more than ever that mankind must move to a humane, intelligent path of action or be removed from the planet. International unity was becoming, more than ever, a political necessity and a matter of life and death.

Ralph Ellison and Wright were close friends at that time, and they often discussed existentialism, especially that of Kierkegaard and Heidegger. In the summer of 1945, Ellison sent Wright, who was thinking of going to Paris, a copy of *Horizon*, the avant-garde British magazine, with an article about new literary developments in France. By this time, Ellison had become as disillusioned and disgusted by American Communist politicians, especially black ones, as Wright had and hoped American complacency could be jostled by "speaking from a station that gets its power from the mature ideological dynamo of France and the Continent."[3] Therefore, when Ellison called his friend's attention to the achievements of the French existentialists, he did so, significantly, out of an interest in writing and commitment, not from a philosophical world view:

> I've been reading some fascinating stuff out of France concerning plays written and produced their during the Occupation. Kierkegaard has been utilized and given a social direction by a group who have organized what is called "Existential Theater," and, from what I read, their psychological probing has produced a powerful art. France is in ferment. Their discussion of the artist's responsibility surpasses anything I've ever seen. . . . They view the role of the individual in relation to society so sharply that the leftwing boys, with the possible exception of Malraux, seem to have looked at it through the reverse end of a telescope. I am sure that over there the war has made the writer more self-confident and aware of the dignity of his craft. Sartre, one of the younger writers, would have no difficulty understanding your position in regard to the Left. He writes: "Every epoch discovers one aspect of. . . . the condition of humanity, in every epoch man chooses for himself with regard to others, to love, to death, to the world (Kierkegaardian categories, aren't they?), and when a controversy arises on the subject of the disarmament of the FFI, or of the aid to be given to the Spanish Republicans, it is that metaphysical choice, that personal and absolute decision, which is in question. Thus by becoming a part of the uniqueness of our time, we finally merge with the eternal, and it is our task as writers to cast light on the eternal values which are involved in these social and political disputes. Yet we are not concerned with seeking these values in an intelligible paradise, for they are only

interesting in their immediate form. Far from being relativists, we assert emphatically that man is absolute. But he is absolute in his own time, in his own environment, on his own earth. The absolute is Decartes, the man who escapes us because he is dead . . . . and the relative is Cartesianism, that coster's barrow philosophy which is trotted out century after century, in which everyone finds whatever he has put in it. It is not by chasing after immortality that we will make ourselves eternal: we will not make ourselves absolute by reflecting in our worlds desiccated principles which are sufficiently empty and negative to pass from one century to another, but by fighting passionately in our time, by loving passionately, and by consenting to perish entirely with it." [4]

This letter is revealing of Ellison's own reasons for becoming interested in Sartre, whose philosophy confirmed his opinion that "man is absolute in his own time, in his own environment," i.e., that the black writer will achieve universality by concentrating on the specific, by dealing with his own experience. This restored his self-confidence and belief in the worth of his craft in the face of the political dictates clamoring for "commitment" under the banner of the CPUSA that he was forcefully rejecting.

Wright was similarly concerned with the responsibility of the artist, as evidenced by his moving answer to the South American artist Antonio Frasconi:

> There is . . . beyond the boundaries of imperious politics, a common ground upon which we can stand and see the truth of the problem . . . . Out of what vision must an artist create? The question seems vague, but when it is conceived in terms of political pressure from the Left or Right, it has vital meaning . . . . I hold that, on the last analysis, the artist must bow to the monitor of his own imagination, must be led by the sovereignty of his own impressions and perceptions[5]

So much for the vindication of independent thinking and personal outlook. But Wright also emphasized responsibility and commitment to truth:

> We must beware of those who seek, in words no matter how urgent or crisis-charged, to interpose an alien and dubious curtain of reality between our eyes and the crying claims of a world which is our lot to see only too poignantly and too briefly[6]

In many ways, the French existentialists were addressing similar problems: the responsibility of the intellectual, the defense of humanistic values, the importance of solidarity, the relationship between truth and freedom. These are clearly the concerns and qualities that Wright so much admired in Sartre. He had found him rather reserved when he first met him at a gathering at the home of his friend Dorothy Norman, the editor of *Twice a Year* and a liberal columnist for the *New York Post*. But later, in 1946 and in 1947, when Wright lived in Paris, he often spoke and wrote of Sartre with the utmost enthusiasm and reverence: "Sartre is the only Frenchmen I've met who had voluntarily made the identification of the French experience with that of mankind." "How rare a man is this Sartre," he noted in his journal after a conversation during which the French philosopher compared the plight of the colonized world to that of the French under Nazi occupation.[7] Again, after another conversation on the role of the intellectual regarding the political and human situation, Wright noted, not without a touch of delighted awe:

> Sartre is quite of my opinion regarding the possibility of human action today, that is up to the individual to do what he can to uphold the concept of what it means to be human. The great danger, I told him, in the world today is the very feeling and conception of what is a human might well be lost. He agreed. I feel very close to Sartre and Simone de Beauvoir. [8]

Wright reiterated—somewhat naively—his respect for Sartre's intelligence and perspicacity in his "Introduction to the *Respectful Prostitute*," which presented the play to the American reader:

> Jean-Paul Sartre, principal exponent of French Existentialism, has brought his keen and philosophical temperament to bear upon the problem of race relations in America . . . . The French mind—especially French minds of the Sartre level—is rigorously logical . . . . The dismally lowered tone of personality expression in America seems ludicrous to the mind of a man who, above all modern writers, is seeking and preaching the integrity of action . . . . It took a foreign mind to see that the spirit of virgins could exist in the personalities of whores. Let us then be thankful for the eyes and mind of Jean-Paul Sartre who, in *La Putain Respectuese*, is helping us to see ourselves . . . . Finally remember that the artist is, in the last analysis, a judge and it is the business of a judge to render judgments[9]

Wright could not but be impressed at this time. He had hardly begun to discover French existentialist philosophy with the help of Dorothy Norman and was only relatively more conversant with the work of the German school, even though, as Ellison's letter suggests, his knowledge of Kierkegaardian categories was more thorough and anterior. This is not to say that Wright did not attempt to study French existentialism. He acquired several introductory treatises, like G. de Ruggiero's *Existentialism* (1946) and Jean Wahl's *Short History of Existentialism* (1949), as well as several books by Sartre in English translation, especially *Existentialism* and *The Psychology of Imagination*, before 1950. Yet *Being and Nothingness* was not translated until 1957, and Wright did not master French well enough to read it in the original. Sartre's metaphysics were, therefore, somewhat unclear to him and less important to his own concerns than such political and social essays as "Anti-Semite and Jew" and "What Is Literature?" and, possibly, than literary works like *Age of Reason, The Reprieve, The Diary of Antoine Roquentin*, and the short stories "Intimacy" and "Men Without Shadows," not to mention Sartre's plays, of which he knew at least *The Respectful Prostitute, Huis-Clos, The Chips Are Down*, and *Les Mains Sales*.

I have dealt elsewhere at some length with Wright's participation in political ventures of the French existentialists under the banner of the Rassemblement Démocratique Révolutionaire from 1949 to 1952. I have also explained how the *Temps Modernes* group perceived Wright as a "representative man" and cast him in that role for a time.[10] It remains to be seen, however, to what extent Wright's reverence for Sartre's stance as a committed intellectual and his experiments as a *romancier à thèse* may have inspired Wright's own efforts in *The Outsider*.

Although the early pencil drafts of the novel no longer exist, the half-dozen successive versions of the manuscript are sufficient evidence that, even though it was planned and begun before Wright's first trip to Paris and his acquaintance with French existentialism, the novel was, in some limited manner, influenced by that way of thinking as well as by that style. It must be remembered that Wright apparently started to write a sort of political thriller much in the vein of his earlier naturalistic novels. Drawing on episodes of the then-unpublished *Lawd Today*, he based the experience of his new protagonist, Cross Damon, on the day-to-day, routine, oppressed, and confined existence of Jake, a Chicago postal worker. Admittedly, the sense of confinement and entrapment in a web of circumstances of such a routine recalls Antoine Roquentin's *"engluement"* and subsequent "nausea." Even more Sartrean, if one turns to the plot, is the underground railway accident that allows Cross to start again from scratch with a new yet-to-be-defined identity. This is the "second chance" given by Sartre to one of the protagonists of *The Chips Are Down*. Yet such occurrences that allow man to "create himself out of nothing" do happen in everyday life, and Wright may have thought of the accident episode before leaving the United States. More probably, his reading the trilogy *Las Chemins de la Liberté* (at least the first volume of it) confirmed Wright in his choice of inserting long philosophical exchanges and considerations in the midst of a well-filled, detective-like plot. Perhaps the example of Sartre should not, in this case, have been followed, since his *romans à thèse* do not make very lively reading. It might have been preferable for Wright to rewrite his own novel as a first-person narrative (as he nearly decided to do after reading Camus' novel *The Stranger*).

Does this mean that the influence of Camus prevailed? It would be quite hazardous to make such a statement.

If one considers the way Wright discovered Camus' writings before he met the man, chronological considerations compel us to state, first of all, that in spite of the many resemblances between *Native Son* and *The Stranger*, there never did exist any kind of contact between the two men that could account for possible influences in either direction. Resemblances are coincidental, more a result of convergence.

Wright first heard of Camus in the spring of 1946, around the time he first met Sartre. The first works by Camus that he read deserve closer scrutiny than I have granted them previously because they set the tone for Wright's perception of the Algerian-born novelist. At the end of 1946, *Twice a Year* printed a lecture Camus had given in the spring of that year in New York under the title "The Human Crisis." Strangely enough, when one considers the bulk of Camus' writings and his general outlook, the views he expressed then were exceedingly despondent and pessimistic, notwithstanding a last-minute appeal to "the best in mankind." Such views must have reinforced Wright's contemporary pessimism regarding the morality of politics and the direction of human history in postwar America, where consumerism and the cult of material success were again rampant. Camus spotted what he called "the clearest symptoms" of the human crisis. He denounced "the rise of terror following upon such a perversion of values that a man or a historical force is judged today not in terms of human dignity but in terms of success."[11] Somewhat unexpectedly, Camus was not indicting man's inhumanity to man in wartime—although he later did so—but the overshadowing of human-oriented goals by the quest for material wealth and "happiness." French intellectuals had, as a rule, leveled accusations of crass materialism against the United States in the 1920s and 1930s: the idea was far from new. Yet Camus made American materialism sound ominous and pervasive. He perceived it as the condition of modern man, as a plague coming to Europe:

> If that unhappy man, the Job of modern times, is not to die of his hurts on his dunghill, then must the mortgage of fear and anguish first be lifted, so that he may again find that liberty of mind without which none of the problems set for our modern consciousness can be solved.[12]

Wright's own categories of fear and anguish were probably more "metaphysical" (more Kierkegaardian) than "intellectual," which is the dimension Camus stresses here, but he could not disagree with Camus' second "symptom," namely, loss of "the possibility of persuasion," of appealing to an individual's feelings of humanity to get a human reaction. "For SS," Camus wrote, "were no longer men, representing men but like an instinct elevated to the height of an idea or a theory."[13] This is precisely what Wright tried to prove in *The Outsider* of Communist leaders like Blount or Blimin; and this is what he had opposed in his analysis of the Trotskyite trials in "I Tried to Be a Communist." A corollary of the lack of human response of "commissars" was indeed mentioned by Camus, who conceptualized it as "the replacement of the natural object by printed matter"—the overwhelming rise of bureaucracy—so that, in short, "we no longer die, love, or kill, except by proxy."[14] Camus ended with a discussion of the substitution of the political man for the living man: "No longer are individual passions possible, but only collective, that is to say abstract, passions"[15] in the new cult of efficiency and abstraction.

Although Damon's opponents and targets in *The Outsider* are precisely the cosmic "blocks" of fascism and political totalitarianism—both based upon an essential repudiation of individual needs and feelings—the protagonist's quest is more specifically oriented toward the creation, if not the discovery, of individual norms, which in his utterly nihilistic criticism of existing social values, he hardly manages to claim at the very end. "Man is nothing in particular": Cross's statement to Houston, which in many ways recalls Sartre's definition of man as "a vacant passion," may thus have been, in deeper ways, supported and corroborated by Wright's reading of "The Human Crisis." Indeed, Camus wrote that the cult of efficiency and abstraction explained why man in Europe today experienced only solitude and silence: he could not "communicate with his fellows in terms of values common to them all." Hence, "since he is no longer protected by a respect for man based on the values of man, the only alternative henceforth open to him is to be the victim or the executioner."[16]

Admittedly, the reasons for Cross's outright "metaphysical egotism" could be found more at the personal than at the societal level, as evidenced by his treatment of his women or comrades at the beginning. One should also consider the racial dimension that prevented him from respecting the nonvalues of so-called American ideals. Yet he might have adhered to the ideals of Communism had he not discovered the ruthless authoritarianism of leaders cultivating what Camus calls "abstraction" when not seeking a sensuous enjoyment of power. It followed that Cross's espousal of Nietzschean theories of a godless, amoral universe can also be explained in the terms used by Camus: no longer protected by human norms, man believes in nothing but himself. Camus concludes:

> If we believe in nothing and nothing makes sense and we are unable to find values in anything, then anything is permitted and nothing is important. Then there is neither good nor evil and Hitler was neither right nor wrong . . . . And since we thought nothing makes sense we had to conclude that he who is right is he who succeeds![17]

As a result, Wright's definition of "man as nothing in particular," which might be construed in the positive, optimistic Sartrean perspective of man as a potentiality to be actualized through existential choice, seems to come closer to Camus' more despondent view of man as neither good nor evil, and deprived of values. This is the path Cross explores as a murderer, although in his heart of hearts he wishes he were neither victim nor executioner. This reading of Camus thus sheds some added light on his final exclamation about being innocent and having experienced the utmost horror. He is innocent because he is not responsible for the human condition, which is "nothing in particular." He is crushed not only by the horror inherent in this metaphysical predicament, but by the realization that, in Camus' terms, "we knew deep in our hearts that even the distinction was illusory, that at bottom we were all victims, and that assassins and assassinated would in the end be reunited in the same defeat."[18]

Camus and Wright parted ways, however, in their unequal emphasis on politics. In spite of his condemnation of fascism and Communism, or at least of the means used by the later, Wright, like Sartre and de Beauvoir, believed that political commitment still represented a means for action, and he eagerly joined in the efforts of the Rassemblement Démocratique Révolutionaire to reject both the United States and the USSR in the name of Europe's freedom of choice. As for Camus, he not only declared that politics must whenever possible be kept in its proper place, which is a secondary one, but also stated emphatically:

> The great misfortune of our time is precisely that politics pretend to furnish us at once with a catechism, a complete philosophy, and at times even a way of loving. But the role of politics is to set our house in order, not to deal with our inner problems. I do not know for myself whether there is or not an absolute. But I do know that this is not a political concern. The absolute is not the concern of all, it is the concern of each . . . . Doubtless our life belongs to others and it is proper that we give it to others when it is necessary, but our death belongs to ourselves alone. Such is my definition of freedom.[19]

Only much later, and only halfheartedly, did Wright thus limit the role of politics in "The Voiceless Ones," a review of Michel del Castillo's *The Disinherited*.[20]

It is evident that Wright's ideology converged with that of the French existentialists, if it was not directly influenced by it at the time. The tone of their respective articles for the "Art and Action" commemorative issue of *Twice a Year* in 1948 is strikingly similar. Wright's "Letter to Dorothy Norman" ends with the declaration that politics and consumerism curtail the definition of man:

> The Right and Left, in different ways, have decided that man is an animal whose needs can be met by making more articles for him to consume . . . . A world will be built in which everybody will get enough to eat and full stomachs will be equated with contentment and freedom, and those who will say that they are not happy under such a regime will be guilty of treason. How sad it is. We are all accomplices in this crime . . . . Is it too late to say something to halt it, modify it?[21]

On the following page, Camus' article, entitled "We Too Are Murderers," begins:

Yes, it is a fact that we have no future, and the present-day world bodes nothing save
death and silence, war and terror. But it is also a fact that we ought not tolerate this,
for we know that man is long in the making and everything worth living for, love,
intelligence, beauty, requires time and ripening.[22]

One would believe that Wright is simply pursuing his argument. As a matter of fact,
Wright's letter, sent to Dorothy Norman on March 9, 1948, was intended for
publication; and Camus' article, originally published in *Franchise* in 1946, largely
developed the concepts of his lecture "The Human Crisis." At the time, such positions
and ideas were in the air in existentialist circles, and it is difficult to attribute the
authorship of any of them to any one intellectual. Even Stephen Spender, in "The
Spiritual Failure of Europe," expressed similar views in his criticism of the Soviet
Union and the United States. He found that the problems of our time were more real in
Europe than elsewhere and thus more likely to be stated and solved there:

> Wherever nations and great interests are powerful, they become victims of illusions
> even if these illusions are euphemistically called political realism. The fundamental
> illusion of power politics is that freedom begins with the protection of the powerful
> group.[23]

To return to the similarity of Wright's and Camus' views in the late 1940s, it is likely
that Wright's composition of his existentialist novel was influenced in subtle ways by
his reading of *The Stranger* in August, 1947. He read the book in the American edition
at a very slow pace, "weighing each sentence," admiring "its damn good narrative
prose," and remarked:

> It is a neat job but devoid of passion. He makes his point with dispatch and his prose
> is solid and good. In America a book like this would not attract much attention for it
> would be said that he lacks feeling. He does however draw his character very well.
> What is of course really interesting in this book is the use of fiction to express a
> philosophical point of view. That he does with ease. I now want to read his other
> stuff. [24]

Wright's remarks are somewhat surprising. On the one hand, he already knew of the
use of fiction to express a philosophical point of view through the novels and theories
of Sartre and de Beauvoir. Thus, when he calls Camus' use "very interesting" and
"done with ease," he refers to the actual blending of message and narrative—something
he himself proved little capable of doing in *The Outsider*, where long political and
metaphysical speeches stand out like didactic asides. On the other hand, when Wright
finds a lack of passion and feeling in *The Stranger*, he refers to a lack of warmth in the
style and the pace of the narration, not in the protagonist, since Meursault's
indifference is precisely one of the motives for his acts. In *The Outsider* Wright's hero
is never "devoid of passion" and acts more upon the compulsion of his egotistical
desires than from the utter existential indifference that characterizes Meursault.

Moreover, Wright's narration is never cold or detached, not because the novelist
wants to please an American audience who, he supposed, likes "feeling," but because
he simply cannot write in Camus' precise but detached fashion. He needs passion and
feeling to carry his narrative along. Wright noted nine days after reading *The Stranger*
that he felt he ought to write his novel in the first person because "there was a certain
note of poignancy missing which a first-person note would supply,"[25] but he made no
real attempt to do so. Either *The Outsider* had reached too definitive a stage, or Wright
felt incapable of changing his own style; *The Stranger's* influence was not enough to
modify significantly the tenor of his own novel. Moreover, had Camus been a
determining influence, it is likely that the scenes dealing with Damon's reaction to his
mother would have been modified in light of Meursault's reactions to his own. Yet it
appears that Wright's motivations for his picture of the mother and son's reciprocal
rejection are to be found in idiosyncratic, personal attitudes, rather than in a detached
attempt to illustrate metaphysical estrangement.

Leaving later political opinions and racial choices aside, it appears that although
Wright and Camus shared a common conception of the role and responsibility of the

artist and intellectual in the modern world, as well as a deep-seated pessimism, their artistic temperaments differed far more than those of Wright and Sartre. Another remark that Wright jotted down in his journal on August 7, 1947, is revealing: "There is still something about this Camus that bothers me. Maybe it is because he is the artist and Sartre and de Beauvoir are not primarily." Wright accurately perceived himself, Sartre and de Beauvoir as less preoccupied with art and less able to achieve the perfect aesthetic adequacy to be found in Camus. He may have felt some regret but could not and would not change his own style of writing.

Simone de Beauvoir was both more congenial and less impressive than Sartre or Camus in Wright's eyes. Not that her thinking was less vigorous than theirs, but her manners were more open and her metaphysical interest always focused upon everyday implications and applications. As a result, Wright found more in common with her than with the two men, insofar as he tended to define Sartre as the metaphysician and Camus as the aesthete.

Since de Beauvoir spoke some English and understood it fairly well, their exchanges were more frequent, too, and Wright knew more about her work and opinions than he did about any other French existentialist. Before reading *The Ethics of Ambiguity* and *The Second Sex*, in 1949 and 1953 respectively, he had been able to ponder de Beauvoir's long and important essay included in the 1948 *Art and Action*. Under the title "Literature and Metaphysics," the first essay provided a theoretical framework for precisely the problems Wright was grappling with when writing *The Outsider*, i.e., the conditions of writing a successful "metaphysical novel." De Beauvoir was convinced:

> There is no doubt that the novel cannot be successful if the writer limits himself to disguising in a more or less alluring fictional cloak a previously constructed ideological framework . . . . It is impossible to see how an imaginary story can serve ideas which have already found their proper mode of expression.[26]

She emphasized the analogous relations between novel writing and metaphysics, the role and value of subjectivity as expressing the temporal form of metaphysical experience, and the aspect of spiritual adventure to be encountered in a novel, which she saw as "an effort to conciliate the objective and the subjective, the absolute and the relative, the intemporal and the historical." Her goal was no less than an attempt to "grasp the meaning at the heart of existence; and if the description of essence belongs to the sphere of philosophy proper, the novel alone makes it possible to evoke the original outpouring of existence in its complete, singular, temporal truth.[27]

Such language was not very different from Wright's definition of a novel's aims and of what it should arouse in its readers, even though he failed to give enough concreteness to his demonstrations in *The Outsider*.

More interesting to him must have been the essay of "Freedom and Liberation," which opposed one of the main objections raised against existentialism, namely, that the precept "seek freedom" proposed no concrete plan of action. De Beauvoir reexamined the concept of freedom to restore its concrete meaning and show that it could be realized only by man's committing himself to the world and embodying his ideal in definite rules of conduct.

Positive freedom was defined as a movement to "unveil being" and turn it into existence: a movement that was constantly being transcended, since man had to "pursue the expansion of his existence and take this effort in itself as an absolute."[28] This expansion was, in many ways, what Wright claimed for Cross Damon. Yet de Beauvoir approved of a personal movement of expansion only insofar as she grounded it in ethics, so as to condemn, in the name of theology, a sort of "happiness" that artificially expanded man's existence through consumerism but really prevented him from transcending it. She analyzed the process of freeing oneself from oppression: there are two ways of transcending the given, to escape (to go on a journey) or to free oneself (from imprisonment), which are very different things, since the present is accepted in the one case, rejected in the other. This led her to criticize Hegel's concept of *Aufhebung*, which is the foundation of his optimism and brings him to regard the future as harmonious development, in the name of realism. She argued that revolt did not integrate itself into harmonious development but constituted a violent disruption, which led Marx to define the proletariat in terms of a negation. Wright actually discussed the concepts and implications of alienation and freedom with Sartre and de Beauvoir. He may have been led to some of his own conclusions about man's responsibility to others and about the limits of individual freedom as incarnate in Damon's end by such assertions as this:

> Freedom need be respected only when it is directed towards freedom and not when it evades itself and falls off from its own principle . . . . And it is not true that the recognition of other people's freedom limits my own. To be free does not mean to have the power to do anything whatsoever; it consists in being able to transcend the given towards an open future; the existence of others as free defines my situation and is even the condition of my own freedom. I am oppressed if I am thrown into prison, not if I am prevented from throwing my neighbor into prison.[29]

One can easily see just how de Beauvoir's conception of other people's freedom meets Sartre's definition of "*l'enfer, c'est les autres*," or in terms of Wright's fiction, how Damon's nihilism can be reconciled with Fred Daniels's belief that he must share his underground vision with others. De Beauvoir writes, "To be free consists in being able to transcend the given towards an open future." Damon discovers this at his own expense, when he realizes that his disregard of others blocks his capacity for change, for establishing a love relationship with Eva especially, i.e., for transcending his personal problems, even though he was miraculously able to recreate his social relationships out of nothing after the train wreck. Damon has no "open future," not because he is chased and killed but because his egotism without norms negates the notion of openness, which is the bedrock of freedom.

It would be easy to multiply examples of interface between the theories of French existentialism and their application to literature, and Wright's own use of certain metaphysical concepts in *The Outsider*, but it may be more revealing to stress some differences.

One can regret that Wright did not pattern *The Outsider* more consistently after the simple plot, classical structure, and terse style of *The Stranger*, but his idiosyncrasies oriented him more toward a mixture of melodrama and rhetorical exposition. Edward Margolies aptly points out in his comparison of Damon and Meursault that "both men kill without passion, both men appear unmoved by the death of their mothers; both men apparently are intended to represent the moral and emotional failure of the age."[30] When writing a notice for the jacket of *The Outsider*, Wright himself specified that "the hero could be of any race." He claimed, "I have tried to depict my sense of our contemporary living as I see it and felt it." He also saw the novel as his first literary effort "projected out of a heart preoccupied with no ideological burden save that of rendering an account of reality" as it struck his sensibilities and imagination. It seems, however, that the motivation and behavior of Meursault are more emblematic of modern man than those of Damon. This may be because the earlier section of the novel is patterned after the naturalistic depiction of black ghetto life in *Lawd Today* and also because Damon's resentment is rooted in racial offense, economic oppression, and a familial atmosphere in which the male is spiritually crushed by women. Damon's "metaphysical resentment" would only come second, or even third, after his hatred for political manipulation and totalitarianism.

Many American critics have found that *The Outsider* was plagued by a problem of motivation. Yet, the gratuitousness of Damon's half-dozen murders poses no problem when it is seen as a prevalent feature of French existentialist fiction and when one recalls that Sartre and Camus refrain precisely from exploring the ambiguous relationship between the condition of freedom and the desire to kill.[31] In the case of Wright's hero, his search for unlimited freedom makes him his own victim when his hatred of others turns into self-hatred. And the root of his compulsive violence must be traced back to the behavior of much earlier Wrightian protagonists like Big Boy and Bigger Thomas, those oppressed and temporarily impotent youngsters who are seized by a compulsion to "blot out" their fellow creatures as they would some insect.

This behavior must be related to the condition of social and racial oppression under which the presence of the "other" (the white man, the capitalist boss) is equivalent to torture and hell, where "*l'enfer, c'est les autres*." But Wright quickly leaves this trend of thinking whereby he might have rejoined the Sartrean perspectives of *Huis-Clos*. The

Outsider set out to prove another existentialist theme: *"l'enfer, c'est soi-même,"* which Wright developed most completely in *The Man Who Lived Underground* before he was aware of it as an existentialist concept. In spite of its rhetoric, *The Outsider* rather aptly reveals the gloomy abysses of man's mind when he is totally outside life. Again, the problem is less the satisfaction of the desires and compulsions of the individual than it is man's need for purification. Trapped in his *mauvaise foi* (although his inauthenticity at the beginning of the novel is rather different from Roquentin's or Meursault's), Damon does not really feel the type of nausea experienced by Sartre's hero—his *engluement* is more the condition of being unable to escape from the social trap—and, in spite of a recurrent use of phrases that may have been borrowed from the French existentialists, the reader is reluctant to believe that Cross can simply decide to be his "own little God" and follow his unrestrained desires. Even the five sections of the novel do not really correspond to Kierkegaardian categories beyond the concept of dread. The final titles, "Despair" and "Decision," are interesting insofar as they recall the mood, if not always the concepts, emphasized both in the gloomy forebodings of Camus' essay on the crisis of man and in de Beauvoir's more spirited analysis of freedom and commitment. Wright's outlook, however, is more unremittingly bleak and somber, and also more narrowly individual than even Camus'. On the whole, the French existentialists were preoccupied with societal survival through the restoration of human values and morality, whereas Damon's trajectory is a negation of all social norms; and this final decision, at the end of his metaphysical journey to the end of night, is more the result of intrinsic dread than the outcome of clearly defined, freely made choice. In the course of Wright's narrative, a world grounded upon the freedom of existentialist choice does not seem possible. Although he symbolically slays the totalitarian and authoritarian monsters of fascism and Communism (presumably for, among other reasons, the greater freedom of mankind), and although he finds in Houston a kindred spirit and an emblematic opposite, Damon never really bridges the gap between himself and others, as is made clear by Eva's suicide when she knows the "horrible truth" about her lover. If Camus' saying "Our life belongs to others but our death belongs to us alone" is true, then Damon is unable to do anything with his death, except to utter a desperate cry of horror that is just as ambiguous as that of Kurtz at the close of *Heart of Darkness*. The "horrible innocence" of Damon—a victim of inhuman society and metaphysical fate as much as of totalitarian ruthlessness—is compounded by his being one of the Nietzschean "new men," one of the godless race who suffer no obligations, since they recognize no values. At this stage, therefore, Wright seems to part ways with the French existentialists. Again, his definition of man as "nothing in particular" does not correspond to Sartre's conception of man as "anything," i.e., as a potentiality to be fulfilled and actualized through choice and action. Wright's view is far more nihilistic than Sartre's; even though Damon's final claim is for human solidarity and compassion, his murderous past and the general atmosphere of *The Outsider* leave us with the impression that this change of heart *in articulo mortis* does not suit the protagonist's previous behavior, that this is a last-minute choice inflicted upon by the novelist.

One may wonder about the reasons for these differences in mood between Wright and the French existentialists, mostly Sartre and de Beauvoir, with whom Wright had so much in common and with whom he worked for years along common political lines. Was it that, for the French intellectuals, existentialism remained less visceral, more conceptual, more "intellectual," in a word, than for the man who had painfully emerged from the deprivations and insecurity described in *Black Boy*? Was it due to Wright's "American" situation—the plight of a modern man in a country of extremes, a country more urbanized than France, which could not fall back on the comfortable traditions of lay humanism to explain theoretically and vindicate what was happening to it? When they expressed their horror at a "valueless universe," the French existentialists often did so in order to excite others to a redefinition of the essential moral and human qualities of social life. When, under the brunt of political disillusionment, Wright explored the implications of a normless existence, he did so with characteristic thoroughness and impetus, with the result that he outdid even Camus' gloomiest forebodings. The results of his attempt are undoubtedly clumsier and psychologically less convincing than the novels of Sartre or Camus; yet for all its aesthetic faults and not too subtle conceptualization, *The Outsider* remains a fascinating piece of writing, and one that still speaks to our present needs. By comparison, *Les Chemins de la liberté* is best regarded as a historical testimony about the mistakes and hopes of the war generation.

Notes

[1] See, among others, J. Saunders Redding, "Home Is Where the Heart Is," *New Leader,* December 11, 1961, pp. 24-25: "The one thing French that caught him was Existentialism, and this held him only long enough for him to write his unqualifiedly bad novel." At a 1964 symposium, transcribed in Herbert Hill's *Anger and Beyond* (New York: Harper, p. 209), Redding was of the opinion that "Existentialism is no philosophy to accommodate the reality of Negro life, especially Southern Negro life," and he agreed with Arna Bontemps, who dismissed Wright's metaphysical attempts as "a roll in the hay with the French existentialists."

[2] See my article, "Richard Wright and the French Existentialists," MELUS, 5 (Summer, 1978), pp. 35-51; also the relevant chapter of *The Unfinished Quest of Richard Wright* (New York: William Morrow, 1973), especially pp. 320-22.

[3] Ralph Ellison, Letter to Wright, August 18, 1945.

[4] Ellison, Letter to Wright, July 22, 1945.

[5] Richard Wright, "Richard Wright to Antonio Frasconi--An Exchange of Letters," *Twice a Year*, 12-13 (Fall-Winter, 1945), p. 258.

[6] "Wright to Frasconi," p. 251.

[7] Wright, Unpublished journal, August 7, 1947.

[8] Unpublished journal, September 7, 1947.

[9] Wright, "Art and Action," *Twice a Year* (1948), p. 14-15.

[10] See Fabre, "Wright and the French Existentialists."

[11] Albert Camus, "The Human Crisis," *Twice a Year*, 14-15 (Fall-Winter, 1946-47), p. 22.

[12] Camus, p. 22.

[13] Camus, p. 23.

[14] Camus, p. 23.

[15] Camus, p. 24.

[16] Camus, p. 24.

[17] Camus, p. 24.

[18] Camus, p. 26.

[19] Camus, p. 29.

[20] Wright wrote: "May it not develop that man's sense of being disinherited is not mainly political at all, that politics serve it as a temporary vessel, that Marxist ideology in particular is but a transitory makeshift pending a more accurate diagnosis, that Communism may be a painful compromise containing a definition of man by sheer default?" See "The Voiceless Ones," *Saturday Review*, 43 (April 16, 1960), p. 54.

[21] Wright, "Two Letters to Dorothy Newman," "Art and Action," *Twice a Year* (1948), 73.

[22] "Two Letters to Dorothy Norman," p. 73.

[23] "Two Letters to Dorothy Norman," p. 79.

[24] Wright, Unpublished journal, August 7, 1947.

[25] Unpublished journal, August 7, 1947.

[26] "Art and Action," p. 89.

[27] "Art and Action," p. 92.

[28] "Art and Action," p. 97.

[29] "Art and Action," p. 100.

[30] Edward Margolies, *The Art of Richard Wright* (Carbondale: Southern Illinois University Press, 1969), p. 135.

[31] See Kingsley Widmer, "The Existential Darkness: *The Outsider*," *Wisconsin Studies in Contemporary Literature*, 1 (Fall, 1960), pp. 13-21. This essay very competently addresses itself to the comparison of some of the conceptual components of the novel with those emphasized by Kierkegaard and other German existentialists on the one hand, and by Sartre on the other.

From *MELUS* V (Summer 1978), 35-51.

Richard Wright's *The Outsider:* Existentialist Exemplar or Critique?

Amritjit Singh

The Outsider (1953) is one of the first consciously existentialist novels written by an American. Richard Wright had been living in Paris for a few years and had not published any book since his autobiography, *Black Boy* (1945). *The Outsider* was his first major work of fiction since *Native Son* (1940), which had received much critical attention and also caused considerable controversy. Wright had started working on *The Outsider* as early as 1947, hoping to make it a "great book," a book, to use his own words, "one can read feeling the movement and rhythm of a man alive and confronting the world with all its strength."[1] In this book, he would deal with the concept of freedom and he decided to familiarize himself with existentialism as part of his preparation. As he learned more about existentialist thought, he felt that it corresponded to his own vision of life and human responsibility. During this period, Wright was, however, exposed to many other influences too. One of his deeply felt concerns at this time was the impact of industrialization on the modern world, especially in Asia and Africa. The Cold War between the East and the West was serious enough, but a deeper problem to Wright was "the total extinction of the concept of a human being which has prevailed for 2000 years," bringing in the worst features of the consumer society.[2] *The Outsider* had its origin, therefore, in Wright's attempt to resolve the dilemma of the individual *versus* society, the mind *versus* materialism.

Wright's view of existentialism was shaped primarily through his responses to Sartre, and it is no coincidence that the two men came to place similar faith in violence in the context of colonialism. Wright's responses were regulated to a great extent by Dorothy Norman, who introduced him to existentialism and the writings of Kierkegaard, Nietzsche, and Heidegger. And it was at her place that he first met Sartre during the latter's visit to the United States in 1946. Later, he met Camus, Sartre, and Simone de Beauvoir in Paris and admired Camus greatly until Camus sided with the French Colonists in the Algerian War. Simone de Beauvoir was more accessible than Sartre and became a closer friend of the Wrights, but French existentialism for Wright was represented primarily by Sartre. Wright and Sartre worked well together on political issues because of their shared Marxist sympathies. Wright was surprised and delighted that Sartre saw a connection between his experience of oppression, the Nazi occupation of France, and that of all oppressed and colonized peoples. The two had, however, arrived at their positions from different directions. As Michel Fabre points out, "since his rupture with the Communist Party, Wright had been a humanist in both ethics and politics, but while he had evolved from politics to morality, Sartre had proceeded from morality to politics."[3] Both believed in committed action, and while Wright's works used violence consistently as a mode of self-expression, Sartre saw it as an unavoidable tool in the hands of the oppressed in their war of liberation against the colonists. In his 1961 Preface to Frantz Fanon's *The Wretched of the Earth*, Sartre makes a frontal attack on Western apathy and complacency towards the Third World. Most Westerners, according to Sartre, felt that they were innocent of the crimes of colonialism because they were not settlers or colonizers. Sartre charges all Westerners with complicity through silence in order to arouse their sense of shame and guilt. Shame, for both Marx and Sartre, is a revolutionary sentiment. Sartre warned that violence by the colonizers would be returned by violence from the colonized; "for violence, like Achilles' lance, can heal the wound it has inflicted."[4] According to Sartre, "to shoot down a European is to kill two birds with one stone, to destroy an oppressor and the man he oppresses at the same time; there remain a dead man and a free man; the survivor, for the first time feels a *national* soil under his feet."[5] Wright's use of violence in *The Outsider* does not, of course, owe itself entirely to existentialist vindications of violence. Violence is endemic to the black American situation; just as to cite the bare facts of black American life is to make an anti-American document, to protest these facts is to incite or invite violence.

The Outsider is no more than a murder mystery if we concern ourselves with the plot in its bare outline. But Wright leaves no doubt in our minds that he intends it to be a serious philosophical work, a novel of ideas. Unlike his earlier work, *The Outsider* is not tied to a realistic sociological portrayal of black American life. The protagonist, Cross Damon, is not merely a black man; he is a thinking, questioning man facing the complexities of twentieth-century life.[6] But, as in *Native Son*, Wright resorts to some transparent devices to build up the intellectual content of his story. The long essay that becomes part of the extended conversation between Damon and Ely Houston, the New York District Attorney, permits Wright, through Damon, to spell out some of his own ideas on modern man and industrialization, religion, and capitalism. In a review, Max Eastman had described the device with some justification as "an ingenious way to compel a lazy-minded nation to read an essay," and also accused Wright of "passing from the Communist conspiracy to the Existentialist racket."[7]

The Outsider is the story of Cross Damon, whose name brings together the Christian ethic of suffering and a Nietzschean demonism.[8] As the book opens, we find Cross drinking compulsively against protests from his friends and co-workers at the post office, where he works in an environment reminiscent of Bartleby's Wall Street office desk. Cross wants to drown the worries that stem from the demands of a separated wife, Gladys, and three children. The situation is complicated now by his involvement with a fifteen-year-old girl, Dot. Dot, pregnant by Cross, is getting ready to exploit the situation to her own advantage. Dot wants Cross to marry her--which he cannot because Gladys refuses to release him in a divorce--or else she will initiate legal proceedings against him for assault and rape. Cross's mother, whose Christian ethic he would like to negate if possible, is in a state of shock at these new developments and urges Cross to find a solution and act quickly.

The gripping tale of Cross's career is divided into five sections: Dread, Dream, Descent, Despair, Decision. The sixth D--"Death"--permeates all the sections. The story moves with a remarkable speed, creating a suspension of disbelief in the reader with regard to its many contradictions and implausibilities. The aloofness and the isolation of Cross from all around him are stressed in the early pages of the novel. Cross would like to open up and relax with someone, and to communicate, but "there was not a single man to whom he cared to confess the nightmare that was his life. He had sharp need of a confidant, and yet he knew that if he had an ideal confidant, before whom he could lay his whole story, he would have instantly regretted it, would have murdered his confidant the moment after he had confided in him his shame."[9] In Dostoevskian passages such as these, Wright tries to make Cross Damon a convincing character--someone who is separated from his friends and family by his pride, his highstrung nature, and his bewildered sensibility. But for these elements in his portrayal in the early pages, Cross of the later sections may be a completely implausible character, likely to appear like a man who has serious problems on hand, but not entirely unique or tough enough to be the dreaded desperado that he later becomes. As in *Native Son*, Wright is careful enough to shape his protagonist's character; and a reader could afford to ignore many passages in Book I only at the cost of missing the essential features of Cross's character. Cross wonders aloud: "Why were some people fated, like Job, to live a neverending debate between themselves and their sense of what they believed life should be? Why did some hearts feel insulted at being alive, humiliated at the terms of existence?" (p. 19). And just as Hawthorne's black-veiled priest senses sin and guilt in others, Cross develops a special intuitive sense of identifying outsiders. He spots other outsiders, people who feel a wall of separation between themselves and the surrounding society because of one reason or the other:

prostitutes, Communists, women and nonwhites in general, or a hunchback such as the District Attorney Ely Houston, whom he meets later on a train journey to New York. He has a keen understanding of the murderous self-hatred that rules the lives of most black Americans and has a clear focus on the problems of modern life and the black man's place in it. Cross's antenna-like sensitivity to all "outsiders" highlights the depth of his alienation and also indicates that it is a social malaise and not a psychic imbalance. The sense of wholeness that Cross appears to have lost defines a situation that is existentialist to the core. The need to authenticate oneself in a stultifying environment leads to an undying craving for freedom.

The plot moves deliberately to dramatize the existentialist theme of freedom. While Cross is still puzzling his way through the latest mess which he has brought upon himself, Gladys has already made sure that she gets a fair share of the blackmail booty. She forces Cross to sign the house and car over to her and demands that he borrow eight hundred dollars from the Postal Union to clear the titles of both. It is when he is returning with this money from the Post Office that he stumbles upon an irresistible opportunity to start his life over again. He is involved in a subway accident which he survives only to learn later from a radio announcement that he is officially dead because he has been mistaken for another fellow passenger. Harassed as he is by his many problems, he jumps at this chance to create a new existence, a new person out of his disposable past:

> What was his past if he wanted to become another person? . . . Now, his past would have to be a deliberately constructed thing. . . . Others took their lives for granted, he would have to mold his with a conscious aim. Why not? Was he not free to do so? That all men were free was the fondest and deepest conviction of his life. . . . He would do with himself what he would, what he liked. (p. 87)

In existentialist terms, there would not be a greater possibility than to have the freedom to act without limitations of any kind. Cross has the freedom to exercise a most fundamental choice, causing him to experience what Kierkegaard describes as "the dizziness of freedom, what occurs when freedom looks down into its own possibility."[10] But Cross, like an existentialist, insists on action, for only in action does existence attain concreteness and fullness. In his *Journals*, Kierkegaard has the following to say:

> What I really lack is to be clear in my mind *what I am to do*. . . . What good would it be to me to be able to develop a theory of the state and combine all the details into a single whole, and so construct a world in which I did not live, but only held up to the view of others![11]

And action for the existentialist is not mere function or mere activism; action properly so-called is intensely personal; it involves the whole man. Action implies freedom. Both Camus and Sartre, who influenced Wright at different times in different ways, are apostles of freedom. For Sartre as for Kierkegaard, freedom and existence are indistinguishable. But freedom itself is an ambiguous phenomenon. It is ambiguous because freedom is often taken to afford possibility, but possibility is to be considered as the opposite of "facticity." Facticity limits and defines possibility, since possibilities exist not in a vacuum but in actual situations. Cross was free to act but he could not exchange his existence for the existence of another. As Martin Heidegger puts it, man is thrown into his situation. By changing one's name or exchanging one's situation, this "thrown-ness" (*Geworfenheit*) cannot be obliterated.[12] And nowhere is this ambiguity of freedom better dramatized than in the action of *The Outsider*. It is a compound irony of Wright's plot and theme that Cross's choice involves the whole man in a perverted, macabre way--it involves remaking the man himself. In existentialist terms, Cross's unlimited possibility is perhaps more "Good God, man is free!" than "Hurrah, man is free!" The rare possibility that is afforded to Cross has only paved the way for a desultory fragmentary existence.

To give himself time to think out his strategy and to make sure all goes well at and after his supposed funeral, Cross checks into a cheap hotel, where he runs into his old friend, Joe Thomas. Afraid that his plans to flee his past might be betrayed, he kills Joe and takes the train to New York in search of a new life, a new meaning for his re-created existence:

> He was empty, face to face with a sense of dread more intense than anything he had ever felt before. He was alone. . . . Nothing made meaning; his life seemed to have turned into a static dream whose frozen images would remain unchanged throughout eternity. (p. 101)

This aloneness, this existentialist alienation, remains with Cross to the end of his days. Existentially, man is alienated from his own deepest being. He is not himself but simply a cipher in the mass existence of the crowd, a cog in the modern industrial world.[13] Each person has to make decisions in his own unique situation and accept responsibility for these decisions.[14] Cross's total aloneness is underscored throughout the novel.

On the train to New York, Cross meets Bob Hunter, a West Indian waiter in the restaurant, and also strikes up a conversation with a Catholic priest and his friend, who turns out to be Ely Houston, the hunchbacked District Attorney from New York City. Cross's fear of discovery permits Wright to introduce some Dostoevskian notes: "Was he being followed on this train? Wasn't this waiter being especially friendly to allay any fears he might have that he was being watched? Hadn't that waiter cursed the white folks with the idea of inducing in him a false notion of security?" (p. 122). Houston's hunchback, like Cross's own racial and intellectual isolation, serves the District Attorney well in empathizing with the outsiders, the outcasts. He has a DuBois-like sense of the Negro's two-ness and claims that "this damned hump has given me more psychological knowledge than all the books I read at the university" (p. 133). Here and elsewhere in the novel, Wright uses dialogue to ensure that his themes and motifs are not missed. In speaking to Houston, Cross expounds his theory of man, which finds a sympathetic chord within Houston:

> "Maybe man is nothing in particular," Cross said gropingly. "Maybe that's the terror of it. Man may be just anything at all. . . . And every move he makes, couldn't these moves be just to hide this awful fact? To twist it into something which he feels would make him rest and breathe a little easier? What man is is perhaps too much to be borne by man. . . ." (pp. 135-36)

On arrival in New York, Cross takes steps to give himself a new name and identity: Lionel Lane, the name of a man who had just been buried in the neighborhood graveyard. He manages to procure Lane's duplicate birth certificate and draft card to close his tracks against possible discovery before he contacts Bob Hunter. Hunter has lost his job as waiter and has just joined the Communist Party to organize the workers. He introduces Cross to Gil and Eva Blount, who would like to use Cross to dramatize discrimination against blacks in housing. Cross moves into the apartment of the Blounts and soon discovers that the Party has tricked Eva, a nonobjective painter with inherited wealth, into marrying Gil, in order to keep her and her wealth within the Party. Cross and Eva are attracted to each other as victims of deception. Soon, Blount's neo-facist landlord, Herndon, discovers Cross in the building. Later in the evening, the confrontation between Blount and Herndon leads to violence wherein Cross kills both. For Cross, both were insects, one a neo-facist and the other a condescending totalitarian. He had earlier killed Joe Thomas for purely practical reasons, but his killing of Herndon and Blount was a conscious choice. Like Bigger Thomas, Cross too must exercise his existentialist choices, must express himself through deadly violence:

> The universe seemed to be rushing at him with all its totality. He was anchored once again in life, in the flow of things; the world glowed with an intensity so sharp it made his body ache. . . . He knew exactly what he had done; he had done it deliberately, even though he had not planned it. (p. 227)

He manages to cover the clues that might expose his complicity, depending on the police to believe the strong possibility of Herndon and Blount killing each other. Cross hopes to discover some meaning in his life through his genuine love for Eva, which she reciprocates to meet her own needs. But the implications of his action trouble him: "As Hilton and Gil had acted toward Bob, so had he acted toward Gil and Herndon; he had assumed the role of policeman, judge, supreme court, and executioner--all in one swift and terrible moment. But if he resented their being little gods, how could he do the same?" (p. 230). When the medical examiner comes up with the theory that a third man may have murdered both Herndon and Blount, both Houston and Cross describe such a man in frightening terms. For Houston, such a man is "a bleak and tragic man. He is the twentieth century writ small." Cross concurs that for such a person, "all ethical laws are suspended. He acts like a God" (p. 283).

But Cross cannot stop with these murders alone. Finding that John Hilton, a Party man, had betrayed Bob Hunter to the Immigration authorities, Cross decides to kill Hilton too. By this time, both the police and the Party have focused on him as a suspect. Houston confronts Cross with his discarded identity but, in the absence of definitive evidence, leaves him to his own punishment:

> "Listen, Damon, you made your own law," Houston pronounced. "And, by God, I, for one, am going to let you live by it. I'm pretty certain you're finished with this killing phase. . . . So, I'm going to let you go. See? Yes; just go! *You're free!* Just like that." Houston snapped his fingers in Cross's face. "I'm going to let you keep this in your heart until the end of your days!. . . You are going to punish yourself, see? You are your own law, so you'll be your own judge. . . ." (pp. 429-30)

But Houston lets Damon go only after he has confronted him with his own reality. Houston, Cross's "double" in the book, lays him bare in a clear and strong description of Cross's *primum mobile*, the desire to be a god among his fellow human beings:

> Desire is the mad thing, the irrational thing. Damon, you peeled off layer after layer of illusion and make-believe and stripped yourself down to just simply naked desire and you thought that you had gotten hold of the core of reality. And, in a sense, you had. But what does one do with desire? Man desires ultimately to be a god. (p. 425)

Some of the animus directed against Communists in the final pages of *The Outsider* has to do with Wright's own experiences with the Party. To some extent, Wright felt close to existentialism because he had come to distrust all forms of authoritarianism. Communism, for him, denies individualism and subjectivity. He charges that the driving force behind Communism is nothing but a lust for naked power:

> [T]o hold absolute power over others, to define what they should love or fear, to decide if they were to live or die and thereby to ravage the whole of their beings--that was a sensuality that made sexual passion look pale by comparison. It was a non-economic conception of existence. (p. 198)

While Bob Hunter's experiences in *The Outsider* were based on the actual case of Hank Johnson, it bears many parallels to the case of Ross Washington, a black party member that Wright had described at length in his essay included in *The God That Failed* (ed. Richard Crossman), and is now also available in *American Hunger*, his second autobiography. Both in *American Hunger* and *The Outsider*, Wright underscores the Communist Party's distrust of intellectuals: "The slightest sign of any independence of thought or feeling, even if it aided the party in its work, was enough to make one suspect, to brand one as a dangerous traitor."[15] This denunciation of Communism links up with the larger theme of *The Outsider*, the tyranny by which one may arbitrarily decide to play the role of God and control the destiny of others.

Wright's handling of the story's ending is perhaps an indication of his deep distrust of the Party's tyranny. While the dispenser of law, Ely Houston, leaves Cross alone to devise his own form of punishment, the Party folks are not prepared to let him go scot-free. They must settle scores blatantly and immediately, leaving little room for psychological retribution or recoupment. Two Party men shadow Cross and finally shoot him down. The final scene, reminiscent in many ways of Bigger Thomas's last meeting with Max, introduces a surprising new element into the conversation between Cross and Houston:

"Nothing . . ." He lay very still and summoned all of his strength. "The search can't be done alone." He let his voice issue from a dry throat in which he felt death lurking. "Never alone. . . . Alone a man is nothing. . . . *Man is a promise that he must never break.*

"Is there anything, Damon, you want me to tell anybody?" His mind reeled at the question. There was so much and yet it was so little. . . .

"I wish I had some way to give the meaning of my life to others. . . . To make a bridge from man to man. . . . Starting from scratch every time . . . is no good. Tell them not to come down this road. . . . Men hate themselves and it makes them hate others. . . . *We must find some way of being good to ourselves . . . Man is all we've got.* I wish I could ask men to meet themselves. . . . We're strangers to ourselves." He was silent for a moment, then he continued, whispering: "Don't think I'm so odd and strange. . . . I'm not. . . . I'm legion. . . . I've lived alone, but I'm everywhere. . . . Man is returning to the earth. . . . For a long time he has been sleeping, wrapped in a dream. . . . " (pp. 439-40; italics mine)

This final scene is also an important clue to our interpretation of the book. Is the book to be seen primarily as a dramatization of an existentialist thesis, or is Wright rejecting existentialist philosophy as inadequate to cope with the problems of the modern world? Or is *The Outsider* perhaps a kind of cathartic exercise, Wright's attempt to purge himself of existentialist attitudes and stances? Growing anxious about his existence, Cross seizes upon an opportunity to foreclose his original identity, and although he is trapped in the process, he appears to have gained an insight into the human situation. He is urged by the Party to be a nonentity and he treats others in the same way; only in death does he gain a semblance of wholeness. Inasmuch as *The Outsider* dramatizes the dilemma of its protagonist, death sets a boundary to everything, and Cross is shown to perceive a unity of existence.

There remains a doubt in the reader's mind, however, about the authenticity of Cross's ultimate assertions about man and life. Internal and external evidence suggests that Wright had written the novel to work out the implications of an existentialist stance, as a conscious stock-taking point in his own intellectual, spiritual, and aesthetic development. The book undoubtedly has the mechanical obviousness of a dogma being rehearsed for possible adoption and lacks the vitality and appeal of *Native Son*, where, partly because of Wright's closeness to the concrete facts of Afro-American existence, one gets the feel of experience lived through, felt on the pulse. To describe Wright's earlier works like *Black Boy* and *Native Son* as existentialist would be to introduce unnecessary semantic confusion into our discussion, but it seems reasonable to suggest that there were enough indications in his earlier work--e.g., his attitude toward God in *Black Boy*, Bigger's half-articulate new sense of himself in the last scene of *Native Son*, and the wide-ranging, nonracial implications of a story like "The Man Who Lived Underground"--to suggest his subsequent gravitation towards the philosophical literature of the alienated and self-determining man.

It would seem unlikely that the novelist in Wright would have stopped with a Nietzschean existentialism. But if we lay aside all that Wright rejects in the pages of *The Outsider*, we are left with little that affirms or lends hope. As Orville Prescott noted in an early review, one may assume that Wright deplores "Cross' moral weakness and irrational behaviour, but that he finds much cogency in Cross' philosophy. That men as brilliant as Richard Wright feel this way is one of the symptoms of the intellectual and moral crisis of our times."[16] For a few years before he wrote *The Outsider*, Wright had been drawn to causes on behalf of colonized nations in Africa and Asia. Fabre tells us that in the early fifties, Wright had been removing himself each day "from purely American pre-occupations by acquiring a more European, more global view of his own situation in particular, of the black situation in general, and the situation of contemporary man."[17] Wright's unpublished article "I Choose Exile" (1950) had strongly underscored the need for Americans to break away from narrow provincialism and to inject a Third-World awareness into a renewed pursuit of the highest American ideals. Is it possible, then, that Wright the political activist cherished goals and sought solutions which clashed with his overwhelming conditioning as a Western intellectual, a very American individualist?[18] Wright's quest for a new humanism remained unfulfilled possibly because as an artist he could not integrate his newly discovered Third-World predilections into his predominantly Western orientation. This inner dichotomy of Wright's is perhaps responsible for the ambivalence that the reader experiences in responding to *The Outsider* as an existentialist novel.

Notes

[1]Quoted in Michel Fabre, *The Unfinished Quest of Richard Wright* (New York: William Morrow, 1973), p. 315.
[2]Ibid., p. 326.
[3]Ibid., p. 322.
[4]Preface to Frantz Fanon, *The Wretched of the Earth*, trans. Constance Farrington (New York: Grove, 1968), p. 22.
[5]Ibid.
[6]Cf. Lorraine Hansberry's review, *Freedom*, 14 (April 1953), 7: "Cross Damon is someone you will never meet on the Southside of Chicago or in Harlem. For if he is anything at all, he is the symbol of Wright's new philosophy--the glorification of--nothingness."
[7]Max Eastman, "Man as a Promise," *Freeman*, 3 (May 4, 1953), 567-8.
[8]Fabre, p. 366.
[9]Richard Wright, *The Outsider* (New York: Harper and Row, 1953), p. 14. All subsequent quotations from the novel are from this edition and have been cited in the text.
[10]John Macquarrie, *Existentialism* (1972; rpt. Harmondsworth: Penguin, 1973), p. 54.
[11]Ibid., p. 175.
[12]Ibid., p. 191. A bit earlier (p. 190), John Macquarrie defines *facticity* thus: "I cannot exchange my existence for the existence of another. I am I . . . . I just happen to be this particular person and no other. I have this particular body; I am of this particular race and colour; I have this particular heredity, this particular intelligence quotient, this particular emotional make-up, and so on. Furthermore, I have been born into this particular historical situation in this particular society, and all kinds of forces are operating in the situation and in the society to shape my life and to limit what I can become."
[13]Ibid., p. 204.
[14]Ibid., p. 103.
[15]Richard Wright, *American Hunger* (New York: Harper and Row, 1977) p. 120.
[16]*New York Times*, 18 March 1953, p. 29. Quoted in John M. Reilly, ed., *Richard Wright: The Critical Reception* (New York: Burt Franklin, 1978), p. 194.
[17]Fabre, p. 316.
[18]For a stimulating discussion of Wright's dichotomous attitude toward the West (or for that matter, toward individualism), see Nina Kressner Cobb, "Richard Wright: Individualism Reconsidered," *CLA Journal*, 21, No. 3 (March 1978), 335-54. Cobb, too, points to "signs of discomfort" in the conclusions of both *Native Son* and *The Outsider*.

From *CLA Journal* 27 (June 1984), 357-70.

Eight Men (1961)

Lives of More than Quiet Desperation

Richard Sullivan

Unhappily, "Eight Men" is a posthumous volume. Richard Wright died in Paris in late November. Still, in his early fifties, he was an American writer of genuine importance, and his best work--some of it contained in this volume--will endure. At times his profound indignation led him into flimsy political philosophizing, which intruded upon his story-telling, understandably, for he was a wounded, sensitive and embattled artist. In "Native Son" and "Black Boy" he illuminated with passion certain aspects of the state of the Negro in this century's American polity. He was a deeply concerned writer, capable of great dramatic intensity, uneven in his achievements, but every instant alive in his awareness of humanity, justice and love, together with their all too frequent negations and denials.

"Eight Men" is a representative book, containing eight stories, some of them published before. Each story centers on a Negro, involved cruelly with his surroundings, beaten down by them; each central figure is in one way or another misunderstood by the world he knows; a few misunderstand and misinterpret that world. Altogether the eight men of these stories have in common a desperate if qualified heroism. They are, at their best and their worst, real men. And the stories are real stories.

A couple of them, rendered largely in dialogue, are technically masterful. One of them, "The Man Who Lived Underground" (the story of a fugitive from justice hiding in a city sewer), is a memorable symbolic piece, worthy of long brooding. Another, "The Man Who Went to Chicago" (which describes the hardships of a migrant worker who comes North), is really a report, half narrative, half essay, the two halves joining impressively. The protagonist in this story says, "I had elected, in my fevered search for honorable adjustment to the American scene, not to submit and in doing so I had embraced the daily horror of anxiety, of tension, of eternal disquiet." Though it is quietly stated, this philosophy of living might be taken from Richard Wright's own experience. One finds it in "Native Son." It is stated, even more explicitly, in the later fragments of autobiography he published in book form. It was a compulsion, a way of living he was destined never to escape entirely, even in his long European exile.

There is not a touch of phoniness or fakery in the book. All eight men and all eight stories stand as beautifully, pitifully, terribly true. Some readers will be shocked by it, for it presents straightforwardly a brilliant American Negro's point of view. Many more readers will be uplifted and encouraged by it; to some it will indeed seem a sign and a token of what is to come and to be welcomed, to be rejoiced at. Because all the way through this is fine, sound, good, honorable writing, rich with insight and understanding, even when occasionally twisted by sorrow.

To a good many readers it will come as an almost inexpressible misery that this book is dedicated to French friends who made the American author "feel at home in an alien land." It is not that those friends are not most estimable and already rewarded; it is that here, in his native land, other friends in the lacking left Richard Wright to perish, like Palinurus, away from a home that must honor him, hereafter, for the sturdy prose he wrote.

From *The New York Times Book Review* (22 January, 1961), 5.

Review of *Eight Men*

Saunders Redding

Of the eight stories in this posthumous collection four are bizarre, three are conventional, one is an autobiographical fragment, and all explore the author's favorite theme--rootlessness. "I am a rootless man," Richard Wright once wrote: "but I am neither psychologically distraught nor in any wise particularly perturbed because of it." With no substantial exceptions, his works--including this one--argue otherwise. Indeed, Wright was painfully distressed by his rootlessness, and this anguish was the living substance of his best books, the stuff of which they were made. But after long expatriation from America, where experience fed his anguish, he came to feel it less. Memory alone was not enough to keep the torment vital. This I suppose accounts for the fact that the best of the stories in "Eight Men" were all written before 1945.

"The Man Who Was Almost a Man," "The Man Who Saw the Flood," and the autobiographical piece, "The Man Who Went to Chicago," are recognizably the old Wright who could snare eternal values in a moment of pure sensation, who could dramatize an idea in a rush of earthy dialogue, and who spoke out his supraconsciousness of being Negro in a way that was, as Dorothy Canfield Fisher said, "honest, dreadful, heartbreaking." Of these three, only "The Man Who Was Almost a Man" can properly be called a story. Its hero is a teenage boy who buys a gun his father does not want him to have. The gun is a symbol. It is the symbol but not the substance of manhood, and to get the substance, to "let him know Dave Saunders is a man," he runs away from home. "The Man Who Saw the Flood" is even simpler in outline. A Mississippi sharecropper, who hopes the flood he has lived through has washed away the road, finds that it has not. Literally and figuratively, the road leads nowhere, but it is the road that he must travel all his life. The last of these three pieces is a straight autobiographical account of Wright's Chicago days, and it, too, is marked by the honest simplicity that characterized the author's earliest books; it, too, drives home a point.

The same cannot be said of the five remaining stories, of which two are eccentric experiments in technique, and three are grotesque in subject matter. In "Man of All Work" and "Man, God Ain't Like That" Wright relies exclusively on dialogue. He uses it to establish the mood, to set the scene, to provide dramatic exposition, to advance the narrative, and to delineate character. And dialogue is not enough. It is not enough because it is not good enough nor flexible enough. Wright cannot make dialogue do all that needs to be done to create an illusion of the reality of the farcical circumstance in which a quite ordinary husband and father ("Man of All Work") masquerades so successfully as a woman as to take a housemaid's job and to be sexually assaulted by the woman-chasing master of the house. In "Man, God Ain't Like That," where character is sketchy and plot implausible, it takes more than dialogue to establish a compelling motive for ritual murder, and to explain the failure of the police to solve it, and to drive home the obscure point of it all--if there is a point.

The most impressive story in "Eight Men" is "The Man Who Lived Underground," and it is an impressive failure. It is a fantastic nightmare of guilt, fear and redemption, of sewage filth, of obscene, senseless murder. It has all the dramatic tension of a first-class Gothic tale; there are descriptive passages of extraordinary vividness, and stylistic ornaments of great glitter, but nothing comes to anything: no passion has meaning, no insight is revealed, no idea truly conveyed, no theme made unmistakably plain. It is as if Gabriel, brandishing his trumpet and filling his lungs with air to blow the blast of doom, managed only a penny whistle's pipe.

"Eight Men" is not one of the books by which Richard Wright deserves to be judged. Those who meet the author for the first time through these stories will have but a faulty acquaintance with him. Those who read "Uncle Tom's Children," "Native Son," and "Black Boy" long ago will read "Eight Men" with sad and growing wonder.

From *New York Herald Tribune Book Review* (22 January, 1961), 33.

Richard Wright: A Word of Farewell

Irving Howe

In the two months since the death of Richard Wright there has appeared, to my knowledge, one serious comment about his life or his work: a memoir by James Baldwin in the socialist paper *New America* reflecting with characteristic honesty that mixture of admiration and estrangement most of the younger Negro novelists felt toward Wright. Otherwise, little has been written in tribute or criticism. Our culture seems almost proud of its capacity for not remembering, and is often most cruel toward those figures it was honoring a few decades ago.

When Wright's first novel *Native Son* appeared in the thirties, it seemed important both as an example of literary naturalism and an outcry of Negro protest. A few years later came *Black Boy*, the story of Wright's boyhood and youth in the deep South and perhaps his single best piece of work. Here, one felt, was the American Negro novelist who would speak without hesitation, who for the first time would tell the truth not only about the familiar sufferings of his people but about their buried responses, those inner feelings of anger and hatred which no white man could reach. And this, I think, Wright did succeed in doing. He told us the one thing even the most liberal and well-disposed whites preferred not to hear: that Negroes were far from patient or forgiving, that they were scarred by fear, that they hated every moment of their humiliation even when seeming most acquiescent, and that often enough they hated *us*, the decent and cultivated white men who, from complicity or neglect, shared in the responsibility for their plight. No Negro writer had ever quite said this before, certainly not with so much force or bluntness, and if such younger Negro novelists as James Baldwin and Ralph Ellison were to move beyond Wright's harsh naturalism and toward more subtle modes of fiction, that was possible only because Wright had been there first, courageous enough to release the full weight of his anger.

Before the implications of this fact, it seemed not very important that his image of Negro life in America was becoming historically dated (which is true) or that he occasionally succumbed to black nationalism (also true) or that he wrote badly (sometimes true). The bitterness and rage that poured out of Wright's books form one of the great American testaments, a crushing necessity to our moral life, forever to remind us that moderate analyses of injustice are finally lies.

And now, after fourteen years of voluntary exile in Paris, chosen, as he once told me, because he could no longer bear to live in the United States and see his children suffer the blows of race hatred, Richard Wright is dead. His life was incomplete, as it had to be, and at the end his work as tentative and fumbling as at the beginning. His later years were difficult, for he neither made a true home in Paris nor kept in imaginative touch with the changing life of the United States. He was a writer in limbo, and his best fiction, such as the novelette "The Man Who Lived Underground," is a projection of that condition. His work, so far as I can tell, is hardly read today by serious literary persons; his name barely known by the young.

Eight Men, Wright's most recent and apparently last book, is a collection of stories written over the last 25 years. Though they fail to yield any clear line of chronological development, these stories do give evidence of Wright's literary restlessness, his wish to keep learning and experimenting, his often clumsy efforts to break out of the naturalism which was his first and, I think, necessary mode of expression. The unevenness of his writing is extremely disturbing; one finds it hard to understand how the same man, from paragraph to paragraph, can be at once so brilliant and inept--though the student of American literature soon learns to measure the price which the talented autodidact pays for getting his education too late. Time after time the narrative texture of the stories is broken by a passage of jargon borrowed from sociology or psychology: perhaps the later Wright read too much, tried too hard, failed to remain sufficiently loyal to the limits of his talent.

The best stories are marked by a strong feeling for the compactness of the story as a form, so that even when the language is scraggly or leaden there is a sharply articulated pattern of event. Some of the stories, such as "Big Black Good Man," are enlivened by Wright's sardonic humor, the humor of a man who has known and released the full measure of his despair but finds that neither knowledge nor release matters in a world of despair. In "The Man Who Lived Underground" Wright shows a sense of narrative rhythm, a gift for shaping the links between sentences so as to create a chain of expectation, which is superior to anything in his full-length novels and evidence of the seriousness with which he kept working.

The main literary problem that troubled Wright in recent years was that of rendering his naturalism a more supple and terse instrument. I think he went astray whenever he abandoned naturalism entirely; there are a few embarrassingly bad experiments with stories written entirely in dialogue or self-consciously employing Freudian symbolism. Wright needed the accumulated material of circumstance which naturalistic detail provided his fiction; it was as essential to his ultimate effect of shock and bruise as dialogue to Hemingway's ultimate effect of irony and loss. But Wright was correct in thinking that the problem of detail is the most vexing technical problem the naturalist writer must face, since the accumulation of detail that makes for depth and solidity can also create a pall of tedium. In "The Man Who Lived Underground" Wright came close to solving this problem, for here the naturalistic detail is put at the service of a radical projective image--a Negro trapped in a sewer--and despite some flaws, the story is satisfying both for its tense surface and its elasticity of suggestion.

For some readers, the obsession with violence they detected in Wright's work was more disturbing than any of his technical faults. As Alfred Kazin has written: "If he chose to write the story of Bigger Thomas [in *Native Son*] as a grotesque crime story, it is because his own indignation and the sickness of the age combined to make him dependent on violence and shock, to astonish the reader by torrential scenes of cruelty, hunger, rape, murder, and flight . . . . " Apart from the fact that something very similar and quite as damning could be said about the author of *Crime and Punishment*, this judgment rests on the assumption that a critic can readily distinguish between the genuine need of a contemporary writer to cope with ugly realities and the damaging effects these realities may have upon him.

The reality pressing upon all of Wright's work is a nightmare of remembrance, and without the terror of that nightmare it would be impossible to render the truth of the reality--not the only, perhaps not even the deepest truth about American Negroes, but a primary and inescapable one. Both truth and terror depend upon a gross fact which Wright faced more courageously than any American writer; that for the Negro violence forms an inescapable part of his existence.

In a sense, then, Wright was justified in not paying attention to the changes that have been occurring in the South these past few decades. When Negro liberals write that despite the prevalence of bias there has been an improvement in the life of their people down South, such statements are reasonable and necessary. But what have they to do with the way Negroes feel, with the power of the memories they must surely retain? About this we know very little and would be well advised not to nourish preconceptions, for it may well be that their feelings are quite close to Wright's rasping outbursts. *Wright remembered*, and what he remembered other Negroes must also have remembered. Perhaps by now the terror and humiliation that fill his pages are things of the past, even in Mississippi; but men whose lives have been torn by suffering must live with their past, so that it too becomes part of the present reality. And by remembering Wright kept faith with the experience of the boy who had fought his way out of the depths to speak for those who remained there.

The present moment is not a good one for attempting a judicious estimate of Wright's achievement as a novelist. It is hard to suppose that he will ever be regarded as a writer of the first rank, for his faults are grave and obvious. Together with Farrell and Dos Passos, he has suffered from the changes of literary taste which occurred during his lifetime: the naturalist novel is little read these days, though often mocked, and the very idea of a "protest novel" has become a target for graduate students to demolish. The dominant school of criticism has little interest in the kind of work Wright did, and it rejects him less from a particular examination than from a theoretic preconception--or to be more precise, from an inability to realize that the kind of linguistic scrutiny to which it submits lyric poetry has only a limited value in the criticism of fiction.

Now I would not pretend to be writing from any established superiority to current taste, for I too find the murk and awkwardness of most naturalist fiction hard to bear. But I believe that any view of 20th-Century American literature which surmounts critical sectarianism will have to give Wright an honored place, and that any estimate of his role in our cultural life will have to stress his importance as the pioneer Negro writer who in the fullness of his anger made it less possible for American society to continue deceiving itself.

Anger and violence may be present in his work, but the Richard Wright I knew, slightly in person and somewhat more through letters, was a singularly good-hearted and sweet man. When I met him in Paris a few years ago, he was open, vigorous and animated, full of shrewd if not always just estimates of the younger writers, actively concerned with the intellectual life of the African students who clustered about him, and, at a time when it was far from fashionable, still interested in the politics of the democratic left.

Richard Wright died at 52, full of hopes and projects. Like many of us, he had somewhat lost his intellectual way during recent years, but he kept struggling toward a comprehension of the strange and unexpected world coming into birth. In the most fundamental sense, however, he had done his work: he had told his contemporaries a truth so bitter that they paid him the tribute of striving to forget it.

From *The New Republic*, 144 (February 13, 1961), 17-18.

The Paradoxical Structure of Richard Wright's "The Man Who Lived Underground"

Patricia D. Watkins

Most critics of Richard Wright's novella "The Man Who Lived Underground" focus on its existential content.[1] However, because these critics generally ground their usually brief analyses on the story's plot rather than close textual analysis, their comments about man's "essence" and "existence" seem inadequate, justifying Robin McNallie's complaint that critics "have settled too easily for broad overviews of 'Man' instead of focusing on the story's particulars"(77). Along the same lines, only a few critics mention—let alone discuss—the story's naturalistic content. When they do mention it, these critics assure their audiences that Wright "surpassed" and "moved beyond" the naturalistic perspective to the more "universal," "sophisticated," and "philosophical" existential perspective.[2] Despite its current low repute, however, naturalism, like existentialism, makes a statement about man's essence and existence. Thus, to focus on the story's existential content while ignoring or minimizing its naturalistic content is necessarily to risk distorting what Wright says in it about man and man's life. More importantly, such a focus disregards a major basis of the story's paradoxical structure—paradoxical because at every level, from the dictional to the philosophical, Wright pairs contradictory and seemingly irreconcilable parts.

At the heart of the paradox is the story's simultaneous existence as a naturalistic (thus deterministic) fable and an existential (thus anti-deterministic) fable. The result of this yoking of fables is a protagonist who is simultaneously portrayed as an animal, whose fate is controlled by forces independent of his will, and a god, whose will becomes, in effect, the First Cause of his fate. The paradoxical structure of the story demands first that the protagonist be considered in terms of his role in both the naturalistic and the existential fables, and finally that the apparent contradictions related to the fables and the protagonist's role in them be reconciled. This structural approach will disclose a more accurate picture of the protagonist's (and, by extension, Wright's conception of man's) essence and existence than has been developed by evaluating the protagonist in terms of one fable alone.

"The Man Who Lived Underground" has all of the features of the classic naturalistic fable. Its working-class protagonist Fred Daniels has been falsely accused of murder. He escapes from the police and takes refuge underground in the sewers. After a few days of tunneling through the sewers and secretly observing the people who live above ground, he leaves the underground and confronts the policemen who earlier forced him to sign a confession of guilt. When Daniels tries to lead them into the sewers so that they can see people as he has seen them, one of the officers shoots and kills him. Thus, Daniels suffers the classic fate of the naturalistic protagonist: He is "wiped out."

Wright's presentation of Daniels' story epitomizes the naturalistic method described by Émile Zola in such works as *The Experimental Novel, The Fortune of the Rougons*, and *Thérèse Raquin*. Wright literally renders Zola's dictum that man be considered an animal. Throughout the story Wright compares Daniels to animals, sometimes explicitly and sometimes implicitly. For example, Wright uses a series of similes that explicitly compare Daniels' actions to those of an insect, a dog, an eel, and a cat (35, 41, 53, 73). Wright implicitly compares Daniels to an animal by writing that Daniels "slithered through" the entrance to the cave that serves as his underground home (41). Wright's placing Daniels underground to "live" is another implicit comparison of Daniels to an animal, most particularly a rat. Mildred W. Everette points out that Daniels lives like a pack rat, burrowing from place to place underground and dragging stolen items to his "underground den" (321). Eventually Daniels dies like the rat that he encountered when he first entered the sewer. As Everette notes, the wording that describes the death of the rat as it spins in the sewer current after Daniels has killed it is the same wording that describes the death of Daniels as he spins after the police officer Lawson has shot him (320).

As Zola also dictated, Wright observes the effect that heredity has on the fortunes and character of his protagonist. A significant role played by heredity is Daniels' inheritance of compulsive animal drives—especially the need to satisfy his hunger and thirst. The need to find food and clean water drives Daniels from one location to another while he is underground. The need to find food influences Daniels' character as well, turning him into a thief who steals a lunch pail from a furnace tender and fruit from a grocer.

Racial identity does not directly determine what happens to Fred Daniels. Rather, environment—specifically, economic and social forces—seems to be a more important determinant of Daniels' fortunes. Before his arrest Daniels worked at the home of a Mrs. Wooten, presumably as a servant. Hence, Daniels is at the lower end of the economic and social scale, like the white night watchman who shares his fate. This fate is to be the victim of policemen who "solve" cases by using brute force. Having falsely accused and then tortured the night watchman, the policemen let him shoot and kill himself; having falsely accused and then tortured Daniels, one of the same policemen shoots and kills him.

On all counts, therefore, "The Man Who Lived Underground" exemplifies the naturalistic fable: it shows man living like an animal and dying like an animal, which is to say that, like an animal, man is the subject of internal and external forces over which he lacks control.

Paradoxically, as Wright compares Daniels to animals, he simultaneously compares him to Christ. This animal/Christ linking is a subparadox within a broader animal/God paradox. The first suggestion that Daniels is Christlike occurs early in the story when he dreams that he can walk on water (42). Less obviously but just as tellingly, references to daylight and darkness, which indicate that Daniels stays underground for three days, reveal his story to be virtually the mirror image of Christ's: Christ was executed, lay dead in a cave for three days, and then rose on the third day; Daniels lives in a cave for three days, rises on the third day, and then is executed.[3]

Daniels' identification with Christ is further suggested in the confrontation of Daniels with the Black worshippers in a church when Daniels returns above ground on the third day. Their paradoxical encounter, during which the worshippers reject the savior that they pray for, is a sustained example of dramatic irony, based on the reader's awareness and the worshippers' lack of awareness that Daniels is a Christ. The congregants sing a hymn that invokes "the Lamb" to "*Tell* me again your story" (75, emphasis added). Daniels comes to them shouting, "... I want to *tell* 'em" (75, emphasis added). Some of the congregation, not recognizing that the invoked spirit has arrived, say of Daniels, "'He's filthy ... He stinks'" (75). Others begin another hymn, which speaks of a "*wondrous sight ... Vision sweet and divine*" (76). The sewer-filthy Daniels is, indeed, a "wondrous sight," and if the congregation recognized him for the Christ that he is, they would see that he is a "vision sweet," even though he does stink. Finally, the congregants sing:

> *Oh, wondrous sight, wondrous sight*
> *Lift my heavy heart above*
> *Oh, wondrous sight, wondrous sight*
> *Fill my weary soul with love* (76)

Love is exactly what Daniels wants to fill these souls with. Though he does not know what to say to the congregation when he confronts them, by the time that he gets to the police station he knows both his message of love and his method for spreading it. Speaking to Lawson he exclaims, "'Mister, when I looked through all of those holes and saw how people were living, I loved 'em...'" (86). Daniels believes that, if the policemen follow him to his underground home, the love that he feels will multiply: "... they would feel what he had felt and they in turn would show it to others and those others would feel as they had felt, and soon everybody would be governed by the same impulse of pity" (89). The Black congregants, however, do not give Daniels the opportunity to deliver the message of love that they pray for. They push him out of the church into the street. Their action provides a final parallel between the situations of Daniels and Christ. Rejected by his own people, Daniels is executed by the centurions of the ruling class. Thus his fate—to die like a rat and to be killed like Christ—is paradoxically the fate of animal and God.

Daniels' divinity is not limited to his Christlike life and death. Rather, it is the broader divinity usually associated with Jean-Paul Sartre's existential dictum "Create yourself and your world." For a humanistic existentialist like Sartre, God is dead. Since there is no God, man is free—obligated, in fact—to define himself and to act based on his own will rather than on some God-given, predetermined idea of what man is and how he should live. In other words, since God is dead, man is free to become his own god. In existential terms Daniels becomes his own god (just as in naturalistic terms he is an animal). Daniels must be considered in existential terms because he experiences the range of emotions—a sense of isolation, anxiety, guilt, and freedom—that are experienced by the typical existential protagonist when he discovers that he exists in a universe without God.

According to Michel Fabre's chronology, Wright wrote "The Man Who Lived Underground" before he received formal instruction on Nietzsche, Kierkegaard, and other existentialists, and before his first meeting with Sartre (299). Thus, in his story Wright may not be consciously working out the major themes of existentialism. Nevertheless, Wright's rendering of existential themes is understandable in terms of standard explanations of twentieth-century existentialism, which, like the existential attitude, seeks to understand how man should live in a chaotic universe on which no God imposes an order that man can comprehend.

No God imposes a comprehensible order on the universe of "The Man Who Lived Underground." In this universe God is dead—or at least absent. Thus, dreaming of a drowning mother and her baby, Daniels loses sight of the baby and begins calling, "*Where is it* and the empty sky and sea threw back his voice" (42). The metaphor has been used by other "empty sky" authors to suggest God's absence from the affairs of men—absence either because He does not exist or because He does not choose to involve Himself. For example, to signify God's non-existence, Nathanael West uses the "empty sky" metaphor in *Miss Lonelyhearts,* wherein the protagonist "searched the sky .... the gray sky looked as if it had been the rubbed with a soiled eraser. It held no angels, flaming crosses, olive-bearing doves, wheels within wheels" (174-75); "... it was canvas-colored and ill-stretched. He examined it ... he found nothing" (204-05). To signify God's lack of involvement, Zola Neale Hurston uses the "empty sky" metaphor in *Their Eyes Were Watching God,* wherein the protagonist "looked hard at the sky for a long time. Somewhere up there beyond blue ether's bosom sat He. Was He noticing what was going on around here? The sky stayed hard looking and quiet .... God would do less than He had in His heart" (264). In the dream of Fred Daniels the empty sky reveals his subconscious awareness (provoked by the corpse of a real baby that he has seen earlier floating in the sewer) that no God will appear to rescue even the most "innocent" of creatures—a baby—from death. Later, while Daniels is waiting to learn the combination of a jewelry store safe, he "looked with a baffled expression at the dark sky" (51). At this point Daniels consciously begins to realize that God is absent.

When the typical existential protagonist realizes that there is no God watching him or watching over him, he feels isolated, alone in the universe. During his three-day ordeal underground, Fred Daniels is constantly aware that he is "alone" (31, 40, 43, 92). In addition, the typical existential protagonist feels angst—a combination of fear and dread—when he realizes that he is solely responsible for his actions because, since there is no God, man lacks a God-given, pre-defined nature that he can use to excuse his actions as well as an absolute standard of good and evil to help him choose among alternative actions. During his three-day ordeal Daniels experiences angst—most clearly as he prepares to emerge from the underground for the last time: "He did not know how much fear he felt, for fear claimed him completely; yet it was not a fear of the police or of people, but a cold dread at the thought of the *actions* he knew he would perform if he went out into that cruel sunshine" (73, emphasis added). Daniels' fear and dread in this case are existential, or ontological. They are not the same as his "ordinary," or situational, fear and dread, which arise when he faces harm (from the rushing sewer waters, for example, or from the police). Instead, they are the angst that arises when he must act.

In addition to feeling alone and anxious, the typical existential protagonist feels guilty. Fred Daniels experiences both "ordinary" and existential guilt. Early in the story, Daniels experiences "ordinary," or situational, guilt when he transgresses religious and social codes, for example, when he wants to laugh at the church congregants the first time that he sees them (32). The guilt that he suffers arises from his wanting to do something that his religious training makes him feel that he should not do. That Daniels has such training, that he is a religious man is clear: Who but a religious man would worry that God might "strike him dead" (32), and of whom but a religious man would it be claimed that "he knew most of the churches in this area [where he was hiding] above ground ..." (32)? Not surprisingly, therefore, Daniels feels guilt when he wants to laugh at the people worshipping God. He feels the same ordinary guilt when he steals the furnace tender's food and while he burglarizes the jewelry shop safe (40, 54).

Unlike his ordinary guilt, the existential, or ontological, guilt of Daniels does not derive from any violation of religious or social codes. It cannot, for existentialists recognize no legal or ethical absolutes against which man can judge his actions and find himself guilty. Rather, as Donald V. Marano explains, existential guilt derives from man's possession of consciousness, which allows him to discern his inherent weakness and inadequacy: his powerlessness to bring himself into existence and his powerlessness to guarantee that he will cease to exist even if he commits suicide; his powerlessness to keep that which is outside himself (for example, the heat from a fire) from impinging on his consciousness unwilled; his physical, intellectual, and moral inability to be or do all that he wants to be or do (42-45). The term *guilt*, therefore, embraces "not only human deficiencies, since they all bespeak discrepancies between what a man is and the what he aspires to be" (46). As Marano concludes, man, because of his finitude, is innately guilty (45).

Fred Daniels first becomes aware of existential guilt as he listens to the church congregation singing:

> He felt that their search for a happiness they could never find made them feel that they had committed some dreadful offense which they could not remember or understand .... Why was this sense of guilt so seemingly innate, so easy to come by, to think, to feel, so verily physical? It seemed that when one felt this guilt one was retracing in one's feelings a faint pattern designed long before; it seemed that one was always trying to remember a gigantic shock that had left a haunting impression upon one's body which one could not forget or shake off, but which had been forgotten by the conscious mind, creating in one's life a state of eternal anxiety. (68)

In other words, Daniels credits the congregation's guilt not to their actual ability to judge themselves guilty of a specific religious or legal violation (in which case their guilt would be "ordinary," everyday guilt) but rather to their consciousness of an innate sense of failure and inadequacy. The guilt that Daniels attributes to them, therefore, is existential guilt.

Daniels recognizes this same existential guilt in the boy who is beaten for stealing a radio stolen by Daniels himself. Watching the beating, Daniels says to himself, "Perhaps it was a good thing that they were beating the boy; perhaps the beating would bring to the boy's attention, for the first time in his life, the secret of his existence, the guilt that he could never get rid of" (69). Likewise, Daniels recognizes existential guilt in the night watchman, who is accused of stealing the jewelry stolen by Daniels: "The watchman was guilty; although he was not guilty of the crime of which he had been accused, he was guilty, had always been guilty" (70). Convinced at last that all men are guilty in a way that is unrelated to any legal or religious infraction, Daniels leaves the underground, enters the police station, and—even though he knows that he has not murdered anyone—confesses, "'I'm guilty'" (85).

Daniels' emotions of isolation, fear, and guilt are predictable consequences of an awareness of the absence of God in the universe. As the existential protagonist accepts the absence of God, he recognizes his freedom to create himself and his world—in short, his freedom to be his own god. Near the end of his second day underground, Daniels takes the first step toward creating himself and his world and hence becoming his own god: He begins rejecting his aboveground values and identity.

One aboveground value that Daniels rejects is money. Given a dime by a woman who mistakes him for a clerk at a grocery store, Daniels "fl[i]ng[s] the dime to the pavement with a gesture of contempt" (49). He shows the same contempt for even larger sums of money when he pastes hundred dollar bills on the walls of his cave. His rejection of the valuation of money above ground is a liberating act. After pasting the money on the walls, Daniels "slapped his thighs and guffawed. He had triumphed over the world aboveground! He was free!" (62).

A second aboveground value that Daniels rejects is time. On his second day underground, Daniels' enslavement to time ends when he prepares to nail valuable watches onto the same dirt wall on which he has just pasted the hundred dollar bills. Taking the watches from a box, he "began to wind them up; he did not attempt to set them at any given hour, for there was no time for him now" (62). Once again, rejecting a value of the world above ground is a liberating act for Daniels, for as he contemplates the watches, he recognizes the restrictions that time places on people who, unlike him, have not escaped time's tyranny: "The gold watches ticked and trembled, crowning time the king of consciousness, defining the limits of living" (66). When he first went underground Daniels realized that he had "to kill time or go aboveground" (35). Because Daniels succeeds in killing time by refusing to acknowledge its existence, he is able to return above ground no sooner than he *wills* to do so. Thus, his ability to reject time, which the people above ground value, helps him to become free.

As Daniels rejects the values of the world above ground, he begins to create his own values, the second step toward "creating his own world." Steeped in his new sense of freedom, Daniels initially concludes that "anything ... was right, any act a man took to satisfy himself, murder, theft, torture" (64). Such an attitude allows him to justify his having taken someone else's money. In his mind, "He had not stolen the money; he had simply picked it up, just as a man would pick up firewood in a forest" (62). The attitude that anything is right also contributes to Daniels' desire to laugh at the boy and the watchman who are accused of having stolen items stolen by Daniels himself (69, 70). Even as he smiles, however, Daniels begins to feel the pity that ultimately characterizes life above ground. He discards the amorality of the Nietzschean superman and assumes the attitude of the existentialist who chooses his actions mindful of the effect that his choices have on humanity: "... every man ought to say to himself, 'Am I really the kind of man who has the right to act in such a way that humanity might guide itself by my actions?'" (20). So writes Sartre to explain how man should evaluate his actions since the death of God eliminates any fixed reference for judging whether an act is "good" or "evil." Such thinking seems to guide Daniels, for he abandons his anything-is-right attitude and replaces it with an attitude of love and pity for mankind, the attitude that he hopes will guide humanity's actions when it sees the new world that he has created underground. This new world is symbolized by his dirt cave, wherein watches, rings, diamonds, and money have lost their value and function merely as decoration.

In addition to creating his own world, Daniels creates himself. He does so after he sheds his aboveground identity—literally his name. When he first goes underground Daniels knows his name and types it on the typewriter that he sees in an office. When he drags the typewriter to his cave, however, his name is "on the tip of his lips," but he cannot remember it. His response is a "vague terror" (61). By the time that Daniels enters the police station, however, not only has he forgotten his name but he no longer cares that he has forgotten it. When asked his name by a policeman, "He had opened his lips to answer and no words came. He had forgotten. But what did it matter if he had? It was not important" (78).

As he sheds his aboveground identity, Fred Daniels acquires a godlike identity. Part of his divinity is the sense of freedom that he attains. Daniels feels *freedom from* the rules and the enslavements (to time, to money) of the world above ground; and he feels *freedom to* make his own rules—initially, to steal and even murder if he chooses to.

Thus, playing God as he stands over the sleeping night watchman, Fred "smiled indulgently; he could send a bullet into that man's brain and time would be over for him ..." (58). Seeing the night watchman being beaten a short time later, Daniels feels "a great sense of power" as he again realizes his godlike ability to control the watchman's fate (70).

Another part of his divinity is the sense of distance from mankind that Daniels feels. This sense becomes evident when Daniels listens to war news on a radio while staring at the stolen diamonds that he has strewn over the floor of his cave. On this occasion Daniels has the illusion of looking down from the sky, godlike, on the actions of men at war with each other (64-65). The violence that the radio announcer reports and the violence that Daniels himself has witnessed and experienced above ground lead to his final avatar—a Christ on a mission of mercy to mankind that ends in his death.

In sum, Daniels experiences or possesses a variety of emotions and attitudes—a sense of isolation, angst, guilt, freedom, creation, and divinity—that are often related to existential protagonists. In one other way, too, is Daniels' experience typical of the existential protagonist's. The pattern of his experience is consistent with the archetypal pattern of the existential fable. As described by William V. Spanos, this fable portrays the protagonist in "flight from a dark, threatening agent who pursues the fugitive protagonist into an isolated corner (often, the underground), where he must confront his relentless pursuer, whereupon, in a blinding moment of illumination he discovers the paradoxically benevolent aspect of his persecutor" (10). Briefly, in "The Man Who Lived Underground" the existential pattern works like this. The police chase Fred Daniels into the underground, ignoring his declaration of innocence and proclaiming him guilty. His underground experience causes Daniels to realize the truth—that he is, in fact, guilty. Because it is the policemen who are responsible for Daniels' going underground and thereby learning the truth, they are malevolent and benevolent. That Daniels' story may be so interpreted is possible because of three paradoxes—oxymora, stated or implied—that define Daniels' perception of the people, artifacts, and atmosphere of the world above ground.

Daniels perceives that the people of the world above ground are dead. Some are physically dead, like the woman whom Daniels is accused of having murdered, the baby that he encounters in the sewer, the corpse that he sees in the undertaking establishment, and the night watchman, who commits suicide. Others in the world above ground are spiritually dead. They are the paradoxical living dead. The oxymoron *living dead* is implied in the description of the crowd that Daniels sees in a movie theater: "These people were laughing at their lives .... They were shouting and yelling at the animated shadows of themselves.... sleeping in their living, awake in their dying" (38). The churchgoers, similarly involved with shadows rather than reality, are also among the living dead. Their pursuit of shadows is apparent in their prayers to an absent God for "a happiness they could never find" (68). The pursuit of shadows by the congregation stands in ironic contrast to their rejection of Daniels, the only real divinity that they will ever see. Their preference for shadows rather than reality links them to the other dead people whom Daniels encounters.

Daniels also perceives a link between death and the artifacts of the world above ground. He drags a number of these artifacts of to his underground home: a gun, a typewriter, a radio, a bloody meat cleaver, money, diamonds, rings, and watches. The oxymoron *serious toys* defines his perception of these items (55). Daniels himself treats the artifacts like toys, using them in "games" of make-believe. With the gun, he pretends to be a gunfighter in a movie; with the typewriter, he pretends to be a secretary in an office; and with the diamonds he pretends to be a rich man talking a morning stroll (58, 61, 63). His games trivialize—that is, reduce to the level of toys—the artifacts as they are used above ground by the people whose roles he plays. The "serious" nature of these "toys" becomes clear, however, when Daniels connects them to all of the dead persons—the physically dead and the spiritually dead—above ground:

> He stood in the dark, wet with sweat, brooding about the diamonds, the rings, the watches, the money; he remembered the singing in the church, the people yelling in the movie, the dead baby, the nude man stretched out upon the white table ... He saw these items hovering before his eyes and felt that some dim meaning linked them

together, that some magical relationship made them kin. He stared with vacant eyes, convinced that all of these images, with their tongueless reality, were striving to tell him something .... (59).

What these images are probably striving to tell Daniels is that the world above ground is "a wild forest filled with death" (62). The artifacts of this world are connected to death if for no reason other than that their disappearance results in beatings and even loss of life for those who are accused of stealing them.

Daniels' perception of the atmosphere of the world above ground is synopsized by the phrase *dark sunshine* (65). This oxymoron stands in the atmosphere of Daniels' underground world. At the beginning of the story, the light of the world above ground is stressed (32, 36, 43, 46, 54), just as the darkness of the underground is stressed (28, 29, 31, 32, 33, 35, 59). At the turning point of the story, however, the world above ground acquires the quality of darkness, and the world underground aquires the quality if light. This turning point is the sequence of events that begins when Daniels drags to his cave the artifacts that he has found above ground. In this sequence, Daniels attaches a light bulb and a string of electric wire to some wiring that runs into his cave. The result is, as Spanos puts it in explaining the existential myth, "a blinding moment of illumination," or as Wright puts it in the story, "the sudden illumination blinded him" (60). The illumination signals the new awareness that Daniels is about to gain, for awakening from a nap that he takes after lighting his cave and decorating it with the stolen artifacts, Daniels realizes that the worshippers in the church, the boy being beaten, and the night watchman being tortured are all guilty. This realization of everyman's guilt is the turning point in Daniels' life, for it makes him ready to stop proclaiming his own innocence, to acknowledge his guilt, and to return above ground. From this point, too, Daniels begins to see the world above ground as not only a place of death and cruelty—suggested by the phrases "dead world of sunshine," "obscene sunshine," "dead sunshine," and "cruel sunshine" (55, 63, 66, 73)—but also a place of darkness, of "dark sunshine." This world is dark in the sense that it does not illuminate but instead cloaks, veils, or obscures the truth—namely, that all men are guilty. In contrast, the "dark light" of the underground allows Daniels to see his—and others'—guilt.

When Officer Lawson burns the confession that Daniels signed three days earlier, Lawson, in effect, nullifies Daniels' new-found knowledge that he, like all men, is guilty. Daniels' response is predictable: "He stared, thunderstruck; the sun of the underground was fleeing and the terrible darkness of the day stood before him" (83). In other words Lawson's act extinguishes the "dark light" of the world underground, which has enabled Daniels to see the truth of everyman's guilt, and restores the "dark sunshine" of the world above ground, which does not allow man to see that truth. The atmosphere of the world above ground reeks of death because of its people and their artifacts. But perhaps the most crucial quality of that world—crucial because there is no remedy for death, although there is a remedy for ignorance—is that it provides only a dark light that does not allow man to see "the *secret of his existence,* the *guilt* that he could never get rid of" (69, emphasis added).

To return to the pattern of the existential fable as Spanos describes it, "The Man Who Lived Underground" portrays a protagonist, Fred Daniels, in flight from the accusation that he is guilty. To escape the policemen who are making this accusation, Daniels goes underground. Before being chased underground, Daniels was like the other dead people above ground: He attended movies (58, 63), believed in a God who watches and watches over mankind, and considered himself innocent as long as he had not violated any law. The dark light of the underground, however, allows Daniels to see the nature of human existence—its tropism (to use Nathanael West's metaphor) toward shadows, or fiction, rather than reality, or truth, and its core of suffering, death, and guilt. The result for Daniels is a blinding moment of illumination, a spiritual birth. Because the policemen forced him underground, they are midwives to that birth. Thus, the agents who initially seem to be wholly malevolent emerge as paradoxically benevolent.

In its structure as well as in its themes of isolation, anxiety, guilt, and freedom, "The Man Who Lived Underground" thus epitomizes the existential fable. A tale of existential triumph and a tale of naturalistic defeat, the story is in the paradoxical position of presenting both a philosophy of determinism and a philosophy that rejects determinism. As a deterministic philosophy, naturalism sees man as merely an animal whose fate is controlled by forces unrelated to his will. In contrast, existentialism presents man as a free agent whose duty is to exercise his will, the possession of which raises him above the level of other animals. "The Man Who Lived Underground" embodies both postures.

One reason that "The Man Who Lived Underground" can embody both naturalistic and existential postures is that Wright has so skillfully crafted his story that the actions that can be attributed to Daniels' will can also be attributed to forces independent of Daniels' will. For example, the existential interpreter can argue that Daniels *wills* to go underground and that Daniels *wills* to return above ground and confront the policemen who have previously tortured him. His decision to return above ground represents a victory of will over animal instinct: "He had to act, yet he was afraid" (72). Once resolved to leave the underground, Daniels moves purposefully and rationally, "his actions ... informed with precision, his muscular system reinforced from a reservoir of energy,"and his mind set on self-preservation—as, avoiding being sucked under by the sewer current, he sighs, "thankful that he had missed death" (72-73). Because Daniels has successfully eluded the police for three days and because they are no longer even looking for him, his decision to return above ground effectively makes Daniels the First Cause of the events that culminate in his death.

On the other hand, the naturalistic interpreter can argue that Daniels' return above ground is caused by insanity, which occurs because Daniels was forced underground. A major sign of Daniels' insanity is his laughter when he sees the boy and watchman being beaten for his thefts and his numerous outbursts of laughter in the presence of the police when he turns himself in to them (77, 81, 90). The existential interpreter can counter that Daniels' laughter is not the inappropriate laughter of an insane man but the wise laughter of the man who gets the cosmic joke—namely, that man's position in the universe is absurd, because no matter how good a life he lives he is guilty and no matter how much he may want to live he is going to die. The naturalistic interpreter and the existential interpreter can continue their rebuttals *ad infinitum,* so tightly has Wright woven the threads of his paradox.

A second reason that "The Man Who Lived Underground" can embody both naturalistic and existential postures is that existentialism recognizes that man *is* a part of nature and is consequently subject to nature's laws. In "Notes from Underground," Dostoevsky's proto-existential underground man (the putative ancestor of Fred Daniels) acknowledges his inability to conquer the laws of nature, which he visualizes as a stone wall: "Of course I cannot break through the wall by battering my head against it if I really have not the strength ..." (853). (However, with the same mettle that Daniels demonstrates when he conquers time, Dostoevsky's underground man immediately makes clear that while his body is subject to nature's laws, his spirit will not be.) The laws of nature to which Daniels is subject are the need to eat, drink, eliminate (a typically naturalistic detail), rest, and sleep. Some of his actions, therefore, are definitely determined by his animal nature. That these actions spring from this source is consistent with naturalism's determinism and compatible with existentialism's anti-determinism.

A final reason that "The Man Who Lived Underground" can embody both naturalistic and existential postures is that existential triumph does not preclude naturalistic defeat. Indeed, the existential hero is *likely* to suffer, for existentialism posits a universe of chaos and death. To triumph in such a setting—that is, to act as he should, existential man must recognize that he is free to act, and he must accept the responsibility for his actions, not attempting to attribute them to some force (for example, God, the laws of society, definitions of "human nature") outside his will. The existential hero triumphs when he breaks free of those forces that would enslave him and acts in order to be himself, whatever self he chooses to be. Thus, when Daniels exercises his will by papering his cave with money, he feels that he has "triumphed over the world aboveground" and senses that he "[i]s free" because he is living the life that he has chosen for himself rather than conforming to the life prescribed for and by the people above ground (62). Again, Daniels triumphs when he exercises his will by choosing to go to the police station and attempting to lead Officers Lawson, Murphy, and Johnson to his underground world. That Lawson kills Daniels does not negate

Eight Men (1961)   149

Daniels' triumph. Rather, Daniels' feat illustrates the fact that one cannot count on others' actions, over which one has no control, to bring about an event. As Sartre puts it, "... no God, no scheme, can adapt the world and its possibilities to my will" (29). Further, Daniels' death underlines the existential truth that the only certainty in man's life is that he will die. Hence, the existential triumph of Daniels is compatible with his naturalistic defeat—the death that he suffers as a result of someone else's will.

Even though key naturalistic revelations about man's essence and existence are assumed in existential theory, it is a mistake to focus exclusively on the existential vision of "The Man Who Lived Underground" and to ignore or minimize the story's naturalistic vision. To do so is to risk misapprehending Wright's portrait of man as it is revealed through Fred Daniels: It is to risk not seeing man as *equally* god and animal, and man's existence as *equally* free and tied to necessity. It is a question of focus and emphasis, the answer residing in the structure of the story, which suggests paradox at every turn. When the paradoxical structure of "The Man Who Lived Underground" is considered, it is clear that man is not simply a god in the existential sense or an animal in the naturalistic sense; nor is man's existence the existence of a god or an animal. Rather—and purely existential interpretations of the story have not revealed this point—the structure of "The Man Who Lived Underground" suggests that man is a paradox whose existence is a paradox. A paradoxical existence is an absurd existence; it makes no sense. In Wright's story man's existence is paradoxical, absurd: In this world innocent men are guilty, men's toys cause death, men reject the savior that they pray for, light leaves men blind while darkness gives sight, dead men live above ground, and a dead man who goes underground comes to life. In this world, too, man is paradoxically, absurdly, both beast and god.

Naturalism is presently out of fashion. It is considered simplistic in its reduction of man to the level of an animal or victim, formulaic in its social protest, and false in its conception of the work of fiction as a kind of scientific experiment in which the writer "objectively" records the details of his protagonist's life and environment. Because of its recognized weaknesses, naturalism is routinely ignored or belittled by Wright's critics. Such dismissal is an error, however, for naturalism, like existentialism, served as an emotional, philosophical, and creative wellspring of Wright's literary career. In "The Man Who Lived Underground" naturalism and existentialism have a synergistic relationship that emphasizes the paradox that Wright, a born naturalistic and existential philosopher, must have seen as inherent in man's essence and existence. Conceivably, one using existentialism as an approach to "The Man Who Lived Underground" could arrive at the same conclusions about man's paradoxical essence and existence that I have reached by using a structural approach. That the former has not been done reveals the danger of not taking into account the structure of a work, which, because it reveals a work to be more than the sum of its parts, necessarily reveals a work to be more than any *one* of its parts. Naturalism is clearly as much a part of "The Man Who Lived Underground" as is existentialism, and both are merely subordinate parts that contribute to the total meaning of Wright's story.

Approaching "The Man Who Lived Underground" from a structural perspective also permits an appreciation of Wright's consummate craftsmanship in constructing a story whose every component—most notably character, story, plot, setting, imagery, diction, and tone—is generated by and integrated within a paradoxical structure. Seen from a structural perspective, "The Man Who Lived Underground" is a warning to any critic of Richard Wright who would peremptorily disregard his naturalism or categorically dismiss his art.

Notes

[1]See, for example, Fabre, "Richard Wright"; Bone 25-31; Gounard; Ridenour; Bakish; Brignano 148-55; Margolies.
Portions of "The Man Who Lived Underground" were originally published in 1942. An expanded version of the story was published in *Cross Section*. All references to the story in this text are to the version appearing in Wright's *Eight Men* (1961).
[2]Ridenour 54; McNallie 83. See also Goede and Widmer.
[3]Daniels' first day underground begins in the daytime and ends when, after encountering the Black worshippers in a church, he sees the light of street lamps

shining through the perforations of a manhole cover and realizes that "it must be night" (33). His second day underground begins as Daniels notices that "daylight spilled from a window above his head" in the basement of a jewelry store (43), and it ends after he burglarizes the store's safe while "moonlight floated in from a wide window"(54). On the third day, Daniels arises from the underground for the final time, stepping "into a hot glare of sunshine" (73).

Works Cited

Bakish, David. "Underground in an Ambiguous Dreamworld." *Studies in Black Literature* 2.3 (1971): 18-23.
Bone, Robert. *Richard Wright.* U of Minnesota Pamphlets on American Writers 74. Minneapolis: U of Minnesota P, 1969.
Brignano, Russell Carl. *Richard Wright: An Introduction to the Man and His Works.* Pittsburgh: U of Pittsburgh P, 1970.
Dostoevsky, Fyodor. "Notes from Underground.", 1864. Trans. Constance Garnett. *The Norton Anthology of World Masterpieces.* Gen. ed. Maynard Mack. 4th ed. 2 vols. New York: Norton, 1980. 2: 846-934.
Everette, Mildred W. "The Death of Richard Wright's American Dream: 'The Man Who Lived Underground.'" *CLA Journal* 17 (1974): 318-26.
Fabre, Michel. "Richard Wright: The Man Who Lived Underground." *Richard Wright: A Collection of Critical Essays.* Ed. Richard Macksey and Frank E. Moorer. Englewood Cliffs: Prentice, 1984. 207-20.
_____. *The Unfinished Quest of Richard Wright.* Trans. Isabel Barzun. New York: Morrow, 1973.
Goede, William. "On Lower Frequencies: The Buried Man in Wright and Ellison." *Modern Fiction Studies* 15 (1969-70): 483-501.
Gounard, J.G. "Richard Wright's 'The Man Who Lived Underground': A Literary Analysis." *Journal of Black Studies* 8 (1978): 381-86.
Hurston, Zora Neale. *Their Eyes Were Watching God.* 1937. Urbana: U of Illinois P, 1978.
Margolies, Edward. "The Short Stories: *Uncle Tom's Children; Eight Men.*" *The Art of Richard Wright.* Carbondale: Southern Illinois UP, 1969. 57-89.
Marano, Donald V. *Existential Guilt: A Phenomenological Study.* Atlantic Highlands: Humanities, 1973.
McNallie, Robin. "Richard Wright's Allegory of the Cave: 'The Man Who Lived Underground.'" *South Atlantic Bulletin* 42.2 (1977): 76-84.
Ridenour, Ronald. "'The Man Who Lived Underground': A Critique." *Phylon* 31 (1970): 54-57.
Sartre, Jean-Paul. "Existentialism." Trans. Bernard Frechtman. *Existentialism and Human Emotions.* New York: Philosophical Library, 1957. 9-51.
Spanos, William V. *A Casebook on Existentialism.* New York: Crowell, 1966.
West, Nathanael. *Miss Lonelyhearts & The Day of the Locust.* 1946, 1950. New York: New Directions, 1962.
Widmer, Kingsley. "Black Existentialism: Richard Wright." *Richard Wright: A Collection of Critical Essays.* Ed. Richard Macksey and Frank E. Moorer. Englewood Cliffs: Prentice, 1984. 173-81.
Wright, Richard. "The Man Who Lived Underground." *Cross Section: A Collection of New American Writing* Ed. Edwin Seaver. New York: Fischer, 1944. 58-102.
_____. "The Man Who Lived Underground." *Eight Men. Cleveland:* World, 1961.27-92.

From *Black American Literature Forum* 23 (Winter 1989), 767-783.

Thematic and Formal Unity
in Richard Wright's *Eight Men*

Robert Butler

When Richard Wright's *Eight Men* was published in 1961 contemporary reviewers generally dismissed it as a regrettable sign of Wright's failing powers as a writer. Saunders Redding, who felt that Wright's long exile in France weakened him artistically because it separated him from his "heart's home" in America, deplored the book's "eccentric experiments in technique" which he felt were a direct result of what he felt was an ennervating case of nihilism which Wright had contracted from the French existentialists.[1] Claiming that "*Eight Men* is not one of the books by which Richard Wright deserves to be judged," he concluded that the book was a sad failure of vision and form:

> It has all the dramatic tension of a first-class Gothic tale; there are descriptive passages of extraordinary vividness, and stylistic ornaments of great glitter, but nothing comes to anything: no passion has meaning, no insight is revealed, no idea truly conveyed, no theme made unmistakably plain. It is as if Gabriel, brandishing his trumpet and filling his lungs with air to blow the blast of doom, managed only a penny whistle's pipe.[2]

Richard Gilman, in a review which John Reilly has observed marked the absolute nadir of Wright's critical reputation,[3] was even harsher in his assessment of *Eight Men*, citing it as evidence that Wright was "simply not a good writer, not even a competent one" because the book's crudely formed vision was "of the sociological order, not the esthetic."[4] Even an ordinarily sympathetic reader like Irving Howe was at best lukewarm in his praise of *Eight Men*, seeing it as an example of the disturbing "uneveness" of Wright's prose and "his often clumsy efforts to break out of the naturalism which was his first and ... necessary mode of expression." Howe's essential complaint about *Eight Men* was that Wright failed to endow the book with coherent form:

> Time after time the narrative texture of the stories is broken by a passage of jargon borrowed from sociology or psychology: perhaps the later Wright read too much, tried too hard, failed to remain sufficiently loyal to the limits of his talent.[5]

Although Wright's literary reputation would soon rebound from the low point it had reached at the time *Eight Men* was published and individual stories such as "The Man Who Was Almost a Man" and "The Man Who Lived Underground" would later receive high praise from a wide range of Wright scholars from the late 1960s to the present, *Eight Men* itself has never received the critical attention and praise it deserves as a remarkable collection of interrelated stories. It is the purpose of this study to argue that *Eight Men*, far from suffering from the nihilistic failure of vision which Redding deplored, is one of Wright's most lucid, affirmative, and philosophically coherent fictive works, embodying a complexly existential vision which Wright carefully develops from story to story. Moreover, *Eight Men* also demonstrates Wright's ability to endow this existential vision with solid literary form by not only structuring his eight stories in a very artful way but also unifying these stories by reinforcing their narrative structure with intricate networks of imagery and symbol. Far from being the crude book which Howe was troubled about, *Eight Men* is a remarkable artistic acheivement, a book which was carefully shaped by a sophisticated writer who was able to envision African American experience in terms which were both thematically powerful and formally coherent.

***

Like Sherwood Anderson's *Winesburg, Ohio* and James Joyce's *Dubliners*--books which Wright greatly admired--*Eight Men* is neither a novel unified by a continuous narrative nor a simple anthology of short stories which are only superficially related. Rather, it is a carefully arranged sequence of thematically related stories which are also unified by strong patterns of imagery and symbol. Starting with "The Man Who Was Almost a Man" and ending with "The Man Who Went to Chicago," the eight stories dramatize a movement from naturalistic victimization by various aspects of environment to an existential triumph over environment by the achievement of enriched consciousness leading to action resulting in the creation of existential selfhood.

For example, Dave Saunders, the protagonist of the first story, fails to attain the manhood he desires and instead becomes a victim of a racist environment. Despite his adolescent bluster that using a gun will make him a "man" who can transcend the role of "mule" which his environment has defined him as, he remains "a boy"[6] and a "fool" (13) when he accepts his culture's macho assumption that manhood can be equated with physical power and that the phallic gun which he purchases for two dollars will give him this power. As the story makes abundantly clear, his mother is absolutely right when she tells him that he is "plumb crazy" (12) for naively thinking that a gun can be anything but trouble for a seventeen-year-old black person in the Deep South. By using the gun in a blind and unskilled way, Dave simply reinforces his culture's stereotype of him as a dumb "mule," one who is neither sufficiently intelligent nor responsible to be trusted with guns but who instead should be beaten by law and custom into the state of a docile work animal. By inadvertently killing the mule, Dave becomes more hopelessly dependent upon the white economic system for he is now required to pay fifty dollars for a dead mule, which will consume two years of his earnings. When Dave is pictured at the end of the story ready to hop a train to the North, his gesture certainly can not be seen as a triumph over a social environment intent on enslaving him because he has not learned anything from his experiences. Because he invests the gun with the power to provide him with manhood and still has difficulty physically using the gun, he continues to ride the "tracks" (21) that a racist American society has devised for him.

The next story, "The Man Who Lived Underground," which begins just as the previous story ended, with a black victim in flight from a hostile white society, carries Dave Saunders's story much further, since it is centered in a character who undergoes the psychological growth which Dave fails to experience. Instead of being limited to the external world which is designed to enslave him, Fred Daniels goes "underground" in his story, transcending the grid of streets in the above-ground city which confuses and traps him. This physical journey, which is an objective correlative to the extraordinary inward journey he undergoes in the story, enables him for a while to move away from the environmental "tracks" which direct Dave Saunders.

One clear indication of Daniels's psychological growth is the attitude he develops toward the things in his subterranean "cave" (25), objects which vividly symbolize the physical powers valorized by conventional American society. Whereas Saunders naively romanticizes the power of the gun and as a result ironically disempowers himself by this crudely simplistic misplacement of values, Daniels "appropriates" (45) symbols of outward power such as guns, money, meat cleavers, and radios, undercutting their meanings and psychologically freeing himself of their ability to control him. Indeed, he comes to see them as nothing more than the "serious toys of the men who lived in the dead world of sunshine and rain" (45). Although he has a chance to gain revenge on the white world and can procure a kind of power over that world by killing a white man who is sleeping in a room which he can observe from his underground hiding place, Daniels conciously resists the temptation to use the gun violence which damages Dave Saunders because he develops the keen awareness that such "power" is illusory and self-destructive. Indeed, he links the use of guns in the above-ground world to "men [who] fire guns in the movies" (51), something which he equates with the pursuit of debilitating fantasy. Unlike Saunders who foolishly uses a gun and then gets laughed at when the gun gets him into trouble, Daniels laughs at the gun he steals and fires it only as a part of an amusing "game" (51) which he safely plays underground.

In the same way, he makes a "mocking symbol" (50) of the money which people in the conventional American society value so highly. By plastering dollar bills on the walls of his subterranean hide-out as a gesture that he is "free" (50) of the compulsions which dominate his society, he has thus "triumphed over the world above ground" (50) through an act of consciousness leading to freedom. He likewise reduces to an absurd joke the clock time which structures social experience, hanging great numbers of watches on his papered walls, richly enjoying a deeply ironic laughter as he does so.

The only symbolic object from the external world which Daniels admires is the typewriter which he steals from an office. But it is important to realize that he imaginatively transforms this object from a business instrument used in the pursuit of monetary rewards to an artistic instrument which can be used to acheive genuine selfhood. "Fascinated" by the typewriter because he perceives it as "something beyond the rim of his life" (44), he uses it to type his name in lower case letters which he then ponders seriously. While he simply laughed at the gun, the radio, the money, the meat cleaver, and diamonds as objects of false worship, he resolves to *use* the typewriter seriously, planning to teach himself how to type. In other words, he is moving from sources of outward power which can destroy his nature to *writing*, a source of inward power which can deepen his consciousness of himself and his world. He thus takes the first steps toward self-creation which Wright himself took when he began to conceive of himself as a writer like H. L. Mencken who could use words, not guns, as "weapons"[7] which could destroy the false values and roles of conventional society.

Fred Daniels, unlike Dave Saunders, has made important initial steps toward fashioning an existential identity because his underground vision has replaced his earlier blind terror of a social world intent on either subjugating or murdering him. Unlike his creator, however, he fails to fashion a durable self which can survive collisions with the public world because he never develops an adequate strategy for acting in that world. Sensing that his underground abode's warm waters are a kind of amniotic fluid which can nourish him, he also realizes that the underground's pestilential gasses can poison him. So he finally understands that whether his cave is a tomb or a womb, he must emerge from it and find a place for himself and a role to play in the surface world. As he realizes mid-way through the story when he observes a man commit suicide, "He had to act" (58). To stay underground forever is a kind of suicide.

But he is never able to act effectively since the consciousness he has developed while underground is too brittle and new to provide him with pragmatic modes of action which can enable him to interact with the social environment without being destroyed by it. Like Plato who gains a vision of truth in a cave separated from the ordinary social world but who can not effectively share this vision with the people who inhabit society, he is unable to make the all-important connection between underground and surface worlds. When he does surface, he is soon overcome by the naive assumption that if he can tell his "story" (67) to the policemen and "force the reality of himself" (66) upon them that he can somehow make them "see" (70) what is wrong with their world and they then can make the necessary steps toward changing it. In the process he will end his own isolation, making them "see what he has seen" and "feel what he has felt," thus creating "fellowship" (71) between them.

The results are predictably disastrous. Emerging from the underground, he is immediately struck by evidence of the painful absurdity of American society as people label him a 'bastard" and a "nigger" (60). Although part of him understands that such a world is "crazy" (57), especially when he observes a policeman senselessly beating a nightwatchman, another part of him innocently believes that he can rationally deal with that world. He therefore runs to the center of the absurdity of his social environment, the police station, hoping to "make a statement" (62) which will establish his innocence and thus heal the breach between himself and society. But this ill-advised impulse results in the police deciding to kill him when he reveals that he has actually observed them beating the nightwatchman who is so traumatized by the experience that he commits suicide. The story ends with Daniels being shot to death by the policeman when he takes them back to his hide-out beneath the streets. Daniels, therefore, finally ends up as a failed artist, one who possesses "vision" but who is unable to effectively communicate that vision to others in a "story" (67) which can not only help the artist to acheive selfhood but also enable him to play an important role in the reconstruction of society. Daniels, ironically, ends up like Dave Saunders, an alienated wanderer in a hostile universe: the story concludes by picturing him as "a whirling object rushing alone in the darkness" (74). For different reasons, the central characters in the first two stories of *Eight Men* end up "lost" (74).

The next four stories in the collection, however, envision their protagonists as gradually moving beyond this victimized condition, acquiring various degrees of existential consciousness necessary to both *see* the world truly and to act productively in that world. The black characters in these stories use a variety of strategies to survive their encounters with a hostile white society. The anonymous black man in "Big Black Good Man," for example, violates the ultimate taboo of his world by getting the night clerk of his boarding house to arrange for him to have sex with a white prostitute with whom he eventually forms a sustained relationship. Olaf Jenson, the night clerk, soon becomes filled with the usual stereotypes about the black man, seeing him as a "black beast" (83) for whom he feels a "primitive hate" (81). By the end of the story he is prepared to kill the black man with a gun he keeps hidden beneath his night desk. But the story concludes with him being physically and emotionally disarmed when the man responds to him with "compassion" (88) rather than hostility, thanking him for helping to arrange for his now humanizing relationship with the white woman by presenting Olaf with the gift of a new shirt. Quite suddenly the stereotypes which have been pushing him into senseless violence are dissolved by this spontaneous act of friendship, leading both to see each other as "good men" rather than adversaries intent on victimizing each other.

In a similar way, the next two stories conclude with black protagonists also successfully navigating the dangers of the white world which threaten them with economic deprivation and death. The black father in "The Man Who Saw the Flood" almost certainly will attempt to find a new life in the North, taking his family out of the South after a flood has ruined their sharecropper's cabin and his white boss has reminded him that he is eight hundred dollars in debt to the company store. Carl, the black husband in "Man of All Work" has to use more ingenious strategies to save his family and their home. After his wife is unable to work because of the recent birth of their child and he has lost his job as a cook when the restaurant in which he had worked goes out of business, he decides to impersonate a woman in order to take a job as a maid working for the Fairchilds, a rich white family. Although this brings about a series of bizarre misadventures, including Mr. Fairchild making a "pass" at him and Mrs. Fairchild shooting him when she discovers this, he is finally able to get from them the two hundred dollars he needs to support his family in exchange for his silence about the whole fiasco.

"Man, God Ain't Like That" also describes a curious victory for a black protagonist over white people. Babu, an African young man who is taken to Paris by John and Lucy Franklin to act as their household servant and a model for their painting, overcomes his misguided worship of whites as "God" when he runs away from their apartment and spends several days examining the true nature of white "civilization" in Paris. Coming to the conclusion that Paris is not a genuine civilization held together by human values but instead "the white man's jungle" (148) in which the powerful victimize the weak, he attains the lucid vision of a black revolutionary. Informing Franklin that his wanderings in Paris have enabled him to "see real good" (149), he then declares "Now it's the black man's turn" (154) to victimize whites and beheads Franklin. He escapes punishment from the Paris authorities by cleverly acting out the role of a religious fanatic who considers Franklin a god. His rantings are dismissed by the police as "delusions" (154) and "pure hysteria" (155) and he is deported back to Africa where he commits himself to "organizing a new religious cult" (154) which doubtlessly is a political movement dedicated to destroying all other white "gods" in Africa.

The final two stories in *Eight Men* present a sharp contrast which goes to the heart of the book's themes. These stories are centered around two opposite kinds of people, characters who are either dominated by environmental forces which destroy their ability to think and act effectively or other characters who possess the superior consciousness and strong will necessary to acheive important victories over their social environments. Saul Saunders, the protagonist of "The Man Who Killed a Shadow," is another version of Dave Saunders: both are essentially blind to the worlds around them and, as a result, are programmed by their societies to perform acts of absurd and self-destructive violence. Like Dave who mistakenly kills a mule when he shuts his eyes and fires a gun without taking proper aim, Saul is so traumatized by socially-induced fear that his vision of reality blurs into "shadows" (155) which confuse him and limit his responses to the world to two equally meaningless reflexes, passivity and violence. In this respect, he closely resembles Bigger Thomas of *Native Son* whose life has "two rhythms"--"indifference and violence."[8]

His passivity leads him to accept his marginal position in a racist world, drifting through "a parade of dirty little towns" which reduce his life from an early age to "an incomprehensible nothingness" (158). His acts of violence are produced by his deepest fear, being caught in a room with a white woman who screams "rape," an act which he equates with "a death sentence" (159). When this does in fact happen at the end of the story, as a forty year old white woman sexually entices him and then screams that he is about to rape her, he is first reduced to a terrified paralysis and then, in an attempt to "do something," (164) he murders her by crushing her skull with a large stick of firewood.

"The Man Who Killed a Shadow" thus concludes in a manner which vividly recalls the endings of both "The Man Who Was Almost a Man" and "The Man Who Lived Underground." Like Dave Saunders, Saul is overcome by reflexive violence when his fears about his manhood are aroused by a racist society. Like Fred Daniels, he is finally interrogated at the police station and is unable either to explain his actions or defend himself with a coherent "story." Arousing the fears of a society which can only accept him as a shadow, he is sentenced to death when he attempts to assert himself with action. Like Fred Daniels, he ends up "surrendering to the world of shadows about him" (169) because he can not formulate a plan of action that will enable him to master his fears and triumph over a society which will not allow him to be a "man."

The final story in *Eight Men*, however, focuses on a person who achieves a true sense of manhood. To emphasize the hero's dramatic achievement of existential selfhood, the story is narrated with first person point of view, the only story in the book not to use third person narration. Indeed, Wright himself becomes the hero of *Eight Men*, speaking to us directly in his own voice about his own liberation in Chicago when he emerged as a writer who could not only lucidly see his environment but also devise a plan of action which could provide him with a clear victory over that environment.

To stress the fact that "The Man Who Went to Chicago" is integrally related to the seven stories preceding it and brings these stories to a thematic culmination, Wright consciously echoes motifs used in the previous stories, subtly transforming their meanings. For example, the devocalized dogs which are used for experimental purposes at the research hospital in which Wright works are clearly reminiscent of the woman whom Saul Saunders devocalizes by slitting her throat. These dogs, which Wright presents as "a symbol of silent suffering," (195) also remind us of the many inarticulate victims of earlier stories who are not able to relieve their suffering by effectively voicing their complaints or telling their stories. In a similar way, the "dark underworld" (204) of the hospital clearly connects not only with the physical underground experienced by Fred Daniels but also epitomizes the mental, emotional, and spiritual underworlds which nearly all of the black characters in previous stories are forced to endure, since they are marginal figures excluded from the mainstream of American life. Then too, the "dread" (178) which Wright feels as a white waitress casually bumps up against him in a restaurant repeats a pattern which unifies all the stories in *Eight Men*--the racially segregated world which Wright depicts throughout the book triggers fear on many levels, ranging from Dave Saunders's "panic" (16) when he inadvertently kills the mule to the "nameless terror" (82) which afflicts Olaf Jenson in "Big Black Good Man." Finally, Wright's description of Communism in "The Man Who Went to Chicago" as a "new faith" (191) reveals a profound longing which most of the central characters in *Eight Men* feel in a variety of ways. This quest for renewal begins in the first story with the protagonist heading North in search of a new life, is then given new psychological meaning in Fred Daniels's underground conversion, and is also given an ironic twist in Babu's organization of "a new religious cult" (154) in Africa after he has killed the white "god" who oppresses him in Paris.

What makes "The Man Who Went to Chicago" an especially effective culminating story for *Eight Men* is the way in which it transforms these motifs to generate new and strikingly affirmative meanings. Because the story's hero has developed a resilient and deeply existential view of life, he can see beyond the traps which ensnare most of the characters depicted in the earlier stories and can also devise for himself a mode of action to engage the world fruitfully without making himself a victim. The "underground" he inhabits, for example, is not a sewer but a hospital which helps to cure him since it becomes for him a metaphor of American life which educates him about the workings of his society and suggests a way in which he can protect himself from the more negative aspects of that society. He is careful to reject the self-defeating strategies used by his co-workers in dealing with the hospital such as the "sullen silence" (193) adopted by Bill and the pointless violence employed by Brand and Cooke. Because his work in the hospital and in other menial jobs as a post office worker, dishwasher, and insurance salesman for a Negro burial society has provided him with a pragmatic "new kind of education" (185), Wright can overcome the fear which paralyzes the central characters of most of the other stories. And because of his "new faith" (191) in both a political program like Communism and an existential belief which enables him to affirm his own selfhood, Wright can act in ways that go well beyond the kinds of action employed by other characters in *Eight Men*. In contrast to loners like Dave Saunders and the nameless black man in "Big Black Good Man," he foresees a time when blacks and other oppressed people will discover bonds of solidarity and carry on a "revolution" leading to "a new and strange way of life" (192). And he categorically rejects the terrible personal violence which deflects the energies and blights the lives of characters like Saul Saunders. He chooses instead to be an activist who organizes people and a writer who can acheive the vision necessary to purposely direct his own energies and the energies of the people whom he will organize.

Unlike Fred Daniels who is overwhelmed by a surplus of awareness but who fails to translate this awareness into fruitful action, Wright acts shrewdly to cross the "boundary line" (171) circumscribing him, all the while protecting himself and the ailing family he must support. Unlike Dave Saunders, he is careful not to quit a job before finding a better job. And unlike Saul Saunders who invokes the wrath of the police by naively telling them too much of the truth, Wright can cleverly dissimulate in front of white people who exert power over him. Admitting that I had "lied to protect myself" (177), he can control people who otherwise might hurt him. Even though he feels that his work in the hospital reduces him to the level of a "slave" (197), he is careful not to erupt in the pointless violence which destroys characters like Saul Saunders. Instead, he converts a condition of outward slavery into a liberating consciousness of this situation, biding his time until he can work to change these circumstances.

In sharp contrast with a failed writer like Fred Daniels who is fascinated by a typewriter but who never masters this instrument to effectively tell his "story" (67), Wright will use a typewriter to fulfill both his personal and political goals. Realizing that there "were but few Negroes who knew the meaning of their lives, who could tell their own story" (175), he commits himself to being the kind of writer who will use his art to help liberate himself and others from "the dark underworld of American life" (204). Centering his art on "our own code of ethics, values, and loyalty" (204), he will work to rejuvenate the self and society. "The Man Who Lived Underground" therefore brings *Eight Men* to a dramatic conclusion by drawing up the themes of the first six stories and transforming them into a lucid and affirmative existential vision.

***

The thematic unity of *Eight Men* is solidly reinforced by its formal unity. Wright consciously employs networks of image and symbol to draw the stories together into a coherent work of art. Three formal patterns are particularly important in the book: images of entrapment, fire symbolism, and ocular imagery. Each forms a complex pattern of associations which then interlock sequentially to bring the book's central themes into sharp, clear focus.

All of the stories in *Eight Men* portray various kinds of paralysis which are dramatized by images of entrapment. Dave Saunders, for example, feels confined by southern culture because it stereotypes him as a "boy" and frustrates his urge to become a "man." When he tries to remedy this situation by purchasing and using a gun, things only get worse, for this results in accidentally killing his boss's mule, thereby getting him into an even deeper economic trap. Even Dave's method of escape is seen as another kind of entrapment since the "road" to Chicago is on "tracks" (21) laid down by others. The train thundering northward is described as "steel grinding upon steel" (21), a machine driven necessarily upon hard rails which rigidly determine its direction and destination. In the same way, Dave is more driven by compulsive reflexes generated by his repressive culture rather than freely willed action devised by a clear mind. The steel gun, like the steel train and the steel tracks, almost certainly will lead to his further entrapment rather than his liberation.

That the northern city is a system of steel traps rather than a promised land offering genuine freedom is clearly borne out by the next story, "The Man Who Lived Underground." Fred Daniels, who at the beginning of the story is "tired of running" (23) and therefore can be seen as a kind of exhausted Dave Saunders, escapes from the police by lifting a steel manhole cover and entering a dark, labyrinthine underworld which at the end of the story traps him and becomes the setting for his death. Although this underground retreat provides a kind of temporary freedom for Daniels and for a while liberates his mind from the restrictive myths of American society, he is never able to fully come to terms with what this underground means and, as a result is trapped in it. Looking at the "walls" of his cave and unable to decide whether it is a womb offering new life or a tomb requiring death, he feels "trapped" (53). Later he is described as standing "paralyzed in the shadows" (59) of the underground and by the end of the story he is taunted by the cave's "shouting walls" and "laughing floor" (74). Indeed, this story concludes like the previous story, with machines suggesting the final entrapment of the main character. Just as Dave Saunders's psychological and physical dead-end is depicted by trains thundering over steel rails, Fred Daniels' paralysis is clearly imaged by "the muffled roar of a powerful motor" (74), the police car leaving the scene after the police have murdered Daniels.

Comparable images of confinement can be found in each of the remaining six stories. Olaf Jenson, the white night clerk in "Big Black Good Man" feels "paralyzed" and "trapped in a nightmare" (83) when his stereotyped notions of black men induce fears in him which lead him to suspect that the nameless black man in the story wants to kill him. The anonymous black man in "The Man Who Saw the Flood" fears that he will be thrown in jail if he runs away from his sharecropper's job but he also suspects that the only alternative to running away is to labor like a slave for the rest of his life in a society which is constructed to deny freedom to black people. Carl, the protagonist of "Man of All Work," can not find employment as a black man but finds that things can get even worse when he "passes" as a black woman. Although this masquerade does result in his getting a job which provides him with enough money to save his home, he ultimately finds the role of black woman even more confining than his position as a black man when his boss tries to make a sexual "pass" at him and his boss's wife shoots him. As he reveals at the end of the story, "I was a woman for almost six hours and it almost killed me" (131). Saul Saunders is probably the most trapped figure in *Eight Men*, since he is physically limited by a series of dead-end jobs and psychologically deadlocked by his inability to see people as anything but "shadows" which evoke his fears. "Hemmed in" (100) on all sides, he explodes in acts of reflexive violence which result in his being executed. And the final story in *Eight Men* completes this dismal vision of social, economic, and psychological entrapment by picturing all of American society as "a system of feudal oppression" (173). Indeed, American society is likened to the condition of laboratory rats in cages.

This pervasive sense of restriction invariably leads to smoldering resentment and violence, both of which Wright expresses with powerful imagery of fire. Fire, which Keneth Kinnamon has described as "a central metaphor of [Wright's] creative imagination,"[9] permeates *Eight Men* and takes many forms, all of which express Wright's deepest concerns about the human costs paid in a society where normal aspirations and healthy appetites have been bottled up and can either explode in fiery violence or slowly smolder, consuming a person's most vital energies. When Dave

Saunders pores over gun catalogues his eyes "glowed" (11), thinking that guns will empower him and enable him to become a "man." But when he *fires* the gun, he soon discovers that, far from being a source of "power," (14) the gun reduces him to the level of a fool and further entrenches him in a condition of southern servitude. These sentiments enflame his resentments, making him "hot all over" (21) as he prepares to hop a freight to what he naively hopes will be a better world in the North.

Images of fire are first used in "The Man Who Lived Underground" to suggest Fred Daniels's desire for illumination as he uses matches to light his way through the subterranean passages into which he flees from the police. But eventually images of fire are used in the story to generate more ominous meanings. When he goes to the basement of the movie house and stares at the "glowing embers" (31) of the furnace, he finds the whole room tinged with the flame's blood-red color. Although he is too inarticulate at this point in the story to realize the significance of this image, Wright makes it clear that the furnace's flame is a symbolic reflector of the frustration and rage which is beginning to "burn" Daniels. In the story's epiphany which describes the police murdering him, their gun fire is described as a "streak of fire" which "ripped through his chest" (74). Failing to adequately light his way through the underground—a symbol of both his inner self and his marginalized position in American society—Daniels is finally destroyed by the fire which symbolizes the anger and violence of his social environment.

Several other characters in the remaining stories are also afflicted by various kinds of "fire." The night clerk in "Big Black Good Man" is nearly overwhelmed by "a flush of heat" which "overspread his body" as he feels "trapped" by his fear of the "black giant" (83) he believes will kill him. Saul Saunders is emotionally singed when a white woman calls him a "black nigger" in a voice that "blazed" (163) at him. The woman, whose "beet red" (163) face and pink panties reflect both her racial hatreds and sexual appetites, pushes Saul beyond his powers of control when she screams, activating his primal fear of being accused of raping a white woman. Overpowered by rage and fear which is depicted by a "hotness bubbling in him" (164), he crushes her skull with a piece of firewood in an attempt to stop the "full blast" (164) of her screaming.

For Wright, the only effective way of coping with the "traps" and "fire" described so powerfully in *Eight Men* is to cultivate the sort of keenly existential consciousness which enables one to see beyond these traps and cool down these fires. In order to develop this theme, Wright uses intricate patterns of ocular imagery, a motif which is deeply embedded in most of his major work, especially in *Native Son* and *Black Boy*.[10] In a sense, all of the characters in *Eight Men* can be divided into two basic types, failed people who are either "blind" or hampered by reduced vision and successful characters who attain a clear and penetrating view of reality which enables them to act effectively in the social world.

Dave Saunders, for example, makes the disastrous mistake of shooting a mule because his eyes are closed and his face averted as he fires his pistol. The strongest sign of hope at the end of his story is the "effort" he makes to hold his "eyes open" (20) as he fires the gun before hopping the freight train. If he is to use power to his advantage, he must develop clear vision or this power may either backfire on him or trample him. Fred Daniels, whose eyes are described as "vacant" (47), "blinded" (48) and "hard" (49) midway through his story, realizes that if he remains "sightless" he will also be "defenseless" (29). Although he undergoes an extraordinary process of illumination in the course of his subterranean adventures which enable him to *see* how black people are victimized in America, his consciousness becomes overburdened by the enormous weight of the implications of what he has witnessed. Listening to the radio which reveals the large-scale violence of a public world disintegrating under the pressures of world war and personally shocked by what he has witnessed underground, he shudders at the grave responsibility he has to reveal the meaning of these horrors to the inhabitants of the above-ground world. At this point in the story the narrator stresses "Fatigue weighed upon his forehead and eyes ... He dozed." (53). When he awakens and acts upon his resolve to reveal his experience to others so that they "would see what he had seen" (71), his vision breaks down, blurred by anxiety and fear. As a result, he blunders badly, entrapping himself again by revealing what he has seen to the wrong people, the police who kill him in an attempt to protect themselves with the *status quo*. The story ends, significantly, with an image of blindness, Daniels sinking into oblivion in the dark sewer, becoming "a whirling object rushing alone in the darkness" (74).

The final two stories contrast a blind man who is a hapless victim of a dark universe with a man who is fully sighted, empowered with an existential vision which enables him to do what Fred Daniels fails to do. A brutally segregated world has destroyed Saul Saunders's vision, providing him with "shadows" (157) which confuse him and force him into self-destructive reflex actions. But the narrator of "The Man Who Went to Chicago" can use his experiences in segregated America as an "education" (185) which provides him with "new eyes" (192). Because of this, his story takes the form of a series of liberating epiphanies which give him the cool, detached vision which he needs as a base for effective action. He can see what others are blind to and, more importantly, can share his vision with others as a way of bringing about socially effective action. For example, while working in a restaurant he is the only one who observes Tillie, the Finnish cook, routinely spitting into the soup. Determined to get her fired because it is a socially responsible thing to do, he is careful not to make Fred Daniels's mistake by sharing his vision with the wrong people and thus victimizing himself. (He desperately needs the job to support his mother, brother and aunt.) To protect himself, he shrewdly prompts a co-worker to complain to the boss about Tillie who is eventually fired when the boss observes her obnoxious behavior.

As the story progresses, Wright's vision widens and deepens. Most importantly, his ability to act effectively keeps abreast of his fast-developing vision. While forced to work as a salesman selling burial insurance policies to South Chicago blacks, a job which is morally repugnant to him, he uses this opportunity to gain a clearer understanding of how blacks are economically and emotionally victimized by a racist and capitalistic society: "Each day I saw how the Negro in Chicago lived" (184). As this "new consciousness" (191) develops, he begins to see signs of hope, even as his outward circumstances worsen. Applying for public assistance at the relief station, he senses that blacks and other disadvantaged people have been "tossed together" in a common condition and are beginning "to sense the collectivity of their lives" (190).

This in turn leads him to significant action, not only as an activist for the Communist party but also as a writer who can make blind people see: "I had felt the possibility of creating a new understanding in the minds of people rejected by the society in which they lived" (141). Unlike Fred Daniels who emerges from a dark underworld only to be blinded by "dead sunshine" (53), he shrewdly exploits his "underground position" (192) to teach people how to see their environment more clearly and develop ways of changing it. Unlike his co-workers Brand and Cooke, who indeed are "branded" and "cooked" by their fiery hatreds, he can transform heat into light, avoiding violence and promoting new understandings. His mind "open and questioning" (191), and his eyes clearly focused on the real world, he has finally escaped the traps which have destroyed most of the central characters in *Eight Men*. Indeed, he has fashioned an existential identity which will help transform the "dark underworld of American life" (204) into a more just society whose citizens are fully sighted men and women instead of Dantean "shadows."

NOTES

[1]Saunders Redding, "Home is Where the Heart Is," *The New Leader*, 44 (December 11, 1961), 25.
[2]Saunders Redding, "Review of *Eight Men*," *New York Herald Tribune Book Review*, (January 22, 1961), 33.
[3]John Reilly, *The Critical Reception of Richard Wright* (New York: Franklin, 1978), xxxvii.
[4]Richard Gilman, "The Immediate Misfortunes of Widespread Literacy," *Commonweal* (April 1961), 130.
[5]Irving Howe, "Richard Wright: A Word of Farewell," *New Republic*, 144 (February 13, 1951), 18.
[6]Richard Wright, *Eight Men* (New York: Pyramid Books: 1969), 10. (All subsequent references to this text are to this Pyramid Books edition. Page numbers are cited parenthetically in the text.)

7*Richard Wright, Black Boy*: A *Record of Childhood and Youth* (New York: Harper and Row, 1966), 272.

8Richard Wright, *Native Son* (New York: Harper and Row, 1966), 31.

9Keneth Kinnamon, *New Essays on Native Son* (Cambridge, England: Cambridge University Press, 1990), 15.

10For a full discussion of how Wright uses ocular imagery in *Native Son,* see James Nagel's "Images of 'Vision' in *Native Son*," *University Review* 35 (December 1969), 109-115 and also James Emmanuel's "Fever and Feeling: Notes on the Imagery of *Native Son*," *Negro Digest* 18 (December 1968). 16-26.

Richard Wright Today

Too Honest for His Own Time

Arnold Rampersad

When the Library of America asked me to edit a volume of Richard Wright, I was pleased to do so. I was also apprehensive. Given the history of his dealings with publishers, some tough decisions would have to be made if justice were to be done to him.

Certainly Wright would be well served by being in the Library of America. His work would appear in beautiful and durable volumes, with the promise of being kept permanently in print. And there could be no doubt about his right to be in such company. Of *Native Son*, Irving Howe has shrewdly declared that American culture was changed "forever" with its explosive appearance in 1940; and *Black Boy* belongs on any definitive short list of American autobiographies. With works twice chosen by the Book-of-the-Month Club, Wright had also enjoyed success and influence unparalleled among black American writers of his era.

Success had come, however, at a price. Certain of his important works, including *Native Son* and *Black Boy*, suffered changes and abridgments that Wright would never have made on his own. The issue for the Library of America was whether we could restore his texts that had been mangled in order to meet the extraordinary demands of his original publishers.

Would the Library of America be prepared to take responsibility with me for undoing changes that were the result, not entirely but in part, of racism—racism that was seldom conscious of itself, that was expressed in subtle, even benign ways, but racism nonetheless? Most of the major areas of textual controversy in Wright's work can be traced to the inevitable conflict that pitted an extraordinarily forceful and brilliant black writer, one who was bent on speaking the unspeakable, against white agents, editors and publishers who, often with what they construed to be Wright's best interests in mind, had very determining ideas of what whites were willing to accept from such a source.

I soon discovered that the Library of America was fully prepared to take on this responsibility. Moreover, it decided to start with two volumes of Wright.

Wright's mixture of brilliance and fearlessness makes virtually every one of his works a challenge. Compared with him, some of the bravest of earlier black writers seem almost timid. There is some truth in the scornful opening of his 1937 essay "Blueprint for Negro Writing," in which he asserts, "Generally speaking, Negro writing in the past has been confined to humble novels, poems, and plays, prim and decorous ambassadors who went a-begging to white America . . . dressed in the knee-pants of servility . . . . For the most part these artistic ambassadors were received as though they were French poodles who do clever tricks."

***

When Wright realized that his first book, four long stories entitled *Uncle Tom's Children*, was "a book which even bankers' daughters could read and weep over and feel good about," he swore that the next one would be different. He would make sure that "no one would weep over it; that it would be so hard and deep that they would face it without the consolation of tears." That is a fair characterization of the almost violent impact of his next book, *Native Son*—and perhaps of Wright's early career as a whole.

Taught early by the writing of H.L. Mencken to appreciate the power of "words as weapons," Wright struck boldly when he encountered falseness or injustice. From his first publications in Chicago as a Communist poet to his death in Paris in 1960 at the age of 52, he took on, at one time or another, white supremacy, organized religion, capitalism, Communism, Fascism and colonialism. Early in his career he also repudiated black cultural nationalism; no major black American writer has written more harshly about black culture. Studious, cautious, he was nevertheless on a mission to speak the truth as he saw it, and this zealotry threatened to bring him into the conflict with everyone who stood between him and the reading public.

Each of Wright's books presented the Library of America with a different set of editorial problems. A fair example is *Lawd Today!*, his first novel, though not published until 1963, three years after his death. Eight major publishers rejected the manuscript when it was submitted to them in 1935 or thereafter. It was finally brought out in 1963 by Walker & Company and treated almost like a foundling, attracting little attention, although—to me at least—it is among Wright's most compelling works, far more accomplished than, for example, his thin psychoanalytic novel *Savage Holiday*, which appeared in 1954.

Lawd Today! casts an important light on Wright's beginning years as a writer. It reveals that at the height of his involvement with the Communist Party, and even as he loyally published propagandistic verse, he had been secretly creating fiction shaped by the existential values and modernist techniques that were anathema to Communists—and affording not a glimpse of the revolutionary potential of the masses. Anticipating the concerns that would mark the first years of his voluntary exile in France after 1947, when he became friends with Jean-Paul Sartre and Simone de Beauvoir, the novel confirms the independence that fired his imagination and intellect from the beginning. Had this work appeared in the mid-1930's, the party almost certainly would not have waited till the early 1940's to expel him.

Why did so many publishers reject the book? For a combination of factors: its status as a first novel, requiring a special faith at a time (the Depression) when publishers had to be unusually cautious; its nihilism, which would have antagonized leftists; and, not least of all, its insistence on the extent to which its main characters, four postal workers in Chicago, are obsessed by sex, including the idea of interracial sex.

Even in 1963, the manuscript apparently troubled the editors at Walker & Company. Ignoring James Joyce's clear influence on Wright—or perhaps not willing to recognize it—the publisher "corrected" many of Wright's innovations in punctuation, capitalization and usage. Words judged obscene were cut; various colloquialisms were polished, presumably to elevate the tone.

The Library of America rejected this version in favor of Wright's last revision. We found this text, finished between 1937 and 1938 (following the various rejections), among Wright's papers at the Beinecke Library of Yale University. The Library of America has been able to restore all elements taken out or modified in the Walker & Company version of 1963. It will, in effect, give readers a new novel.

Uncle Tom's Children offered no comparable difficulties, but *Native Son* required a major salvage operation. At the very moment that the book was set to appear from Harper & Brothers in 1939 came the electrifying news that the Book-of-the-Month Club was interested in *Native Son*—provided that certain revisions were made. Poor all of his life and eager for a financial windfall, Wright assented. The appearance of *Native Son* as a main selection in 1940 led to sales of almost 215,000 copies within three weeks. However, this book was significantly different from the one Wright had been set to publish.

In the section considered most offensive by the club's selectors, Wright's central character, Bigger Thomas, and a male friend casually masturbate ("polishing my nightstick," Bigger says) as they await the start of a movie. Also questioned was a scene shortly afterward, when Bigger and his friend hungrily view a newsreel featuring Mary Dalton, the attractive young millionaire's daughter Bigger will soon kill. She is shown on vacation, and as Mary's boyfriend chases her on a beach, the announcer leers: *"Ha! He's after her! There! He's got her! Oh boy, don't you wish you were down there in Florida? . . . . Ah, the naughty rich!"* To Bigger, who knows that he will soon be working in the Dalton household, Mary is "a hot-looking number, all right." His friend assures him insouciantly that "them rich white women'll go to bed with anybody, from a poodle on up. They even have their chauffeurs."

Although the published version of *Native Son* would play down Bigger's sexuality, Wright had intended to make it quite clear that Bigger is indeed sexually stirred by Mary Dalton. Watching the rear-view mirror as he drives her car, he sees "a faint sweep of white thigh." While Mary and her boyfriend, Jan Erlone, make love on the back seat, Bigger reacts: "Filled with a sense of them, his muscles grew gradually taut. He sighed and sat up straight, fighting off the stiffening feeling in his loins."

Taking the drunken Mary upstairs at home after Jan has left her, "He tightened his arms as lips pressed against hers and he felt her body moving strongly. The thought and conviction that Jan had had her a lot flashed through his mind. He kissed her again and felt the sharp bones of her hips move in a hard and veritable grind." (Wright even has Bigger thinking of Mary Dalton while he is having sex with his girlfriend, Bessie.)

Strongly objecting to such writing, as well as to several other sexual references, the Book-of-the-Month Club asked Wright to cut the masturbation episode and the newsreel account of Mary Dalton, to shorten his account of Bigger's sexual intercourse with Bessie and to delete at least one detail of what Bigger regarded as foreplay. The speeches of his lawyer and the district attorney were also to be cut. Wright apparently did not resist any of these requests, although he was later to reject an offer for a film version (the proviso was that all of the main characters be white). The club, satisfied with the changes, decided to take the novel.

The Library of America decided to reject the Book-of-the-Month Club text of 1940—that is, *Native Son* as readers have always known it. Instead, it has published the version Harper was prepared to publish in 1939.

It might be argued, of course, that the masturbation scene is in bad taste. (Even Wright's editor had called the scene "a bit on the raw side.") But it is also true that in making Bigger almost asexual and unresponsive where Mary Dalton is concerned, the Book-of-the-Month Club version made him less human, less alive and almost incomprehensible. And quite apart from its meaning in the novel itself, Bigger's vibrant sexuality had historic significance. Never before in American literature, except in scurrilous attacks on black men as rapists or likely rapists, had black male sexuality been represented with such frankness.

Wright understood that, with few exceptions, there could be no serious discussion of race in the United States without reference to sexuality (a fact attested to by works as far apart as William Faulkner's *Absalom, Absalom!* and Spike Lee's *Jungle Fever*). To nullify Bigger's sexual drive was to dilute or even to sabotage the central power of *Native Son* as a commentary on race in this country.

Four years later, in 1944, Wright's autobiography, *Black Boy*, once again brought him into creative conflict with the Book-of-the-Month Club. Again, Harper had accepted his manuscript for publication and set it in page proofs before the club voiced its interest and its objections. First called "Black Confessions" and then "American Hunger," the manuscript comprised two sections. "Southern Night" told of Wright's life until 1927, when he fled the South for Chicago; "The Horror and the Glory" traced Wright's experiences in Chicago, including his membership in the Communist Party and his subsequent break with it in the name of artistic and intellectual freedom. The club asked Wright to drop the entire second section.

Again, Wright agreed. The book appeared in the spring of 1945, renamed *Black Boy*. ("It is honest," he wrote his editor, Edward Aswell, about the title. "Straight. And many people say it to themselves when they see a Negro and wonder how he lives.") The changes in *Native Son* almost emasculated Bigger Thomas; the changes in *Black Boy* worked to de-intellectualize Wright, to return him to his childhood and adolescence. Moreover, *Black Boy*, as published, made the white South the only true villain of the text. In this way, Wright's broader criticism of the United States was blunted, as was his criticism of radical socialists, a touchy issue in 1945 as the Allied victory approached. In his journal, Wright recorded his firm belief that Communist pressure had prompted the club's demands.

One part of the deleted section appeared as "I Tried to Be a Communist" in the *Atlantic Monthly* in 1944 and another in *Mademoiselle* (of all places) in 1945. However, it was not until 1977, long after Wright's death, that the entire second section was brought out by Harper & Row as *American Hunger*. Like the posthumously published *Lawd Today!*, it has failed to make much of an impression. Without the preceding material, *American Hunger* is more a memoir of a period than an integral part of a life story. Offering a limited vision of Wright, it sometimes makes him seem alternately quarrelsome and egotistical.

Once again, the Library of America decided to publish the book that Harper was set to bring out before the club intervened. For the first time, Wright's remarkable autobiography is offered as he intended it, tracing his life from his birth in the deep South to his break with the Communist Party in the North and the start of his new life as a free artist and intellectual.

The Outsider, Wright's long, prophetic political novel of 1953, called for yet another set of decisions. The Book-of-the-Month Club was not an issue here; apparently it foresaw no great interest in a novel about a despairing black intellectual who takes on a new identity following a train wreck, only to be drawn into a doomed interaction with Communists. The novel, which builds steadily to a clamorous denunciation of the rival totalitarianisms of Communism and Fascism, also offers a dire—and accurate—prediction of a worldwide revival of religious fundamentalism in response to the spiritual gloom spawned by these monoliths.

Faced with a manuscript of almost 800 typewritten pages, Wright's new editor at Harper, Jack Fischer, demanded that it be cut by one-third. The relationship quickly became antagonistic, especially after Wright discovered that Fischer was depending on the advice of a consultant. Sex was not the issue—there was little of it, although Wright's hero, Cross Damon, does make love to a white woman, the widow of an unscrupulous Communist leader (killed by Damon) who had married her on orders from the party. Among the sections marked for elimination were most of those written in the stream-of-consciousness manner, some freighted with philosophic arguments and several involving black characters, who somehow seemed less important to Fischer than they did to Wright.

***

Wright refused to drop any of the episodes. Instead, by compressing various scenes he reduced the manuscript by roughly one-sixth. Still later, again urged by Fischer, he made more cuts. Moreover, a careful collation further revealed that while inserting these changes, a copy editor at Harper quietly removed two additional pages and several other passages and words from the manuscript. No one sought permission for these cuts from Wright, who was given only two days to read the final galleys. The volume appeared without the two pages.

The Library of America decided against restoring any of the material deleted by Wright at Fischer's insistence. Fischer almost certainly improved *The Outsider* by demanding that it be cut; Wright served himself well by refusing to drop whole sections. However, the cuts made without Wright's approval were another matter altogether. The Library of America decided to publish the final typescript of the novel as submitted by Wright. It restored all the passages pulled by the copy editor, as well as his or her other changes.

The Library of America has insured that most of Wright's major texts are now available as he had wanted them to be read. Whether future printings by other publishers will follow the Library's lead remains to be seen. I hope that Harper Collins, which retains the copyright for most of Wright's major works, will go back to the texts it had originally intended to publish in the case of *Native Son* and *Black Boy*. In a way, our work is a tribute to Harper's courage and foresight in agreeing to bring out Wright's work with a minimum of interference. Most important of all is the opportunity we now have to hear a great American writer speak with his own voice about matters that still resonate at the center of our lives.

From *The New York Times Book Review* (December 29, 1991), 3.

The Problematic Texts of Richard Wright

James W. Tuttleton

It is an event of great cultural importance to have, at last, the best of Richard Wright in The Library of America series.[1] Thus far, with respect to black writers, only W.E.B. DuBois has been represented, although it is only fair to the Library to remark that the best black writers are modern, and considerations of copyright and high royalty fees have delayed the appearance of many twentieth-century writers—both white and black.

In a manner of speaking, the reprint of a writer's work in The Library of America may be perceived as a sign of greatness, even an admission to the "canon of classic texts." At the very least it is a great honor, for most readers probably assent to the project's claim of offering "the only definitive collection of America's greatest writers." *Definitive* is a loaded word, about which I shall say more, but whatever his flaws, Richard Wright belongs, in my judgment, in this distinguished group—which includes, at least in the Library series, such familiars as Twain, Crane, Parkman, William and Henry James, Lincoln, Cather, Wharton, Cooper, and Franklin, among others. *Native Son* is Wright's best novel; but *Uncle Tom's Children* and his autobiography *Black Boy* are also compelling narratives that served to revolutionize black writing in America. Irving Howe, in "Black Boys and Native Sons," has even gone so far as to say that "the day *Native Son* appeared, American culture was changed forever." And so, in a sense it was. A new work of great imaginative power rearranged the tradition of American fiction; and, with respect to black writing, it made previous novels by black writers like Charles Chestnutt, DuBois, Nella Larsen, and Rudolph Fisher seem mild by comparison. Younger black writers also found a new model for the naturalistic representation of their experience; and in quick order other grim portraits of black life appeared in Chester Himes's *If He Hollers Let Him Go* (1945), Ann Petry's *The Street* (1946), Curtis Lucas' *Third Ward Newark* (1946), and Willard Motley's *Knock on Any Door* (1947). Equally as important, after *Native Son*, white readers no longer found it possible to luxuriate in an illusion of black docility, passivity, and contentment.

Richard Wright, the grandchild of slaves and child of an illiterate sharecropper and backcountry schoolteacher, was born in 1908 on Rucker's Plantation near Roxie, Mississippi. He had all the disadvantages of being black in the Jim Crow Mississippi of that time; and the bitter effects of racial animosity toward blacks and legal segregation were compounded by a grinding poverty that would have stunted nearly anyone's development. Making ends meet required the family frequently split up, and Richard and his brother were placed for a while with their grandparents in Natchez while the parents searched for work. Eventually his father, a brutal man, abandoned the family, and his mother moved the boys about continually—to Memphis, Tennessee, Jackson, Mississippi, and Elaine and West Helena Arkansas—as she shifted from job to job, laboring as a cook or cleaning woman for white families. There was never enough money for rent or food. A dominant motif of Wright's autobiography is in fact the constant hunger he suffered. Again, for a time, Wright was placed in a Methodist orphanage in Memphis; and for a while he lived with his Uncle Silas Hoskins.

(Hoskins was lynched in 1917 in Elaine—only because, it seems, he had a successful business coveted by whites.)

It would be tedious to rehearse the family's many moves, or Wright's chronic hunger as a child, his makeshift schooling in one town or another, or the menial labor and odd jobs—as delivery boy, salesclerk, dishwasher, and bellboy—by which the growing boy tried to help out his mother and grandmother, who were in continual ill health. For them the strict fundamentalism of Methodist and Seventh-day Adventist Christianity was completely sustaining, but the religious prohibitions of his family, their moral strictness, and the manifest hypocrisy of Southern racial relations alienated and estranged the boy, even while he was filled with a lifelong sense of anxiety and dread. Great curiosity and omnivorous reading—in thrown-away issues of the *Atlantic Monthly*, *Harper's*, and *American Mercury*—saved him from the common fate. Mencken's iconoclastic *Prejudices* and *A Book of Prefaces* taught him to see "words as weapons"; he began to haunt the public libraries and to cultivate a burning ambition to write.

Black poverty in the rural South is horrific enough in Wright's account of it in *Black Boy*. The North, with its more liberal racial attitudes and industrial capacity beckoned to the Wrights, as it did to the thousands of rural blacks. But the Wrights' move to Chicago in 1927 plunged young Richard into evils almost as great. And the urban poverty he experienced, particularly after the Crash of 1929, was equally as appalling. But he eked out a life of sorts, supporting his mother and aunt as a dishwasher, ditch digger, postal clerk, and insurance agent. He read extensively in Conrad, Twain, James, Proust, Dostoevsky, and others. But, as he told an interviewer for *L'Express* in 1960, "Theodore Drieser first revealed to me the nature of American life, and for that service, I place him at the pinnacle of American literature."

The Communist organizers in the League of Struggle for Negro Rights captured Wright's attention in the 1930s, and he quickly became an ardent member of the local John Reed Club. Joining the Communist Party in 1934, he developed friendships with many proletarian writers and social critics—including Nelson Algren, Jack Conroy, Arna Bontemps, and James T. Farrell. His literary talent opened opportunities for him in *Left Front*, *Anvil*, and *New Masses*, and between 1934 and 1937, Wright was an impassioned activist at writers' congresses and in Midwest literary groups. Wherever he went he argued for racial equality and espoused his Communist faith. Yet he cooled to the Chicago branch of the Party in 1937 when it tried to infringe on his personal freedom as a writer. Moving in that year to New York, he pursued his literary career as the Harlem editor of the *Daily Worker*, to which he contributed more than 200 articles. His first breakthrough came with the publication of *Uncle Tom's Children* in 1938. *Native Son*, a Book-of-the-Month-Club selection, followed in 1940, and, with the many accolades it earned him, his career took off.

Wright's subsequent life seemed foreordained by his popular success in America. His works were translated into French, Italian, German, Dutch, and other languages. The power of the novel made him in constant demand as a spokesman for racial equality, and he toured the country as a platform speaker and panelist. His distinction as a portrayer of black life in America led naturally in 1941 to *12 Million Black Voices: A Folk History of the Negro in the United States*; and, after some disagreement over its content, his best-selling autobiography *Black Boy: A Record of Childhood and Youth* appeared in 1945.

Although he had quietly broken with the Communist Party in 1942, his political views brought him under FBI surveillance, which continued throughout most of his lifetime, and he had constant passport difficulties in traveling abroad. In 1946, he took a month-long trip to France, at the invitation of Jean-Paul Sartre and Claude Lévi-Strauss, where he formed friendships with Gertrude Stein, Simone de Beavoir, André Gide, and many others, In Paris he was introduced to the *Négritude* movement sponsored by Léopold Sédar Senghor and Aimé Césaire. What particularly pleased him about France was its greater racial tolerance and openness to new ideas. In 1947, racial prejudice in the Greenwich Village housing market provoked his ire, and he decided to move permanently to France, taking with him his wife Ellen and daughter Julia. In Paris he became a spokesman for the American colony of blacks (and for African blacks in Paris), and he founded and joined many literary and liberal political organizations. The Existentialism of Sartre and Camus was then all the rage, and

Wright began to read in the philosophy of Heidegger, Husserl, and Jaspers. This Existentialism, in ill-digested clumps, unfortunately mars his novel *The Outsider* (1953).

At the same time, his friendship with George Padmore, the Trinidadian author of *Pan-Africanism or Communism?*, heightened his interest in Africa, and in 1953 he toured Ghana, Sierra Leone and other countries—producing in 1954, out of this experience, *Black Power: A Record of Reactions in a Land of Pathos*. As fascinated as he was by black Africa, it must be said that his reactions are those of a Western intellectual. During this period Wright's political and cultural interests interfered, in my view, with his imaginative work. *Savage Holiday* (1954), a novel about a white psychopathic murderer, was a weak performance. Harper rejected it, and he was obliged to bring it out as an original paperback by Avon. Somewhat like the later Faulkner, Wright saw himself as an important public spokesman on national and international issues. As a cultural reporter for the Congress of Cultural Freedom, he attended the Bandung (Indonesia) Conference of non-aligned nations and listened to Nehru, Sukarno, Sihanouk, Nasser, and others declaim on the state of international relations in the Cold War Era. *The Color Curtain: A Report on the Bandung Conference* appeared in 1956. *Pagan Spain* (1957), a travel book, *White Man, Listen!* (1957), a collection of essays based on his lectures about race, and *The Long Dream* (1958), a novel set in Mississippi, represent the final phase of his declining career. He was in ill health in the last years of his life , probably as a result of amoebic dysentery picked up in Africa, but he died in fact of a heart attack in Paris in 1960, as he was completing the proofs of *Eight Men* (1961), his last collection of stories.

Richard Wright: Early Works begins with *Lawd Today!*, a work not very well known—principally because it was not published in Wright's lifetime. Completed in 1935 and originally entitled *Cesspool*, the novel was rejected by several publishers. An account of one day—an anniversary of Lincoln's birthday—in the life of a black postal worker, it portrays in Jake Johnson an arrogant, irresponsible, vain and cruel man who begins the day by beating up his wife (the section is called "Commonplace"); he ends it, in a drunken rage, by nearly killing her (in "Rats' Alley"). In between, Jake is shown hanging out at Doc Higgins' Tonsorial Palace, overborrowing from a loan shark, malingering at the Post Office (the "Squirrel Cage" section), and drinking himself into a violent rage at a ghetto whorehouse, where he is rolled of the $100 he has just borrowed. No publisher would take the novel in 1936, and it languished in manuscript until it posthumously appeared in 1963. Professor Rampersad has thought it important enough to include here; and indeed, its structural form, rhythmic dialogue, contrapuntal themes, and suggestive symbolism give a clear foreshadowing of the Wright who would emerge, fully matured, in *Native Son*. As a reflection of the social and moral inferno in which these hollow men live, *Lawd Today!* is Wright's version of Eliot's *The Waste Land*, construed as the bitter end of Lincoln's dream of black emancipation.

Uncle Tom's Children, a fully achieved work of fiction, contains five long stories, preceded by an autobiographical sketch, "The Ethics of Living Jim Crow." Wright was a dedicated Communist at the time he wrote these tales, and each introduces, more or less, the Marxist viewpoint. But they are by no means mere propaganda, which is no doubt why Wright got into trouble with the Chicago branch of the Party, which hinted, ominously, of purging the "bastard intellectuals" in their midst. (His troubles with Party orthodoxy are recounted in his essay "I Tried to Be a Communist" [1944], which was reprinted in *The God That Failed*.) Each of these stories focuses on a black protagonist who reacts against brutalization by whites not so much on the basis of ideology as on an instinctive desire for freedom from social oppression and on the intuition of a better way of life. As the children of Uncle Tom, each of them has learned "to lie, to steal, to dissemble," to "play that dual role which every Negro must play if he wants to eat and live."

"Fire and Cloud" is, in my view, the best of the five. It tells the Depression story of a black minister, the Rev. Taylor, whose people are starving but who cannot persuade the white power structure to provide relief in the form of food. When the Communist organizers urge a demonstration, the Mayor and Police Chief urge Rev. Taylor to discourage his people from attending. He is a Christian, has always been a "good nigger," and is necessarily worried that if he leads his people into the town square, a bloodbath will await them. But before he can decide what to do, he is seized by Klan rednecks, taken out into the countryside, and horsewhipped until he is unconscious. On the following morning, having had a "vision," he walks with most of the town's 10,000 blacks into the square—a multitude so numerous that the Mayor and the police back down, capitulate, and agree to provide food for the starving. While the story is meant to be an illustration of Lenin's saying—that *"Freedom belongs to the strong!"*—its literary power inheres in Wright's masterly presentation of the poignant helplessness of those who have nowhere else to turn. All of the tales suggest a complex grasp of racist social relations in the pre-World War II South, yet Wright's command of the nuances of emotion in his inarticulate characters, their impulses and bewildered striving, is equally compelling. His ear was true to the dialect of Mississippi blacks, at least as I knew it forty years ago, and his expert use of biblical symbolism and Christian allusion is richly counterpointed with his own idiosyncratic Marxist perspective.

In the writing of *Uncle Tom's Children*, Wright was later to claim that he had

> made an awfully naïve mistake. I found that I had written a book which even bankers' daughters could read and weep over and feel good about. I swore to myself that if I ever wrote another book, no one would weep over it; that it would be so hard and deep that they would have to face it without the consolation of tears. It was this that made me get to work in dead earnest.

The response of reader sympathy for his characters meant less to Wright than administering a shock that would stun readers into an amelioration of the conditions of black existence. In *Native Son*, he exploded a bomb.

This narrative of a deprived black boy living in a rat-infested tenement who commits two more or less unintended murders naturalizes Dostoevsky and Drieser in a Chicago tenement setting. Bigger Thomas becomes the chauffeur for a rich white man and is sexually attracted to his promiscuous daughter. After a night on the town, when Mary Dalton and her Communist boyfriend Jan Erlone get drunk and make love in the back seat of the car, Bigger Thomas has to put the comatose Mary back to bed. In trying to keep her quiet, he accidentally smothers her, and, to cover up this crime, stuffs her body into the furnace. Framing the boyfriend, Bigger then fakes a kidnap note to mislead the police, but—when he is discovered—he runs. During the manhunt, he hides out in several abandoned buildings, murders his girlfriend, but is nevertheless caught and brought to trial. Modeling his narrative on *An American Tragedy*, Wright constructed a novel so as to rationalize the meaning of Bigger's experience through the speeches presented by the defense lawyer, a Communist named Boris A. Max. Needless to say, the sociological conditions of black urban poverty and white racism are invoked as the proximate cause of the murder of the two women. Thus white society is put on trial and Bigger Thomas is made out, at least implicitly, to be a victim of the social forces conspiring to diminish black life in America. But setting aside this unconvincing defense, the novel is still a work of horrifying and sobering import.

Wright was later to say, in "How Bigger Was Born" (reprinted here) that while his "contact with the labor movement and its ideology" (his euphemism for Communism) made him feel "the pinch and pressure of the environment" that produces a Bigger Thomas, he did not mean to say that "environment *makes* consciousness." But Bigger has too little self-consciousness to have any comprehensible view of why he is a murderer. Like Drieser, Wright constructed his novel out of newspaper accounts of the trial of one Robert Nixon, who had murdered a white woman, Nixon was defended by two black lawyers. In the novel, Wright changes the defense to a Leftist white lawyer, for no black attorney would have mounted the sociological defense of Bigger that Max provides. Wright's attention to Bigger's shapeless inner life and the prolixity and dubiety of Max's courtroom speechifying have led some of Wright's defenders to transform the book into a psychological novel, of sorts, so as to deflect attention from its social message. Yet this maneuver robs the novel of its force as a document of social protest and misrepresents Wright's ideological sympathies in the late thirties.

In understanding Wright's development into a Communist, his autobiography is immensely illuminating, for its portrait of abject poverty and of racial prejudice in the South produced in him such smoldering rage that not even the ministrations of family or the consolations of religion could be adequate. In 1943, when he completed the manuscript, he intended to call his autobiography *American Hunger*. In the draft he sent to his agent Paul Reynolds, the manuscript contained two sections: "Southern Night," dealing with his life in the South; and "The Horror and the Glory," dealing with his Chicago life and membership in the Party. The Book-of-the-Month-Club was interested in it, but they recommended to Wright's editor at Harper, Edward Aswell, that only the first part be published. Wright agreed and renamed the autobiography *Black Boy*; it dealt with only his Southern years. Not until 1977 was the second part published by Harper and Row—under the title *American Hunger*. In the Library of America text, we now have the whole of Wright's original manuscript—presented under the title *Black Boy (American Hunger)*.

As rich as is the content of Wright's autobiography (not to speak of *The Outsider*), some of the textual decisions by the Library of America deserve comment. As a first principle of professional editing, it ought to be the objective *to present that form of the text that represents the author's final intention*. According to this principle, then, a text editor should incorporate any changes on the manuscript, galleys, page proofs (and pages of already published editions) that reflect the last wish of the author with respect to the form in which his work should appear. *Black Boy (American Hunger)*, in the Library of America edition, is not a form of the text of his autobiography that Wright ever approved. An argument can be made that Wright merely acquiesced, under pressure from Harper and the book club, in a change that otherwise he would not have made. And in fact Wright privately complained in his journal that "pressure from Communists" had induced the club to request deletion of the second part. (I have seen no evidence for this belief.) Yet in after years, when he had attained international fame, Wright never moved to reissue his autobiography in the form in which he had originally written it. The second part—already mined for magazine articles—only appeared posthumously, in 1977, as a separate text, with the approval of Mrs. Ellen Wright, who controls the literary estate.

These textual considerations also raise a question about the form of *Native Son* as well. Professor Rampersad remarks in a note that "This text of *Native Son* is the last version of the text that Wright prepared without external intervention, and in all the others cases these texts are the last, or last-known, versions that Wright approved." His reference to external intervention deserves clarification. When Aswell sent a copy of the Harper proofs to the Book-of-the-Month Club, Dorothy Canfield Fisher (and perhaps other judges of the Club) objected to a passage, early in the novel, where Bigger and a friend masturbate in a movie theater, while watching a newsreel clip about Mary Dalton as a rich Chicago socialite and left-wing sympathizer. The Club was inclined to accept the novel if that passage were deleted. Wright then agreed to excisions deemed to be obscene. In the Library of America text, these excisions have been restored as instances of unwarranted external interference. But Wright approved the deletion, rewrote the scene, and modified later particulars (not always with perfect consistency) to harmonize with his changes. Do not these changes represent his final intention? Moreover, in later years, to my knowledge, Wright never complained of the editorial suggestions supplied by Aswell or the Club. And he never moved to reissue the novel in its manuscript form.

In reaction to the Library's editorial decision, James Campbell, in "The Wright Version," has raised a question—in the *Times Literary Supplement* for 13 December 1991—about whether Wright "would have approved the work of re-editing which has been carried out on his two most famous books." Rampersad, in his view, "appears to have overstepped his brief." Rampersad has not, to my knowledge, replied to this accusation. But Mark Richardson, who describes himself as having assisted in the research for the Library edition, replied in the *TLS* for 24 January 1992 that the Library's decisions were sound because "Wright would not have revised the two books if the Book Club hadn't asked him to." Likewise, Ellen and Julia Wright, the novelist's widow and daughter, announced rather grandly in a *TLS* letter of 31 January that

> It is important to us that Bigger Thomas, who was "castrated" because deprived of his sexual life in the edited 1940 text, is made whole again—and made human—by the reinstatement of the masturbation scene at the beginning of *Native Son* and of references to his guilt-ridden desire for rich, white Mary prior to the panic which leads him to smother her accidentally. Likewise it is important to have reinstated

American Hunger as an integral part of *Black Boy* because of the psychological importance of viewing Wright's account of his disillusionment with Communist Party politics as only one in a series of betrayals, the first of which takes place in *Black Boy* when young Richard is disowned by his father over the kitten episode.

There is no question that readers will want to know about these variant versions. The question, in relation to serious bibliographical and editorial practice, is where these variants belong—in a restored text or in footnotes? The fact is that Rampersad's restored passages are, in the lingo of professional text editors, *rejected substantives*. Wright agreed to reject them and did so. His reasons are not fully clear. He may have assented because he knew that Club sponsorship would vastly increase the book's sales. But he may just as well have felt that he did not wish to be judged an obscene writer. Just as possible, he might, on reconsideration, have concluded that the aesthetic merit of his text suffered from the scene in which Bigger masturbates. We really cannot know.

What we do know is that he agreed to make changes, did make them, and never afterward—to my knowledge—complained that he had been coerced by his publishers. We need to have these restored passages—but they belong in the notes, not in the text. When later editors, on their own authority, undertake to restore canceled material, they do not honor the author's final intention and do not produce "definitive texts." While we now live in a more liberal age, where almost any obscenity can be claimed to have aesthetic merit or socially redeeming value, the imposition on a text of an editor's modern attitudes really serves to create a different book from the one the author finally intended, a book different from the one that made its impact on the reading public of his time.

Notes

[1]The set is in two volumes: RICHARD WRIGHT: EARLY WORKS. The Library of America. $35.00 includes *Lawd Today!*, *Uncle Tom's Children*, and *Native Son*. RICHARD WRIGHT: LATER WORKS. The Library of America. $35.00, includes *Black Boy* (*American Hunger*) and *The Outsider*. Arnold Rampersad, author of the acclaimed biography *The Life of Langston Hughes*, wrote notes for both volumes and oversaw (I presume) the text selection.

From *The Hudson Review* XLV (Summer 1992), 261-271.

The Library of America Edition of *Native Son*

Keneth Kinnamon

The publication a little over a year ago of a generous selection of Richard Wright's works by the Library of America is a literary event of the first magnitude. As we all know, prior to that time, W.E.B. Du Bois had been the only black author published in "the only definitive collection of America's greatest writers." Now Wright joins a very select company of thirty American writers, including the following novelists: Willa Cather, James Fenimore Cooper, Stephen Crane, Theodore Dreiser, William Faulkner, Nathaniel Hawthorne, William Dean Howells, Henry James, Jack London, Herman Melville, Frank Norris, Harriet Beecher Stowe, Mark Twain, and Edith Wharton. Even those of us who have reservations about the process of canonization or perhaps the concept of canon itself must be a little impressed, even as we wonder what problems of chronology or literary property required Wright to wait for inclusion on such lesser lights as Cather, Crane, Howells, London, Norris, Stowe, and Wharton. Let us assume that there were such problems, for Wright is the most recent of all the writers yet included in the Library of America, with the sole exception of Flannery O'Connor (whom I have not listed among the novelists because I consider her primarily a practitioner of the short story). Let me add parenthetically that Wright might have been included much earlier, for I wrote to Daniel Aaron in 1987 nominating Wright and volunteering my services as an editor. I received no reply; obviously I should have written to Gila Bercovitch, who, along with Max Rudin, has been so energetic and effective in promoting the Wright volumes.

Like most cultural events, Wright as Library of America author has a long background, but I shall focus on that part of it concerning textual issues in *Native Son*. The history of scholarship on this subject requires a bit more autobiography, for which I ask your indulgence. Thirty years ago, as I was beginning my dissertation on Wright, the reference book *American Literary Manuscripts* listed three repositories for Wright materials: the James Weldon Johnson Collection in the Beinecke (not the Wright Archive, of course, acquired many years later), the Hartford Theological Seminary (an erroneous listing referring to another Richard Wright), and the Fales Collection of the New York University Library. In the last named I made an interesting discovery while examining the recently acquired bound page proofs of *Native Son*, revised as of 1 December 1939. As I explained in a note published early in 1965 in the *Bulletin of the Society for the Libraries of New York University*,

> a rapid examination . . . revealed that slightly less than two thirds of the pages of proof seem to be identical with the corresponding pages of the first edition, but of the remaining pages, about one hundred consist of printed yellow paper pasted on the blank white sheets. Some minor textual variations exist between these latter and the corresponding pages of the first edition.

> More importantly, on twenty-three pages the printed yellow paper is pasted over part of the printed white page. The resulting revised version corresponds to the first

edition, but since in some cases the original page proof version may be read by looking through the back of the white sheet interesting comparisons are possible.

At this point the typescript of my note discussed some of the deleted sexual scenes so familiar to all of you. But a funny thing happened on my note's way to publication. In a manner oddly and ironically reminiscent of what happened to the very work I was discussing, the editor of the *Bulletin* deleted the examples my discussion provided of sexual scenes deleted from the novel. The lacuna was indicated by three asterisks in otherwise blank space. Unfortunately for this impecunious graduate student with a wife and three small children subsisting on a Harvard teaching assistant's stipend eked out by his wife's day care of children of other impecunious students, the deletion in my scholarly note did not result in its selection by the Book-of-the-Month Club.

Since the Wright papers did not come to Yale until 1976 and since in any event I was busy with other Wright projects, I did not pursue textual matters concerning *Native Son* until a quarter century after my initial discoveries. In 1987 I began researching the composition of the novel for my introduction to *New Essays on Native Son* (1990), appearing in a somewhat different form as "How *Native Son* Was Born" in a collection of such genetic studies, *Writing the American Classics*, published the same year. I first presented the results of my research as "Sex, Politics, and Editorial Intervention in *Native Son*" on 7 July 1989 at the Wright symposium sponsored by the Gorky Institute of World Literature in Moscow, and I repeated the lecture in two other conferences later in 1989 and, in a fuller version, at various universities and another conference in 1990, the fiftieth anniversary year of the publication of the novel. The first of these was at Columbia at the end of January, where Arnold Rampersad, then recently appointed editor of the Library of America edition, was in the audience. We met for breakfast the following morning and discussed my work on the text. Four months later, at the first convention of the American Literature Association in San Diego, Gila Bercovitch contacted me to discuss my textual work and to inform me of the work of her staff, especially Mark Richardson, which was already well under way independently of my efforts.

So much for autobiography. With the appearance of the Library of America edition of Wright in October 1991, preceded by much publicity beginning in mid-August, autobiography ends and history begins. Let me state clearly that although my work and that of Rampersad, Richardson, and associates reach generally similar conclusions, their work is based on more thorough research in a wider range of primary sources. Its demonstration that the Book-of-the-Month Club played a larger role and Harper editor Edward Aswell a smaller one in the changes made in the text than I had thought is an important corrective.

The press coverage before and after publication of the Library of America edition has been voluminous, and much of it has focused on the deletion of explicit sexual scenes in *Native Son*. I have read over thirty reviews, essays, interviews, and letters to the editor appearing in such places as *The New York Times, The Washington Post, The Chicago Tribune, The Los Angeles Times, TLS, The New Yorker, The Hudson Review,* and *The New Republic* by such distinguished scholars, critics, and novelists as Rampersad himself, Cyrus Colter, John A. Williams, Charles Johnson, Alfred Kazin, Herbert Mitgang, Louis Menand, James W. Tuttleton, and Andrew Delbanco. Ellen and Julia Wright have also spoken out. As I said at the beginning of this paper, it was a literary event of the first magnitude.

The issue most thoroughly debated, of course, was whether or not the cuts of explicit sexual material demanded by the Book-of-the-Month Club should have been restored in the Library of America edition of *Native Son*. The view of the large majority of those who have expressed an opinion, twenty-two individuals, favor the Library of America edition over the 1940 edition. Rampersad speaks for many when he urges that "in making Bigger almost asexual and unresponsive where Mary Dalton is concerned, the Book-of-the-Month Club has made him less human, less alive and almost incomprehensible." Rampersad adds that the cuts diluted the power of the novel as racial commentary by denying the intimate connection between race and sex. Chicago novelist Leon Forrest agrees that "with this edition, we get more of Bigger's humanity and psychological motivation." Other reviewers echoed these points. In an excellent essay Andrew Delbanco emphasizes Wright's daring presentation, for the first time in

American literature, of "the full, urgent sexuality of a young black man" in a highly physical novel that insists on "the imperatives of the body." Jack Miles, Louis Menand, and several others show how restoration of deleted passages resolves inconsistencies, as I had also demonstrated. Not all who endorsed the restorations agreed that they enhanced the protagonist's humanity by affirming his sensuality. John A. Williams claims that the masturbation scene tends "to minimize whatever sympathy the reader feels for Bigger at this early point in the novel," noting that some black parents already object to their children reading the tamer Bigger of 1940. Nevertheless, Wright is positive about the negative effects of racism. In one of the most thoughtful commentaries, Cyrus Colter praises the Library of America edition but notes that the 1940 version still displays "Wright's powerful chemistry" as a "resourceful and intrepid author."

On the other hand, four writers clearly prefer the novel as originally published by Harper; the new edition, they believe, should present the deleted passages in the notes, not the text. Charles Johnson objects to Wright's "heavy-handed" treatment of sexual material: "Wright struggled mightily and only with partial success to make Bigger's brief moment of masturbation work as social metaphor . . . It's [sic] omission is, perhaps, an example of how a good editor can save a great writer from belaboring his point." Eugene Miller is of like mind but less temperate expression in his "Open Letter to Jerry Ward, Keneth Kinnamon, Arnold Rampersad and the Wright Circle," where he caricatures the views of Kinnamon and Rampersad as the black superstud stereotype: "If Wright meant to indicate such an equation, he could easily have written Bigger as a former day Wilt Chamberlain." James Campbell develops the most cogent argument in favor of the 1940 text. Believing that the Book-of-the-Month Club objected only to the masturbation scene, Campbell believes that all other changes were entirely voluntary, and some of these had nothing to do with sex. Even the deleted masturbation scene may have met with Wright's voluntary rather than coerced approval. Thus the 1940 edition was indeed the final approved version, even though Wright believed that he had completed the novel weeks earlier with the bound page proof Harper submitted to Book-of-the-Month. Furthermore, so far as we know Wright did not object to the 1940 version of *Native Son* in the numerous reprints after original publication. So says James Campbell. James Tuttleton in *The Hudson Review* follows a similar line of reasoning. Both Campbell and Tuttleton would agree that the 1940 version had a fifty-year life span not easily ended by a new version of dubious bibliographical authenticity because it was not in fact the final version approved by the author.

What is my own view? Initially I fully supported the restoration of deleted passages, which I had considered to have powerful interpretive implications when I discovered them in 1962, not knowing about editorial and Book-of-the-Month Club intervention. As I examined proofs and correspondence at Yale, Princeton, and Schomburg in 1987, I became convinced that Wright did not freely endorse the deletion of sexual and political passages. The coercive power of the Book-of-the-Month Club as explained by the Library of America edition seemed to me to settle the case, for I believed and still believe that the uncensored version is closer to authorial intention in its graphic power than the tamer version published in 1940. But from the point of view of the textual bibliographer, are the bound page proofs sent the Book Club a suitable copy text.? What constitutes authorial intention? Indeed, what constitutes authorship? My oversimplified thinking about these matters was complicated by reading the great textual scholar Jack Stillinger's fascinating recent book *Multiple Authorship and the Myth of Solitary Genius*. Stillinger argues that there is really no such things as solitary authorship, for spouses, friends, colleagues, agents, editors, and others participate in varying degrees in books ostensibly the product of the single person whose name appears on the spine and the title page. As we all know, our books and articles almost never appear in print in exactly the same form we present them to a journal, and often we find them better for editorial intervention. Certainly Wright was grateful to Edward Aswell for his help on other occasions, as Hemingway was to Maxwell Perkins and Faulkner was to Saxe Commins. If the authorship of *Native Son* belongs in part to his friends the Newtons, Ralph Ellison, Theodore Ward, Margaret Walker, perhaps others as well, why not also his agent Paul Reynolds and his editor Aswell? And if Reynolds and Aswell, why not the Book-of-the-Month Club also? Is authorship destabilized as the text becomes finally stabilized as a published book? These are unsettling questions as we try to determine authorial intentions.

But literary and social as well as authorial issues are at work here, complicated by issues of race and audience. My present preference, still somewhat tentative, is anathema to many textual scholars. I want a version of *Native Son* that restores all the coerced sexual cuts but retains all other changes made by Wright for the 1940 edition. This would be a synthetic copy text never approved by Wright, but more faithful to his intentions, I believe, than either the 1940 or the 1991 texts of *Native Son*. If someone can offer proof that Wright did in fact complain after 1940 about the sexual cuts, my case would be stronger. Neither Mark Richardson nor Ellen and Julia Wright respond to Campbell's emphasis on this point. At my request Michel Fabre very recently asked Ellen Wright if her husband ever mentioned the matter to her. She did not recall that he did, which does not prove that he did not. And certainly he could have complained about that meddlesome Dorothy Canfield Fisher to Aswell or Reynolds or later to Chester Himes or Ollie Harrington or others. Even if he never mentioned it to anyone, he may have been too busy with current projects or resigned merely to suffer in silence. On the other hand, he may have decided that the Book-of-the-Month Club did help him produce a better book, as Campbell believes. The issue cannot be settled until new hard evidence is adduced.

Meanwhile, we can all indulge our personal preferences for 1940, 1991, 1991 with some of 1940, or 1940 with some of 1991. Are we, in the process of choosing, ourselves sharing in the multiple authorship of that American classic *Native Son*?

The Library of America Edition of *The Outsider*

Yoshinobu Hakutani

Critics have largely regarded the Harper Edition of *The Outsider* published in 1953 as existential. They have also noted parallels between Wright and European existentialist novelists in the treatment of the metaphysical rebel, calling Cross Damon's philosophy most consistently nihilistic.[1] It would be quite tempting to compare *The Outsider* with Camus's *The Stranger*, for instance if they were the products of the same age and the particular philosophy they dealt with was in vogue. It is well known that Wright lived and wrote *The Outsider* in France, where he maintained a close contact with such influential writers as Camus, Sartre, and de Beauvoir. Moreover, Camus's philosophy can conveniently be placed side by side with Wright's protagonist, who contemplates human existence through his exhaustive reading of Nietzsche, Hegel, Kierkegaard, and Dostoevsky. One suspects, however, that the comparison of the two novels would never have been made unless the two novelists were both caught up in the philosophical context of existentialism. This meant that the literary likeness was taken for granted.

Even a casual examination of *The Outsider* and *The Stranger* would reveal that the two novels are of a different order. Meursault kills a man; he is charged with a murder, tried, and convicted in a world of court, jury, and judge. Damon, on the other hand, kills more than one man, not only an enemy but a friend, a mentor, and an ally, and is responsible for the suicide of a woman he loves. But he is never charged with a crime, brought to a trial, or convicted. Unlike Meursault, who encounters his death in the world of daylight in Algiers, Damon is himself murdered by two men, the agents of the Communist Party, on a dimly lit street in New York. Although the two novels appear existential, giving attention to the crucial details that differentiate the narratives make them radically different in their ideology and action.

Thanks to Arnold Rampersad's edition of *The Outsider* published by the Library of America, such differences became even more apparent. For the Harper edition, as Rampersad has shown, the original length of 741 typescript pages was shortened to 620 pages, a 16.3 percent deduction of the original manuscript. The difference between the two versions is partly stylistic but it has to do, in a larger measure, with Wright's intention about character and ideology. Most of the block cuts suggest that the novel as originally conceived is not as avowedly existentialist as critics have characterized the Harper edition. The original version suggests that Cross Damon is not a black man in name only. Not only is his plight real, but all the incidents and characters he is involved with, which at times appear to be clumsily constructed symbols, nonetheless express well-digested ideas. He is not "pathetically insane" as a reviewer described him.[2] The novel bewildered black reviewers as well, not because of Wright's philosophy, but because Wright seemed to have lost contact with his native soil.[3] But a detailed comparison of the two versions will show not only that Cross Damon as originally portrayed is not simply an embodiment of a half-baked philosophy, but that he is a genuine product of American society.

Wright's intention in the Harper edition of *The Outsider* is to express a version of existentialism in which human action is taken as the result of an individual's choice and will. Earlier in the novel Damon's wife Gladys complains to her husband that white people intimidate her. He in turn admonishes her that one must exert one's will to exist. "It's up to us to make ourselves something," he argues. "A man creates himself."[4] Initially Damon is attracted to his Communist mentor Gil Blount for his ideology and action. After his death Damon realizes that Blount epitomized "a modern man." "Life, to him," Damon reflects, "was a game devoid of all significance except that which he put into it" (*Outsider*, p. 370). Damon, however, killed Blount because Blount attempted to wield the Communists' power over Damon's will.

Corollary to Damon's idea of self-creation is his abhorrence of human dependency on others. Damon loses his interest in Gladys because, as Wright observes, "it was the helplessness of dependence that made her fret so. Men made themselves and women were made only through men" (*Outsider*, p. 51). In order to characterize modern man as self-reliant and autonomous, Wright deleted a number of passages in which people are portrayed as passive and dependent on others. Both editions of the novels begin with a scene where Damon, tired with his long work at the post office, tries to rest his body on one of his companions. But his friend, a short man, chides him, saying, "Hell, naw! Stand on your own two big flat feet, Cross!" (*Outsider*, p. 1)[5] The opening scene is, indeed, identical between the two versions except for the three sentences allusive to a racial feature of black men: "Tiny crystals trembled whitely between their dark faces. The shoulders of their overcoats were laced with icy filigrees; dapples of moisture glowed diamondlike on their eyebrows where the heat of their blood was melting the snow . . . . " (*Later Works*, p. 371). This passage is deleted, since Damon and his black friends, conscious of their racial background, give the impression that having been born black is responsible for their plight. Such an implication is contrary to Wright's portrait of an existentially self-made man.

Among the sequences and incidents cut out of the original manuscript, the extended Hattie episode, which runs fourteen pages in two scenes, is the longest. Hattie is a young black widow who is lost in her life and is trying to cling to others for help. Damon finds himself easily tempted by this lonely women but he staves off her temptation. Even before this event, Wright also deletes a sentence from Damon's conversation with Ely Houston, a district attorney he happens to meet on the train: Damon says to Houston, "The American Negro, because of his social and economic situation, is a congenial coward" (*Outsider*, p. 505). Even though Damon characterizes the African-American as a helpless victim of American society rather than a courageous, self-sufficient individual, he is not aware that he himself remains a coward. The irony in Wright's portrayal of Cross Damon rests in that fact that while Damon disparages black women like Gladys and Hattie as weak and dependent, he himself does not always act like a strong man. The original manuscript thus includes an episode in which Damon, pursued by the Communist agents, desperately tries to save his life by begging Hattie to hide him in her apartment and promising to give her 250 dollars for her help. An existentialist like Meursault in *The Stranger* and Raskolnikov in *Crime and Punishment* would not stoop to such an action as does Wright's protagonist.

Cross Damon as originally conceived strikes one as an egotist, a selfish individual, rather than an indifferent, audacious human being compelled to do something in the face of the void. For this reason, Wright seems to have excised the two opening paragraphs of the Book Four, entitled "Despair." In this passage Damon confesses his selfish motive for murdering Blount and Herndon. Damon accomplished his goal, Wright observes, "as much for a dawning reference for her as for the protection of his self-love" (*Later Works*, p. 618). The difference between a self-centered man like Damon and a modern anti-hero like Meursault is that whereas Meursault is convinced of the essential absurdity of existence, Damon is not. If one considers human life inherently meaningful as does Damon, then it follows that his action to seek love, power, and freedom on earth is also meaningful.

In the original version of the novel, the character of Eva Blount, Damon's love, is strikingly similar to that of Damon. He falls in love with Eva because both have suffered from a loveless marriage. He sympathizes with her, for he discovers that she, too, is a fearful individual and that she had been deceived into marrying her husband because of a political intrigue. Damon is also tormented by the envenomed abstraction of racial and political myths. He is strongly attracted to her partly because a black man's desire for a white woman is taboo. In stark contrast to an existentialist, Eva is as passionately in search of meaning in existence as is Damon. "Her sense of guilt," Wright says, "was throwing her on his side; she had long been wanting to be free of Gil and now that she was free she wants to unburden her guilt on to someone else, on to Herndon" (*Later Works*, p. 642). Significantly enough, Wright eliminates this passage to make Eva as selfless and passive a person as Damon. As a result, she is portrayed "as calm as marble. Balling a handkerchief in her right fist, she sat looking bleakly in front of her. His eyes caught hers and he saw in them a glint of recognition. Yes, she's with me. She thinks I'm a victim too . . . " (*Outsider*, pp. 253-54).

Despite the fact that Eva has fallen prey to the Communists as has Damon, Wright's aim in the Harper version is to endow her character with courage and autonomy. To strengthen her individualism, Wright omits two sentences from Eva's diary in which she expresses an outrage against the Communists: "The Party lifted me up in its hands and showed me to the world, and if I disown them, they'll disown me . . . What a trap!" (*Outsider*, p. 594). Such a passage intimates that she has been deprived of freedom and independence and become a helpless victim of the Communists. Omitting this passage makes Eva akin to Damon and hence more attractive to him. His affinity for her, in turn, whets his craving for freedom and independence from a totalitarian philosophy. While his intimate relationship with Eva constitutes a credible event in *The Outsider* as a naturalistic protest novel, it also plays a crucial role in Wright's dialectics between oppression and freedom.

Wright's chief interest in *The Outsider* thus lies in an exposition of what freedom means to certain individuals. As Damon disparages Gladys and Hattie, he repudiates his own mother not only because she is the product of the traditional Christianity in the South that taught black children subservient ethics but because she failed to challenge the lack of freedom and individualism that prevailed in African-American life. To make Mrs. Damon freer of religious dogma, Wright cuts out a long speech by her in which she admonishes her son to abide by God's law. "If you feel you can't master yourself," she warns him, "then take your problems to God . . . . Oh, God, to think that at twenty-six you're lost . . . " (*Later Works*, p. 391). It is only natural that he should find his peace of mind in a liberal woman like Eva. Wright also takes pains to show how religion gets in the way of achieving freedom. In his flight to New York he meets a priest he regards as "a kind of dressed-up savage intimidated by totems and taboos that differed in kind but not in degree from those of the most primitive of peoples." The priest's demeanor shows Damon that good and evil are not discovered by "the edicts of any God" but by human actions, for it is only the individual who is responsible for the consequences of his actions (*Later Works*, p. 494).

To Damon, law, like religion, is created to inhibit human actions. A truly liberated individual does not control his or her actions under the law. Instead, an existentialist creates his or her own law and abides by it. For this reason, Wright deletes a long passage in which Damon discusses how law has the capacity of inhibiting individuality and creativity in human life but at the same time providing the freedom of choice. "Implied in law," Damon asserts, "is a free choice to each man living under the law; indeed one could almost say a free challenge is embedded in the law" (*Later Works*, p. 700). Since this ambivalence in Damon's interpretation of law is embodied in Houston, Wright also deletes several sentences that specifically refer to Houston: "Cross shrewdly suspected that Houston, a self-confessed outlaw, knew this, felt it; and it was what had made him become an active defender of the law; he had to represent the law in order to protect himself against his own weakness and fear" (*Later Works*, 700). Wright makes such an omission to strengthen his argument that one's moral obligation is to the individual and not to society, as well as to justify his murder of the men who had deprived him of individual freedom.

Wright's emphasis on the autonomy of human action is also reflected in the style of the novel. While Wright partly intended the book to be a social protest, his chief aim was to mold a black man's life upon existential tenets. As Damon's statement in the original manuscript that the black person in America is a victim of the social and economic environment is excised from the Harper edition, other descriptions of naturalistic determinism are also deleted. The subway accident in which he is involved makes him feel as if he were imprisoned in himself. He was "so swamped . . . by himself that he could not break forth from behind the bars of that self to claim himself" (*Later Works*, p. 488). A stranger who witnessed the accident tells Damon: "Brother, your blood is the tomato sauce. Your white guts is the spaghetti. And your flesh is the meat, see? You'd be surprised how like a plate of meatballs and spaghetti you look when you get minced up in one of those subway wrecks" (*Later Works*, p. 470). Such a description is omitted, for it is a cynical remark about the hopelessly victimized condition of a human being.

To make *The Outsider* akin to existential novels by Sartre and Camus, Wright also eliminated much of the profane and sexually allusive language. The Harper edition, for instance, deleted an expression Eva writes in her diary as she accuses the Communists of having deceived her into marrying her husband: "Goddam this deception!" (*Later Works*, p. 595). In describing the ground where Joe, a friend which Damon kills, lies, Wright originally wrote: "some of the grounds spilled over a bloodstained Kotex which still retained the curving shape of having fitted tightly and recently against the lips of some vagina; there was a flattened grapefruit hull whose inner pulpy fibres held a gob of viscous phlegm" (*Later Works*, p. 485). The quoted passage was changed to "some of the grounds that gleamed in the light of the street lamp" (*The Outsider*, p. 115). Similarly, the passages including such sentences as "Sarah's breasts heaved" and "her lips hung open and she breathed orgiastically" are deleted (*Later Works*, p. 556).

At a crucial point in the development of the story Wright is at the pains of revising the original manuscript to express an existential philosophy. On the one hand, Wright comes to recognize a close relationship between Damon's actions and his social and psychological backgrounds; on the other, he also tries to demonstrate in Damon's life a nihilistic view of the world stated earlier in the book that "man is nothing in particular" (*Outsider*, p. 135). As the story progresses, however, the feeling of isolation and loneliness increasingly dictates Damon's action. Reading Eva's diary makes him realize that Eva's love for him came out of her sympathy for his oppressed life just as his love for her was intensified by his compassion for her predicament. This revelation leads to his statement on his death bed, a clear contradiction of his earlier view of man: "I wish I had some way to give the meaning of my life to others . . . . To make a bridge for man to man . . . Man is all we've got . . . . I wish I could ask men to meet themselves" (*Outsider*, p. 439).

Though Damon's final vision makes the Harper version of *The Outsider* less existential than originally intended, it suggests that Wright is ambivalent in expressing his view of human existence. In both versions, he intended to portray an outsider as an individual with courage and audacity, but as the story unfolds Damon finds himself increasingly alienated and realizes that, however imperfect society may be, he cannot live without relating to others. It is ironic that Wright's hero is determined to be an outsider but in his heart he wants to be an insider. A character like Cross Damon is sometimes larger than the author's occasional philosophy and he is able to speak for himself. Wright the philosopher only gets in his way; Wright the artist remains true to him. In the end, the interest of the story lies not in Wright's mind but in his heart, the genuine feelings Wright himself had experienced in American society.

Notes

[1]See Charles I. Glicksberg, "*Existentialism in The Outsider,*" *Four Quarters*, 7 (January 1958), 17-26; "The God of Fiction," *Colorado Quarterly*, 7 (Autumn 1958), 207-220. Michel Fabre specifically indicates that Wright's composition of *The Outsider* "was influenced in subtle ways by his reading of *The Stranger* in August 1947. He read the book in the American edition at a very slow pace, 'weighing each sentence,' admiring 'its damn good narrative prose.'" See Fabre, "Richard Wright, French Existentialism, and *The Outsider*," in Yoshinobu Hakutani ed., *Critical Essays on Richard Wright* (Boston: G.K. Hall, 1982), p. 191.
[2]James N. Rhea, *Providence Sunday Journal*, March 22, 1953.
[3]See Saunders Redding, *Baltimore African American*, (May 19, 1953), 15-16; Lloyd Brown, "Outside and Low," *Masses and Mainstream*, 6 (May 1953), 62-64.
[4]Richard Wright, *The Outsider* (New York: Harper, 1965 [1953]), p. 51. Subsequent page references are to this edition.
[5]Richard Wright, *Later Works*, ed. Arnold Rampersad (New York: Library of America, 1991), 369. Subsequent page references are to this edition.

Authority, Gender, and Fiction

Eugene E. Miller

Richard Wright's fictional works as published recently in the Library of America edition do, as the editor, Arnold Rampersad, hoped, promote new lines of inquiry, at least for *Native Son*: the question of Wright's (or any writer's) authority over his text, the question of gender approaches to a literary work, and the question of the nature of fiction.

Rampersad has valorized this new version partly on grounds that it makes *Native Son* "available as [Wright] had wanted [it] to be read" and allows us "to hear a great American writer speak with his own voice" (*New York Times Book Review*, 29 Dec 1991). Jerry Ward agrees: "The unexpugated texts of this novel and other works bring us closer to what Wright meant" (*Richard Wright Newsletter*, Fall 1991). But these assessments are problematical, for they are at odds with au courant deconstructionist feminist criticism, which manifestly claims the death of authors' and critics' expropriational rights to texts and their meanings. A novel's meaning is as much as anything a matter of what its writer did *not* say, or subtext; hence, Wright's patriarchal authority over the gender meanings of the text must be abrogated. Even Wright's statement that all is Bigger's viewpoint, not his, no longer has authority.

Ambiguity, the speech and reticence of symbols, in literature has long been recognized as the playing field of literary study, and the "intentional fallacy" (today, *phallacy*?) is exposed and discounted. It is safe to say that the new edition will not make much difference to feminist criticism, yet because the passages restored to *Native Son* are sexual, this new edition invites gender analysis.

So far, the comments about it have indicated that the restorations also restore Bigger's manhood, that they create, as Keneth Kinnamon, apparently with straight face, phrases it in his introduction to *New Essays on Native Son*, a "harder" Bigger, less congenial to sentimental bankers' daughters than even the 1940, model. The changes resulting in the version published in 1940, according to Rampersad, "almost emasculated Bigger," "nullify Bigger's sexual drive," "make him almost asexual" and therefore "less human, less alive and almost incomprehensible." The restorations provide Bigger with "vibrant sexuality."

One obvious problem with this presentation of what Wright meant, based on what he wrote, is that it premises also the curious view that prior to this "unexpugated" new edition, to quote Jerry Ward again, ". . . a crucial element of characterization was missing in the . . . *Native Son* we had been reading for fifty years"; that the "removal of explicit reference to Bigger's sexuality" had been wholesale. In an age of explicit, "steamy" sexual-imagery overkill, perhaps it is possible to miss in the 1940 edition the references to Bigger's sexuality in passages such as

> . . . he leaned over [Mary], excited, looking at her face in the dim light, not wanting to take his hands from her breasts . . . . he tightened his fingers on her breasts, kissing her again, feeling her move toward him. He was aware only of her body now, his lips trembled . . . .

and

> [Bessie] was undressing. He got up and began to undress . . . . He went to her, folding her in his arms . . . . he felt her as a fallow field beneath him . . . and he floated on a wild tide, rising and sinking, with the ebb and flow of her blood . . . .

Another problem, at least for feminist readers, is that this view of Bigger's supposedly cut-and-now-restored testicles encourages an admirative connection between male sexual activity in any form and the meaning of masculinity—a connection not unrelated to an erstwhile stereotype known as the black superstud. Wright's dealings with it in such fictions as "Big Boy Leaves Home," "The Man Who Killed a Shadow," *The Outsider*, and *The Long Dream*, as well as explicit references to it in *Native Son*, seem to indicate that *he* was not admirative of it.

Furthermore, as gender criticism (i.e., feminist) is now theorized, and insofar as in literary scholarship a theoretic starting point is today considered de rigueur, a gender approach to this new edition reveals conflict not only between Rampersad's view of Bigger's "restored" sexuality as "vibrant" and what established gender study practices might reveal, but a problem within such gender criticism itself. A non-negotiable principle of current gender criticism applied to literature is that men reify women, turning them into mere objects of phallic domination, prestige prizes in macho competitions. One of the major cuts restored in the new edition of *Native Son* deals with Bigger and one of his friends masturbating in a movie theater (masturbation being more offensive to bankers' daughters, it would seem from Kinnamon's comments, than mere decapitation and rape). A gender study of this episode suggests not that Bigger's sexuality is particularly "vibrant," or that the passage re-masculates him but that he is androgynous. After all, one part of Bigger does dominate, in a sexual competition with another male, another part; he is not described as being sexually aroused prior to the act; his male member is simply seized and forced into compliance:

> "I'll bet you ain't even hard yet," Jack whispered.
> "I'm getting hard."

In addition, Bigger refers to his penis as a thing, a "nightstick." Such an appellation complicates the genderal reading because it both reduces the penis to an impersonal thing, as men are said to do to women, and yet associates it with an instrument of domination, which power women are said not to have.

Other components of the scene thicken this genderal interpretation. Bigger—or maybe it's Jack (the names yet!)—thinks that a passing woman movie patron "saw us." The rejoinder is that

> "If she saw it she'd faint."
> "Or grab it, maybe."

In the first part of the episode, Bigger's "absent" hand can be seen acting as the male agent, seizing upon the equally "absent" hapless male member, working its will upon it, regardless. But, circularly, the "male"—first the male member, then the hand—is altered into its opposite gender, then back again: The hand, usually acting as female organ, here masculinely "feminizes" the male organ and then is explicitly associated with the female. Obviously "male" does not come off (excuse the expression) as what feminist gender theory posits. It is the female that is empowered here, dominating the phallus that is conventionally, theoretically taken as the sign of male dominance.

At least one feminist-based study of the 1940 *Native Son*, contrary to intent, reveals this pattern. Alan Frances (*Modern Fiction Studies*, Autumn 1988) contends that the rat which Bigger kills in the novel's initial scene is a symbolic penis that he then dangles in front of his sister, securing for himself a much enjoyed phallic dominance. Ignored in this analysis is the considerable beating he has given the rat, reducing it to a bloody, lifeless pulp by clobbering it with a frying pan and crushing its head with his foot. Considering the attack on this phallicized head, his own member seems treated no differently from the way he treats Mary and Bessie. Feminist criticisms of the 1940 edition have also argued that Bigger's killings of Mary and Bessie are disguised attempts at killing off the feminine, the internalized castrating female, in himself (or in Wright). But the restored masturbation scene sets up a pattern of attempts at killing off the masculine instead, not an uncastration of Bigger that restores him to either superstudery or oppressive maleness.

Perhaps the new edition and the editorial commentary on it so far can then lead to a new genderal look at *Native Son*, if "gender" also means "men's studies." A men's studies approach to *Native Son* has not yet occurred, in part because men's studies has been feminist-based and hence accepting not only of feminist theories of men but also of the feminist axiom that all approaches to literature, among other things, have until recently been men's studies. Rampersad's remarks that the new edition invites new study of Bigger in terms of his sexuality, as Wright saw it, with the additional implications that Wright thus intended us to see Bigger as a man, fully masculine, raise the intriguing question of just how we are to know this masculinity. That is, most gender studies of men start with an a priori theory of masculinity, by which images are identified as "masculine." But what theory of masculinity can be applied to *Native Son* to help us see what *Wright* meant by masculinity if we don't already have Wright's theory?

In "How 'Bigger' Was Born," the authority of which must be accepted if we accept the authority of the fictional *Native Son*, Wright indicates that Bigger and his story are not just "masculine." The novel is "a scheme of images and symbols" representative of a sub-group, "a vast, muddied pool of human life," men *and* women whose personalities and the actions expressing them are warped by what a civilization with "no spiritual sustenance . . . whose metaphysical meanings have vanished" has imposed on them or made available to them as expressive instrumentalities. The passages restored to this new edition quantitatively add to images of Bigger's sexuality, but they would have to have the same meaning he implied to all the behaviors of a large segment of the world's population symbolized in Bigger—skewed, not really vibrant, the behavior of humans "who lived by violence, through extreme action and sensation, through drowning daily in a perpetual nervous agitation," by which "they felt their lives had meaning." Clearly this is a condition Wright mourns, not advocates as truly human, masculine sexuality.

In terms of current gender approaches, such a view places Wright at least on the edges of the radical profeminist camp, which sees "masculinity as a distinctive social role that is continually imposed on a naturally benign being in order to maintain a patriarchal social order" (Ken Clatterbaugh, *Contemporary Perspectives on Masculinity).* But Wright never imaged an ordered, satisfying fulfillment of male sexuality, although implicitly he seems to have had such a notion and came closest to working it out in *The Long Dream.*

Closely related, equally complicated questions this new edition raises concern Wright's view of fiction. Could Wright's own gender theory be derived for *Native Son*, a fiction? In "How 'Bigger' Was Born" and *American Hunger,* he told us his efforts as a writer were to create in words something never seen before—in *Native Son*, the illusion of Bigger's "elusive core of being, that individual data consciousness which in every man and woman is like no other." Theories are generic; fictional creatures (and for Wright, apparently, actual individuals) are unique.

Also, the new edition has Bigger at the movies seeing a newsreel depicting Mary and Jan cavorting on a Florida beach. Kinnamon would have Wright in the restored passages "presenting Bigger as a typically highly sexed nineteen-year old [he tells Mr. Dalton he's twenty] . . . titillated by a newsreel" which explains Bigger's "otherwise implausible speculation" in the 1940 edition that "maybe [Mr. Dalton] had a daughter who was a hot kind of girl." Of course, the newsreel scene in the newly restored edition has the implausible detail of the commentator's giving Mary's specific street address and also has Bigger thinking "maybe Mary Dalton was a hot kind of girl," a decidedly pointless and repetitious "maybe" on Bigger's part, given what the commentator has explicitly said about "'the naughty rich'" and if the newsreel is indeed all that sexually arousing (Bigger has just masturbated).

What this new edition's restorations make possible is a reconstruction that does not redundantly emphasize anything as mundane as Bigger's sex drive. It is significant that Wright did not simply cut the newsreel image, as he did the masturbation scene, at the request of Book-of-the-Month Club editors. He evidently wanted to retain the film image more than he did the onanism. In spite of his conscious commitment to naturalistic realism, he carefully replaced the factual newsreel with not only a fictional movie, but one whose hokieness is more obvious to the reader than to Bigger. The movie is an image more clearly than the newsreel, not a reflection of any reality, although Bigger accepts it as a window into the unknown Dalton world. It is he in the 1940 edition—not an anonymous voice as in this new version—that makes connections between flickering shadows, Mary Dalton, and the kind of woman she is. Mary becomes, by this change, more a hallucination than flesh when she first enters the story. Wright seems to have been trying to say something—perhaps, ironically, not totally complimentary—about art, fiction, the human imagination's participation in the reality it responds to; or about Bigger's naïveté in the "reading" of images as reality. Bigger's obviously a deconstructionist twenty-some years ahead of his time, a mutated banker's daughter appropriating images into his own perspective, as is revealed after he has actually met Mary, in his "remote" musings about "how different this rich girl was from the one he had seen in the movies. This woman he had watched on the screen had not seemed dangerous and his mind had been able to do with her as it liked." This is precisely an action on Wright's own images he was determined to forestall.

The new edition of *Native Son* does raise interesting, perhaps unanswerable, questions about the author's intended meaning, the problems of genderal interpretations, and the physics of fiction. In "How 'Bigger' Was Born," Wright admitted his inability to explain everything about his novel, and suggested another way in which it might be seen in fictional genderal terms:

Always there is something just beyond the tip of the tongue that could explain it all
. . . . an imaginative novel represents the merging of two extremes . . . at once something private and public by its very nature and texture . . . . As I wrote . . . one image, symbol, character, scene, mood, feeling evoked its opposite, its parallel, its complementary, and its ironic counterpoint.

From *African American Review* 27 (Winter 1992) 687-691.

The Invisible Woman in Wright's *Rite of Passage*

Robert Butler

With the publication of the Library of America editions of Richard Wright's major works in 1991 an important new phase of Wright scholarship has begun, the arduous tasks of first recovering and then evaluating the texts which Wright actually wrote and which editors often altered because they were uncomfortable with certain aspects of Wright's extraordinary vision of African American life. The recent publication of *Rite of Passage*, a novella which Wright completed in 1945 and later tried to include in *Eight Men* shortly before his death, is another significant step in restoring Wright's work for contemporary readers. This book, which Arnold Rampersad in the Afterword rightly claims "is unmistakably a story from the heart of Wright's, consciousness and creativity" (117), was discovered in the Rare Archives Room at the Beinecke Library at Yale and is now made available by Harper Collins in a relatively inexpensive hardcover edition.

Anyone familiar with Wright's fiction can immediately recognize in this story unmistakable signs of Wright's style and vision. From the opening scenes in which the protagonist, Johnny Gibbs, is awakened from his daydreams by the loud "BRAAAAAAAAAG" (2) of a school bell and later by the equally jarring BRRIIINNNNNNNNG! (23) of a doorbell announcing the presence of people who will destroy the central character's young life, the reader is clearly reminded that this book is cut from a bolt of imaginative cloth very similar to that used in *Native Son, Black Boy, The Outsider,* and *Eight Men.* Like Bigger Thomas, Johnny Gibbs seeks "a new life" (57) in violence because he finds himself trapped in a society which denies him most of the things which build and sustain human identity -- family, friends, work, and self-esteem. Feeling a deep sense of "estrangement" (52) from the dominant white culture because it is intent on convincing him that "he was nothing, a nobody" (52), he rebels and, like Cross Damon and Fred Daniels, retreats into an underground world, a juvenile gang whose meeting place is in the basement of a school, a "dirty room" behind the furnace which gang members characterize as the "hole" (61) Like all of Wright's central characters, and particularly the hero of *Black Boy/American Hunger,* Johnny is driven throughout the story by various forms of "hunger" ranging from his need for physical nourishment to his profound desire for kinship and love.

Rite of Passage, like "Big Boy Leaves Home" and so much of Wright's other best work, stresses the existential fragility of its protagonist's identity with a narrative that describes how his life is completely transformed by a single dramatic event. Like Dave Saunders who is detached from a relatively stable and familiar life when he accidentally kills his boss's mule and like Bigger Thomas, Cross Damon, and Fred Daniels whose lives are forever changed when they are accused of breaking the laws of racist societies which systematically deny them any legal protection, Johnny Gibbs finds his old life suddenly dissolved when he returns home from school one day to discover that he is in fact a foster child who has been living since infancy with people who are not his biological parents. Due to a bureaucratic "policy" (25) which defies any rational explanation, he is ordered to move to a new foster home of people he has never met. He is therefore confronted by the same painful dilemma which troubles the protagonist of *Black Boy* -- should he accept an identity arbitrarily constructed and imposed upon him by a social world which is unable to perceive him as a human being or should he rebel absolutely, completely rejecting the standards of conventional society and begin the task of building a radically isolated self? Not surprisingly, he chooses the latter alternative and by the end of the book is described as "alone," attempting "to make a life for himself by trying to reassemble the shattered fragments of his lonely heart" (115).

Put another way, *Rite of Passage* is a powerful inversion of the Alger myth. Wright, who as Michel Fabre has aptly observed, was as a young man "an avid reader of Horatio Alger" (51), and who wrote a review of the complete works of Horatio Alger in the same year that he completed *Rite of Passage*, cleverly echoes and reverses the Alger myth throughout the book. In the story's first chapter Johnny Gibbs seems a likely candidate for Algeresque success since he is a bright, hard-working boy on the margins of American life. A straight-A student, he is much more interested in his report card than the knives which some children bring to school. Education means to him precisely what it means to all of Alger's heroes; it is not only an effective means of achieving material success but, more importantly self esteem and personal transformation. Furthermore, school provides Johnny with another essential component of the Alger myth, a patron who will help him rise in life by developing his moral and intellectual character. Mrs. Alma Reid, the white teacher who assures Johnny that "The world was rosy and he was happy," (3) lives "far away" (33) in a world quite removed from Johnny's "smelly ramshackle apartment" (6) and inspires him to move upward in life. Like Alger's rich gentlemen, Mrs. Reid is a custodian of morality who is interested in helping hard-working, intelligent boys like Johnny to climb the ladder of American success.

When Johnny discovers that he is in fact an orphan and that his apparently solid identity has no basis in fact, he quickly falls off the ladder of success and plunges into a world which is "dark, alien and unreal" (28). In such a universe Johnny is a marginal figure who "had no plans" (29). He becomes generally like the boys at school who carry knives, people whom he had previously not identified with and "smiled superiorly" (3) at. Joining a juvenile gang because it provides him with at least the illusion of connection with others, Johnny becomes a grim inversion of the Alger hero, a gang leader who must now live on the violent fringes of society, eking out a bare subsistence engaged in activity which is anathema to the Alger hero, stealing.

In these ways *Rite of Passage* displays most of the trademarks of Wright's best-known work and some readers therefore might argue that it was not published for a good reason; namely that it is simply a pale imitation of novels like *Native Son*, and a novella like "The Man Who Lived Underground." Such an argument would be false for two reasons: 1) *Rite of Passage* is anything but a "pale imitation" of Wright's previous work but is instead characterized by an unusual energy, power, and artistic skill which make it an important piece on its own merits, and 2) It does possess a very distinctive feature which is either missing or radically understated in Wright's other work, a sensitive and revealing treatment of important gender issues which are particularly relevant to contemporary readers. Wright, who has been strongly criticized in recent years for stereotyping female characters and generally ignoring or undervaluing the crucial roles which black women have played in African American culture, centers *Rite of Passage* in a serious meditation on how "feminine" values can play an enormously positive role in Johnny's development while aggressively "masculine" values will lead to his destruction. Readers who feel justifiably uncomfortable with the ways in which gender is envisioned in novels like *Lawd Today!* and *The Outsider* will therefore find *Rite of Passage* an intriguing book which may cause them to re-evaluate Wright's treatment of important gender issues.

Unlike "The Man Who Lived Underground" which has no significant female presence and *The Long Dream* which portrays women as either extensions of male desire or annoying encumbrances blocking male fulfillment, *Rite of Passage* insists that women play a pivotal role in the lives of its male characters. Furthermore, it stresses that if men grow up without the nurturing of women and if they do not honor the "feminine" side of their own personalities, then the most disastrous consequences will result. Johnny Gibbs, from an early age onward, is essentially confronted by two worlds with two opposite value systems: 1) A life-giving world presided over by women which is focused on two important institutions, the school and the home, and 2) A destructive world controlled by men which assumes two equally deadly forms, the street and the gang.

At the beginning of the book Johnny's life is defined by the school and home, both of which are directed by women who nurture him and provide him with a sense of possibility. His teacher, a white woman whose "silver voice caressed his ears" (1) helps to bring out Johnny's best self by encouraging him to do well in school: "Her approval made him glow with pleasure" (3). Johnny's classroom, which in the book's opening scene is irradiated with "a flood of sun" (1), is portrayed as a heathy setting for mental growth and emotional warmth. Totally at ease in school, Johnny is "happy" (3), convinced that his life will take very different "directions" (5) from his classmate Billy who has already joined a gang and is deeply impressed with the gun his brother has brought home from the army. Indeed, his teacher's name, Alma Reid, allegorically defines the school as a positive environment which nurtures the soul by teaching him to "read" himself and the world in a confident, secure way. It is not surprising therefore that Johnny is offended when he sees the peaceful and vital world of school violated when a student brings a knife to class, feeling strongly that "nobody ought to bring a thing like that to school" (3). Knives for Johnny at this point in his life are part of the dangerous world of the streets, from which he instinctively recoils.

When his day at school is over, Johnny moves to another nurturing environment which is also presided over by women, the apartment which his family rents in Harlem. Hungry now for physical food, Johnny anticipates a satisfying meal at home and is not disappointed when he enters the apartment and sees his mother busily preparing one of his favorite meals. Although the apartment building is "a smelly, ramshackle tenement" (6), his mother has made their home within this building a place of order, warmth, and growth. As he enters the apartment, Johnny is cheered not only by the prospect of enjoying a good supper, but also by his mother's warm smile as she directs him to wash before dinner.

The secure and healthy identity promoted by school and home, however, is quickly dissolved when Johnny learns that he is in fact a foster child and must move to a new "home" that evening. Finding out that the woman he thought was his mother is not his "blood" (14) mother and Sis is not his "real" (13) sister, Johnny reacts as strongly to his situation as does Bigger Thomas after killing Mary Dalton or Fred Daniels after he has been falsely accused of murdering a woman -- he moves in a flash from a familiar "old" life to a radically insecure and threatening "new" existence. Given the choice of an inauthentic life premised upon the fiction that his new foster parents will provide him with a loving family and a more troubling but genuine life that he can forge for himself on the streets, he quickly chooses the latter alternative, running away from home and taking a subway to 42nd Street. What the city provides him with is a terrifying Gothic world closely resembling Bigger Thomsas's South Side of Chicago. Such an "unstable" and "unreal" (30) place is a powerful reflector of Johnny's fear and alienation. Replete with "yellow streetlamps glowing in the hazy dark" (36), "cold wind" (30), and tall buildings whose windows look like a "thousand vacant eyes" (40), the city becomes a complete reversal of school and home, a landscape of nightmare which threatens to reduce Johnny to complete paralysis.

Recoiling from such a "naked reality" (29) which strips him of everything he has previously valued and identified himself in terms of, Johnny reluctantly becomes part of a youth gang when his friend Billy sees him aimlessly wandering the streets and invites him to become part of "The Moochers." The exclusively male world of the gang initially promises him a new existence anchored in a fresh sense of self and community:

> Yes, this was his passport to his new life, to the new and strange gang of boys upon whom he would have to depend for his food, for friendship. If, for any reason, they rejected him, he would be once again on the cold windswept streets (57).

This "new life" promising a "new self" (57), ironically, is very similar to the false "new life" which Bigger Thomas *thinks* he achieves when he kills Mary Dalton. Just as Bigger's "new life" is in fact a destruction of his most humane self and quickly leads to his death, Johnny's new life as a gang member is simply a dead-end which will result in his destruction. The gang's predatory and senseless violence, which Billy wrongly claims will convert Johnny into a "man" (51), can only turn him into an animal or a corpse. Significantly, most of the gang members are described as "ghosts" (99), "rats" (111), "beasts" (79) or "robots" (107). And Johnny's gang name, appropriately enough, is "Jackal" (85), signifying his loss of humanity and his becoming part of a grimly Darwinian world which will lead, sooner than he thinks, to his downfall. The gang which takes a special delight in jumping "a university teacher" (103) and chides Johnny when his educated diction makes him "sound like a schoolteacher" (113), is a complete reversal of the world of school. Instead of stimulating his growth and offering him an open future, it forecloses his prospects and moves him either to an early death or imprisonment.

Wright's distaste for this grotesquely masculine world based upon violence, competition, and death is vividly revealed in his description of two important scenes of graphic violence late in the novel, Johnny's savage fight with the gang's leader, Baldy, and the gang's mugging of a white man in Central Park. (These two scenes are so strongly written that they may have been the main reason why Wright had difficulty publishing the book in the mid-1940s.) It is important to remember that Wright stresses that only a part of Johnny's divided self participates in these two episodes. While his outer nature is forced by circumstances to engage in violence, his inner nature draws back from the action and longs for more humane options. His fight with Baldy is "forced upon him" (72) and, although part of him becomes a fierce beast which goes "wild" (79) during the fight, another part of him is repulsed by the scene. In the same way, Johnny does not really want to participate in the Central Park mugging but goes along with the gang because he is fearful of their response to his objecting to their actions. As he walks to the park with them, he secretly wished "to flee to the shelter of one of those dark, looming houses and knock on the door and be admitted into the warmth of a home where people lived with smiles and trust and faith" (102). Like most of Wright's protagonists and heroes, he has two conflicting selves, a humane self seeking love and community and an artificially imposed social self forced into acts of suicidal violence.

It is important to realize that Wright consistently associates Johnny's best self with feminine values and influence while he links his worst self with masculine values and influence. Irresponsible flight, for example, is connected with Johnny's biological father who quickly abandons his mother after she becomes pregnant, thus forcing her to give up Johnny to a foster home. And compulsive violence is always associated with male figures like Billy's brother who endangers his family by bringing home his army gun and Baldy who erupts in terrible violence whenever his ego is threatened. Johnny's humane self, however, is activated whenever he thinks of the women who have touched his life in positive ways. Soon after he runs away from home after being told that the "City" (18) authorities have placed him in another foster home, he has the strong desire to talk with someone and immediately thinks of his teacher, Mrs. Reid. When he imagines his biological mother, whom he discovers has gone insane and become institutionalized, his moral nature is activated and he feels "enormously guilty" (51). Although this guilt is irrational, it does help to counterbalance the destructive rage boiling in him when he finds out about his father's abandonment and society's arbitrarily moving him to another foster home.

In the novel's final scenes, Johnny's humane self is vividly dramatized by his desire for female presence and influence. As he trudges the "empty silent streets" (102) with the gang as they make their way to Central Park to randomly beat up and rob white people, Johnny's inner self "yearned to sink to his knees to some kind of old black woman and sob: Help me. . .I can't go through with this!" (102) After he has participated in the mugging, he hears the voice of a "Negro woman" (103) screaming her disapproval of the gang's behavior by shouting in denunciation "You Boys! You Boys!" (107) Although it is highly unlikely that this woman is objectively real since only Johnny hears her repeated calls and nobody actually sees her, she is crucially important in the story because she is the voice within Johnny, a moral voice like the voices of Mrs. Reid and his foster mother which direct him away from crime and violence and encourage him to respond to the world in productive, humane terms.

The active presence of this "feminine" voice within Johnny, therefore, endows *Rite of Passage* with a very measured and qualified hope. As the gang "huddled together, panting" (107) like pack animals trapped in a cycle of inward compulsion and outward conditioning, Johnny is "alone" (117) in a positive sense because the macho values which control the gang have not yet swallowed up his entire personality. He surely has not become Baldy who is finally described as a psychopath and he has not yet fully become Jackal, a jungle animal. He is repulsed by the gang's nihilistic behavior and, more importantly, wants to share his humane, "feminine" self with them:

> Again Johnny wondered if he ought to tell them about the woman; he turned his head and looked over the park, but no one was in sight. Had he imagined that he had seen and heard the woman? No, he had seen her, had heard her. He found himself identifying with the woman, pictured her running and looking for them, and he wanted her to find them (108).

Identifying more strongly with the woman and what she represents than the gang and what it represents, Johnny is only superficially taken in by a macho ethic and still has a chance of remaining human in an increasingly brutal world. Moreover, he has a strong desire to tell the gang about the woman and wishes that she may "find" them; that is, redeem them by rejuvenating the feminine side of their personalities.

One might say that Johnny finally becomes more than a bit like Wright himself, who dedicated his masterwork to his mother because she activated within him an artist's voice as she took him on her knee when he was a child and taught him "to revere the fanciful and the imaginative" *(NS* II). By nurturing a humane and creative voice within Wright that enabled him to tell his "story" and share it with others, Wright's mother provided him with resources which enabled him to find imaginative alternatives to the social environment which crushes so many of his characters.

Wright's problems with women have been well documented by his biographers and his difficulties in portraying feminine experience in some of his works have been stressed by many recent critics. But a significant part of Wright's life and art have been unfortunately obscured by these observations, however valid they might sometimes be. Perhaps one of the most valuable aspects of the literary recovery and publication of *Rite of Passage* is that its very explicit treatment of the high premium which Wright placed on feminine values might cause us to take a fresh look at how women figure generally in Wright's work and especially in his masterpiece, *Native Son*. (We should remember, for example, that Bigger's inhumanity is most vividly revealed when he "blots out" not only two women but the feminine side of himself and that his salvaging of a human identity begins when he acknowledges guilt over these actions and is able to touch his mother and sister in love.)

Although Johnny Gibbs's humanity is not apparent to anyone on the scene in Central Park when he participates in a gang mugging, the reader is well aware that he is a tragically divided person rather than a vicious animal because the reader realizes that Johnny's mind is "still full of the running and invisible woman he had seen and heard" (109). Because he sees this woman and her humane voice arises from the deepest levels of his own consciousness, he has not yet been consumed by the macho values which could turn him into a robot, beast, or ghost. Perhaps it is time now for Wright's readers to pursue the "invisible woman" in Wright's best work and thus become more aware of a critically important, but often neglected, dimension of his vision.

WORKS CITED

Fabre, Michel. *The Unfinished Quest of Richard Wright*. New York: William Morrow and Company, 1973.
Wright, Richard. *Native Son*. New York: Harper and Brothers, 1940.
Wright, Richard. *Rite of Passage*. New York, 1994

Selected Bibliography

PRIMARY WORKS

Fiction

Uncle Tom's Children. New York: Harper and Brothers, 1938.
Native Son. New York: Harper and Brothers, 1940.
The Outsider. New York: Harper and Brothers, 1953.
Savage Holiday. New York: Avon Books, 1954.
The Long Dream. New York: Doubleday, 1958.
Eight Men. Cleveland: World, 1961.
Lawd Today! New York: Walkers and Co., 1963.
Rite of Passage. HarperCollins, 1994.

Nonfiction

"Blueprint for Negro Writing." *New Challenge 2* (Fall 1937): 53-65.
"The Ethics of Living Jim Crow." *American Stuff: A WPA Writer's Anthology*. New York: Viking Press (1937): 39-52.
"How Bigger Was Born" (pamphlet). New York: Harper, 1940.
Twelve Million Black Voices. New York: Viking Press, 1941.
"I Tried to Be a Communist." *Atlantic Monthly*, August 1944, 61-70.
Black Boy. New York: Harper, 1945.
Black Power. New York: Harper, 1954.
The Color Curtain. Cleveland: World, 1954.
Pagan Spain. New York: Harper and Row, 1957.
American Hunger. New York: Harper and Row, 1977.

SECONDARY WORKS

Bibliographies

Fabre, Michel, and Charles T. Davis. *Richard Wright: A Primary Bibliography*. Boston: G.K. Hall, 1982.
Kinnamon, Keneth (with the help of Joseph Benson, Michel Fabre, and Craig Werner). *A Richard Wright Bibliography: Fifty Years of Criticism and Commentary, 1933-1982*. Westport: Greenwood, 1988.
Reilly, John. "Richard Wright: An Essay in Bibliography." *Resources for American Literary Study* (Autumn 1971): 131-180.

Books

Bakish, David. *Richard Wright*. New York: Ungar, 1973.
Brignano, Russell. *Richard Wright: An Introduction to His Works*. Pittsburgh: University of Pittsburgh Press, 1970.
Butler, Robert. *Richard Wright's Native Son: the Emergence of a New Black Hero*. New York: Twayne, 1990.
Fabre, Michel. *The Unfinished Quest of Richard Wright*, translated by Isabel Barzun. New York: Morrow, 1973.
_____. *Richard Wright: Books and Writers*. Jackson: University of Mississippi Press, 1990.
Felgar, Robert. *Richard Wright*. Boston: Twayne, 1980.
Gayle, Addison. *Richard Wright: Ordeal of a Native Son*. New York: Doubleday, 1980.
Joyce, Joyce Ann. *Richard Wright's Art of Tragedy*. Iowa City: University of Iowa Press, 1986.
Kinnamon, Keneth. *The Emergence of Richard Wright: A Study in Literature and Society*. Urbana: University of Illinois Press, 1972.
Lynch, Michael F. *Creative Revolt: A Study of Wright, Ellison, and Dostoevsky*. New York: Peter Lang, 1990.
McCall, Dan. *The Example of Richard Wright*. Carbondale: Southern Illinois University Press, 1969.
Reilly, John. *Richard Wright: The Critical Reception*. New York: Burt Franklin, 1978.
Walker, Margaret. *Richard Wright: Demonic Genius: A Portrait of the Man, A Critical Look at His Work*. New York: Warner/Amistad Books, 1988.
Webb, Constance. *Richard Wright: A Biography*. New York: Putnam, 1968.
Williams, John A. *The Most Native of Sons*. Garden City, N.J.: Doubleday, 1970.

Chapters in Books

Baker, Houston. *Long Black Song: Essays in Black American Literature*. Charlottesville: University Press of Virginia, 1972.
Baldwin, James. *Notes of a Native Son*. Boston: Beacon Press, 1955.
_____. *Nobody Knows My Name: More Notes of a Native Son*. New York: Dell, 1961.
Bell, Bernard. *The Afro-American Novel and Its Tradition*. Amherst: University of Massachusetts Press, 1987.
Bone, Robert. *The Negro Novel in America*. New Haven, Conn.: Yale University Press, 1958.
Cleaver, Eldridge. *Soul on Ice*. New York: Dell, 1968.
Cooke, Michael. *Afro-American Literature in the Twentieth Century: The Achievement of Intimacy*. New Haven: Yale University Press, 1984.
Davis, Arthur P. *From the Dark Tower: Afro-American Writers, 1900-1960*. Washington: Howard University Press, 1974.
Ellison, Ralph. *Shadow and Act*. New York: Random House, 1964.
Gayle, Addison. *The Way of the New World: The Black Novel in America*. Garden City: Doubleday, 1975.
Gloster, Hugh M. *Negro Voices in American Fiction*. Chapel Hill: University of North Carolina Press, 1948.
Howe, Irving. *A World More Attractive*. New York: Horizon, 1963.
Scruggs, Charles. *Sweet Home: Invisible Cities in the Afro-American Novel*. Baltimore: Johns Hopkins Press, 1993.
Smith, Valerie. *Self-Discovery and Authority in Afro-American Narrative*. Cambridge: Harvard University Press, 1987.

Collections of Essays

Abcarian, Richard. *Richard Wright's "Native Son": A Critical Handbook*. Belmont: Wadsworth, 1970.
Bloom, Harold, ed. *Richard Wright*. New York: Chelsea House, 1987.

_____. Richard Wright's *Native Son*. New York: Chelsea House, 1988.
_____. *Bigger Thomas*. New York: Chelsea House, 1990.
Baker, Houston. *Twentieth Century Interpretations of "Native Son."* Engelwood Cliffs: Prentice-Hall, 1972.
Fabre, Michel. *The World of Richard Wright*. Jackson: University of Mississippi Press, 1985.
Gates, Henry Louis and K.A. Appiah, ed. *Richard Wright: Critical Perspectives Past and Present*. New York: Amistad, 1993.
Hakutani, Yoshinobu, ed. *Critical Essays on Richard Wright*. Boston: G.K. Hall, 1982.
Kinnamon, Keneth. *New Essays on Native Son*. Cambridge, England: Cambridge University Press, 1990.
Macksey, Richard, and Frank Moorer. *Richard Wright: A Collection of Critical Essays*. Engelwood Cliffs: Prentice-Hall, 1984.
Trotman, James C. *Richard Wright: Myths and Realities*. New York: Garland, 1988.

Articles

Adell, Sandra. "Richard Wright's *The Outsider* and the Kierkegaardian Concept of Dread." *Comparative Literature Studies* 28 (Fall 1991): 379-95.
Alexander, Margaret Walker. "Natchez and Richard Wright in Southern American Literature." *The Southern Quarterly* 29 (Summer 1991): 171-75.
Andrews, William L. "In Search of a Common Identity: The Self and the South in Four Mississippi Autobiographies." *The Southern Review* 24 (Winter 1988): 47-64.
Baldwin, James. "Everybody's Protest Novel." *Partisan Review* (June 1949): 25-39.
Baldwin, Richard E. "The Creative Vision of *Native Son*." *Massachusetts Review* 14 (1973): 278-90.
Brivic, Sheldon. "Conflict of Values: Richard Wright's *Native Son*." *Novel VII* (Spring 1974): 231-45.
Bryant, Earle V. "The Sexualization of Racism in Richard Wright's 'The Man Who Killed a Shadow.'" *Black American Literature Forum* 16 (Fall 1982): 119-121.
Bryant, Jerry. "The Violence of *Native Son*." *Southern Review* 17 (April 1981): 303-19.
Butler, Robert James. "The Quest for Pure Motion in Richard Wright's *Black Boy*." *MELUS* 10 (Fall 1983): 5-17.
_____. "The Function of Violence in Richard Wright's *Native Son*." *Black American Literature Forum* 20 (Spring-Summer 1986): 9-25.
_____. "Farrell's Ethnic Neighborhood and Wright's Urban Ghetto: Two Visions of Chicago's South Side." *MELUS* 18 (Spring 1993): 103-11.
Campbell, James. "The Wright Version." *Times Literary Supplement* (Dec. 13 1991): 14.
Cobb, Nina Cresser. "Richard Wright and Individualism Reconsidered." *CLA Journal* 21 (1978): 335-54.
Davis, Thaddeus. "The Metamorphosis of Richard Wright's *Black Boy*." *American Literature* 5 (May 1985): 199-214.
Ellison, Ralph. "Richard Wright's Blues." *The Antioch Review* (Summer 1945): 20-35.
_____. "Remembering Richard Wright." *Delta* 18 (April 1984): 1-13.
Emmanuel, James. "Fever and Feeling: Notes on the Imagery of *Native Son*." *Negro Digest* 18 (Dec. 1968): 16-26.
Fabre, Michel. "Margaret Walker's Richard Wright: A Wrong Righted or Wright Wronged?" *Mississippi: Quarterly* 42 (Fall 1989): 429-60.
France, Alan W. "Misogyny and Appropriation in Wright's *Native Son*." *Modern Fiction Studies* 34 (Autumn 1988): 413-423.
Gallagher, Katherine. "Bigger's Great Leap to the Figurative." *CLA Journal* 27 (March 1984): 293-314.
Gibson, Donald. "Wright's Invisible *Native Son*." *American Quarterly* 21 (Winter 1969): 728-39.
_____. "Richard Wright's *Black Boy* and the Trauma of Autobiographical Rebirth." *Callaloo* 9 (Summer 1986): 492-98.

Graham, Maryemma. "Richard Wright." *Callaloo* 9 (Summer 1986): 21-30.

Hakutani, Yoshinobu. "*Native Son* and *An American Tragedy*: Two Different Interpretations of Crime and Guilt." *The Centennial Review* 23 (Spring 1979): 208-26.

_____. "Richard Wright's *The Outsider* and Albert Camus's *The Stranger*." *Mississippi Quarterly* 42 (Fall 1989): 365-378.

Hernton, Calvin. "The Sexual Mountain and Black Women Writers." *Black American Literature Forum* 18 (Winter 1984): 139-45.

Jackson, Esther Merle. "The American Negro and the Image of the Absurd." *Phylon* XXIII (1962): 359-71.

Jan Mohamed, Abdul R. "Negating the Negative as a Form of Affirmation in Minority Discourse." *Cultural Critique* 7 (Fall 1987): 245-66.

Joyce, Joyce Ann. "Style and Meaning in Richard Wright's *Native Son*." *Black American Literature Forum* 16 (Summer 1982): 112-15.

Kent, George E. "Richard Wright: Blackness and the Adventure of Western Culture." *CLA Journal* 12 (June 1969): 322-43.

Kinnamon, Keneth. "How *Native Son* Was Born." *Writing the American Classics*, ed. James Barbour and Tom Quirk. Chapel Hill: University of North Carolina Press, 1990.

_____. "Richard Wright's Use of *Othello* in *Native Son*." *CLA Journal* 12 (June 1969): 358-59.

Lenz, Gunter. "Southern Exposures: The Urban Experience and the Reconstruction of Black Folk Culture and Community in the Works of Richard Wright and Zora Neal Hurston." *New York Folklore* 7 (Summer 1981): 3-39.

Mackethan, Lucinda. "Black Boy and Ex-Colored Man: Version and Inversion of the Slave Narrator's Quest for Voice." *CLA Journal* 32 (Dec. 1988): 123-47.

McLuskey, John. "Two Steppin': Richard Wright's Encounter with BlueJazz." *American Literature* 55 (1983): 332-44.

Miller, James A. "Bigger Thomas's Quest for Voice and Audience in Richard Wright's *Native Son*." *Callaloo* 9 (Summer 1986): 501-06.

Nagel, James. "Images of 'Vision' in *Native Son*." *University Review* 35 (Dec. 1969): 109-15.

Pudaloff, Ross. "Celebrity as Identity: Richard Wright, *Native Son*, and Mass Culture." *Studies in American Fiction* 11 (Spring 1983): 3-18.

Redden, Dorothy. "Richard Wright and *Native Son*. Not Guilty." *Black American Literature Forum* 10 (Winter 1976): 111-16.

Reilly, John. "Richard Wright Preaches the Nation: *12 Million Black Voices*." *Black American Literature Forum* 16 (Fall 1982): 116-19.

Scott, Nathan. "Search for Beliefs: The Fiction of Richard Wright." *University of Kansas City Review* XXIII (1956): 19-24.

Scruggs, Charles. "The Importance of the City in *Native Son*." *Ariel* 9 (1978): 37-47.

Siegel, Paul. "The Conclusion of Richard Wright's *Native Son*." *PMLA* 89 (May 1974): 517-23.

Singh, Amritjit. "Richard Wright's *The Outsider*: Existentialist Exemplar of Critique?" *CLA Journal* 27 (June 1984): 357-70.

Skerrett, Joseph T. "Richard Wright: Writing and Identity." *Callaloo* 2 (October 1979): 84-89.

Tate, Claudia C. "*Black Boy*: Richard Wright's 'Tragic Sense of Life.'" *Black American Literature Forum* 10 (1976): 117-19.

Tremaine, Louis. "The Dissociated Sensibility of Bigger Thomas in Wright's *Native Son*." *Studies in American Fiction* 14 (Spring 1986): 63-76.

Ward. Jerry W. "Richard Wright's Hunger." *Virginia Quarterly Review* 5 (1978): 148-53.

_____. "The Wright Critical Paradigm: Facing a Future." *Callaloo* 9 (Summer 1985): 25-43.

Wertham, Frederic, M.D. "An Unconscious Determinant in *Native Son*." *Journal of Clinical Psychopathology and Psychotherapy* 6 (Winter 1944): 111-15.

Williams, Sherley Ann. "Papa Dick and Sister Woman: Reflections on Women in the Fiction of Richard Wright." In *American Novelists Revisited: Essays in Feminist Criticism*, edited by Fritz Fleischmann. Boston: J.K. Hall, 1982.

Witt, Mary Anne. "Rage and Racism in *The Stranger* and *Native Son*." *The Comparatist* 1 (1977): 35-47.

Index

About the Editor

ROBERT J. BUTLER is Professor of English at Canisius College, where he is also Director of College Honors. He has published numerous articles on African-American literature and contemporary American authors. In addition, he is the author of *Richard Wright's Native Son: The Emergence of a New Black Hero* (1990) and coeditor of *The City in African American Literature* (1995) with Yoshinobu Hakutani.